THE CAMBRIDGE COMPANION TO
AMERICAN METHODISM

A product of trans-Atlantic revivalism and awakening, Methodism initially took root in America in the eighteenth century. In the mid-nineteenth century, Methodism exploded to become the largest religious body in the United States and the quintessential form of American religion. This *Cambridge Companion* offers a general comprehensive introduction to various forms of American Methodism, including the African-American, German Evangelical Pietist, holiness, and Methodist Episcopal traditions. Written from various disciplinary perspectives, including history, literature, theology, and religious studies, this volume explores the beliefs and practices around which the lives of American Methodist churches have revolved, as well as the many ways in which Methodism has both adapted to and shaped American culture.

Jason E. Vickers is Associate Professor of Theology and Wesleyan Studies at United Theological Seminary in Dayton, Ohio. He is the author of *Minding the Good Ground: A Theology for Church Renewal* (2011), *Wesley: A Guide for the Perplexed* (2009), and *Invocation and Assent: The Making and Remaking of Trinitarian Theology* (2008), and he is co-editor (with Randy L. Maddox) of *The Cambridge Companion to John Wesley* (2009).

CAMBRIDGE COMPANIONS TO RELIGION

This is a series of companions to major topics and key figures in theology and religious studies. Each volume contains specially commissioned chapters by international scholars, which provide an accessible and stimulating introduction to the subject for new readers and nonspecialists.

Other Titles in the Series

AMERICAN ISLAM Edited by Juliane Hammer and Omid Safi

AMERICAN JUDAISM Edited by Dana Evan Kaplan

KARL BARTH Edited by John Webster

THE BIBLE, 2nd edition Edited by Bruce Chilton

BIBLICAL INTERPRETATION Edited by John Barton

DIETRICH BONHOEFFER Edited by John de Gruchy

JOHN CALVIN Edited by Donald K. McKim

CHRISTIAN DOCTRINE Edited by Colin Gunton

CHRISTIAN ETHICS Edited by Robin Gill

CHRISTIAN MYSTICISM Edited by Amy Hollywood and Patricia Z. Beckman

CHRISTIAN PHILOSOPHICAL THEOLOGY Edited by Charles Taliaferro and Chad V. Meister

CLASSICAL ISLAMIC THEOLOGY Edited by Tim Winter

JONATHAN EDWARDS Edited by Stephen J. Stein

FEMINIST THEOLOGY Edited by Susan Frank Parsons

THE JESUITS Edited by Thomas Worcester

JESUS Edited by Markus Bockmuehl

C. S. LEWIS Edited by Robert MacSwain and Michael Ward

LIBERATION THEOLOGY Edited by Chris Rowland

MARTIN LUTHER Edited by Donald K. McKim

MEDIEVAL JEWISH PHILOSOPHY Edited by Daniel H. Frank and Oliver Leaman

MODERN JEWISH PHILOSOPHY Edited by Michael L. Morgan and Peter Eli Gordon

MOHAMMED Edited by Jonathan E. Brockup

POSTMODERN THEOLOGY Edited by Kevin J. Vanhoozer

PURITANISM Edited by John Coffey and Paul C. H. Lim

THE QUR'AN Edited by Jane Dammen McAuliffe

KARL RAHNER Edited by Declan Marmion and Mary E. Hines

REFORMATION THEOLOGY Edited by David Bagchi and David Steinmetz

RELIGIOUS STUDIES Edited by Robert A. Orsi

FRIEDRICH SCHLEIERMACHER Edited by Jacqueline Mariña

SCIENCE AND RELIGION Edited by Peter Harrison

ST. PAUL Edited by James D. G. Dunn

THE TALMUD AND RABBINIC LITERATURE Edited by Charlotte E. Fonrobert and Martin S. Jaffee

HANS URS VON BALTHASAR Edited by Edward T. Oakes and David Moss

JOHN WESLEY Edited by Randy L. Maddox and Jason E. Vickers

THE CAMBRIDGE COMPANION TO

AMERICAN METHODISM

Edited by Jason E. Vickers
United Theological Seminary, Ohio

CAMBRIDGE
UNIVERSITY PRESS

32 Avenue of the Americas, New York, NY 10013-2473, USA

Cambridge University Press is part of the University of Cambridge.

If furthers the University's mission by disseminating knowledge in the pursuit of education, learning, and research at the highest international levels of excellence.

www.cambridge.org
Information on this title: www.cambridge.org/9781107401051

© Cambridge University Press 2013

First published 2013

Printed in the United States of America

A catalog record for this publication is available from the British Library.

Library of Congress Cataloging in Publication data
The Cambridge companion to American Methodism / edited by Jason E. Vickers, United Theological Seminary, Ohio.
    pages   cm. – (Cambridge companions to religion)
Includes bibliographical references and index.
ISBN 978-1-107-00834-2 (hardback) – ISBN 978-1-107-40105-1 (paperback)
    1. Methodist Church – United States.   I. Vickers, Jason E., editor of compilation.
BX8235.C36   2013
287.0973–dc23   2013003968

ISBN 978-1-107-00834-2 Hardback
ISBN 978-1-107-40105-1 Paperback

Contents

Illustrations *page ix*

Contributors *xi*

Acknowledgments *xv*

Abbreviations *xvii*

Introduction 1
JASON E. VICKERS

Part I *The Making and Remaking of American Methodism*

1 American Methodism: A Theological Tradition 9
JASON E. VICKERS

2 Early American Methodism 44
RUSSELL E. RICHEY

3 American Methodism in the Nineteenth Century:
Expansion and Fragmentation 63
DOUGLAS M. STRONG

4 American Methodism in the Twentieth Century: Reform,
Redefinition, and Renewal 97
WENDY J. DEICHMANN

Part II *The Religious Culture of American Methodism*

5 Revivalism and Preaching 119
MICHAEL K. TURNER

6 Sacraments and Life-Cycle Rituals 138
KAREN B. WESTERFIELD TUCKER

7 Discipline and Polity 156
DOUGLAS M. KOSKELA

8 Clergy 171
E. BROOKS HOLIFIELD

9 Laity 188
JENNIFER L. WOODRUFF TAIT

10 Asceticism 208
MAURA JANE FARRELLY

11 Healing 227
CANDY GUNTHER BROWN

12 Spiritual Biography and Autobiography 243
TED A. CAMPBELL

13 Education 261
STAN INGERSOL

Part III *Methodists and American Society*

14 Methodists and Race 281
MORRIS L. DAVIS

15 African-American Methodists and the Making
of the Civil Rights Movement 296
DENNIS C. DICKERSON

16 American Methodist Women: Roles and Contributions 316
LACEYE C. WARNER

17 Methodists and War 335
ANDREW J. WOOD

18 American Methodists and Popular Culture 352
CHRISTOPHER J. ANDERSON

Index 371

Illustrations

1   Bishop Richard Allen, the African Methodist Episcopal
    Church   *page* 11
2   Thomas O. Summers, Methodist Episcopal Church, South   19
3   Ordination of Francis Asbury (1784)   51
4   Bishop Benjamin T. Roberts, the Free Methodist Church   78
5   Procession at 1968 Uniting Conference   99
6   Methodist Camp Meeting (1836)   124
7   Peter Cartwright, the Methodist Episcopal Church   178
8   Cover from anti-tobacco pamphlet (1883)   211
9   Amanda Berry Smith   234
10   Advertisement for Wesleyan University (1883)   269
11   Bishop Robert E. Jones, the Methodist Episcopal Church   291
12   Truman Commission: Channing Tobias (CME), Dorothy Tilly
     (ME), and Sadie Tanner Mossell Alexander (AME)   304
13   Phoebe Palmer, the Methodist Episcopal Church   326
14   Bishop Matthew Simpson, the Methodist Episcopal Church   336
15   Chicago Methodists viewing a film at Community
     Methodist Episcopal Church   359

The editor wishes to express his deep appreciation to Christopher J. Anderson, Methodist Librarian and Coordinator of Special Collections at Drew University, Madison, New Jersey, for his assistance in obtaining these images, and to Drew University and the General Commission on Archives and History for allowing their use in this volume.

The Truman Commission image was obtained from the Sadie T. M. Alexander Papers and is used here with permission from the University of Pennsylvania Archives.

Contributors

Christopher J. Anderson is Methodist Librarian and Coordinator of Special Collections at Drew University, Madison, New Jersey. He is the co-editor of the *International Journal of Religion and Sport, Volume 1* (2009).

Candy Gunther Brown is Associate Professor, Department of Religious Studies, Indiana University, Bloomington. She is the author of *The Word in the World: Evangelical Writing, Publishing, and Reading in America, 1789–1880* (2004) and *Testing Prayer: Science and Healing* (2012) and editor of *Global Pentecostal and Charismatic Healing* (2011).

Ted A. Campbell is Associate Professor of Church History at Perkins School of Theology, Southern Methodist University, Dallas, Texas. His publications include *Methodist Doctrine: The Essentials,* 2nd edition (2011); *Wesleyan Beliefs: Formal and Popular Expressions of the Core Beliefs of Wesleyan Communities* (2010); *John Wesley and Christian Antiquity: Religious Vision and Cultural Change* (1991); *Christian Confessions: A Historical Introduction* (1996); and *Charles Wesley: Life, Literature & Legacy* (co-edited with Kenneth G. C. Newport, 2007).

Morris L. Davis is Associate Dean for Academic Affairs and Associate Professor of the History of Christianity and Wesleyan/Methodist Studies at Drew University, Madison, New Jersey. He is the author of *The Methodist Unification: Christianity and the Politics of Race in the Jim Crow Era* (2008).

Wendy J. Deichmann is President and Associate Professor of History and Theology at United Theological Seminary, Dayton, Ohio. She is co-editor of *Gender and the Social Gospel* (2003) and the author of numerous articles on the history of Christian missions and the social gospel movement.

Dennis C. Dickerson is James M. Lawson, Jr., Professor of History at Vanderbilt University, Nashville, Tennessee. He is the author of *African Methodism and Its Wesleyan Heritage: Reflections on AME Church History* (2009); *A Liberated Past: Explorations in A.M.E. Church History* (2003); and *Religion, Race, and Region: Research Notes on A.M.E. Church History* (1995).

Maura Jane Farrelly is Assistant Professor of American Studies and Director of the Journalism Program at Brandeis University, Waltham, Massachusetts. She is the author of *Papist Patriots: The Making of an American Catholic Identity* (2012).

E. Brooks Holifield is Emeritus Professor of American Church History, Candor School of Theology, Emory University, Atlanta, Georgia. He is the author of *God's Ambassadors: A History of the Christian Clergy in America* (2007) and *Theology in America: Christian Thought from the Age of the Puritans to the Civil War* (2003).

Stan Ingersol is the denominational archivist of the Church of the Nazarene. He is the co-author of several books, including *Here We Stand: Where Nazarenes Fit in the Religious Marketplace* (1999) and a new denominational history, *Our Watchword and Song: The Centennial History of the Church of the Nazarene* (2009).

Douglas M. Koskela is Associate Professor of Theology and Associate Dean of Undergraduate Studies in the School of Theology at Seattle Pacific University, Seattle, Washington. He is the author of *Ecclesiality and Ecumenism: Yves Congar and the Road to Unity* (2008) and co-editor of *Immersed in the Life of God: The Healing Resources of the Christian Faith: Essays in Honor of William J. Abraham* (2008).

Russell E. Richey is Professor of Church History Emeritus and former Dean of the Candler School of Theology at Emory University, Atlanta, Georgia. He is the author or co-author of numerous works, including *American Methodism: A Compact History* (2012), *The Methodist Experience in America: A History* (2010), and *Doctrine in Experience: A Methodist Theology of Church and Ministry* (2009).

Douglas M. Strong is Dean of the School of Theology and Professor of the History of Christianity at Seattle Pacific University, Seattle, Washington. He is the author of *Perfectionist Politics: Abolitionism and the Religious Tensions of American Democracy* (1999) and *They Walked in the Spirit: Personal Faith and Social Action in America* (1997).

Michael K. Turner is Associate Professor of the History of Christianity at Hood Theological Seminary, Salisbury, North Carolina.

Jason E. Vickers is Associate Professor of Theology and Wesleyan Studies, United Theological Seminary, Dayton, Ohio. He is the author of *Minding the Good Ground: A Theology for Church Renewal* (2011), *Wesley: A Guide for the Perplexed* (2009), and *Invocation and Assent: The Making and Remaking of Trinitarian Theology* (2008), and he is the co-editor (with Randy L. Maddox) of *The Cambridge Companion to John Wesley* (2009).

Laceye C. Warner is Executive Vice Dean, Associate Professor of the Practice of Evangelism and Methodist Studies, and Royce and Jane Reynolds Teaching Fellow at Duke Divinity School, Durham, North Carolina. She is the author of *Saving Women: Retrieving Evangelistic Theology and Practice* (2007), co-editor (with Paul Chilcote) of *The Study of Evangelism* (2008) and (with Sarah Lancaster) of *Wesley Study Bible* (2009), and co-author (with Bishop Kenneth Carder) of *Grace to Lead: Practicing Leadership in the Wesleyan Tradition* (2010).

Karen B. Westerfield Tucker is Professor of Worship at Boston University School of Theology, Boston, Massachusetts. Dr. Westerfield Tucker is the author of

American Methodist Worship (2001), the editor of *The Sunday Service of the Methodists: Twentieth-Century Worship in Worldwide Methodism* (1996), and co-editor (with Geoffrey Wainwright) of *The Oxford History of Christian Worship* (2006).

Andrew J. Wood is Lecturer in Wesleyan Studies and Church History, United Theological Seminary, Dayton, Ohio.

Jennifer L. Woodruff Tait is Affiliate Professor of Church History at Asbury Theological Seminary, Wilmore, Kentucky, and Managing Editor of *Christian History* magazine. She is the author of *The Poisoned Chalice: Eucharistic Grape Juice and Common-Sense Realism in Victorian Methodism* (2011).

Acknowledgments

The editor thanks his colleagues at United Theological Seminary for encouraging and supporting his work on this project. In addition, he would like to thank his research assistants, Chad Clark and Jordan McKenzie, for their help with the proofreading, formatting, and indexing of this volume.

Abbreviations

AC	Annual Conference
AME	African Methodist Episcopal
AMEZ	African Methodist Episcopal Zion
ASWPL	Association of Southern Women for the Prevention of Lynching
BCP	Book of Common Prayer
BSCP	Brotherhood of Sleeping Car Porters
CME	Colored Methodist Episcopal Church or Christian Methodist Episcopal Church after 1954
CN	Church of the Nazarene
COCU	Consultation on Church Union
CORE	Congress of Racial Equality
DS	District Superintendent
EA	Evangelical Association
EC	Evangelical Church
EUB	Evangelical United Brethren
FCNC	Fraternal Council of Negro Churches
FEPC	Fair Employment Practices Commission
FM	Free Methodist
FMC	Free Methodist Church
FOR	Fellowship of Reconciliation
GC	General Conference
GCCUIC	General Commission on Christian Unity and Interreligious Concerns
GCSRW	General Commission on the Status and Role of Women
IAHR	International Association of Healing Rooms
LHFMS	Ladies Home and Foreign Mission Society
LMM	Layman's Missionary Movement
MC	Methodist Church
MD	Medical Doctor
MEA	Methodist Experience in America

MEC	Methodist Episcopal Church
MECS	Methodist Episcopal Church, South
MEF	Ministerial Education Fund
MFSA	Methodist Federation for Social Action
MFSS	Methodist Federation for Social Service
MOWM	March on Washington Movement
MP/MPC	Methodist Protestant Church
NCNW	National Council of Negro Women
n.d.	no date
NNC	National Negro Congress
NUL	National Urban League
NWCTU	National Woman's Christian Temperance Union
PM	Primitive Methodists
SCLC	Southern Christian Leadership Conference
SNCC	Student Nonviolent Coordinating Committee
SSU	Sunday School Union
UBC	United Brethren in Christ
UEC	United Evangelical Church
UM	United Methodist
UMC	United Methodist Church
UMW	United Methodist Women
WC	Wesleyan Church
WCTU	Woman's Christian Temperance Union
WFMS	Women's Foreign Missionary Society
WHMS	Woman's Home Missionary Society
WMC	Wesleyan Methodist Connection
WMS	Woman's Missionary Society
WTS	Wesleyan Theological Society
YMCA	Young Men's Christian Association

Introduction

JASON E. VICKERS

For almost two hundred and fifty years, Methodism has been one of the most dynamic, diverse, and culturally significant forms of religion in America. To be sure, Methodism was not the first English religious movement to arrive in America. That distinction belongs to the Puritans. However, it was not long before Methodism exploded onto the American religious landscape, and it soon rivaled Puritanism "in its force and intensity," as well as in its ability "to mobilize followers, to generate new modes of communication and organization, and to instill habits of industry, sobriety, and mutual accountability." By the mid-nineteenth century, the Methodists were "the largest religious body in the United States and the most extensive national organization other than the Federal government."[1]

Despite its phenomenal rate of growth and its pervasive influence in American culture, Methodism was until very recently underrepresented in the scholarly study of religion in America.[2] In a way that resembles the meteoric growth of Methodism itself, a slow beginning has now given way to a veritable explosion of scholarly interest and work. Indeed, the last twenty-five years have witnessed the development of a significant scholarly literature and conversation related to American Methodism. This literature is multidisciplinary in nature, including contributions in social, political, cultural, and intellectual history, the sociology and psychology of religion, theology, and more. There is also a great deal of diversity with respect to the topics and themes that scholars are exploring. For example, in addition to period,[3] regional,[4] and denominational studies,[5] there are now hundreds of monographs and articles that explore Methodism and race;[6] Methodism and gender;[7] Methodism and alcohol;[8] American Methodist missions;[9] and American Methodist worship, to name just a few.[10] Moreover, there is a fast growing list of outstanding critical biographies of significant people in the history of American Methodism.[11]

Among the many lessons to be learned from this recent scholarly work, two are especially worth noting. First, American Methodism is not a static form of religion. Throughout its history, Methodism has continually adapted to and agitated for change within American culture.[12] In other words, Methodism has been deeply shaped by the tensions and transitions in American culture across space and time, but it has also played a leading role in advocating for social and political change and thereby shaping American culture.

Second, American Methodism is not a monolithic form of religion. On the contrary, American Methodism comprises of a dynamic and diverse group of churches and denominations. In early American Methodism, for example, theology, ethnicity, and race contributed to the formation of African-American and German Evangelical-Pietist churches that represent American Methodism as much as the larger and predominantly white Methodist Episcopal Church.[13] Over time, disagreements over whether and how best to adapt to American culture and over whether and how best to agitate for change led to the formation of other American Methodist groups and churches, a development best illustrated by the division of the Methodist Episcopal Church over slavery and by the churches and denominations that resulted from the holiness controversies of the mid- to late nineteenth century.[14]

The present volume *reflects* these and other interpretive insights that have emerged in the scholarly study of American Methodism over the last quarter century. It does so by taking a multidisciplinary approach to the subject, highlighting the dynamic and diverse nature of American Methodism, paying close attention to the relationship between Methodism and American culture, and introducing readers to the most important scholarly literature related to a wide range of themes and topics (the endnotes in each chapter contain a gold mine of bibliographic information for additional research and study). However, it also *builds upon* recent interpretive trends insofar as each chapter compares and contrasts a range of American Methodist groups or denominations in an effort to provide a more textured and nuanced reading of the whole. This volume also advances the conversation by attending to themes or topics that are less prominent in the scholarly literature to date, including clergy and laity, Methodism and popular culture, healing, asceticism, and war.

Another way in which this volume contributes to the scholarly conversation has to do with understanding and appreciating American Methodism *as a theological tradition.* American Methodism has been perceived for too long as a form of religion that revolves around pragmatic concerns rather than around deeply engrained theological sensibilities. For example, Charles Wood, an ordained elder in the United Methodist Church and long-time professor of Christian doctrine at

Southern Methodist University in Dallas, Texas, began a recent book on Methodist theology with the following remark:

> It is widely believed that a walk through the Methodist doctrinal pond would hardly get one's feet wet. It is not only other Christians who have this impression of us, of course; many Methodists share it, and take it either as a point of pride (the dominant view, so far as I can see) or as a reason for self-reproach (a minority view, whose influence waxes and wanes periodically).[15]

When American Methodism is not being perceived as theologically or doctrinally superficial, it is frequently characterized as involving a "bewildering spectrum of doctrinal diversity."[16] Taken together, these two caricatures have discouraged scholars from working to identify the theological sensibilities and doctrinal commitments that have animated American Methodists across the centuries. Thus, despite the considerable progress made in the scholarly study of American Methodism over the last twenty-five years, an account of American Methodism as a theological tradition has yet to appear.

With a view toward correcting this misreading and the oversight that results from it, the present volume begins with an account of American Methodism as a theological tradition. Contrary to the widespread notion that Methodism is either too theologically shallow to be compelling or too diffuse to constitute a theological tradition, Chapter 1 maintains that both the dynamism and the appeal of Methodism stem from doctrinal commitments and theological sensibilities that have persisted across space and time.

Following this initial chapter on American Methodism as a theological tradition are three chapters that correspond roughly to the eighteenth, nineteenth, and twentieth centuries. These chapters combine to provide the reader with a wide-ranging overview of the history of American Methodism in its many forms. They attend to the evolution of Methodism from a movement within the wider horizon of trans-Atlantic revivalism to a Church with an episcopal form of government (Chapter 2), to the fragmenting of Methodism into several Churches and/or denominations (Chapter 3), and to the many and varied attempts to reunite and renew Methodism in the twentieth century (Chapter 4). These three chapters also introduce the reader to many significant materials, persons, practices, and events in the history of American Methodism, including the so-called "Christmas Conference" of 1784, books of Discipline, Richard Allen, Francis Asbury, and Phoebe Palmer, the holiness movement, camp meetings, and much more.

The second section of the book takes a closer look at the religious culture of American Methodism. Chapters 5 and 6 provide an overview of the liturgical or cultic life of American Methodism as it inheres in preaching, the sacraments, and life-cycle rituals. Chapter 7 compares and contrasts approaches to church government or polity in several American Methodist churches/denominations. Chapters 8 and 9 examine evolving notions about the roles and contributions of clergy and laity in American Methodism. Chapters 10 through 13 highlight a range of practices and commitments at the heart of American Methodist life, including asceticism, healing, the reading and writing of spiritual biographies and autobiographies, and learning through higher education.

The third section of this volume considers the ways that Methodists have responded to major issues, movements, and developments in American society. Chapters 14 and 15 provide an overview of the ways in which American Methodists have responded to issues and developments related to race, including but not limited to slavery, Jim Crow, and the Civil Rights Movement. Chapter 16 examines the roles and contributions of American Methodist women, giving special attention to the ways in which Methodist women have thought about and advocated for gender equality in church and society. Chapter 17 provides a framework for thinking about the ways that Methodists have responded to or participated in wars, and Chapter 18 considers the ways in which American Methodists have interacted with popular culture.

Finally, by way of introduction, the reader should note that every effort has been made to present American Methodism in a way that honors its theological, political, and denominational diversity. For example, the authors were encouraged to include examples or illustrations from a variety of time periods as well as from a wide range of American Methodist churches and denominations. While some topics lent themselves to this more than others, all of the authors strived to provide as much comparative analysis as possible. Moreover, the authors themselves represent a wide range of American Methodist denominations, including the African Methodist Episcopal Church, the Church of the Nazarene, the Free Methodist Church, the United Methodist Church, and the Wesleyan Church, as well as a wide range of theological and political views.[17]

Notes

1 Nathan O. Hatch and John H. Wigger, "Introduction," in *Methodism and the Shaping of American Culture*, edited by Nathan O. Hatch and John H. Wigger (Nashville, TN: Kingswood Books, 2001), 11.

2 For an account of the relative neglect of Methodism in the scholarly study of religion in America, see Nathan O. Hatch, "The Puzzle of American Methodism," *Church History* 63:2 (1994): 175–189.

3 Examples of period studies include Dee E. Andrews, *The Methodists and Revolutionary America, 1760–1800: The Shaping of an Evangelical Culture* (Princeton, NJ: Princeton University Press, 2000); Russell E. Richey, *Early American Methodism* (Bloomington, IN: Indiana University Press, 1991); Lester Ruth, *Early Methodist Life and Spirituality* (Nashville, TN: Kingswood Books, 2005); and John H. Wigger, *Taking Heaven by Storm: Methodism and the Rise of Popular Christianity in America* (Urbana, IL: University of Illinois Press, 1998).

4 For exemplary regional studies, see Cynthia Lynn Lyerly, *Methodism and the Southern Mind, 1770–1810* (New York: Oxford University Press, 1998); Beth Barton Schweiger, *The Gospel Working Up: Progress and the Pulpit in Nineteenth Century Virginia* (New York: Oxford University Press, 2000); Randall Stephens, *The Fire Spreads: Holiness and Pentecostalism in the American South* (Cambridge, MA: Harvard University Press, 2008), and Brian K. Turley, *A Wheel within a Wheel: Southern Methodism and the Georgia Holiness Association* (Macon, GA: Mercer University Press, 1999).

5 Recent examples of denominational studies include James T. Campbell, *Songs of Zion: The African Methodist Episcopal Church in the United States and South Africa* (Chapel Hill, NC: The University of North Carolina Press, 1998); *Our Watchword and Song: The Centennial History of the Church of the Nazarene*, edited by Floyd Cunningham (Kansas City, MO: Beacon Hill Press, 2009); Dennis C. Dickerson, *A Liberated Past: Explorations in AME Church History* (Nashville, TN: A.M.E. Sunday School Union, 2003); and Othal Hawthorne Lakey, *The History of the CME Church* (Memphis, TN: CME Publishing House, 1996).

6 For example, see Morris L. Davis, *The Methodist Unification: Christianity and the Politics of Race in the Jim Crow Era* (New York: New York University Press, 2008); and Peter Murray, *Methodists and the Crucible of Race, 1930–1975* (Columbia, MO: University of Missouri Press, 2004).

7 See Jean Miller Schmidt, *Grace Sufficient: A History of Women in American Methodism 1760–1968* (Nashville, TN: Abingdon Press, 1999); A. Gregory Schneider, *The Way of the Cross Leads Home: The Domestication of American Methodism* (Bloomington, IN: Indiana University Press, 1994); and Susie C. Stanley, *Holy Boldness: Women Preachers; Autobiographies and the Sanctified Self* (Knoxville, TN: University of Tennessee Press, 2002).

8 For example, see Jennifer Woodruff Tait: *Poisoned Chalice: Eucharistic Grape Juice and Common-Sense Realism in Victorian Methodism* (Tuscaloosa, AL: The University of Alabama Press, 2011).

9 For example, see J. Steven O' Malley, *On the Journey Home: The History of Mission of the Evangelical United Brethren Church, 1946–1968* (New York: General Board of Global Ministries, The United Methodist Church, 2003); and Russell E. Richey, "Organizing for Missions: A Methodist Case

Study," in *The Foreign Missionary Enterprise at Home: Explorations in North American Cultural History*, edited by Daniel H. Bays and Grant Wacker (Tuscaloosa, AL: The University of Alabama Press, 2003), 75–93.

10 See Karen B. Westerfield Tucker, *American Methodist Worship* (New York: Oxford University Press, 2011).

11 See Edith Blumhofer, *Aimee Semple McPherson: Everybody's Sister* (Grand Rapids, MI: Eerdmans, 1993); Sandy Dwayne Martin, *For God and Race: The Religious and Political Leadership of AMEZ Bishop James Walker Hood* (Columbia, SC: University of South Carolina Press, 1999); Howard A. Snyder, *Populist Saints: B. T. and Ellen Roberts and the First Free Methodists* (Grand Rapids, MI: Eerdmans, 2006); Charles Edward White, *The Beauty of Holiness: Phoebe Palmer as Theologian, Revivalist, Feminist and Humanitarian* (Grand Rapids, MI: Francis Asbury Press, 2008); and John H. Wigger, *American Saint: Francis Asbury and the Methodists* (New York: Oxford University Press, 2009).

12 On adaptation and agitation within American Methodism, see David Hempton, *Methodism: Empire of the Spirit* (New Haven, CT: Yale University Press, 2006).

13 See Russell Richey et al., *American Methodism: A Compact History* (Nashville, TN: Abingdon Press, 2012). Also see *Methodist and Pietist: Retrieving the Evangelical United Brethren Heritage*, edited by J. Steven O' Malley and Jason E. Vickers (Nashville, TN: Kingswood Books, 2011); and Harry V. Richardson, *Dark Salvation: The Story of Methodism as It Developed among Blacks in America* (Garden City, NJ: Anchor Press/ Doubleday, 1976).

14 For more on the holiness movement and the churches that resulted from it, see Randall J. Stevens, "The Holiness/Pentecostal/Charismatic Extension of the Wesleyan Tradition," in *The Cambridge Companion to John Wesley*, edited by Randy L. Maddox and Jason E. Vickers (Cambridge: Cambridge University Press, 2010).

15 Charles Wood, *Love that Rejoices in the Truth: Theological Explorations* (Eugene, OR: Wipf & Stock, 2009), 1.

16 E. Brooks Holifield, *Health and Medicine in the Methodist Tradition: Journey Toward Wholeness* (New York: Crossroad, 1986), 4.

17 Three of the authors are not members of any American Methodist body.

Part I

The Making and Remaking of American Methodism

1 American Methodism: A Theological Tradition

JASON E. VICKERS

The purpose of this chapter is to provide an account of American Methodism as a dynamic and living theological tradition. What follows is not a short history of American Methodist theology, but a conceptual argument about the theological sensibilities that inhere in deep, if sometimes subtle, ways in American Methodism across space and time. More specifically, it is an argument that, at the heart of American Methodism, are theological sensibilities that 1) took shape initially in the religious culture of revivals and awakenings, 2) evolved over time into five distinct theological languages, and 3) are presently awaiting dogmatic development.[1]

Before turning to the origins of American Methodist theology in revivals and awakenings, it may help to say a brief word about the terms *American Methodist, doctrine,* and *theology.* In the account that follows, *American Methodist* denotes the African-American Methodist Episcopal, Brethren, Evangelical, Methodist Episcopal, United Methodist, and Wesleyan-holiness traditions. *Doctrine* denotes what American Methodists have believed, taught, and confessed not only in official doctrinal statements, but also in catechisms, sermons, hymns, personal testimonies, and even architecture. *Theology* is a broader term that denotes the work of ongoing reflection upon the doctrines of Methodism. At times, the work of theological reflection takes the form of criticism, revision, and expansion. At other times, it involves retrieving or renewing doctrines that have been obscured, distorted, or otherwise rendered inoperative.

THE MAKING OF AMERICAN METHODIST THEOLOGY: REVIVALS AND AWAKENINGS

The theological sensibilities around which early American Methodism coheres can be traced, not to the work of a single great theologian, but to the religious culture of revivals and awakenings. It is not simply that

American Methodist theology originates *within* this culture; the whole history of American Methodist theology, with all of its twists and turns and with all of its methodological and material diversity, can be read as a series of creative adaptations of the theological sensibilities that took shape in this formative period. If this sounds bizarre, then it is no doubt because the standard histories have focused more on explaining the affective trappings of the religious culture of revivals and awakenings than on discerning the theological sensibilities that animated it in the first place.[2]

Evangelical Sensibilities

In the culture of revivals and awakenings, American Methodists were concerned primarily with proclaiming the Gospel. They proclaimed the Gospel through evangelism, personal conversation, letter writing, obituaries, spiritual biographies and autobiographies, and a host of other ways.[3] Above all, however, early American Methodists were committed to the proclamation of the Gospel through preaching.[4] In their explanatory notes to the *Discipline*, Bishops Francis Asbury and Thomas Coke stressed, "The preaching of the Gospel is of *first* importance to the welfare of mankind."[5]

More than anything else, the commitment to preaching shaped early American Methodist theological sensibilities. As will be evident shortly, subsequent generations of American Methodists would go on to experiment with other types of theology, including philosophical and systematic theology. In doing so, they would sometimes lose the vital connection between preaching and theology. By contrast, when early American Methodists undertook theological reflection, they almost always did so with a view toward the work and the goal of preaching. Consequently, early American Methodist theology was primarily homiletical theology.

One way that preaching shaped early American Methodist theology has to do with the role of the Bible. As *the* source of preaching, the Bible was the wellspring of American Methodist doctrine and theological reflection. For instance, early American Methodist doctrinal and theological vocabulary consisted primarily of concepts and metaphors derived directly from Scripture rather than from philosophical or other sources. Moreover, early American Methodists were committed to scriptural reasoning, which is to say, to adhering closely both to the language and the logic of Scripture. Thus, Bishops Asbury and Coke urged early American Methodist preachers to "choose the plainest text you can," and having done so, to "take care not to ramble, but keep to your text."[6] They also warned the preachers that the Gospel is not a matter of "fine metaphysical reasoning."[7]

Another way that preaching deeply shaped early American Methodist theology has to do with a commitment to simplicity and

Figure 1. **Bishop Richard Allen, the African Methodist Episcopal Church,** Methodist Library Image Collection, Drew University, Madison, New Jersey.

intelligibility. Compared with other Protestants at the time, Methodists had a reputation for plain speaking. Thus Richard Allen, the founder of the African Methodist Episcopal Church, observed,

> The Methodists were the first people that brought the glad tidings to the colored people.... We are beholden to the Methodists, under God, for the light of the Gospel we enjoy; for all other denominations preached so high-flown that we were not able to comprehend their doctrine.[8]

The commitment to simplicity and intelligibility led early American Methodists to focus their theological attention on three doctrines having to do with the Christian life. First, they emphasized the universality of sin. In other words, they stressed that all human beings were estranged from God and from one another. Second, they insisted that, in the crucifixion, death, and resurrection of Jesus Christ, God had supplied a way for people to be reconciled to God and to one another. Third, they highlighted the work of the Holy Spirit in bringing people to saving faith in Jesus Christ (justification) and in bringing them to new life in Christ (regeneration and sanctification).[9]

If many early American Methodists emphasized doctrines related to the Christian life, they also recognized that these doctrines depended upon other Christian doctrines, including the doctrine of God, the doctrine of creation, the doctrine of the church, and the like. In other words, they understood that the doctrinal emphases described earlier presuppose and entail other doctrinal commitments. They were well aware, for instance, that the doctrine of the universality of sin trades on a doctrine of creation and a doctrine of human nature. Similarly, they knew that the saving significance of Christ's death and resurrection is related to doctrinal commitments having to do with the person of Jesus.[10] Consequently, they deeply embraced the full range of Christian doctrines enshrined in their Articles of Religion, a reality perhaps best reflected in the practice of requiring public affirmation of these doctrines for church membership and ordination. This practice originates in early American Methodism and persists in most American Methodist churches right down to the present day.[11]

The strong commitment to the basic doctrines contained in their Articles of Religion and/or other official doctrinal statements notwithstanding, the concern for preaching led early American Methodists to adopt a deflationary view of doctrine and theology. For example, despite frequently insisting that Christ's death and resurrection was of saving significance only if Jesus was divine, they typically stopped short of engaging in extended reflection on the nature of Christ's divinity or the relationship between Christ's divinity and the divinity of the Father and the Holy Spirit.[12] Similarly, early American Methodists did not focus their attention on the relationship between Christ's divine and human natures. In these and many other areas of theology, they preferred to travel light.

If early American Methodists were not especially interested in systematic or dogmatic theology, then it was not because they were intellectually lazy. Within the religious culture of revivals and awakenings, the criterion of good preaching was sincere repentance and conversion, not technical precision or comprehensiveness in doctrinal or theological matters. Thus, early American Methodists insisted that the knowledge needed for faith and therefore for salvation was of *a different kind* than the knowledge contained in the medieval *Summa* or the theologies of Protestant scholasticism. In other words, the priority of preaching deeply shaped how early American Methodists thought about theological knowledge.

In the context of preaching, true theological knowledge was saving or *experiential* knowledge. Initially, this knowledge had to do with a personal encounter with Jesus Christ in the present. Once again, Bishop Asbury and Coke's *Notes* are illustrative. After convincing people of their need for God, Methodist preachers were to bring them to "a *present* Saviour," showing "the willingness of Christ *this moment*" to bless them and to bring "a present salvation *home* to their souls."[13]

With a view toward helping people obtain saving or experiential knowledge, early American Methodists developed and deployed a range of Scriptural metaphors, images, and concepts. The persuasive power of early American Methodist theology was partly a function of the creative use of these metaphors, images, and concepts in sermons and personal testimonies. For example, in a personal testimony about coming to faith, Bishop Daniel Payne, an early leader in the African Methodist Episcopal Church, made effective use of the metaphor of giving one's heart to Jesus, saying: "Here I too gave my *whole heart*, and instantly felt that peace which passeth all understanding, and that joy which is unspeakable and full of glory."[14] Other prominent metaphors included putting one's trust in Jesus and surrendering to Jesus, both of which came to popular expression in the twentieth century in the beloved American Methodist hymn "I Surrender All."[15]

If the persuasive power of early American Methodist theology was partly a function of the creative use of metaphors designed to facilitate an experiential or saving knowledge of Jesus Christ, then it was also a function of a closely related theme, namely, the presence and work of the Holy Spirit. Thus, early American Methodists stressed that people could not put their trust in Jesus without the help of the Holy Spirit. However, the really explosive aspect of early American Methodist theology was the insistence that, precisely because the Holy Spirit was involved, coming to faith involved not merely the giving of the heart to Christ, but also its renovating, cleansing, and filling with love for God and neighbor.

A particularly poignant example of the insistence that the knowledge that really matters is an experiential knowledge of Christ that involves the renovating work of the Holy Spirit in the human heart can be seen in the opening paragraph of Nathan Bangs' *Letters to Young Ministers of the Gospel* (1826), a work whose primary purpose was to stress the importance of the study of doctrine for Methodist clergy. Bangs writes,

> It will ... be assumed that you are convinced satisfactorily of your call to the sacred work of ministry, that you have experienced the renovating power of the Holy Ghost upon your heart, and consequently that you have not now to learn the first principles of religion. But if, indeed, you be destitute of that knowledge of God through Jesus Christ which can be acquired *only by experience,* all the study in the universe, even were you master of the whole circle of the sciences, will never qualify you for the holy work of the ministry.[16]

Early American Methodists also developed and deployed an array of Scriptural metaphors, images, and concepts with a view toward helping people to understand and experience the renovating and sanctifying work of the Holy Spirit. For example, they frequently deployed the metaphor of regeneration or new birth to capture the transformative dimension of coming to faith in Jesus Christ.[17] In other words, they insisted that justification involved a *real* change wrought by the Holy Spirit in the lives of believers. Moreover, they developed and deployed the concepts of assurance, restoration, renovation, divine indwelling, cleansing, entire sanctification, full salvation, Christian perfection, and perfect love in an effort to help people experience the breadth and depth of the work of the Holy Spirit.

The emphasis on the transforming work of the Holy Spirit meant that people did not have to lead spiritually defeated lives. Perpetual estrangement from God and from one's fellow human beings was not inevitable. With the help of the Holy Spirit, people could know, trust, love, and obey Jesus and, through him experience peace, joy, and happiness in God the Father. They could also begin to know and to love one another as God intended. This was the good news of the Gospel proclaimed by early American Methodists.

Radical Sensibilities

While the emphasis on a present encounter with the living Christ and the transforming work of the Holy Spirit in the human heart gave the Methodist message a decidedly evangelical orientation, another emphasis gave it widespread appeal and a politically and socially radical orientation. Within the religious culture of revivals and awakenings, early

American Methodists were keen to insist that the Gospel is *for every-one*. They stressed that the Gospel did not belong to any special class of people who, for one reason or another, were elected by God for salvation. Rather, the Gospel was for the rich *and* the poor, the enslaved *and* the free, black *and* white, men *and* women, the old *and* the young, and the educated *and* the illiterate.

Across space and time, the emphasis on the universality of the Gospel has easily been the single most distinguishing feature of American Methodist theology. It also helps to explain the stunning growth of American Methodism from the late eighteenth through the mid-nineteenth century. During this period, the idea that the Gospel is for everyone was especially attractive to people at the margins of American society, many of whom found a theological and spiritual home in Methodism.[18] For instance, Harry V. Richardson notes that the message that "the Gospel was meant for every creature" was behind "the heavy participation of blacks in early Methodist meetings."[19] The same holds for poor whites, for women and children, and for immigrants struggling to make their way in the new world.

In addition to giving the Methodist message its universal appeal, the idea that the Gospel is for everyone gave rise to radical social and political sensibilities in American Methodism.[20] In the name of the universality of the Gospel, American Methodists opposed slavery and Jim Crow, played leading roles in the Civil Rights Movement, advocated for women's rights and women's ordination, and worked tirelessly on behalf of the poor and oppressed.[21] In other words, they did not simply insist that all people should be able to hear the Gospel; they also insisted that all people should be able to enjoy the full benefits of receiving the Gospel, including peace, joy, happiness, and full inclusion in the life of the church. Thus, American Methodists have a long history of opposing anything that limits the ability of a specific group or class of people to receive the Gospel and to flourish as human beings made in the image and likeness of God.

Like evangelical sensibilities, radical social and political sensibilities permeated every branch of American Methodism. A good test case for this is the holiness branch of the tradition. Often perceived to be more socially and politically conservative, the various holiness groups were actually among the most radical, especially when it came to poverty. For example, they frequently opposed pew rentals, alcohol, tobacco, gambling, and expensive clothing precisely because these things prevented the poor from receiving the Gospel and from flourishing in its light. B. T. Roberts, the primary founder of the Free Methodist Church, went so far as to make effective communication of the Gospel to the poor a criterion for discerning the true church, saying,

> There are hot controversies about the true Church. What constitutes it, what is essential to it, what vitiates it? These may be important questions, but there are more important ones. It may be that there cannot be a Church without a bishop, or that there can. There can be none without a gospel, and a gospel for the poor. Does a church preach the gospel to the poor – preach it effectively? Does it convert and sanctify people? Are its preaching, its forms, its doctrines, adapted *specially* to these results? If not, we need not take the trouble of asking any more questions about it. It has missed the main matter. It does not do what Jesus did, what the Apostles did.[22]

The holiness churches also have an impressive record of being among the earliest and strongest advocates for women in ministry. Especially noteworthy on this front have been groups like the Church of God (Anderson, IN), the Church of the Nazarene, the Pilgrim Holiness Church, and the Salvation Army. At times in their history, these groups could boast as high as 40 percent women ministers, "a phenomenal figure by standards of what has been achieved elsewhere in Christendom."[23] Moreover, within these groups, women were able themselves to advocate for an ethic "aimed towards addressing social issues and alleviating social problems."[24]

At this stage, it must be admitted that early American Methodists did not always enact their radical sensibilities with respect to race, gender, and poverty. For instance, while the early American Methodist record on slavery includes impressive displays of moral outrage and organized opposition, it also includes dramatic instances of moral failure and willful neglect.[25] Similarly, holiness churches have frequently struggled to sustain their commitment to the poor, and virtually all American Methodist churches have been inconsistent in their advocacy for women in ministry.

In a very profound way, however, American Methodists' failure to enact their radical sensibilities actually helps to validate the claim that a deep impulse toward radicalism lies at the heart of the American Methodist theological tradition. From the beginning, American Methodists were deeply aware of their social and political failures, ranging from knowing their own complicity in evil to the apathy and indifference that so frequently besets well-established churches. Thus, there emerged alongside the record of failures a powerful record of prophetic self-critique.[26] For example, after extolling Methodists for preaching the

Gospel in a way that "colored people" could easily understand, Bishop Allen went on to admonish them for abandoning "the simplicity of the Gospel that was among them fifty years ago" in order "to conform more to the world and the fashions thereof." Finally, using a metaphor prominent in the culture of revivals and awakenings, he urged them to repent and return to "the good old way" and to "walk therein."[27]

Ecumenical Sensibilities

If early American Methodist theology was evangelical and radical, then it was also ecumenical.[28] Initially, American Methodists were primarily concerned with clarifying their relationship to two other groups. First, they entered into dialogue with John Wesley and the Anglican theological tradition. Having begun life as a missionary movement loosely affiliated with the Church of England via Wesley, American Methodists soon distanced themselves from the so-called "Established Church." After the Revolutionary War, they declared their independence from Wesley and from the Church of England, becoming an autonomous church at the Christmas Conference in Baltimore, MD, in 1784. Leading up to that event and for many years afterward, American Methodists wrestled with the extent to which they were Wesleyan or Anglican in theological orientation. For example, they debated the status of the theological materials that Wesley had sent to them, including Wesley's own sermons and *Notes on the New Testament*, a redacted version of the Thirty-Nine Articles of Religion of the Church of England, and a redacted version of the Book of Common Prayer (the *Sunday Service*). In 1808, they gave dogmatic status to the Articles of Religion, now twenty five in number, by instituting a "restrictive rule" that made them normative for teaching and prohibited the changing or altering of them in any way. And while historians disagree sharply over whether the restrictive rule included Wesley's sermons and *Notes on the New Testament*, they tend to agree that Wesley's influence declined rather significantly in many quarters of American Methodism throughout the nineteenth and well into the twentieth century.[29]

Second, early American Methodists frequently entered into dialogue with their Calvinist co-laborers in the revivals. Over against the Calvinist doctrines of double unconditional election and limited atonement, they insisted on the doctrine of the unlimited atonement, affirming that Christ died for all. Similarly, they stressed that, in Christ, God had elected everyone to salvation. If some people were not saved, then it was because they freely rejected God's offer of salvation and not because God had eternally predestined them to damnation.

In the mid- to late nineteenth century, American Methodists, having severed their ties with the Church of England and having developed a deep opposition to Calvinism, began to explore a more positive basis for ecumenical dialogue. They did this primarily by attempting to establish their own dogmatic theological tradition. Especially noteworthy here is the work of John Miley (MEC) and Thomas O. Summers (MECS), each of whom produced a two-volume, systematic theology.[30] Aware that they represented a new form of Protestant Christianity, Miley and Summers aligned American Methodist doctrine and theology with the ancient orthodox faith of the church represented by the Nicene Creed and Chalcedonian Definition. In other words, they strengthened the commitment to basic orthodoxy that was prevalent in early American Methodism by providing more nuanced and extensive treatments of the doctrines of the Trinity and the person and work of Christ.

While it is difficult to assess the extent to which these early works in American Methodist dogmatic theology influenced the thinking and understanding of clergy and laity, we know from various Methodist *Disciplines* that Miley and Summers were required reading in Methodist ministerial preparation for decades. For example, Miley was required reading in the AME Church from 1896 through 1920; in the AMEZ Church in 1900 and again in 1909; in the MEC from 1892 through 1904; and in the MPC from 1908 to 1916. Summers was required in the CME Church from 1902 to 1906 and again from 1926 through 1934; in the MECS in 1894, 1898, and 1902; and in the MPC from 1888 through 1916.[31]

By the late nineteenth century, however, many American Methodists had a growing sense that their religious and cultural situation was changing. Once determined to sever ties with the Established Church in England, American Methodists had awakened a century later to a new reality: they were the most well-established Protestant church in America. Further complicating matters was the fact that America itself was coming of age intellectually, politically, economically, and culturally. In response, many American Methodists sensed that they needed to use their growing financial and material resources to update their strategies for sharing the Gospel. Thus, they began founding colleges and bible schools aimed at equipping Methodist clergy with the kind of knowledge and training necessary for effective witness in a fast-changing world.[32] Their goal was to use their new position and resources to communicate the Gospel more effectively to an American audience that was increasingly oriented toward the future.

The change in Methodist sensibilities can be seen in part by comparing the works of Miley and Summers. While both authors explicate

Figure 2. **Thomas O. Summers, Methodist Episcopal Church, South,** Methodist Library Image Collection, Drew University, Madison, New Jersey.

the ancient ecumenical foundations for Methodist doctrine and theology, Summers' work, which had been written earlier, is primarily *preservationist* in tone.[33] By contrast, Miley clearly believed that Christian doctrines needed to be updated in order to bring them into line with the intellectual, moral, and political sensibilities of the late nineteenth century. For example, he rejected several classical theories of the atonement in favor of a moral government theory that cohered both with his wider Arminian theology and with the political sensibilities of his late-nineteenth-century American context.[34] Thus, Miley was already pointing the way toward a more *progressive* understanding of the theological task.[35]

THE REMAKING OF AMERICAN METHODIST THEOLOGY: THE LIBERAL TURN AND ITS EFFECTS

While it has become customary to think of evangelicalism and liberalism as radically different forms of Christianity, liberalism initially sprang from evangelical soil. This is especially true within American Methodism. For many American Methodists from the late nineteenth through the mid-twentieth century, theological liberalism did not undermine evangelical sensibilities; it extended them in new and powerful ways to meet the challenges of a new day.

In its classical expression, theological liberalism revolves around two methodological commitments. First, theological liberals are committed to facilitating dialogue between theology and other domains of inquiry and learning, most notably history, philosophy, and the natural sciences. Second, theological liberals are committed to experience as a reliable source for the knowledge of God and to the appropriation of arguments from natural theology.

Almost from the beginning, American Methodists' evangelical sensibilities led them to embrace a form of the methodological commitments at the heart of theological liberalism. For example, the concern for evangelistic effectiveness led Nathan Bangs to stress the importance of facilitating dialogue between theology and other domains of learning. Thus, immediately after he insisted on the supreme importance of personal experience relative to knowledge of "the whole circle of the sciences," Bangs added, "Every science, the knowledge of which may enable us the better to understand and illustrate the sacred Scriptures, to defend and enforce the truths of Christianity, should be the object of our pursuit."[36] He then urged young Methodist clergy to read widely across the full range of intellectual disciplines, recommending specific texts in history, geography, natural and moral philosophy, poetry, and the philosophy of language. Similarly, the concern for evangelistic effectiveness led early American Methodists to develop a favorable disposition toward natural theology. For instance, in his 1837 "Lectures on the Relative Claims of Christianity and Infidelity," Henry Bascom, a Methodist pastor from Kentucky who would become a professor at Augusta College and then president of Transylvania University, argued for the truth of Christianity "based exclusively on the principles of Natural theology."[37]

Taken together, the commitment to a deflationary view of doctrine and theology, to personal experience, and to evangelistic effectiveness entailed that American Methodists did not have to become liberal in their outlook. Insofar as liberalism has to do with intellectual virtues like fair-mindedness and a ready willingness to take a wide range of arguments and evidence seriously, American Methodists were liberal-minded from the beginning. Of course, there is a difference between being liberal-minded in these general ways and being committed to liberalism as a distinct research program in theology. Yet, precisely because they shared these basic evangelical sensibilities and a deep commitment to intellectual virtue, American Methodists soon discovered kindred spirits in the great luminaries of liberal theology. All that was needed was access to the epicenter of the fast-emerging liberal theological tradition.

Here, too, American Methodism's evangelical heritage played a crucial role in various groups of American Methodists coming to explore and ultimately to embrace liberal theology. Evangelicals of German origin were scattered throughout the Methodist movement in America. To be sure, the heaviest concentration was in the Evangelical Association, but there was a strong German-speaking population in the Methodist Episcopal Church as well, most notably in and around Cincinnati, Ohio. As early as the 1820s, reviews of works by leading German theologians began appearing in Methodist periodicals, including the *Methodist Review, Methodist Quarterly Review*, and *United Brethren Review*. By the mid- to late nineteenth century, these journals, which were read by clergy and educated laity alike, featured a steady conversation with many of the leading voices of the liberal theological tradition, including Albrecht Ritschl, Friedrich Schleiermacher, David F. Strauss, and Karl Ullmann, to name just a few.

Even more important than the publication in English of reviews of German theological works was the willingness of American Methodists to study theology in Germany. Especially noteworthy on this front was Borden Parker Bowne, the eventual founder of Boston Personalism, whose theological journey began in the home of parents known for their evangelical and radical sensibilities. Gary Dorrien writes,

The Bownes were deeply pious, morally serious Methodists. Margaret Bowne's piety was a type of Wesleyan sanctificationist mysticism, devoted to the attainment of a sinless state of grace, and her bookshelves contained long rows of the monthly Methodist *Guide to Holiness,* which she studied assiduously. Joseph Bowne, a farmer, local preacher, and justice of the peace, shared his wife's concern with personal sanctification, though not her mysticism; he was personally reticent, but outspoken in his opposition to slavery and alcohol.[38]

As a student at Halle and Göttingen, Borden Parker Bowne brought American Methodism into conversation with liberalism directly at its source. Most important, in Göttingen, he discovered a kindred spirit and friend in the post-Hegelian idealist philosopher Rudolf Hermann Lotze (1817–81), whose insistence on "the primacy of feeling over thought" appealed immediately to Bowne's evangelical sensibilities. He was especially persuaded by Lotze's view that "the existence and teleological agency of a personal deity in history is disclosed to human agents principally through feeling," making it the touchstone of his own emerging theological views.[39]

A year after he returned to America, Bowne accepted an invitation to chair the philosophy department at the recently founded Boston University, a position that he would hold for the next thirty-five years. During that time, Bowne wrote seventeen books and hundreds of journal articles aimed at facilitating a conversation between personal idealist metaphysics and Christian theology.[40] He was also greatly interested in facilitating a conversation between Christian theology construed along Personalist lines and evolutionary science.

The emergence of a school of thought known as Boston Personalism was partially a testament to Bowne's charismatic ability to recruit faculty colleagues and students into the conversation. Alfred C. Knudson, Edgar S. Brightman, Francis J. McConnell, and Ralph T. Flewelling all came on board in the early twentieth century. Later, Boston Personalism would extend to a second and even to a third generation in the work of Peter Bertocci, Rufus Burrow, Jr., Paul Deats, Harold DeWolf, Georgia Harkness, John Lavely, Walter Muelder, and S. Paul Shilling.[41]

Despite its name and its philosophical rigor, the influence of Boston Personalism was not confined to a regional or a professional academic audience. For example, from his position at the University of Southern California, Ralph Flewelling founded an academic journal called *The Personalist* and helped to promote Boston Personalism on the west coast. Reaching beyond academic circles, Francis McConnell, a prominent Methodist bishop, introduced a large popular audience to Personalist ideas. However, it was through their students, including Martin Luther

King, Jr., that Boston Personalism evolved into "one of the few profound and inspiriting schools of progressive American Christianity."[42]

In retrospect, Borden Parker Bowne's significance within American Methodism far exceeds the establishment and promotion of an influential school of thought. More than anyone else, Bowne paved the way for American Methodists to explore and develop a variety of liberal programs in theology. He did so in large part by making the case that theological liberalism was essential for evangelistic effectiveness. If American Methodists wanted to reach a new age with the good news of the Gospel, then it was crucial that their message be intellectually credible and relevant.[43]

Bowne's example and the popularity of Boston Personalism helped to inspire a growing number of American Methodist theologians to explore and ultimately to embrace and to promote a range of options in liberal theology. Especially deserving mention here is Georgia E. Harkness. A Methodist from New York, Harkness enrolled at Boston University in 1918, received her doctorate under Edgar Sheffield Brightman in 1923, and went on to study during sabbatical leaves with many of the leading liberal philosophers and theologians of her day, including Alfred North Whitehead at Harvard in 1926, D. C. Macintosh at Yale from 1928–29, and Reinhold Niebuhr and Paul Tillich at Union in 1935 and 1936–37. In 1940, Harkness became the first female to obtain a professorship in an American seminary when she accepted an appointment at Garrett Biblical Institute. At Garrett and later at the Pacific School of Religion, she made significant contributions in ecclesiology, ecumenical theology, and theological ethics, becoming both a noted Christian pacifist and advocate for women's rights in church and society.[44]

In Harkness's work, the diverse nature of theological liberalism becomes manifest. Having begun her theological career as a Personalist, she became a "chastened liberal" of the Nieburhian realist type. Looking back on this period of extraordinary intellectual ferment, Schubert M. Ogden, a leading United Methodist liberal theologian, summarized the range of options within liberalism that had emerged, saying,

> We have aligned ourselves with that 'liberal' tradition in Protestant Christianity that counts among the great names in its history those of Schleiermacher, Ritschl, Hermann, Harnack, and Troeltsch, and more recently, Schweitzer and the early Barth and, in part at least, Bultmann. It is to this same tradition that most of the creative figures in the last century and a half of American theology also belong. For we must remember here not only the names of Bushnell, Clark,

and Rauschenbusch, not to mention those of 'the Chicago School' and Macintosh, but those of the brothers Niebuhr and (if America may claim him!) Tillich as well.[45]

Regardless of which type of liberalism was being pursued, American Methodist theologians during this period agreed that compatibility with either ancient ecumenical Christianity or with the Methodist theological tradition was not their primary orienting concern. Rather, their primary orienting concern had to do with their own intellectual integrity and a strong sense of accountability to God. As Ogden says,

> What makes this long and diverse tradition essentially *one* is that those who have belonged to it have been profoundly in earnest about being modern men [sic] in a distinctively modern world. Although they have been concerned to stand squarely within the tradition of the apostolic church, they have exhibited no willingness whatever to sacrifice their modernity to their Christianity. They have insisted, rather, on living fully and completely within modern culture and, so far from considering this treason to God, have looked upon it as the only way they could be faithful to him.[46]

For many people, the appeal to intellectual integrity did not diminish the fact that, from their perspective, the liberal turn marked a dramatic departure from the theological sensibilities that inhered in early American Methodism. For example, in his classic work, *The Varieties of Religious Experience* (1902), William James observed,

> When I read in a religious paper words like these: 'Perhaps the best thing we can say of God is that he is *the Inevitable Inference*,' I recognize the tendency to let religion evaporate in intellectual terms. Would martyrs have sung in the flames for a mere inference, however inevitable it might be? ... Yet the intellect, everywhere invasive, shows everywhere its shallowing effect. See how the ancient spirit of Methodism evaporates under those wonderfully able rationalistic booklets ... of a philosopher like Professor Bowne.[47]

For James, Methodism in its liberal mode was like a "beautiful picture of an express train" that was "supposed to be moving" but failed to depict "the energy or the fifty miles an hour." Put simply, the "vital element" was missing. Methodism now lacked "solidity or life." This was, he noted, the outcome of a transition from a world of "individualized feelings" to a world of "generalized objects." In other words, American Methodism no longer had to do primarily with "personal destinies."[48] To be sure, American Methodist liberals spoke frequently of religious experience(s), but they did so in increasingly abstract and impersonal ways.

Two years later, in *Methodist Theology v. The Methodist Theologians*, George W. Wilson set out to demonstrate that Methodist theologians such as Borden Parker Bowne, D. W. C. Huntington, and W. F. Tillett had abandoned the theological sensibilities that had made the Methodists "a distinctive people."[49] In an introduction to the volume, Bishop W. F. Mallalieu warned that the liberal turn represented a yielding to "the unevangelical, un-Wesleyan, and un-Scriptural tendency of the present times."[50] Wilson himself stressed that Methodism was being lost in "a sea of vain speculations and the decrease of those experiences and interpretations of God's Word which have confounded all human philosophy and make heaven resonate with redemption's song."[51]

Wilson went on to complain that Methodism was now "born in a university" rather than on "ten thousand altars with fire kindled from the skies."[52] In the university setting, "lectures" had "supplanted Gospel services" and Methodist theologians "demanded that Divine manifestations ... not transcend reason." As a result, a growing number of Methodists had suppressed their "spiritual impulses," "clipped" the "wings of their faith," and "doubted the supernatural." Most alarming, however, was the fact that "New England Methodism, where much of this new theology is born," was now "slowly dying." Revivals, Wilson lamented, were "scarce." To be sure, American Methodists now had "wood, brick, stone and mortar ... in beautiful proportions," but many churches could not report "a single conversion in a year," and "remarkable conversions" were "becoming rare."[53] Liberal theology, Wilson cautioned, offered "no key to the divine life."[54]

Wilson concluded by suggesting that to recover from the "abyss" of liberal theology, "Methodism needs only to be true to herself." Methodists, he urged, needed once again to 1) "preach explicitly, strongly, constantly, believingly its glorious doctrines"; 2) "return to the simplicity of the Gospel"; 3) "develop its affectional life which in spiritual life is superior to reason"; 4) "encourage holy enthusiasm"; and 5) "live in the supernatural." He then added, "Perfect *love*," and not "perfect *reason*," had given the Methodists their "hold upon the masses," and it would "do so again."[55]

Deep concern over theological liberalism surfaced in other branches of American Methodism as well. In an article for *The Evangelical*, H. B. Hartzler warned members of the Evangelical Association about trends at Garrett Biblical Institute, saying,

Prof. H. F. Rall, of Garrett Biblical Institute, was president of Iliff School of Theology before going to Garrett. He is a German and was educated in Germany. He unloaded his German U-boat theology upon Iliff and is now doing the same at Garrett. He is the supremely moving spirit in the Commission on the Course of Study for our young preachers, and is more than any one responsible for the un-Methodistic, anti-Biblical, faith-wrecking infidel character of this course.[56]

In holiness circles, Benjamin Franklin Haynes, a former Methodist Episcopal Church, South pastor, active participant in the late-nineteenth-century holiness movement, and first editor of the Pentecostal Church of the Nazarene's *Herald of Holiness* addressed anxiety over liberal Protestant methods of biblical interpretation. In a series of editorials, Haynes insisted that "no progress in Higher or Lower or any other kind of Criticism" could change "one single phrase or fact or feature" of the "great, original, changeless ... and eternal, duplex truth about man's Sin and his Need." Yet, while Haynes was emphatic about the reliability of Scripture with respect to "the great and fundamental truth about sin and salvation," he was also careful to note that this truth was among "*those few things* immutable and eternally settled."[57]

Above all, people like Wilson and Haynes were calling for a return to the theological sensibilities of their Methodist forebears. Echoing Asbury, Wilson urged Methodists not to be sidetracked by "metaphysical disquisitions and refinements," but to remain focused on the "simplicity of the Gospel" and the need for direct, personal encounter with Jesus Christ.[58] Similarly, Haynes exhorted his readers not to be overly concerned about liberal methodologies for interpreting Scripture, but to remember that Scripture's primary purpose was to point all people to the living Christ. Thus, he says,

> All Scripture is His, is of Him, is for Him, is through Him, is by Him, reveals Him, is inseparably joined to Him in honor and integrity and validity. ... The inspired Word centers in, revolves around, points to and reveals Christ as its center and source. ... All true preaching of the Word is to honor Christ. *There is a path from any and every passage of this Bible to the very Christ himself.*[59]

The efforts of Methodists like Wilson and Haynes to recover the theological sensibilities of a previous generation mostly fell on deaf ears. For better or worse, liberalism had succeeded in focusing the conversation on the meaning and credibility of Christian doctrines. Thus, in the decades following, a growing number of American Methodists began to focus their attention and energy on articulating and defending the doctrine of the divine inspiration of Scripture. However, the inspiration of Scripture no longer had primarily to do with the Spirit's work in bringing people to a life-changing encounter with Jesus Christ. Rather, it became the favored strategy for demonstrating the rationality and truthfulness of Christian doctrines over against liberalism. In other words, in their doctrine of Scripture, many self-avowed evangelicals within American Methodism had shifted their focus from soteriology to epistemology.[60]

Nazarene theologian H. Orton Wiley was keen to observe what had happened. In the name of Methodism's evangelical heritage, a "reactionary party" had resorted to "a mere legalistic defense of the Scriptures," which "depended upon logic rather than life." Wiley continued,

> They divorced the written Word from the Personal Word and thus forced it into a false position. No longer was it the fresh utterance of Christ, the outflow of the Spirit's presence, but merely a recorded utterance which bound men [sic] by legal rather than spiritual bonds.... The views of God attained were merely those of a book, not those of a living Christ which the book was intended to reveal.... The Bible thus divorced from its mystical connection with the Personal Word, became in some sense a usurper, a pretender to the throne.[61]

For Wiley, the growing influence of Fundamentalism among American Methodist evangelicals and especially within holiness denominations was a matter of significant concern.[62] In response to theological liberalism, Fundamentalism was threatening to obscure the theological content and vision of an earlier form of American Methodist evangelicalism.

Despite its growing popularity, Fundamentalism did not exhaust American Methodist evangelicalism in the mid-twentieth century. On the contrary, the evangelical sensibilities that flourished in early American Methodism continued to function as a theological leaven in the tradition.[63] This was especially true at the local parish level, where revivals and evangelistic preaching continued to focus the hearts and minds of American Methodists on the basic content of the Gospel, which is to say, on the Incarnation and atonement, and on the work of the Holy Spirit in justification, regeneration, and sanctification. At the denominational level, the uniting of the Evangelical Association and the United Brethren Church to form the Evangelical United Brethren Church (1946) occasioned the production of a new Confession of Faith that embodied the evangelical sensibilities of early American Methodism without being in any way Fundamentalist in content or tone.[64] Finally, a number of American Methodist theologians continued to give expression to earlier evangelical sensibilities through the production of dogmatic or systematic theologies, including Wiley's own three-volume *Christian Theology* and S. J. Gamertsfelder's *Systematic Theology*.[65]

POSTLIBERAL TRAJECTORIES: THE QUEST FOR COHERENCE

By the 1960s American Methodism, like America itself, was on the brink of fragmentation. Theological liberals were prioritizing experience and reason over against the insistence of conservative theologians that Scripture and tradition were of supreme importance. The threat of incoherence was especially alarming to Albert C. Outler. A Methodist (later United Methodist) theologian and early church historian, Outler had personally represented the Methodist Church at Vatican II. A few years later, he would advocate for the union of the Methodist and Evangelical United Brethren churches in 1968, and he would be the natural choice to preach at the first worship service of the newly formed United Methodist Church.[66] Over time, Outler would personally inspire numerous American Methodist theologians to get involved with the work of the National and World Council of Churches and other ecumenical activities.[67]

In the early to mid-1960s, however, Outler was especially concerned about the growing theological fragmentation of Methodism. Determined to heal the mounting tension between theological liberals and conservatives, he developed and deployed a three-part strategy.[68] First, he urged Methodists to return to their roots, most notably, to the long-neglected writings of their founder John Wesley. To aid them in doing so, Outler published a major volume on Wesley that consisted of a lengthy and learned introduction followed by an anthology of Wesley's writings.[69] He could not have anticipated the impact of this volume. In the decades following its publication, an entire generation of American Methodist historians and theologians would heed Outler's call to rediscover Wesley.[70] Indeed, the response to the call to rediscover Wesley was so overwhelming that American Methodists soon began identifying their theological perspective as Wesleyan rather than Methodist.[71]

While Outler deserves credit for inspiring a golden age in Wesley studies, this was not his primary intention. Outler's main purpose in pointing Methodists to Wesley had to do with overcoming the theological fragmentation of Methodism. Hence, the initial appeal to Wesley simply set the stage for the second and third parts of his strategy, both of which he surfaced and advanced through a particular reading of Wesley.

The second part of Outler's strategy can be seen in his emphasis on the deeply ecumenical character of Wesley's theology. In Wesley, Outler discovered and promoted someone deeply influenced by ancient ecumenical sources. Thus, he repeatedly urged Methodists to follow Wesley's lead "back to the sources" and then forward into the future.[72] Like his initial appeal to Wesley, this strategy was also well received, as Methodist historians and theologians began searching far and wide for the ancient ecumenical sources of Wesley's theology.[73] Most recently, this strategy has evolved from a quest for Wesley's ancient ecumenical sources into a search for family resemblances between Wesley and ecumenically significant theologians like Thomas Aquinas.[74]

From the standpoint of its reception by American Methodists, Outler's third strategy was arguably his most influential. Outler urged Methodists to emulate Wesley not only in returning to ancient ecumenical sources, but also in theological method. Wesley, he proposed, did not set reason and experience over against Scripture and tradition. Rather, he appealed judiciously to Scripture, tradition, reason, and experience in a theological method that Outler dubbed "the quadrilateral."[75]

For many American Methodists, the quadrilateral was simple and compelling. United Methodists in particular were quick to endorse the proposal at the highest level of church government. At the General Conference of 1972, they voted to include the quadrilateral in a new section of the *Book of Discipline* called "Doctrine and Doctrinal Standards."[76] The quadrilateral has also been well received in holiness circles.[77] A particularly dramatic example of this can be seen at Spring Arbor University, a Free Methodist school, where the components of the quadrilateral are prominently inscribed on the four columns of a clock tower that stands at the center of campus.

Unfortunately, what initially seemed like a simple and brilliant way to heal the theological tensions between liberals and conservatives only paved the way for a fresh round of controversy. Thus, from 1972 to 1988, United Methodist conservatives worked for legislative change to the "Doctrine and Doctrinal Standards" statement in the *Book of Discipline*. The problem had to do with the failure of the 1972 statement to acknowledge the primacy of Scripture in cases where Scripture appeared to contradict beliefs held or claims advanced in the name of tradition, reason, or experience. The result was the development of a new statement, "Doctrinal Standards and Our Theological Task," which acknowledges the primacy of Scripture and which was approved by the General Conference of The United Methodist Church in 1988.[78]

The 1988 statement notwithstanding, the quadrilateral failed to produce the kind of theological cohesion that Outler originally envisioned. If anything, it obscured the original theological sensibilities that were once at the heart of American Methodism. Compared to the theological vision of early American Methodism, the quadrilateral is a methodological construct that is too unwieldy to bring coherence. In other words, Scripture, tradition, reason, and experience are all extremely large categories that, apart from particular renderings, offer no specific theological content or theological vision, not to mention the kind of egalitarian social vision for which nineteenth- and early-twentieth-century American Methodists were so well known.[79]

At the same time that Outler was proposing a way forward that centered on recovering John Wesley's ecumenical spirit and theological method, a very different trajectory was emerging in the form of liberation theologies. For many liberation theologians, the problem with theological liberals and conservatives was that both groups were so preoccupied with the questions and concerns of the economically and culturally privileged that they failed to notice the political and social concerns of marginalized peoples throughout the world. To be sure, liberation theologies were not confined to American Methodism. However, a striking number of highly influential liberation theologians were either deeply shaped by or actively affiliated with a branch of American Methodism. For instance, James Cone, widely recognized as the founder of black liberation theology, was reared in the AME Church. Jacquelyn Grant, an early and still prominent leader in Womanist theology, is also from the AME Church. Rebecca Chopp, Catherine Keller, and Marjorie Hewitt Suchocki of the United Methodist Church, and Diane LeClerc and Susie Stanley of the holiness movement, are influential feminist theologians. Andrew Sung Park, a United Methodist theologian, represents a form of Asian-American liberation theology that revolves around the concept of *han*. United Methodists Theodore Jennings and Douglas M. Meeks have advanced a liberationist perspective oriented around concern for the poor.

Some American Methodists have discerned in the various forms of liberation theology a departure from the theological sensibilities of Methodism. From another perspective, however, liberation theologies can be viewed as a recovery and creative extension of the radical sensibilities that inhered in early American Methodism. This is precisely how many American Methodist liberation theologians understand their work.[80] To use a metaphor that southern Methodists from the late nineteenth through the mid-twentieth centuries would have recognized, liberation theologies can be seen as a reconfiguration of the American Methodist theological loom.[81] The threads, namely, the insistence that the Gospel is for all and that reception of the Gospel is radically transformative, remain the same even if the resulting patterns are somewhat different. Hence, one can discern in the new liberationist patterns the old appeal to experience, though here it is not an appeal to a philosophical conception of experience (as in liberalism), but to the experiences of groups of people previously excluded from theological conversation.

While a strong case can be made that liberation theologies represent a recovery of early American Methodism's radical sensibilities, they remain highly controversial in many quarters. For Methodist theologians who are deeply committed to the ancient ecumenical faith of the church enshrined in the Nicene Creed and Chalcedonian Definition and to the doctrines at the core of Methodism itself, liberation theologies can appear to be a form of social ethics lacking in dogmatic theological content.[82] Similarly, for Methodists with strong evangelical sensibilities, liberation theologies can appear tone-deaf to the vital role of conversion and spiritual formation in the life of faith. Consequently, like Outler's appeal to Wesley, liberation theologies have been enthusiastically embraced by some American Methodists, but they have ultimately failed to bring cohesion and repair to the fragmentation that currently besets the American Methodist theological tradition.

Despite the stinging criticisms by first generation liberation theologians and numerous obituary notices, theological liberalism has continued to exert influence in American Methodism, most notably in the form of Process theology. To be sure, Process thought did not originate in American Methodism. However, a majority of Process theologians have been affiliated with one of the branches of American Methodism. Inspired by the empirical and pragmatic philosophies of Alfred North Whitehead and Charles Hartshorne, Process theology has flourished in United Methodism in the work of John Cobb, Catherine Keller, Jay McDaniel, Mary Elizabeth Moore, Bryan Stone, and Marjorie Suchocki, in holiness circles in the work of John Culp, Michael Lodahl, and Thomas Jay Oord, and in African Methodism in the work of Monica Coleman and Henry James Young.[83]

Like Boston Personalists before them, Process theologians make experience the basis of a highly creative form of philosophical theology. Also like Boston Personalists, they emphasize the immanence of God, love as essential to God's nature, and the interrelatedness or interconnectedness of all things. Unlike Boston Personalists, however, Process theologians do not limit the concept of experience to "experience that is conscious, sensory, and value-based." Rather, they insist on a more inclusive notion of experience, acknowledging "the validity of uncon scious and nonsensory experience."[84] American Methodist Process theologians are also continuing the grand liberal tradition of facilitating dialogue between Christian theology and other domains of learning. Thus, they are presently involved in interreligious dialogue and in the dialogue between theology and ecology.[85]

The last forty years have also witnessed a concerted effort to recover, promote, and extend American Methodism's evangelical sensibilities. Among theologians, William J. Abraham, Kenneth J. Collins, William M. Greathouse, Joel Green, Elaine Heath, Henry Knight, Rebekah Miles, Joy Moore, Thomas C. Oden, Alan Padgett, Douglas Powe, Stephen Seamands, Don Thorsen, Laceye Warner, and Laurence Wood have all made important contributions on this front. In the United Methodist Church, this effort can be observed in the work of an array of renewal groups, including Aldersgate Renewal Ministries, the Confessing Movement, the Institute on Religion and Democracy, and Good News. Each of these groups is highly active in the life of the church, publishing newsletters, promoting special events, and hosting websites devoted to renewal.[86] In addition, the Foundation for Theological Education and the John Wesley Fellows program has worked to encourage and support the theological education of United Methodists with evangelical sensibilities, many of whom are now teaching in Methodist colleges and seminaries.[87] In holiness circles, historians and theologians have worked to recover and promote American Methodism's evangelical sensibilities primarily through the Wesleyan Theological Society (WTS) and the *Wesleyan Theological Journal*. Founded in 1965, WTS was the product of an "evangelical renaissance" among Wesleyan-holiness scholars that began in the 1940s and 1950s.[88]

Finally, one additional strategy for recovering and promoting evangelical sensibilities within American Methodism is especially worth mentioning. Beginning in the 1950s and 1960s, a significant number of American Methodist theologians discerned a way forward in the work of the Swiss Reformed theologian Karl Barth. Initially, Barth's theology found a ready reception among Methodist theologians at Candler School of Theology and Perkins School of Theology, though his influence in those schools has waxed and waned over the years. From the 1970s down to the present day, however, Barth has been especially influential at Duke Divinity School, most notably in the work of Stanley Hauerwas and William H. Willimon.

Efforts to recover and promote American Methodism's evangelical heritage have been successful to a degree. However, there has also been a strong tendency on the part of advocates for evangelicalism to focus their efforts on the epistemic status of Scripture on the one hand, and on controversial ethical issues on the other, most notably, homosexuality. As a result, the material doctrinal emphases that were at the heart of early American Methodist evangelical sensibilities are often put on the back burner. To be sure, those who have turned to Karl Barth for help have been more attentive to the doctrine of the Trinity and to Christology, but they have also failed to develop a serious *Methodist* option in dogmatic theology.[89] Thus, like the quadrilateral and liberation theologies, evangelical renewal groups have failed to bring theological depth and healing to American Methodism.

AMERICAN METHODISM: A TRADITION
AWAITING DOGMATIC DEVELOPMENT

One way to think about American Methodism today is to envision it as a living and dynamic theological tradition in which five distinct languages are spoken, including evangelicalism, radicalism, ecumenism, liberalism, and Wesleyanism. All five of these languages have been present from the beginning, though in varying degrees.[90] For example, in the period of revivals and awakenings, evangelicalism, radicalism, and ecumenism were more widely spoken than liberalism and Wesleyanism. From the late nineteenth century through the mid-twentieth century, however, liberalism became increasingly more pronounced, with Wesleyanism coming to the fore in the late twentieth century.

Each of these languages revolves around an orienting concern or set of concerns that distinguish it from the others. Evangelicalism revolves around a deep commitment to a short list of material doctrines deemed essential for coming to faith in Christ and for experiencing the transforming power of the Holy Spirit in one's life, as well as to the vital role played by Scripture in that process.[91] Radicalism revolves around an abiding concern for the social and political implications of the Gospel. Ecumenism is animated by a deep concern for dialogue with the orthodox faith of the Christian church embodied in ecumenical creeds and councils, with the works of significant theologians, and with representatives of other Christian traditions today. Liberalism is chiefly concerned with developing arguments from natural theology and with fostering dialogue between theology and other domains of learning. Wesleyanism revolves around a concern to recover and reappropriate John Wesley's theology for Methodism today.

While each of these theological languages can be distinguished from the others on the basis of its orienting concern, they are rarely found in isolation. On the contrary, hybridity is one of the defining features of American Methodist theology today. For example, consider the ways in which the language of Wesleyanism has combined with the other four theological languages described previously.[92] In the work of Kenneth Collins, Wesleyanism and evangelicalism are combined in a dramatic and powerful way.[93] By contrast, Randy Maddox's work fosters a compelling conversation between John Wesley and Eastern Orthodoxy, which is to say, between Wesleyanism and ecumenism. Theodore Jennings represents yet another form of hybridity, combining Wesleyanism with social and political radicalism.[94] Still another form emerges when Methodist theologians combine Wesleyanism and theological liberalism.[95]

Many American Methodist theologians are truly multilingual in their approach, combining three or more of these languages. Two particularly good examples of this can be seen in the work of United Methodist theologians Catherine Keller and William Abraham. On the one hand, Keller's work combines radicalism (in the form of feminist theology), liberalism (in the form of Process theology), and Wesleyanism on a grand scale. On the other hand, Abraham's work combines evangelicalism, Wesleyanism, ecumenism (in the form of an ongoing dialogue with the full canonical heritage of the undivided church and with Methodism and Pentecostalism after Wesley), and liberalism (in the form of an ongoing dialogue with analytic philosophy and especially with epistemology). These are, of course, only two examples among many that could be given. Indeed, the sheer variety of combinations that have emerged in recent years reflects the extent to which American Methodist theology is truly a dynamic and living tradition.

However, insiders to American Methodism know that radical diversity also raises a thorny issue, namely, whether there is a nameable coherence among these theological languages. In other words, what makes all five languages, as well as the many combinations thereof, distinctively Methodist? In wrestling with this question, American Methodist theologians generally fall into two camps. On the one hand, many American Methodist theologians conclude that Methodist theology is like farming: they may not be able to provide a good working definition of what is essential to it, but they know it when they see it. On the other hand, not a few American Methodists have significant doubts about whether there is any real coherence to be shown. For this group, American Methodist theologians are more like the workers at the tower of Babel than they are the disciples at Pentecost.

For those who are not satisfied with either of these responses to the issue of coherence, another possibility is on the horizon. Picking up where theologians like Miley and Summers left off, American Methodists need to resume the difficult and demanding work of fostering a serious Methodist option in dogmatic theology. In other words, the time has come 1) to identify the material doctrines that are constitutive of the Methodist theological tradition and 2) to engage in theological reflection upon those doctrines in a way that honors the orienting concerns associated with the five theological languages described earlier.

While this work will be time consuming, even multigenerational, the raw materials necessary to get started are ready to hand. First and foremost, Methodist theologians can begin to pick out the doctrines that are constitutive of their tradition by consulting the official or canonical doctrines lodged in the disciplines of the various Methodist traditions. Second, Methodist theologians who recognize that lists of official or canonical doctrines often do not exhaust what is actually believed, taught, and confessed will want to explore the largely untapped resource that is the very rich tradition of Methodist catechisms.[96] Third, they will also want to pay close attention to the doctrinal material contained in Methodist liturgical rites, most notably rites pertaining to the sacraments, ordination, healing, marriage, and death. With few exceptions, these materials have not received the attention they deserve.[97] Fourth, Methodist theologians will need to explore the doctrinal content of their various hymn traditions.

Of course, the work of discerning the doctrines constitutive of the Methodist theological tradition is only the first step in the development of a serious Methodist option in dogmatic theology. Once Methodist theologians have done this, they will need to begin the creative and constructive work of reflecting theologically on these materials in a way that honors both the deep theological sensibilities that inhere in the Methodist tradition, as well as the orienting concerns represented by the five theological languages that have emerged from those sensibilities across space and time. For example, Methodist dogmatic theologians might wish to take their initial cues from their evangelical inheritance by working unapologetically from the standpoint of the third article of the Creed. In other words, they might undertake the work of theological reflection from the standpoint of the eschatological outpouring of the Holy Spirit in creation and in the life of the church, patiently showing the myriad ways in which that outpouring leads to loving communion with God the Father in and through Jesus Christ, with one's neighbors, and with the whole of creation. They might also honor their evangelical heritage by accentuating the doctrines of justification by faith, regeneration, and entire sanctification and Christian perfection, and by working to construct theology in a way that assists people in coming to faith, in worshipping the Triune God, and in bearing witness to Jesus Christ in word and deed on behalf of the world.

Those who undertake the work of cultivating a serious *Methodist* option in dogmatic theology will also need to honor the radical sensibilities and concerns that inhere in the Methodist tradition by discerning and exploring the social and political implications of their doctrines. Indeed, any theology that stops short of this work will fail to embody one of the deep animating impulses at the heart of American Methodism. Similarly, a Methodist dogmatics will need to honor the ecumenical sensibilities and concerns that inhere in the Methodist tradition by engaging in ecumenical dialogue with the ancient faith of the Christian church, with the Magisterial Reformers, with the Wesleys, and with representatives of other Christian traditions down through the centuries. Likewise, the cultivation of a distinctively Methodist option in dogmatic theology will honor the orienting concerns represented by liberalism. After all, American Methodists have been committed to fostering dialogue between theology and other domains of learning and interested in arguments and insights from natural theology from the beginning. Moreover, honoring the orienting concerns of liberalism will help to distinguish a Methodist dogmatic theology from its Reformed and Lutheran counterparts.

Finally, the challenge facing the Methodist dogmatic theologian is not that she lacks for enough good doctrinal and theological material with which to work. If anything, she has an overabundance of doctrinal and theological material at her disposal. The real challenge has to do with discerning and naming the deep theological sensibilities that can *heal* and once again *animate* a tradition that many perceive as fragmented beyond repair. In the end, such work belongs to the dogmatic theologian.

Notes

1   In this essay, the terms *revival* and *awakening* refer to a religious culture that centered on multiday indoor and outdoor preaching events, personal conversion and testimony, and other movements of the Spirit loosely regulated by church authorities. In this broad sense, the religious

culture symbolized by revivals and awakenings persists from the first appearance of Methodism in America right down to the present day. The identification of the five distinct theological languages and a discussion of the need for dogmatic development will occur in the final section of this chapter. The languages metaphor is inspired by Russell E. Richey's argument that four languages characterized early American Methodism: popular Evangelical, Wesleyan, Episcopal, and republican. The languages identified in the final section below differ from Richey's in two important ways. First, they are specifically theological languages, whereas Richey's languages include languages that express explicitly political sensibilities. Second, the languages identified here are characteristic of American Methodism across space and time, whereas Richey's argument focuses on early American Methodism. See Russell E. Richey, *Early American Methodism* (Bloomington, IN: Indiana University Press, 1991).

2 For the experiential and psychological dimensions of the culture of revival, see Ann Taves, *Fits, Trances, and Visions: Experiencing Religion and Explaining Experience from Wesley to James* (Princeton, NJ: Princeton University Press, 1999).

3 See the chapter by Ted A. Campbell in this volume.

4 See the chapter by Michael K. Turner in this volume.

5 *Doctrines and Discipline of the Methodist Episcopal Church in America* (n.p.: Methodist Episcopal Church, 1798), 85, emphasis added.

6 *Doctrines and Discipline* (1798), 85.

7 *Doctrines and Discipline* (1798), 85.

8 Richard Allen, *The Life Experience and Gospel Labors of the Rt. Rev. Richard Allen* (Nashville, TN: Abingdon Press, 1960), 30.

9 For more on these emphases in early American Methodist theology, see Leland Scott, "The Message of Early American Methodism," in *The History of American Methodism*, vol. 1., edited by Emory Stevens Burke (New York: Abingdon Press, 1964), 291–359.

10 Early American Methodists routinely stressed the importance of the divinity of Jesus. For more on this, see Jason E. Vickers, "Christology," in *The Oxford Handbook of Methodist Studies*, edited by William J. Abraham and James E. Kirby (New York: Oxford University Press, 2009), 554–572. Also see Lester Ruth, *Early Methodist Life and Spirituality: A Reader* (Nashville, TN: Kingswood Books, 2005), ch. 1.

11 For an overview and comparative analysis of the official Methodist doctrinal statements of a wide range of American Methodist churches, see Ted A. Campbell, *Methodist Doctrine: The Essentials*, 2nd ed. (Nashville, TN: Abingdon Press, 2011).

12 See Jason E. Vickers, "Begotten from Everlasting of the Father: Inadvertent Omission or Sabellian Trajectory in Early American Methodism?" *Methodist History* (July 2006), 251–261.

13 *Doctrines and Discipline* (1798), 86, emphasis original.

14 As quoted by Harry V. Richardson in *Dark Salvation: The Story of Methodism as It Developed among Blacks in America* (Garden City, NY: Anchor Press/Doubleday, 1976), 105 (emphasis in original).

15   Written by Judson W. Van De Venter (1855–1939), a Methodist evangelist from Pennsylvania, this hymn is included in the current hymnals of
every major Methodist body in America. Together with other hymns and
songs that deploy such metaphors, the popularity of this hymn reflects
the enduring nature of the religious culture of revivals and awakenings.

16   Nathan Bangs, *Letters to Young Ministers of the Gospel on the Importance
and Method of Study* (New York: N. Bangs and J. Emory, 1826), emphasis
added.

17   Examples of the emphasis on regeneration are abundant in every branch
of American Methodism. For a little known but exemplary text in the
United Brethren tradition, see S. D. Faust, *Regeneration* (Dayton, OH:
United Brethren Publishing House, 1902).

18   See Nathan O. Hatch, *The Democratization of American Christianity*
(New Haven, CT: Yale University Press, 1991); also see John H.
Wigger, *Taking Heaven by Storm: Methodism and the Rise of Popular
Christianity in America* (Urbana, IL: University of Illinois Press, 2001).

19   Richardson, *Dark Salvation*, 47–48.

20   For more on early American Methodism's radical social and political
sensibilities, see Cynthia Lynn Lyerly, *Methodism and the Southern
Mind, 1770–1810* (New York: Oxford University Press, 1998).

21   For more on these themes, see the chapters by Morris Davis, Dennis
Dickerson, and Laceye Warner in this volume.

22   As quoted by Donald W. Dayton in "Good News to the Poor: The
Methodist Experience After Wesley," in *The Portion of the Poor: Good
News to the Poor in the Wesleyan Tradition*, edited by M. Douglas
Meeks (Nashville, TN: Kingswood Books, 1995), 85.

23   Donald W. Dayton, "Piety and Radicalism: Ante-Bellum Social
Evangelicalism in the U. S., in *From the Margins: A Celebration of the
Theological Work of Donald W. Dayton*, edited by Christian T. Collins
Winn (Eugene, OR: Pickwick Publications, 2007), 38.

24   Rebecca Chopp, "Anointed to Preach, Speaking of Sin in the Midst
of Grace," in *The Portion of the Poor: Good News to the Poor in the
Wesleyan Tradition* (Nashville, TN: Kingswood Books, 1995), 100.

25   See Christine Leigh Heyrman, *Southern Cross: The Beginnings of the
Bible Belt* (New York: Knopf, 1997); also Donald G. Mathews, *Slavery
and Methodism: A Chapter in American Morality, 1780–1845* (Princeton,
NJ: Princeton University Press, 1965).

26   See "The Tension Regarding Racialization," in Chapter 3 of this volume.

27   Allen, *Gospel Labours*, 30.

28   In this section, the term *ecumenical* simply refers to the work of engaging in theological dialogue with other Christian traditions or churches.

29   For the disagreement over the referent of doctrinal standards, see Richard
P. Heitzenrater, "At Full Liberty: Doctrinal Standards in Early American
Methodism," in *Doctrine and Theology in The United Methodist
Church*, edited by Thomas A. Langford (Nashville, TN: Kingswood Books,
1991), 109–124; and Thomas C. Oden, "What Are 'Established Standards
of Doctrine,': A Response to Richard Heitzenrater," in *Doctrine and
Theology in The United Methodist Church*, 125–142. Nashville, TN:
Kingswood Books, 1991. On Wesley's diminishing influence, see Randy

L. Maddox, "Respected Founder/Neglected Guide: The Role of Wesley in American Methodist Theology," *Methodist History* 37 (1999): 71–88.

30 See John Miley, *Systematic Theology*. 2 vols. (New York: Hunt & Easton, Cincinnati: Cranston & Stowe, 1892–1894); and Thomas O. Summers. *Systematic Theology: A Complete Body of Wesleyan Arminian Divinity*. 2 vols., edited by J. J. Tigert (Nashville, TN: Publishing House of the Methodist Episcopal Church, South, 1888).

31 Randy L. Maddox provided these data through email correspondence with the author on Monday, October 29, 2012.

32 For more on the founding and mission of Methodist schools, see the chapter by Stan Ingersol in this volume. For the clergy's response to perceived intellectual and cultural changes, see E. Brooks Holifield, *God's Ambassadors: A History of the Christian Clergy in America* (Grand Rapids, MI: Wm. B. Eerdmans Publishing Company, 2007).

33 Summers' work was edited and published posthumously by J. J. Tigert.

34 See John Miley, *The Atonement in Christ* (New York: Phillips and Hunt, 1879).

35 For more on the progressive character of Miley's theology, see Robert E. Chiles, *Theological Transition in American Methodism* (Landham, MD: University Press of America, 1983).

36 Bangs, *Letters to Young Ministers of the Gospel*, 14.

37 As quoted by E. Brooks Holifield, *Theology in America: Christian Thought from the Age of the Puritans to the Civil War* (New Haven, CT: Yale University Press, 2003), 259.

38 Gary Dorrien, *The Making of American Liberal Theology: Imagining Progressive Religion, 1805–1900* (Louisville, KY: Westminster John Know Press, 2001), 372. Also see Francis J. McConnell, *Borden Parker Bowne: His Life and His Philosophy* (New York: AMS Press, 1929).

39 Dorrien, *Imagining Progressive Religion*, 372–373.

40 For example, see Borden Parker Bowne, *Studies in Christianity* (Boston: Houghton Mifflin, 1909).

41 For an excellent introduction to the theology of personalist idealism, see Gary Dorrien, *The Making of American Liberal Theology: Crisis, Irony, & Postmodernity, 1950–2005* (Louisville, KY: Westminster John Knox Press, 2006), 9–57.

42 Dorrien, *Imagining Progressive Religion*, 392.

43 Bowne successfully defended his work as well as the work of his colleagues against accusations of heresy in large part by framing the conversation in terms of evangelistic effectiveness and credibility.

44 For more on Harkness, see Gary Dorrien, *The Making of American Liberal Theology: Idealism, Realism, and Modernity, 1900–1950* (Louisville, KY: Westminster John Knox Press, 2003), 390–414. For a collection of some of Harkness's most important writings, see *Georgia Harkness: The Remaking of a Liberal Theologian*, edited by Rebekah Miles (Louisville, KY: Westminster John Knox Press, 2010).

45 Schubert M. Ogden, *Christ without Myth: A Study Based on the Theology of Rudolf Bultmann* (Dallas, TX: Southern Methodist University Press, 1961), 131.

46 Ogden, *Christ without Myth*, 132–133.

47   William James, *The Varieties of Religious Experience* (New York: Touchstone, 1997), 389, n. 9.

48   James, 389–390.

49   George W. Wilson, *Methodism v. The Methodist Theologians* (Cincinnati, OH: Jennings & Pye, 1904), 5.

50   Wilson, *Methodism v. The Methodist Theologians*, 12.

51   Wilson, *Methodism v. The Methodist Theologians*, 7.

52   Wilson, *Methodism v. The Methodist Theologians*, 346–348.

53   Wilson, *Methodism v. The Methodist Theologians*, 330–331.

54   Wilson, *Methodism v. The Methodist Theologians*, 345.

55   Wilson, *Methodism v. The Methodist Theologians*, 347–348.

56   H. B. Hartzler, "Alarming and Humiliating," *The Evangelical*, March 5, 1919, p. 7. For more on the reaction to liberalism in the Evangelical Association, see William Naumann, "Doctrine and Theology in the Evangelical Association/Church," in *Methodist and Pietist: Retrieving the EUB Heritage*, edited by J. Steven O' Malley and Jason E. Vickers (Nashville, TN: Kingswood Books, 2011), 93–107.

57   Benjamin Franklin Haynes, "Old, New and Eternal," in *Herald of Holiness*, June 5, 1912, p. 4, emphasis added.

58   Wilson, *Methodism v. The Methodist Theologians*, 340–341.

59   Benjamin Franklin Haynes, "Christ the Center and Source," in *Herald of Holiness*, April 8, 1914, p. 4, emphasis added.

60   For more on the soteriological conception of Scripture that had been a hallmark of early American Methodism, see Donald W. Dayton, "The Pietist Theological Critique of Biblical Inerrancy," in *From the Margins*, 193–206.

61   H. Orton Wiley, *Christian Theology*, 3 vols. (Kansas City, MO: Beacon Hill Press, 1940), 1:141–142.

62   See Paul M. Bassett, "The Fundamentalist Leavening of the Holiness Movement, 1914–1940 – in the Church of the Nazarene: A Case Study," *Wesleyan Theological Journal* 13:1 (1978): 65–91.

63   For an account of this, see Riley Case, *Evangelical and Methodist: A Popular History* (Nashville, TN: Abingdon Press, 2004).

64   Following the 1968 union of the EUB Church and the Methodist Episcopal Church, this Confession of Faith was included alongside the latter church's Articles of Religion in the newly formed United Methodist Church's *Book of Discipline*. For more on the Confession of Faith, see Jason E. Vickers, "The Confession of Faith: A Theological Commentary," in *Methodist and Pietist*, 109–138.

65   See H. Orton Wiley, *Christian Theology*; and Solomon J. Gamertsfelder, *Systematic Theology* (Cleveland, OH: Evangelical Publishing House, 1921). Gamertsfelder combined many evangelical and liberal emphases. For more on his work, see William H. Naumann, "Solomon J. Gamertsfelder, Theologian," *Telescope Messenger* (Center for the Evangelical United Brethren Heritage, United Theological Seminary) 18, no. 1 (2008):1–5; and Ted A. Campbell, "Progressive Evangelicalism: The Theological Matrix of Garrett-Evangelical," *AWARE* (Winter 2005): 2–3.

66 Albert C. Outler, "Visions and Dreams; the Unfinished Business of an Unfinished Church," in *The Wesleyan Theological Heritage: Essays of Albert C. Outler*, edited by Leicester R. Longden and Thomas C. Oden (Grand Rapids, MI: Zondervan, 1991), 253–262.

67 See Geoffrey Wainwright, *Methodists in Dialogue* (Nashville, TN: Kingswood Books, 1995). In addition to ongoing Methodist participation in ecumenical dialogue through the National and World Council of Churches, Outler's legacy can be seen in the recent consultations between Wesleyan and Eastern Orthodox theologians. Papers from these consultations have now been published in the following volumes: *Orthodox and Wesleyan Spirituality*, edited by S. T. Kimbrough, Jr. (Crestwood, NY: St. Vladimir's Seminary Press, 2002); *Orthodox and Wesleyan Scriptural Understanding and Practice*, edited by S. T. Kimbrough, Jr. (Crestwood, NY: St. Vladimir's Seminary Press, 2006); and *Orthodox and Wesleyan Ecclesiology*, edited by S. T. Kimbrough, Jr. (Crestwood, NY: St. Vladimir's Seminary Press, 2007).

68 See Jason E. Vickers, "Albert Outler and the Future of Wesleyan Theology: Retrospect and Prospect," *Wesleyan Theological Journal* 42:2 (2008): 56–67.

69 *John Wesley*, edited by Albert C. Outler (New York: Oxford University Press, 1964).

70 Outler was aided significantly in this work by the historian Frank Baker.

71 This shift in terminology is problematic on a number of levels. Most notably, it has led to a preoccupation with Wesley and, comparatively speaking, to an ignoring of the Methodist theological tradition after Wesley. Insofar as the term *Wesleyan* is supposed to signal a renewed commitment to John Wesley, it is worth remembering that Wesley himself preferred the name *Methodist* in part because of the ridicule and scorn that accompanied the term. For more on Outler's influence in Wesley studies, see the Introduction to *The Cambridge Companion to John Wesley*, edited by Randy L. Maddox and Jason E. Vickers (New York: Cambridge University Press, 2010).

72 See Albert C. Outler, *Theology in a Wesleyan Spirit* (Nashville, TN: Tidings, 1975).

73 For an excellent example of this Outler-inspired trend in Wesley studies, see Randy L. Maddox, "John Wesley and Eastern Orthodoxy: Influences, Convergence, and Differences," *Asbury Theological Journal* 45:2 (1990): 25–53.

74 For instance, see Edgardo Colon Emeric, *Wesley, Aquinas, and Christian Perfection: An Ecumenical Dialogue* (Waco, TX: Baylor University Press, 2009).

75 For the first usage of this term, see *John Wesley*, Outler, ed., iv. For a later, expanded account, see Albert C. Outler, "The Wesleyan Quadrilateral – In John Wesley," in *Doctrine and Theology in The United Methodist Church*, 75–90.

76 For an account of the proceedings leading up to this, see Albert C. Outler, "Introduction to the Report of the 1968–1972 Theological Study

Commission," in *Doctrine and Theology in The United Methodist Church*, 20–25.

77   For example, see Don Thorsen, *The Wesleyan Quadrilateral: A Model for Evangelical Theology* (Lexington, KY: Emeth Press, 2005).

78   For more on this statement, see Richard P. Heitzenrater, "In Search of Continuity and Consensus: The Road to the 1988 Doctrinal Statement," in *Doctrine and Theology in The United Methodist Church*, 93–108.

79   See William J. Abraham, *Waking from Doctrinal Amnesia: The Healing of Doctrine in The United Methodist Church* (Nashville, TN: Abingdon Press, 1995). Also see Andrew P. Thompson, "Outler's Quadrilateral, Moral Psychology, and Theological Reflection in the Wesleyan Tradition," *Wesleyan Theological Journal* 46:1 (2011): 49–72.

80   *Methodist and Radical: Rejuvenating a Tradition*, edited by Joerg Rieger and John J. Vincent (Nashville, TN: Kingswood Books, 2004). Also see Donald W. Dayton, *Discovering an Evangelical Heritage* (New York: Harper & Row, 1976); and Susie Stanley, "Empowered Foremothers: Wesleyan/Holiness Women Speak to Today's Christian Feminists," *Wesleyan Theological Journal* 24 (1989), 103–116.

81   In the cotton mills so prevalent in the American South, looms were used to weave cloth. My grandparents, Elbert F. and Martha Vickers, like many of the members of their beloved Wesleyan Church, spent most of their lives in this oppressive setting. The noise of the looms stole their hearing at an early age, and the stigma of working in a cotton mill robbed them of any chance for social standing in society. In the Wesleyan Church, however, they were able to put their musical talents to use and to develop a sense of social worth and belonging. They would not have understood liberation theology, but in many ways, they embodied it. For more on the history of Methodism, cotton mills, and the American South, see Liston Pope, *Millhands and Preachers* (New Haven, CT: Yale University Press, 1965).

82   For a carefully nuanced example of this, see Andrew C. Thompson, "From Societies to Society: The Shift from Holiness to Justice in the Wesleyan Tradition," *Methodist Review* 3 (2011): 141–72.

83   For an introduction, see Bruce G. Epperly, *Process Theology: A Guide for the Perplexed* (London: T&T Clark, 2011).

84   Thomas Jay Oord, "Wesleyan Theology, Boston Personalism, and Process Thought," in *Thy Nature and Thy Name Is Love: Wesleyan and Process Theologies in Dialogue*, edited by Bryan P. Stone and Thomas Jay Oord (Nashville, TN: Kingswood Books, 2001), 386.

85   For example, Nazarene theologian Michael Lodahl has made important contributions in both of these areas. See his *Claiming Abraham: Reading the Bible and Qur'an Side by Side* (Grand Rapids, MI: Brazos Press, 2010); and *God of Nature and of Grace: Reading the World in a Wesleyan Way* (Nashville, TN: Kingswood Books, 2004).

86   For an account of this phenomenon, see Thomas C. Oden, *Turning Around the Mainline: How Renewal Movements Are Changing the Church* (Grand Rapids, MI: Baker Books, 2006).

87   For more on this, see http://www.johnwesleyfellows.org/.

88 http://wesley.nnu.edu/wesleyan-theological-society/our-history/ The Wesleyan Theological Society and *Wesleyan Theological Journal* have also helped to recover and promote American Methodism's radical and ecumenical sensibilities for holiness churches.

89 A good case can be made that overdependence on Barth is one of the chief reasons that American Methodists have failed to develop their own dogmatic tradition.

90 For example, all five languages are on display in Nathan Bangs' *Letters to Young Ministers of the Gospel* (1816).

91 On this account, Fundamentalism is a reactionary form of evangelicalism in which the conception and role of Scripture is primarily epistemological rather than soteriological.

92 For a full list of the ways in which Methodist theologians have combined Wesleyanism with other theological languages, see William J. Abraham, "The End of Wesleyan Theology," *Wesleyan Theological Journal* 40:1 (2005): 7–25.

93 The work of Kenneth J. Collins is especially noteworthy, including *The Scripture Way of Salvation: The Heart of John Wesley's Theology* (Nashville, TN: Abingdon Press, 1997); *John Wesley: A Theological Journey* (Nashville, TN: Abingdon Press, 2003); and *John Wesley's Theology: Holy Love and the Shape of Grace* (Nashville, TN: Abingdon Press, 2007).

94 See Theodore Jennings, *Good News for the Poor: John Wesley's Evangelical Economics* (Nashville, TN: Abingdon Press, 1990). Also see *Sanctification and Liberation: Liberation Theologies in the Light of the Wesleyan Tradition*, edited by Theodore Runyon (Nashville, TN: Abingdon Press, 1981).

95 See John Cobb, *Grace and Responsibility: A Wesleyan Theology for Today* (Nashville, TN: Abingdon Press, 1995).

96 See William McDonald, "What Shall We Do for the Rising Generation: Methodist Catechisms, 1745–1928," *Wesleyan Theological Journal* 43:2 (2008): 177–192.

97 See Karen B. Westerfield Tucker's chapter in this volume. For important exceptions, see Don E. Saliers, *Worship as Theology: Foretaste of Glory Divine* (Nashville, TN: Abingdon Press, 1994); also see Geoffrey Wainwright, *Doxology: The Praise of God in Worship, Doctrine and Life* (Oxford: Oxford University Press, 1980).

2 Early American Methodism

RUSSELL E. RICHEY

In 1787, the young Methodist Episcopal Church (MEC) rearranged and "methodized" its *Discipline*. Its earlier 1784-Christmas-Conference-produced version had followed the curious order and replicated much of the contents of British Methodism's foundational document, the "Large Minutes." Retaining John Wesley's question-answer format, the MEC prefaced the 1787 *Discipline* with history, asking about "the Rise of Methodism (so called) in Europe and America." Answering question 3, the MEC *Discipline* Americanized the answer to Mr. Wesley's mission statement. "What may we reasonably believe to be God's Design, in raising up the Preachers called Methodists?" The *Discipline* answered:

> To reform the Continent, and spread scripture Holiness over these Lands. As a Proof hereof, we have seen in the Course of fifteen Years a great and glorious Work of God, from New York through the Jersies, Pennsylvania, Maryland, Virginia, North and South Carolina, even to Georgia.

By dating the "great and glorious Work of God" from their arrival, the preachers credited themselves with the decisive role. Candor might have led them to the acknowledgment that laity – women, men, youth, whites, African Americans, rich, poor – were often the initiators of Methodist organization and expansion.

Indeed, the prior two questions and answers broadened Methodist agency considerably. To the first, "What was the Rise of Methodism, so called, in Europe," the *Discipline* repeated Mr. Wesley's three-sentence narration from the "Large Minutes" of John and Charles Wesley and the Holy Club. To question 2, "What was the Rise of Methodism, so called, in America," the *Discipline* provided the first historical account of the American movement:

> *Answ.* During the Space of thirty Years past, certain Persons, Members of the Society, emigrated from England and Ireland, and

44

settled in various Parts of this Country. About twenty Years ago, Philip Embury, a local Preacher from Ireland, began to preach in the City of New-York, and formed a Society of his own Countrymen and the Citizens. About the same Time, Robert Strawbridge, a local Preacher from Ireland, settled in Frederick County, in the State of Maryland, and preaching there formed some Societies. In 1769, Richard Boardman and Joseph Pilmoor, came to New-York; who were the first regular Methodist Preachers on the Continent. In the latter End of the Year 1771, Francis Asbury and Richard Wright, of the same Order, came over.[1]

This "official" history made clear that American Methodism had emerged spontaneously. Boardman, Pilmore, and Asbury, commissioned by Wesley, came to resource an already-launched movement. The *Discipline* neglected to credit Barbara Heck with prompting Embury or Elizabeth Strawbridge with effecting the first conversion. Nor did the *Discipline*-drafting young white preachers who constituted the new church's conference think it important to mention that these early societies included African Americans. Still, implicitly the history acknowledged that growing the little Methodist movement was and would be an all-hands operation. Similar affirmations can be made of other early Methodist movements, including the United Brethren, the AME, and the AMEZ.

A spontaneously spreading, all-hands operation would long remain Methodism's signature thanks to the document the little history prefaced, the *Discipline*. It provided a template, as had Wesley's "Large Minutes" and related publications, for an activist, entrepreneurial, evangelistic enterprise energized from above and from below, balancing organization and Spirit, locating authority with preachers but empowering laity, centralizing decision making with conference (hence preachers) but ordering the movement from the ground up, and prescribing rules but eliciting emotional display. The tensions in Mr. Wesley's designs may have been more dynamically equipoised and productive in North America because colonial Methodists got used to being on their own.[2] Indeed, the spontaneous beginnings and the sheer distance separating colonial Methodists from Wesley and the British conference generated a kind of balance between and among three creating, shaping, promulgating Methodist factors – communities of witness, itinerating preachers who went out from and returned to conference(s), and the Wesley-ordered connection – the discipline and doctrine that he had prescribed, scattered through various publications of his but eventually held together for Americans in the little handbook for the Christian life, individual and corporate, the *Discipline* (Beginning in 1792, the MEC titled its book *The Doctrines and Discipline of the Methodist Episcopal Church.*)

SPONTANEOUS START-UPS

Sharing this triadic pattern – communities of witness and an order of itinerating preachers held together by discipline and doctrine – was the movement that coalesced around the German Reformed pastor William Otterbein and the Mennonite preacher Martin Boehm. The itinerating Otterbein heard Boehm at a revivalistic "great meeting" in 1767 in Lancaster County (PA) and recognized their kinship ("Wir sind Brüder!") as sharing a vibrant piety (see below).[4] Trained at the Pietist theological center of Herborn, recruited for the colonial synod and in good standing for the duration of his ministry, Otterbein held a number of German Reformed pastorates, the last in Baltimore (1774–1813). Remaining always a pastor, he itinerated broadly, raising up others to range widely over scattered adherents and occasionally gathering these itinerating preachers. Boehm, on the other hand, was excommunicated by the Mennonites and thus was freed to travel. In 1785, Otterbein (and Boehm) gave form to what would eventually be the United Brethren with "The Constitution and Ordinances of The Evangelical Reformed Church of Baltimore."[5] The document, published the same year as the MEC's *Discipline*, held together itinerating preachers and communities of witness with the confessional, churchly, apologetic, orthodox, covenantal, and christocentric doctrines and practices of Herborn Pietism.

Pietism – a transatlantic, transconfessional, diffuse religious reform in its Herborn, Mennonite, Wesleyan, and other expressions – keyed the aforementioned triadic impulse. It did so reclaiming one or another standard of doctrinal orthodoxy (e.g., Lutheran or Calvinist) understood to be a return to Scripture. Scriptural piety was to be expressed fully in conversion, not simply a forensic alteration in one's status with God but a discernible inner redemptive experience. Transformed, a reborn Nicodemus, a re-creation in Christ, the convert's character and life manifested its new identity in fruits of the Spirit, including especially testimony – by praise, hymn, or letter. Small groups networked and resourced those reborn and those seeking rebirth. Various termed (conventicles, religious societies *collegia pietatis*), these little-churches-within-the-church featured Bible study, witness, prayer, hymn singing, and other empowering spiritual disciplines. Readily spawned by laity given space for group leadership, the communities of witness raised up "converted" preachers and came to expect the church's leadership to be so authorized, whatever other standards for ministry might apply. Such expectations could and did issue in powerful critiques of stolid religious institutions and uninspiring clergy.

Steeled by such sentiments, the giants of Methodism, indeed of British evangelicalism, John and Charles Wesley and George Whitefield, had labored in the colonies. The Wesleys had fled in some disgrace. In six wildly successful evangelistic tours, the grand itinerant Whitefield had introduced his Calvinistic Methodism but did not organize societies to sustain his revivals. Instead, the little spontaneous Methodist efforts of Heck and Embury in New York City and the Strawbridges in Frederick County (MD) provided real foundations. Robert Strawbridge itinerated in Maryland, in Virginia, and into Pennsylvania establishing what would mature as societies in Baltimore, Georgetown, Washington, DC, and Leesburg. Several converts became local preachers. Numbered among his contributions to Methodist leadership were Jacob Toogood (African American), William Watters, and Freeborn Garrettson. Outreach from New York owed much to Captain Thomas Webb. After colonial military service, he had returned to England, was converted, and, when back in America, stumbled on the New York society. His efforts keyed Methodist beginnings at Albany and Schenectady, on Long Island, in the Philadelphia area (Chester and Bristol), in New Jersey (Trenton, Burlington, and New Mills), and in Delaware (Wilmington and New Castle).

The New York movement wrote John Wesley describing the situation and requesting help – "a man of wisdom, of sound faith, and a good disciplinarian."[6] In response, Wesley sent over successive pairs of itinerants. Richard Boardman and Joseph Pilmore in 1769, Francis Asbury and Richard Wright in 1771, Thomas Rankin and George Shadford in 1773, and James Dempster and Martin Rodda in 1774. Several preachers came to the colonies on their own, including Robert Williams.

The British emissaries – Pilmore and Boardman, then Asbury, then Rankin –experienced the little spontaneously initiated Methodist efforts to be out of compliance with normative Wesleyanism. Running American societies according to the General Rules, holding property under the Model Deed and Trust Clause, regularizing itinerancy, remaining within the Church of England and therefore refraining from baptizing and celebrating Communion – these touchstones of Wesleyan order proved a challenge for the British preachers. For instance, a quarterly conference of late 1772, convened by Asbury as Wesley's assistant, wrestled with the question "Will the people be contented without our administering the sacrament?" "Indeed yes," Methodist preachers working the South, Pilmore and Williams, assured cooperating Anglican clergy like Devereux Jarratt, who frequented Methodist gatherings and administered the Lord's Supper. "No," seemingly replied Strawbridge, who also continued celebrating the sacraments. Six months later, in June 1773, Rankin, replacing Asbury as "general assistant" and disciplining his charge from Wesley, convened the first annual conference. Rankin complied, posing three queries demanding assent to Wesleyan order, the third of which registered the gathering's tone, "if any preachers deviate from the [Large] Minutes we can have no fellowship with them till they change their conduct?" The conference reiterated the prohibition against administering the sacraments and prohibited Williams from printing more of Mr. Wesley's books, a restraint indicating another act of American initiative and independence. Rankin appointed the ten preachers from New York to Virginia, himself and Shadford to New York and Philadelphia with the plan to switch in four months. Four, including Asbury and Strawbridge, were sent to Baltimore. Maryland accounted for 500 of the overall 1,160 Methodist numbers, a testimony to Strawbridge's success.

WARS: AGAINST SLAVERY AND AGAINST BRITAIN

The conference minutes do not register how many of that number were African Americans. That record of membership by race begins with the 1786 minutes, tallying a tenth of the overall 18,791 as black. However, from the start the preachers commented on the biracial character of early Methodism.[8] African Americans responded enthusiastically to their acceptance and inclusion in Methodist classes, to the Wesleyan message of love, free grace, and liberty, and to the strong antislavery preaching. And in 1780, colonial Methodism went on record requiring preachers to free slaves and issued a similar expectation of members generally:

> Does this conference acknowledge that slave-keeping is contrary to the laws of God, man, and nature, and hurtful to society; contrary to the dictates of conscience and pure religion, and doing that which we would not others should do to us and ours? – Do we pass our disapprobation on all our friends who keep slaves, and advise their freedom? Answ. Yes.[9]

Some whites on conversion and by conviction indeed freed their slaves and Methodist antislavery contributed significantly to manumissions in the middle colonies/states. However, Methodist antislavery proved and would continue to prove highly controversial.

Also controversial was Methodism and Mr. Wesley during the Revolution. As colonial-British relations worsened Wesley cautioned Rankin and company to be "peace-makers," striving for neutrality. Wesley failed to heed his own counsel, issuing in 1775, *A Calm Address to Our American Colonies*, the first of several loyalist pamphlets.[10] Several of his preachers echoed Wesley's strong Tory sentiments. Two of these, Webb and Martin Rodda, collaborated with the British militarily, the latter actually gathering a loyalist force on the eastern shore of Maryland. These loyalist publications and actions and its identity as a movement within Anglicanism tarred Methodism as pro-British. Some Methodists experienced persecution, most notably Freeborn Garrettson. Asbury went into hiding. But Methodists also served the revolutionary cause, including Thomas Ware, later a preacher, under arms, and Jesse Lee, as a noncombatant and chaplain. Rankin and others of Wesley's appointees, save for Asbury, returned to England.

The flight of Anglican priests and the prospect of success for the revolutionary cause led Methodists in the South to recognize that "the Episcopal Establishment is now dissolved" and to plan for a movement unconnected with the Church of England or with Mr. Wesley. The regularly called conference of May 1779, meeting in Fluvanna (VA), proceeded to organize as an independent church, to ordain some of their number, to establish them as a presbytery, to authorize celebration of the sacraments, and to draw up some (minimal) liturgical and disciplinary rules.[11] This independence-tracking portion of Methodism reported 6,086 members, almost three-quarters of the 8,577 total. Anticipating the regular Fluvanna conference, Asbury called a late April 1779 "preparatory" conference for "the convenience of the preachers in the northern stations" and because it was deemed "unadvisable" for him to travel away from his Delaware safekeeping. The "preparatory" measure, then ineffective, had been to forestall self-ordinations, assumption of sacramental authority, and independence. Hence, Quest.10 asked, "Shall we guard against a separation from the Church, directly or indirectly? The answer: by all means."[12]

The 1780 Asburian conference, technically no more "regular" than its predecessor, listed its first question as "What preachers do now agree to sit in Conference on the original plan as Methodists?" Later actions disapproved of "the step our brethren have taken in Virginia" and deemed them no longer "Methodists in connection with Mr. Wesley and us till they come back." They also set conditions for reunion, namely, suspension of "all their administrations for one year" and meeting together in Baltimore.[13] The Asburian cabal sent a delegation to Virginia (Asbury,

Garrettson, and Watters), and the Virginians reluctantly accepted the terms and healed Methodism's first schism.

THE METHODIST EPISCOPAL CHURCH

The dramatics of separation and reconciliation strengthened Asbury's role as "general assistant in America."[14] The experience of the two conferences had, however, led the preachers to like the convenience of a conference toward the North and one toward the South. This resulted in what John Tigert termed the "Baltimore system" of governance, multiple conference sessions whose final legislative word came from its Baltimore meeting, represented by a single set of minutes.[15] So, waiting for some ecclesiastical deliverance from Mr. Wesley, the Americans continued aggressive evangelization across the colonies and legislated and functioned in conference(s) in a very independent, churchlike fashion.

Deliverance came by delegation and instruction. The delegation – the Rev. Dr. Thomas Coke as superintendent and Richard Whatcoat and Thomas Vasey as elders – were all ordained as such by Wesley in a letter "To Dr. COKE, Mr. ASBURY, and our Brethren in *NORTH-AMERICA*."[16] Recognizing the new political and ecclesiastical situation consequent of the Revolution, Wesley had "drawn up a little Sketch" for a new church order, appointed "Dr. Coke and Mr. Francis Asbury, to be joint *Superintendents* over our Brethren in North America," drafted a liturgy for the new church, and exhorted American Methodists to be "at full liberty, simply to follow the Scriptures and the Primitive Church." These provisions, Richard P. Heitzenrater notes, revised or provided analogues of documents constitutive of the Church of England. For example, Wesley's "liturgy," *The Sunday Service for the Methodists in North America*, was a revision of the Book of Common Prayer (BCP), and his twenty-four Articles of Religion a revision of the Church of England's thirty-nine Articles of Religion. In keeping with the traditions of the Established Church, Wesley provided a Psalter, *A Collection of Psalms and Hymns for the Lord's Day*. Wesley's *Sermons* and *Notes on the New Testament* served the boundary-setting functions of the Anglican Book of Homilies and "Canons."[17] The "little Sketch," a revised "Large Minutes," became the *Discipline* and held all these church-defining documents together.

Wesley apparently thought that the Americans would simply receive and live into these texts, accepting as well the plan for Coke to ordain Asbury as superintendent. Church by such regal (Wesleyan) decree did not suit Asbury and others at a quarterly conference at Barratt's

Figure 3. **Ordination of Francis Asbury (1784)**, Methodist Library Image Collection, Drew University, Madison, New Jersey.

Chapel, Delaware, where Coke and his British colleagues appeared. The Revolution had taught the Americans a little about constitution making, and Asbury, having earned leadership by the preachers' affirmation and having little incentive to become Coke's suffragan or auxiliary wanted superintendents-by-election. So the Americans proposed the calling together of the preachers, essentially to be a constitutional convention. They sent Garrettson off to summon the preachers to the late December 1784 "Christmas Conference." The gathering did elect Coke and Asbury superintendents, the former "ordaining" the latter to deacon, elder, and then superintendent on successive days, using the *Discipline*'s revised Anglican service for ordination of bishops. By its three-fold ordering of ministry (others ordained to the first two orders), by acceptance of Wesley's several Anglican-light church-constituting documents, and through selection of its middle name (Methodist *Episcopal* Church), the conference proclaimed itself an episcopal church. The Christmas Conference kept no minutes, so whether or not African-American preachers Harry Hosier and Richard Allen attended cannot be proved. However, among its several important acts was a courageous set of antislavery mandates providing explicit guidelines for staged emancipation. Prefiguring troubles to come, the *Discipline* also called for white oversight of African-American gatherings, and it failed to provide for lay voice in conference.[18]

CONFERENCING

On paper the equipoise between and among communities of witness, the itinerating preachers, and the connecting discipline and doctrine might look different after MEC organization – with its preachers-only conference, Wesley-like appointive power in the superintendents, and presiding elders exercising authority on local levels. But a community might see and hear a preacher only once in six weeks, a presiding elder (P.E.) once a quarter, and a bishop only if traveling through. Compensating for this very occasional and tenuous ministerial oversight was a system of gatherings prescribed for the ordering of the Christian life, individually and corporately. In effect, Methodism structured itself with a series of conferences, occasions for conversation about the way of holiness. Indeed, conferencing was perceived of as one of the "instituted" means of grace.[19] A more constitutionally astute and theologically shaped movement might have labeled each level in this series a "conference," but Wesley had labeled gatherings as he adopted them.

The basic level, in the colonies and new church, was the *class*, the small group typically overseen by a white male leader. A member belonged to a class rather than to a local church, congregation, or society. In other words, the class functioned as the membership unit. In the class, members held themselves and one another to the demanding disciplines of the way of holiness. These disciplines are elaborated in detail in the fittingly described *Discipline*. In the cities classes were connected to a *society*. More typically, classes on itinerant preaching circuits belonged and reported to quarterly meetings or quarterly conferences, and those oversaw societies as well. From 1780 on, American Methodists arrayed the *quarterly meeting* as two-day events, preferably Saturday and Sunday.[20] Religious festivals from the start and sacramental occasions after 1784, the quarterly meeting licensed leaders, recommended persons for ordination, collected donations (quarterage), heard appeals in disciplinary cases, and affected other business of Methodism at a local level. Before the advent of camp meetings, the quarterly meeting drew huge crowds, particularly in warm weather, and became a two-day festival for preaching, love feasts, and sacraments. After camp meetings emerged, Methodists routinely adopted and staged them as one of the warm-weather quarterly meetings, effectively conjoining their revivalistic, business, and sacramental affairs. In the quarterly meeting – attended by black and white, female and male, young and old, members and leaders – Methodism most fully exhibited the range of duties and services that the "Articles of Religion" defined as "church."

The annual conference had, even before 1784, exercised a governing, legislating, rule-creating role. Strangely, the Christmas Conference did not attend to constitutional details with respect to conference such as composition, call, powers, presidency, authority, and voting. The first *Discipline* merely carried over the Large Minutes' exhortation about proceeding spiritually in conference and Wesley's who, what, how questions that identified money coming in and preachers going out. The 1787 "methodized" *Discipline* brought those sections together and added the responsibility of electing and ordaining bishops, elders, and deacons. Further formalization came at the 1792 and 1796 General Conferences. The latter reduced what had been the increasing number of conferences (seventeen in 1792, nineteen in 1793), establishing geographical boundaries for six. Though the number would increase again and again, boundaries made annual conference into membership units.

The fourth conference level, General Conference, emerged only after other measures for connectional governance failed. Bishop Coke, who exercised oversight roles in Ireland, the West Indies, Canada, and the United States, returned in 1787 with explicit written directions from Wesley for "a General Conference of all our preachers in the United States, to meet at Baltimore on 1st May 1787," and for appointment of Richard Whatcoat as "Superintendent with Asbury" and of Freeborn Garrettson for British North America. Three conferences had been appointed for 1787, and all three were rescheduled so that the third could meet in Baltimore in July. At the second gathering, in late April at Rough Creek, Virginia, James O'Kelly and Jesse Lee led opposition to Coke, to Wesley's exercise of authority, and to the nomination of Whatcoat. The Baltimore affair, really just the third annual conference, elected no new superintendents. It qualified Coke's authority, stipulating in the *Annual Minutes* to the first question – who are the superintendents – the answer: "Thomas Coke, (when present in the States), and Francis Asbury." It also removed from the 1784 *Discipline* the designation of superintendents as Wesley's "Sons in the Gospel, ready in Matters belonging to Church-Government, to obey his Commands."[21] After the 1787 conferences, Coke and Asbury decided that "bishop" rather than "superintendent" better described their office, a decision ratified in the 1788 conferences and *Discipline*.

Meeting in more than one conference and expanding in numbers and territory, Methodism struggled with decision making under the Baltimore system. In 1788 alone, Methodism added 11,481 members and nineteen circuits by extending its penetration beyond the upper South or Chesapeake, creating new circuits in South Carolina, western

Pennsylvania, Kentucky, (West) Virginia, Ohio, New York, and Georgia, and establishing significant toeholds beyond the Appalachians and Alleghenies. That year the church did its business in eighty-five circuits and seven conferences, the last of which was in Philadelphia, not Baltimore. In 1789, eleven conferences met, with Baltimore located in the middle of the schedule rather than the end where decisions could be finalized. Thus collapsed the Baltimore system of governance, a casualty of Methodist growth.

With its work so extended and conference government so fragmented, would Methodism have but one voice, that of Francis Asbury? In 1789 and 1790 the church experimented with a council, in effect an executive committee, initially composed of the bishop(s) and presiding elders (Asbury's appointees who served at his pleasure). Though unpopular, it provided briefly for efficient decision making – regularizing publishing, authorizing a magazine (the *Arminian Magazine*), promoting education (including finances for Cokesbury College), envisioning Native American missions, and issuing guidelines for worship. Leading a campaign against the Council were Irish-born P. E. James O'Kelly and Jesse Lee. They favored a general conference with Lee proposing that it be delegated (a democratic principle that would have to wait). Coke, who was supportive of the Council but whose visits to America (1787, 1789, and 1791) did not permit his attendance at the two meetings, also favored a general conference.

The first General Conference met in Baltimore, November 1–15, 1792. It established itself as the ongoing legislative authority for the church, deciding to convene again in four years as a body of the "preachers in full connection." It determined that annual conferences would also be so constituted, bringing together two or more of the districts under the purview of the presiding elders. The latter office General Conference also formalized, but it limited terms in one place to four years due to concern over the concentration of power with presiding elders.

NEW METHODISMS

Early in the 1792 General Conference, P. E. James O'Kelly, more concerned with the authority of the bishops, offered a motion permitting preachers who were "injured" by the bishop's appointment the "liberty to appeal to the conference" and the right, if the appeal was sustained, to another appointment. In a long and intemperate debate, O'Kelly invoked the rhetoric of republicanism, of the Revolution, of American liberty, and of democracy. When the motion failed, O'Kelly and his supporters bolted to form a rival movement. His Republican Methodists prospered in lower Virginia and upper North Carolina (O'Kelly's district), and their appeal threatened to split Methodism in two. In apologetic tirades, O'Kelly lambasted Asbury and espoused a new polity protective of liberty, grounded in Scripture alone, and explicitly antislavery.[22] Asbury worked diligently to counter the schism at both the intellectual and relational levels. He responded, implicitly, by editing and publishing, in Wesley-like fashion, *The Causes, Evils, and Cures of Heart and Church Divisions*. He commissioned Nicholas Snethen, his "silver trumpet," to refute O'Kelly. In several tracts, Snethen portrayed the Republicans as schismatic, heretical (particularly on the Trinity), driven by O'Kelly's megalomania, and excessively critical of Asbury. At the 1796 General Conference's direction, Asbury and Coke answered O'Kelly, annotating the *Discipline* to explain and provide Scriptural warrant and defense for Methodist polity and practice (including bishops and appointed presiding elders). In 1801, O'Kelly renamed the movement the Christian Church, and it later coalesced with others of a restorationist bent.

The separation of black Methodists from the MEC proceeded slowly. Their issues were not with Asbury but with white attitudes generally, the segregation of classes by race, and the MEC's steady retreat from its early antislavery resolve. In the early 1790s Richard Allen took important steps along the way toward independence, walking out of St. George's and establishing Bethel Church as an African-American congregation in Philadelphia. In a 1794 "Public Statement" Bethel explained why it required separate accommodations. The same year, other black Philadelphians organized African Zoar, a congregation that would remain MEC and therefore represent a second option for black Methodists. The 1800 General Conference authorized the ordination of black deacons (an action not published). Allen and Daniel Coker of Baltimore were among the earliest to hold this office. That General Conference also issued a widely distributed pastoral letter imploring a state-by-state antislavery campaign of petitions to legislatures.[23] Its southern reception – publicly burned in Charleston – motivated the 1804 General Conference to publish a version of the *Discipline* without the section on slavery. That self-censorship became policy in 1808 as that General Conference authorized "each annual conference to form their own regulations relative to buying and selling slaves." By 1816, admitting that "little can be done to abolish a practice so contrary to the principles of moral justice," the MEC deemed "the evil ... to be past remedy" and moved to qualify a prohibition against slaveholders holding office. That year, Black Methodists led by Allen and Coker gave up on the MEC, constituted the African Methodist Episcopal Church (AME), and selected Allen as their bishop.[24]

Three other late-eighteenth- and early-nineteenth-century schisms challenged the bishops and episcopal order. William Hammet, ordained by Wesley, served in the West Indies and with Coke's assistance settled in Charleston. He built a strong following there, resisted the authority of Asbury and Coke over his congregation, and in 1792 broke away to found the Primitive Methodists. The movement drew support in the Carolinas but dissipated after Hammet's death in 1803. At the northern reaches of the denomination, a group of "Reformed Methodists" led by Pliny Brett, who had itinerated from 1805 to 1812, sought church government and local authority similar to Congregationalism. They protested episcopacy, emphasized the attainability of entire sanctification, and repudiated war and slavery. Formally organized in 1814 at a convention in Vermont, they drew several thousand adherents across New England, New York, and Canada. By the Civil War, most of the Reformed movement had affiliated with the Methodist Protestants (see below). Another separate Methodist body, also with the name Primitive Methodists, developed around the eccentric figure of Lorenzo Dow, who exported camp meeting revivalism to Britain after 1805 and imported the export as a distinct denomination beginning in 1829. The Primitives, also critical of established MEC order, developed strength in Pennsylvania and especially in Canada.

Two German-American movements, the United Brethren (UBC) and Evangelical Association, also coalesced in this time frame. An 1800 meeting of the "United Ministers" adopted a new name, *Vereinigten Bruderschaft zu Christo* (United Brethren in Christ), agreed to meet annually, approved believer's as well as infant baptism, selected their two founders, Otterbein and Boehm, as bishops, and empowered them to appoint preachers to circuits upon consultation with pastors and circuits.[25] The German Reformed recognized the break and began expulsion of UBC members, the first of whom was George Geeting (in 1804), who along with Christian Newcomer and Andrew Zeller succeeded to leadership, the latter two later became bishops. Geeting served as the church's secretary. A stabilizing figure, Newcomer led the UBC in unity explorations with both the MEC and the EA, as his journal indicates.[26] Newcomer related warmly to Bishops Francis Asbury and William McKendree, just as Otterbein and Boehm had done earlier. Rules adopted by 1813 expected preachers to have a renewed heart and to pursue holiness and a church ordered "by doctrine and life, by prayer and a godly walk."[27] With Asbury's encouragement, the MEC Philadelphia

[margin handwritten notes: challenge to the episcopal order (discipline and polity)]

Conference translated the MEC *Discipline* into German in 1807–1808, but the UBC paid little heed to it. Negotiations with the MEC formalized in letters continued from 1809 to 1814. Methodists objected to the UBC's term episcopacy and less resolute itinerancy. By 1815, when the UBC gathered for its first General Conference, unity with the MEC was off the table.

The UBC refined its confessional statement in 1815 and again in 1819. Even so, its doctrinal formulations and religious practices continued to reflect its Reformed and Mennonite past. The UBC kept centralized power lean, maintained term episcopacy, elected its presiding elders, appointed preachers through a stationing committee, ordained in one stage (to elder), and kept ministerial identity in the congregation. Class meetings, which were structured loosely, remained voluntary. The UBC prospered in southeastern Pennsylvania, Maryland, and northern Virginia, and the Miami River valley in Ohio.

In most of these areas, the Evangelical Association (EA) competed with the UBC. Like the latter, the EA developed gradually without a transition crisis. By contrast to the UBC, the EA tracked MEC doctrine and discipline closely. Jacob Albright, catechized Lutheran, found a spiritual home with the Methodists after his 1791 conversion experience. The Methodists promptly licensed him as an exhorter.[28] Beginning in 1796, Albright itinerated through German-speaking communities, preaching salvation through a renewed heart rather than through traditions, liturgies, and catechisms. After expulsion by the Lutherans in 1797, he gathered converts into classes, held camp meetings, and raised up other preachers. A conference in 1803 recognized Albright as leader, ordained him, commissioned two other preachers as associates, and constituted itself as a society. The first regular EA annual conference in 1807 was attended by five itinerants, three local preachers, and twenty class leaders. They called themselves the *Neuformirten Methodisten Conferenz* (Newly Formed Methodist Conference), authorized a German translation of the MEC *Discipline*, and elected and ordained Albright as bishop.[29] The *Discipline* fell to George Miller, Albright's chief assistant, to complete, as Albright died the next year (1808). Despite affinities, the desire to become the German-speaking conference of the MEC went nowhere with Asbury, who objected to the EA's persistent use of the German language. In 1814, George Miller retired. John Dreisbach, elected presiding elder and charged with denominational oversight, convened a General Conference (1816), which approved a new name, *Evangelische Gemeinschaft* (Evangelical Association), authorized negotiations with the UBC, reshaped the *Discipline*, authorized a hymnal, but elected no bishop. For the next twenty years, two presiding elders, Dreisbach and Henry Niebel, led the EA. In 1839, the church selected its second bishop, John Seybert, a former Lutheran. In contrast to the UBC, the EA clung firmly to the German language well into the twentieth century.

MEC REORGANIZATION

Composed of those in full connection (after 1800) who found themselves able to attend, General Conference met frequently in Baltimore and increasingly was dominated by the most proximate and larger annual conferences, Philadelphia and Baltimore. In 1804 members of those two conferences overwhelmed the other five conferences, 70 to 42; in 1808, the ratio was still 63 to 66. Defined by their membership and geographical contours, conferences increasingly behaved like states, and the distant ones resented not being represented proportional to their membership. An 1804 memorial for equal conference representation was endorsed by the four more distant conferences (New York, South Carolina, New England, and Western) but opposed by Philadelphia, Baltimore, and Virginia. The 1808 General Conference, guided by Asbury, established a committee of two persons from each conference to deal with the concern. Ezekiel Cooper drafted a plan with a bishop for each conference, or failing that, the election of presiding elders. Joshua Soule proposed a delegated General Conference, its power limited in several crucial areas, among them being modification of "our present existing and established standards of doctrine" and alteration of the plan of an "itinerant general superintendency." Soule's proposal, with this set of "Restrictive Rules" at its heart, came eventually to be regarded as the constitution of the church.[30]

Ironically, by defining General Conference by annual conference representation, Soule indeed altered the episcopacy, making bishops presiders only, no longer empowered to initiate legislation, create committees, and make motions. American-born William McKendree, elected in 1808, expanded episcopal leadership in other ways, most notably by creating cabinets of presiding elders in conference and by setting General Conference agendas. The latter he established in 1812, apparently without advance notice to Asbury, with an agenda-outlining address.[31] An Episcopal Address would thereafter begin General Conference's work.

Asbury's death en route to the 1816 MEC General Conference created a sense of crisis. Coke had also died, leaving William McKendree as his successor. General Conference worried over deviance on discipline, dress, sacramental practice, pew rental, and doctrine, detecting heresies of Arianism, Socinianism, and Pelagianism. It elected Enoch George and Robert Richford Roberts to the episcopacy, selected Joshua Soule as book agent, authorized a magazine (the variously titled *Methodist Magazine*, launched in 1818), and established the Course of Study, a reading regimen for candidates for the ministry that continues to the present day. It also took up again the question whether presiding elders should be elected.

Nathan Bangs, Soule's successor as book agent, really led the translation of crisis into program by the reorganization of the MEC and the transformation of Methodism from an aural/oral into a textual community.[32] Books, newspapers, tracts, Sunday school materials, and magazines thereafter defined Methodism's triadic pattern – texts, papers, and tracts serving its communities of witness, the order of itinerating preachers creating Sunday school and missionary society instead of Wesley's class, books and magazines for preachers and *Christian Advocate*(s) for people mediating Methodism's adhesive discipline and doctrine.

Bangs became Book Concern head in 1820, but he had already published books defending Methodist doctrine, ministry, and episcopacy. Under his leadership the MEC established a Missionary Society in 1819, an endeavor stimulated by the initiative of John Stewart (part African American and part Native American) among the Wyandotte in Ohio. A Women's Auxiliary, constituted three months later, would be but one of the women's benevolent and service enterprises through which Mary Morgan Mason paralleled Bangs's organizational fecundity.[33]

To build constituency and encourage conference and local auxiliaries, Bangs used the *Methodist Magazine*. But his founding of the *Christian Advocate* in 1826, which capitalized on others' success with local papers, most dramatically established Methodism as a textual community. Within two years its 25,000 subscribers and far more readers made the *Advocate* the authoritative Methodist voice and the most widely distributed serial in the nation. A bishop might be heard by one small group here and another there. The *Advocate* put the entire adult membership – a church exploding west and south – on the same page. For the MEC's children, Bangs launched in 1823 a monthly periodical called the *Youth's Instructor and Guardian*. He also flooded the church with Sunday school materials after 1827, when the MEC dropped out of the Calvinist-dominated American Sunday School Union and established its own Sunday School Union (SSU). And for the preachers whose promotion helped (the women and men) establish missionary societies, sustain Sunday schools, and subscribe to the *Advocate* and other literature, the Book Concern rolled out the books required by the Course of Study. So Bangs and company made Methodism into one big educational system, a text-defined community. The founding of colleges for men and women would come in the late 1820s and 1830s as Methodism increasingly settled into roles that shaped American society.

REFORMERS

Communication systems that served Methodist machinery helped conquer the continent and promoted respectability that could also critique power and perceived abuses thereof. In 1821, William Stockton, a New Jersey and later Philadelphia printer, founded such a reform medium, the semimonthly *Wesleyan Repository and Religious Intelligencer*, succeeded in 1824 by the Baltimore periodical, *The Mutual Rights of Ministers and Members of The Methodist Episcopal Church*. Through the paper, Stockton, other laity, and ministers advocated for the democratic reform of the church. They specifically called for the election of presiding elders, lay representation, local preacher rights, fair procedures in church trials, and checks on episcopal tyranny. The maturation of this reforming impulse would soon result in a new denomination, the Methodist Protestants.[34]

William Stilwell, a white elder in charge of two African-American congregations, Asbury and Zion, led the formation of a short-lived denomination (the Stilwellites), which shared concerns with the Methodist Protestants and with which surviving remnants united. Stilwell aided the New York black Methodists in efforts to chart a middle way between separation from and continued subservient status within the MEC. James Varick had a leadership position among black Methodists for some three decades, ran a school in his home and later in his church, and was one of the five black deacons ordained in 1806 and 1808. This cadre led New York African Americans in successive New Year's Day antislavery and antislave-trade celebrations. They also pressed for control over Zion and for elders' ordination. These would become strategic issues after 1818, when they started a new building and found themselves competing with the AME's beginning to work in the New York area.

Gathering twenty-two preachers in a conference (1821), they asked the Philadelphia and New York annual conferences to set apart "a Conference for African Methodist preachers, *under the patronage of the white Methodist Bishops and Conference.*"[35] Philadelphia assented. New York pled that the decision belonged to General Conference. Stilwell encouraged independence. A committee had been working on *The Doctrines and Discipline of the African Methodist Episcopal Church in America.* Organizing on this platform and on Philadelphia's posture, New York black Methodists met in their first conference on June 21, 1821, with white elders William Phoebus, as president, and Joshua Soule, as secretary. Lacking a bishop, the conference ordained no elders. The following year Stilwell and two other renegade Methodist elders ordained a number of elders, among them James Varick and Christopher Rush, Zion's first two bishops. When the 1824 MEC General Conference failed to embrace this new conference, its distinct denominational identity was secured. Varick convened the first General Conference of the AMEZ Church in 1826, which reelected him to the episcopacy. Varick died the next year, just days after New York's deadline for freeing all slaves. Rush succeeded Varick as superintendent, leading the AMEZ until his health failed in 1852.

Notes

1   *Discipline*/MEC 1787, 3. Reproduced in Russell E. Richey, Kenneth E. Rowe, and Jean Miller Schmidt, eds. *The Methodist Experience in America: A History* (Nashville, TN: Abingdon Press, 2010), 10. The latter will be cited as MEA 1 and its companion volume, *The Methodist Experience in America: A Sourcebook* (Nashville, TN: Abingdon Press, 2000), will be cited as MEA 2 followed by the document date.
2   David Hempton, *Methodism: Empire of the Spirit* (New Haven, CT: Yale University Press, 2005).
3   On this triad, see Russell E. Richey, *The Methodist Conference in America: A History* (Nashville, TN: Kingswood Books, 1996).
4   MEA 1, xvii-iii, 1–4.
5   MEA 2, 1785b.
6   MEA 2, 1768.
7   MEA 2, 1773.
8   MEA 2, 1769, 1771, 1784c, 1788.
9   *Minutes*, MEC 1780.
10 MEA 2, 1775b.
11 MEA 2, 1779.
12 *Minutes*/MEC 1779 (Delaware).
13 *Minutes*/MEC 1780.
14 *Minutes*/MEC 1779 (Delaware).
15 Jno. J. Tigert, *The Making of Methodism: Studies in the Genesis of Institutions* (Nashville, TN: Methodist Episcopal Church Publishing House, 1898) and *A Constitutional History of American Episcopal Methodism*, (Nashville, TN: Methodist Episcopal Church Publishing House, 1908) 122–124; 523–531.
16 MEA 2, 1784a.
17 Richard P. Heitzenrater, *Wesley and the People Called Methodists* (Nashville, TN: Abingdon Press, 1995), 288–290. Karen Westerfield Tucker, *American Methodist Worship* (Oxford: Oxford University Press, 2001).

18   For a list of Christmas Conference accomplishments see MEA 1, 51–52.
19   *Discipline*/MEC 1785, 25.
20   *Minutes*/MEC/1780, 12.
21   *Minutes*/MEC/1787, 26; *Discipline*/MEC 1785, 3.
22   MEA 2, 1792a.
23   MEA 2, 1800a.
24   MEA 2, 1816, MEA 1, 91–101.
25   MEA 2, 1800b.
26   MEA 2, 1813c.
27   MEA 2, 1813a.
28   MEA 2, 1791b.
29   MEA 2, 1807.
30   MEA 2, 1808.
31   MEA 2, 1812a.
32   MEA 1, 103–140.
33   MEA 1, 124–126.
34   For more on this, see Chapter 3 in this volume.
35   MEA 2, 1821a; MEA 1, 592, n9.

3 American Methodism in the Nineteenth Century: Expansion and Fragmentation

DOUGLAS M. STRONG

When Peter Cartwright – often lifted up as the quintessential symbol of the frontier circuit-riding itinerant – published his autobiography in 1856, he provided his readers with an illuminating overview of Methodism during the first half of the nineteenth century. Cartwright rendered an insightful perspective, for instance, on the 1816 quadrennial Methodist Episcopal Church (MEC) General Conference, the first of many of these national delegated conventions to which he was elected. Looking back, he recognized the historical import of that meeting, acknowledging the symbolic significance of the passing of Francis Asbury, American Methodism's first bishop, just prior to the Conference.[1] Left to carry on in Asbury's absence was William McKendree, chosen at the previous General Conference to assist the aging Asbury. The church's first native-born bishop, McKendree personified Methodist expansion in the trans-Appalachian Western frontier, from which he had carried out his ministry. As the "senior bishop" for the next nineteen years, McKendree helped to shape many aspects of the post-Asbury era.

Cartwright observed a number of other momentous features related to the 1816 General Conference. Most evidently, the MEC reported exponential growth – in numbers, administrative structure, and territory. Statistically, the denomination gained thirty thousand members in 1815 alone; Cartwright understandably interpreted this expansion as a time of "general prosperity." The numerical advancement necessitated the development of a larger, more integrated institutional configuration. Although the MEC's formal organization as a denomination dated back to 1784, for a number of years it still functioned more like a revival movement or missionary order under the direction of a determined, single-minded leader. With continuing enlargement, however, the personalized oversight characteristic of Asbury's administration and the minimalist structures of early Methodism were no longer adequate.[2] Thus, the 1816 General Conference and its successors created many new annual conferences (regional judicatories) to service the ever-increasing Methodist members, circuits, and preachers. Likewise, during the quarter century after Asbury's demise, new bishops were elected to work alongside McKendree (Enoch George and Robert Roberts in 1816; Joshua Soule and Elijah Hedding in 1824; John Emory and James O. Andrew in 1832) and then, following McKendree's death, as a more collective episcopate (Beverly Waugh and Thomas Morris in 1836 and Leonidas Hamline and Edmund Janes in 1844). The greater number of bishops indicated the perceived need for more supervisory leadership of the spreading denomination.

This numerical and structural expansion paralleled the territorial expansion of the nation, especially westward, and the church moved rapidly into each and every new area of European American settlement. Along the way, Methodists also incorporated Indian tribes, slaves, free blacks, Mexican Americans, and (eventually) newly arrived Asian immigrants and European immigrants from non-Anglo-Saxon backgrounds. Women, too, were drawn to Methodism; they outnumbered men in society membership and class meeting attendance, and these groups were some of the few places in nineteenth-century American culture where women were able to "find a voice." Indeed, more than any other institution, Methodism came to epitomize the breadth of American society, by evangelizing a broad sweep of the dominant (white) culture along with more marginalized (Native American, African American, Latino, and Asian American) cultures. While other religious sects also gained supporters, nineteenth-century Methodism nevertheless stood out as America's most representative religious group; by 1830, the MEC was the largest and the most geographically widespread denomination, a place it held for nearly the rest of the century.[3] In numbers, Methodism grew twentyfold (1,939 percent), from 64,894 members in 1800 to 1,259,906 in 1850. (During the same period, the nation's population increased 437 percent.) The Methodist share of the total population during the first half of the century went from 1.2 percent to 5.4 percent. In just one quadrennium (from 1832 to 1836), Cartwright reported, the MEC added six new conferences and 59,000 members; he confidently declared that the MEC, "in point of prosperity and increase of number in her ministry and membership, stands without an equal in the Protestant world since the day of the apostles." No wonder church historians have dubbed the nineteenth century as "the Methodist age in America."[4]

INSTITUTIONAL GROWTH AND DEVELOPMENT

Methodism's pattern of interlocking conferences – "General" (national representative gatherings every four years), "Annual" (regional associations divided by states or other large territories, and the meetings held once a year with all of the appointed elders in that region), "Quarterly" (combined preaching services, sacramental meetings, and business sessions held in "districts" overseen by "presiding elders"), and weekly (preaching services and small accountability groups, called "class meetings," in local "societies" or congregations) – proved to be an efficient, highly effective, and well-organized structure for growth. Each level of conference ("conferring") expressed an ongoing spiritual conversation among Methodist believers – fellow seekers after a life of holiness, through the power of God's Spirit, as mediated by the Christian community. On the local level, these various occasions for personal testimony and worship were conducted periodically by circuit-riding itinerant clergymen, appointed by the bishop, and weekly by stewards, exhorters, and class leaders (all of whom were lay people, sometimes including women). Camp meetings, grafted by Asbury and others into the denominational ethos as a providentially well-suited "means of grace," also continued to infuse Methodism with emotional energy and enthusiasm throughout the early nineteenth century, especially as they were combined with district-wide Quarterly Conferences.[5]

Through this system, Methodist classes and preaching circuits kept pace with (and sometimes preceded) the expansion of settlement: In 1833, circuits were organized in Iowa and Wisconsin; in 1836, Methodist preachers followed the newly opened National Road into Indiana; in 1837, Martin Ruter was appointed superintendent of the Texas Mission; in 1847 (even *before* the Gold Rush), William Roberts developed Methodist societies in San Francisco and, in 1849, in the Pacific Northwest; in 1849 (*during* the Gold Rush), William Taylor preached in the streets of San Francisco; in 1853, Benigno Cardenas preached the first Methodist sermon to Latinos in Mexican territory in Santa Fe; also in 1853, David Blaine started the first church of any kind in Seattle; in 1854, the first church ever established in the city of Chicago was founded; the same year, William Goode began Methodist work in Nebraska and, four years later, in Colorado; and, in 1864, the first Methodists arrived in Montana. Cartwright referred to this westward spread as the "progress and prosperity of the Methodist Episcopal Church."[6]

The same theme of expansion occurred among German-speaking Methodists – whether in the MEC or in the two German language Pietist denominations: the United Brethren in Christ (UBC) and the Evangelical Association (EA). The MEC developed ministry among German transplants wherever they settled, especially in the Ohio valley and further west, under the enterprising direction of William Nast, himself an immigrant from Germany. The UBC followed an extension pattern similar to what occurred in the MEC after Asbury's death, as the first generation leadership of Philip Otterbein and Jacob Boehm passed from the scene, to be replaced in 1813 by the very competent second-generation bishop Christian Newcomer. Newcomer, like the nineteenth-century MEC bishops, rode a continuous circuit, ceaselessly evangelizing throughout the Middle Atlantic and Midwest, especially in Ohio. Membership in the UBC mushroomed from approximately ten thousand in 1813 to forty-seven thousand in 1850; new conferences were established; and strong prohibitions against slavery and any connection with secret societies were enacted in the 1820s. In like manner, the EA deployed John Dreisbach and John Seybert (the first bishop after Jacob Albright, elected in 1839) as able second-generation leaders. The Association formed a number of new conferences among ethnic Germans in the Midwest and also took an abolitionist stand regarding slavery.[7]

African-American Methodism thrived as well in the early nineteenth century. After their founding (narrated in the previous chapter), the African-American Methodist denominations grew, but not especially rapidly, at first; the AME Church expanded from seven thousand to seventeen thousand in a twenty-two-year period (1826–1848), and the AMEZ Church increased from 1,689 members to 4,600 members in a twenty-nine-year period (1831–1860). Nonetheless, AME bishops Richard Allen (who served until his death in 1831) and, later, Morris Brown and William Quinn, furnished their church with exceptional leadership as the AME Church initiated its ministry throughout the northern and midwestern states. The denomination's work in Ohio (and, eventually, further west) began with the establishment of Allen Temple AME Church in Cincinnati in 1824. The AME Church even started congregations in twelve southern states, but black-run organizations were suppressed in the South after several slave revolts. AMEZ Church work was concentrated mostly in the northeastern United States, though some AMEZ congregations sprang up as far afield as California by the early 1850s. In addition to congregations in the AME and AMEZ Churches (self-identified African-American denominations), a few black congregations within the MEC were formed in northern and border state areas.[8]

The largest number of African-American Methodists prior to the Civil War, in both the North and the South, held their membership in majority white congregations of the MEC, even though these white-dominated churches practiced segregated seating and usually required communicants of color to receive the sacrament after all the whites were served. Despite the overt racism, many African Americans were designated as licensed local preachers and exhorters. In 1844, 13 percent of the MEC membership was African American, and one-third of all southern African-American Christians (about 120,000) were Methodists. At the same time, African-American slaves also participated in the "invisible institution" of fervent, clandestine Christian worship that took place in the "brush arbors" of southern plantations, in addition to their attendance at the legally recognized church services. Indeed, the stunning proliferation of black Methodists (along with black Baptists) in the antebellum period, considering the outright prejudice they faced and the onerous restrictions on assembly and free travel they endured, can be explained by the distinctive ways in which African Americans appropriated the Christian faith and made it their own – particularly in terms of its cultural expression.[9]

Among Methodists of all ethnic backgrounds, the uniform message preached during the early nineteenth century was conversion to Christ and living a sanctified life. Peter Cartwright personified this born again/holiness gospel when he stated that "real religion" consists of the Holy Spirit "bearing witness with our spirits that we are the children of God," which results in an affective expression of faith, a "sensible evidence of a change of heart." Indeed, when Cartwright ran in 1846 as the Democratic nominee for Congress from Illinois against Whig nominee Abraham Lincoln, his main campaign issue was Lincoln's unsuitability for office because of his rationalistic religious skepticism. Cartwright's problem with his Whig opponent was Lincoln's unwillingness to affirm a palpable conviction of sin and an explicit new birth encounter with Jesus. Consequently, Cartwright referred to Lincoln as an "infidel." Though Cartwright eventually lost the race against Lincoln, at least the voters in his district – most of whom were well aware of Cartwright's religious agenda because of his years of colorful preaching around the circuit – recognized that his insistence on evangelical conversion was typical Methodist fare.[10]

Methodism grew at an energetic rate in the early national period and with that growth came competition and opposition. In the religious landscape of the first half of the nineteenth century, Methodism shared the territory with – and disputed with – Baptists, Calvinists (Presbyterians and Congregationalists), and (less prevalently) Restorationists (Campbellites), Universalists, Unitarians, and Mormons. Sermons were preached and tracts published against all these groups and vice versa.

Methodists refused to cooperate with the Unitarians and Universalists because their doctrinal differences were considered beyond the pale, or with Campbellites and Mormons, because of their perceived unorthodoxy and sectarianism (that is, their insistence that no group but their own could be considered to be Christian). The Mormons especially frustrated the Methodists, because they tended to work in the same areas and Methodism was the religious tradition that provided the largest number of early Mormon adherents (at least 28 percent). According to Peter Cartwright's (unflattering) account of his interaction with Joseph Smith, the circuit rider claimed that Smith admitted to him that: "among all the Churches in the world, the Methodist was the nearest right."[11]

With Presbyterians, Congregationalists, and Baptists, though, Methodists extended more cooperation – even while disagreeing and competing with them – particularly in evangelistic efforts like camp meetings. In this regard, Methodists were part of the nineteenth-century "evangelical consensus," groups that accepted each other as fellow Christians because they shared a biblically centered, regeneration-focused piety, but who were "denominated" differently – characterized by competition but usually not by condemnation.[12]

Despite, or perhaps assisted by the competition, Methodists flourished throughout the American continent, accounting for a third of all church members by mid-century. The ballooning numbers needed to be serviced – more conferences, more bishops and presiding elders, and many thousands more preachers.[13] Significant changes occurred during the second quarter of the century as the denomination gained size: Larger, more elaborate church buildings were constructed; many of the circuit riders dismounted and became stationed pastors who were appointed to one or two sizeable churches with a parsonage; class meetings for spiritual accountability were supplemented with, and then replaced by, Sunday school classes for religious instruction; and publishing enterprises – especially the Methodist Book Concern under the direction of Nathan Bangs – produced a multitude of books and periodicals such as the various regional editions of the *Christian Advocate*, the *Sunday School Advocate*, the *Methodist Magazine and Quarterly Review*, the *Ladies' Repository*, *Zion's Herald* (Boston), *Wesleyan Journal* (Charleston), *Der Christliche Apologete* (edited by William Nast for the German-speaking MEC), *Der Christliche Botschafter* and the *Evangelical Messenger* for the EA, the *Religious Telescope* (for the UBC), *Mutual Rights* (for the MPC) and the *True Wesleyan* (for the WMC). Methodists also began scores of colleges during the same period. The 1820 General Conference encouraged each annual conference to develop liberal arts colleges under their own auspices. Though starting late, the Church quickly outpaced other denominations' higher education efforts. Of those schools founded by the MEC, the earliest were McKendree (the first, in 1828), Randolph-Macon, and Wesleyan (Connecticut).[14]

Meanwhile, Methodists also gained a vision for evangelizing cross-culturally by engaging in missionary efforts, both domestically and abroad. Domestically, the MEC sponsored "home missions" in urban settings ("city missions") such as the Five Points Mission in Manhattan, ministry to sailors ("Mariners' Bethels"), and ethnic-specific ministries such as the German Mission Annual Conference and the Indian Mission Annual Conference. The Church's extensive mission work with Native Americans started with John Stewart, an African-American lay preacher who felt called to evangelize the Wyandot tribe in Ohio, beginning around 1818. Stewart's work helped to inspire the formation of the Mission Society of the Methodist Episcopal Church in 1819. The Society's first sponsored missionaries went to various native tribes: In 1822, A. J. Crawford was sent to minister to the Cherokee in the southeast; in 1833, Jason Lee was sent to the Flathead tribe in Oregon and John Clark to the Chippewa in Michigan. Then, in the late 1830s, Alfred Brunson worked with the Sioux Mission – and many others followed. Methodist class meetings offered Indians communal support while camp meetings built upon the same kind of emotional exhilaration they had known in their traditional spirituality.[15]

Methodist missionary activity among Native Americans left a mixed legacy. On the one hand, missionaries often assumed that Christian evangelistic efforts should go hand in hand with the imposition of certain standards of (Western) "civilization." However, other missionaries took stands in support of native concerns; most noticeably, a number of Methodists lived among the natives and risked their careers to stand alongside the Cherokee, Creek, and Choctaw when they were forcibly removed in the 1830s (by the Jackson administration) from Georgia to Oklahoma on the "Trail of Tears." In particular, a group of young circuit riders remained loyal to their Cherokee coworkers and fought against their oppression.[16]

In addition to home missions, Methodists also became zealously involved with foreign missions – similar to other nineteenth-century Protestants. The earliest foreign effort of the Mission Society was the creation of the Liberian Mission. Melville B. Cox, the first MEC missionary to go to Liberia in 1833, only lived for a few months, but his successor, John Seys, was able to build a long-lasting mission. (Daniel Coker, one of the founders of the AME Church, actually preceded the official MEC mission in Africa when he arrived in 1820 and evangelized in both Liberia and Sierra Leone, but he was not under the direction of any mission board.) MEC foreign mission work also began in South America (most successfully in Buenos Aires) and then in China (1847), Germany (1849), and India (1856). Women accomplished much of the financing of Methodist missions; they established their own women's auxiliaries to the Mission Society for this purpose, beginning in New York City. The other Wesleyan denominations also started foreign mission endeavors: the Missionary Society of the EA, authorized by the EA General Conference in 1839, and the UBC Home and Foreign Mission Society, begun in 1853.[17]

All of this denomination building did not occur without internal controversy, which Peter Cartwright commented upon in his autobiography. Several matters of concern especially bothered Cartwright as he surveyed the Church's developments over the first half of the nineteenth century: the increasing tension over denominational authority and control and the increasing tension over the issue of slavery, which exposed the underlying racism of the Church.[18]

THE TENSION REGARDING AUTHORITY

Cartwright reflected back on the denominational struggle that occurred regarding the concentration of MEC power in the hands of the clergy, and more particularly, how that struggle had manifested itself through the large division in 1830 known as Methodist Reform. From the beginning of American Methodism, there had been challenges to centralizing control from the likes of Robert Strawbridge, James O'Kelly, and Lorenzo Dow (see Chapter 2). While Asbury had been able to minimize much of the mischief caused by Strawbridge and O'Kelly, "Crazy" Dow's idiosyncratic, antiestablishment (but evangelistically successful) ministry continued unabated into the post-Asbury years; Dow's unwillingness to abide by any bishop's appointed assignment perturbed Methodist officialdom until his death in 1834. His unconventional antics – humorous anecdotes, emotional displays, and droll jesting – were deliberately designed to contrast with the "staid" services of predestination Calvinists. Dow's tactics also represented an unbridled example of early Methodism's entrepreneurial, antielitist spirit. Though at cross-purposes with the increasingly consolidated organization of the MEC, Dow's self-professed "eccentricity" was nonetheless emblematic of many aspects of the nineteenth-century Methodist ethos. Indeed, an accusation of being eccentric was considered a badge of honor among those early national period people who resisted existing structures, who wanted to distinguish themselves from the undemocratic privileged few who exercised power in both church and state.[19]

Less extreme than Dow, but still demonstrating democratic pro-
clivities, was a group of reformers in the 1820s that eventually broke
away from the MEC to create the Methodist Protestant Church (MPC).
Methodist reform leaders, such as Nicholas Snethen, Asa Shinn, and
Gideon Davis, felt that the MEC hierarchical system (and especially
the bishops and presiding elders) revealed the arbitrary power of an
unelected religious cabal – a structure similar to Roman Catholicism
that was prone to abuse and did not befit a church operating in the democratic milieu of Jacksonian America. At MEC General Conferences
during the 1820s, proposals were made for lay representation at annual
conferences and the election of presiding elders, instead of their appointment by bishops. These sentiments regarding the reform of church government gained traction through a publication, *The Mutual Rights of
Ministers and Members of the MEC*. Eventually, many of the reformers
were expelled from the MEC, especially local preachers and laymen,
and others left on their own accord. Whether thrust out or eased out of
the MEC, these innovators established the MPC in 1830 as a denomination without bishops or presiding elders, with preachers appointed by
an elected "President" of conference (and those appointments could be
appealed), and with laity and clergy equally represented in denominational meetings, an egalitarian polity that they viewed as being truly
"Protestant." Inconsistent with their democratic ideals, however, the
new church took a conservative position on the slavery issue, a conces-
sion to southern members that later caused serious disruption.[20]

THE TENSION REGARDING RACIALIZATION

In his description of the years between Asbury's death in 1816 and the
writing of his biography on the eve of the Civil War, Peter Cartwright
also observed growing problems related to slavery and racial prejudice
in the church – in addition to his observations about problems regarding
denominational control. Though Methodism's early commitment to antislavery was strong and although the Wesleyan message of free grace for
all resonated well with African Americans, nonetheless compromise on
the issue started early. Most white Methodists, South and North, adjusted
their formerly resolute views regarding the evils of slavery. In 1856, as
Peter Cartwright reflected back on the previous forty years of Methodism,
he wrote that he did "not recollect a single Methodist preacher, at that day
[1816], that justified slavery. But O, how have times changed!"

> Methodist preachers in those days made it a matter of conscience
> not to hold their fellow-creatures in bondage, if it was practicable

to emancipate them, conformably to the laws of the state in which they lived. Methodism increased and spread; and many Methodist preachers, taken from comparative poverty, not able to own a negro, and who preached loudly against it, improved, and became popular among slaveholders; and many of them married into those slaveholding families, and became personally interested in slave property (as it is called). Then they began to apologize for the evil; then to justify it, on legal principles; then on Bible principles; till lo and behold! It is not an evil, but a good! It is not a curse, but a blessing!

Cartwright described the slow devolution from an antislavery position to a slavery-supporting position. Even in the earlier years, Cartwright's statement that Methodists were expected to emancipate their slaves "if it was practicable," betrayed the way in which the Church allowed for a loophole. The compromising reached such an extreme that one prominent southern preacher, William Winans, proposed in 1838 that ministers had a Christian duty to acquire slaves.[21]

As in American society more generally, African Americans initiated the opposition to slavery in the church. Denmark Vesey, a Methodist class leader in Charleston, South Carolina, plotted a slave revolt in 1822 and received ample assistance from his AME congregation. A few years later, in 1829, David Walker, a former slave who was active in an AME Church in Boston, wrote a theologically profound "Appeal," encouraging blacks to stand up against white hegemony, and especially to challenge the unchristian attitudes commonly expressed in dominant Christianity. A number of escaped slaves, such as Sojourner Truth, Frederick Douglass, Harriet Tubman, and the Rev. (later Bishop) Jermain Loguen (all AMEZ), used explicitly religious rationales to protest slavery via various means – preaching, public speaking, political activism, and conducting fugitives on the underground railroad.[22]

Among white MEC members, a small, but vocal minority took a radical position against slavery. When William Lloyd Garrison (a Baptist) founded the American Anti-Slavery Society in 1833, a number of Methodists were "abolitionized" – that is, they became convinced that slaveholding was sin (not just an evil) and, therefore, lobbied for the immediate and uncompensated manumission of all slaves. Orange Scott, a prominent presiding elder in the New England Conference, left his pastoral appointment and became a traveling agent for the American Anti-Slavery Society. He and others argued forcefully for abolition at annual conference sessions and at the General Conferences of 1836 and 1840. This increasing agitation resulted in censure of abolitionist delegates for their "reproachful" attitudes and a suppression of debate by

Some pastors revolted from the MEC to make a new group, not called a church if they wanted to escape ... episcopal ... ? the MEC.

The Nineteenth Century: Expansion and Fragmentation 73

the bishops on any discussion in conferences related to slavery (known as the "gag rule").[23]

By 1842, Scott and several others in New England and New York expressed complete frustration with the denomination. They withdrew from the MEC and, the next year, founded the Wesleyan Methodist Connection (WMC) – deliberately not calling themselves a "church," a structure that they deemed to be inherently hierarchical and undemocratic. The WMC seceders declared that they were "dissolving their connection with Episcopacy and Slavery," because they believed these two concerns were "well calculated to sustain each other" – thereby linking Methodism's problematic issues of the proper limits of authority and racialization. In 1847, WMC pastor Adam Crooks courageously planted an abolitionist congregation called "Freedom's Hill" in Alamance County, North Carolina. Wesleyan Methodists such as Luther Lee and Laura Haviland championed political abolitionism (by actively campaigning for the antislavery Liberty Party), risked themselves as station keepers on the underground railroad, and even endorsed women's rights as a parallel concern to abolition. (Interestingly, for instance, the WMC chapel in Seneca Falls, N.Y., hosted the first Women's Rights Convention in 1848; and, in 1853, Luther Lee promoted "Woman's Right to Preach the Gospel" at an ordination service.)[24]

Many northern Methodists feared that all of New England and perhaps large portions of New York and Ohio would leave the MEC in order to go along with the new WMC; this anxiety provided a foreboding backdrop for the fateful General Conference of 1844. The immediate causative issue for the eventual church schism, though, came from a situation in which one of the bishops, James O. Andrew, who inherited slaves from his wife's family, was asked to resign or at least to pledge to free his slaves. Andrew refused to do either, and many of his southern colleagues took the stance that, in the mocking words of Peter Cartwright, "slavery was no impediment to the official relation of a bishop." Northern Methodists had been willing to compromise when members, preachers, and even presiding elders held slaves, but not a bishop. The General Conference delegates now recognized the inevitability of division. Under the guidance of Bishop Joshua Soule, the southerners withdrew and, at their own General Conference held in Louisville in 1845, formed a separate organization, the Methodist Episcopal Church, South (MECS).[25]

METHODISM IN THE CIVIL WAR ERA

It is well known that two denominations resulted from the Methodists' sectional conflict of the mid-1840s; more accurately, there were several:

The MECS, a generally pro-slavery denomination; the WMC, which, along with the previously organized AME and AMEZ, were abolitionist denominations; and the MEC (the original organization), a deliberately moderate denomination that tried to avoid a firm position on the slavery issue for as long as possible.[26] Because of the desire to hold onto the support of the border conferences, especially in Kentucky and parts of Virginia (now West Virginia), the MEC did not take a strong stand against slavery (even after the withdrawal of the southern portion of the Church) until the General Conference session held just a few months before Lincoln's election. Meanwhile, the MPC split yet again in 1858 (the 1830 split-off was caused by conflict over episcopal power), this time into northern and southern branches over the slavery issue – though these MPC factions reunited soon after the war, in 1877.[27] Throughout the 1850s, the Southern Methodists continued to justify the morality of slavery, partly by extending their evangelistic efforts among the bondsmen, organized as "plantation missions" by the Rev. William Capers. Meanwhile, the AME, AMEZ, and WMC continued to agitate for immediate abolition. It was during this decade that the AME assisted with the formation of the "British Methodist Episcopal Church," established originally for the spiritual support of fugitive slaves who fled to Canada.[28]

As the various Methodist bodies moved toward the tumultuous election year of 1860, they became, along with Baptists and Presbyterians (who also split into northern and southern branches and had abolitionist splinter groups), the "broken churches that prefigured the broken nation." Historian C. C. Goen concluded that the stakeholders of these three largest culturally influential Protestant church traditions demonstrated a "failure of moral leadership" when they could not find a way to make a united witness against the evil of American slavery; consequently, the denominational schisms were both portents and catalysts "of the imminent national tragedy." Peter Cartwright predicted such a calamitous end result when he warned in 1856 that if "compromise [continued to] succeed compromise" then "it will end in a dissolution of this blessed Union, civil war will follow, and rivers of human blood [will] stain the soil of our happy country."[29]

At the beginning of the Civil War, the relatively unified MEC that Asbury bequeathed to his Wesleyan heirs when he died in 1816 was now divided into no fewer than eight "Methodist" denominations.[30] By the 1860s, border communities and annual conferences were so fragmented by the various divisions of nineteenth-century Methodism that, in the case of the relatively small town of Martinsburg, [West] Virginia, and its surrounding county, for example, one could find an MEC congregation, an MECS congregation, an AME congregation, two MPC congregations [North and South] – and because that county had a large German presence, both a UBC and an EA congregation.[31]

Not surprisingly, when war erupted in 1861, the MEC generally supported the Union cause (though not uniformly), while most of the MECS supported the Confederacy.[32] Both provided troops, chaplains, and prayers against the "enemy" – those who only a few years previous had been their colleagues in ministry. In the North, the interdenominational U.S. Christian Commission was created, with the help of Bishop Janes, to supply relief (often done by Methodist women) and chaplaincy services to the soldiers. Nearly five hundred MEC pastors volunteered as regimental chaplains. Lincoln spoke very highly of northern Methodist support, stating that the MEC, "by its greater numbers ... sends more soldiers to the field, more nurses to the hospitals, and more prayers to heaven than any. God bless the Methodist Church!" In the South, the MECS also gave more chaplains to the war effort than any other denomination. Both armies reported frequent outbreaks of spiritual renewal and religious revival in their ranks.[33]

After the war, Gilbert Haven, a strong advocate for full social equality for African Americans, helped to establish the Freedman's Aid Society, which offered literacy education as part of the Reconstruction effort. The Society began at Trinity MEC in Cincinnati in 1866 to assist former slaves, and became an official part of the denomination in 1872 (the same year that Haven was elected to the episcopate); it created scores of educational institutions, including colleges such as Central Tennessee, Clark, Claflin, Rust, and Meharry Medical College. The MEC also continued to provide pastoral support for African Americans, but it bowed to racist pressure when it organized separate annual conferences for black members, beginning with the Delaware and Washington conferences. During the war, and increasingly afterward, the MEC expanded southward, starting racially integrated work in many places throughout the South; however, intensified Jim Crow feelings in the 1870s led the MEC to segregate their southern biracial congregations. African-American Methodists, such as Hiram Revels, a prominent presiding elder and Reconstruction-era senator from Mississippi, strenuously opposed these regressive measures.[34]

In the meantime, many whites in the southern Church identified with the "lost cause." The MECS incurred the loss of significant membership and property in the war and for several years appeared to be a beleaguered denomination. Nonetheless, after the demise of the Confederacy, the MECS still presented the largest, most cohesive, transsouthern organization, so a number of southerners looked to the MECS to perpetuate their regional identity.[35] The southern Church soon recovered its former size and influence, especially under the guidance of bishops Holland McTyeire and Atticus Haygood. The MECS energetically supported temperance, encouraged revivals, began to introduce lay representation into various structures of the Church, developed Sunday schools throughout the connection, and, in 1872, established a "great Southern Methodist university" in Nashville, which soon received a substantial endowment and took the name of Vanderbilt.[36]

African-American Methodists in the South no longer wanted to be a part of the MECS, especially given its continuing identification with white Dixie. Some former slaves became members of the AME Church, the AMEZ Church, or the MEC, all of which advanced their work in the South after the Civil War. The AME Church, for instance, founded the South Carolina Annual Conference of their denomination in 1865, out of which originated other southern AME judicatories. Bishop J. W. Hood of the AMEZ established many congregations in North Carolina. The AME and the AMEZ each had over 300,000 communicants in the South by 1884.[37]

A large number of African Americans in the South, most of whom had been a part of the MECS, organized themselves in 1870 (with the blessing and financial assistance of the MECS, in an atmosphere of "warmest sympathy and support") as another new denomination, the Colored Methodist Episcopal Church (CME). (The CME renamed itself the Christian Methodist Episcopal Church in 1954.) The CME Church's election of Isaac Lane in 1873 seemed providentially arranged, because he did much to promote the ministry of the new church, including an interest in providing higher education for African-American Methodists in the South; hence, it is fitting that the denominational college in Jackson, Tennessee, carries his name.[38]

THE TENSION REGARDING SANCTIFICATION AND INCREASING RESPECTABILITY

In addition to the tensions related to authority and racialization, a third tension became apparent during and after the Civil War era – regarding the degree to which the traditionally Wesleyan experience of holiness ought to be preached and what the implications of that sanctification experience should be for Methodist lifestyles during a time of growing affluence within the church and the broader society. As early as the 1830s, partly due to Methodist influence but also resulting from the optimistic postmillennialism characteristic of the period, the doctrine of

How much do we stress holiness?

Christian perfection received new attention from a variety of Protestants, including some who were not Methodists, such as Asa Mahan, Thomas Upham, and especially the famed Presbyterian/Congregationalist evangelist Charles G. Finney. Holiness became the watchword for a large number of American Christians.[39]

Also at this time, Phoebe Palmer, a Methodist in New York City, encouraged the experience of entire sanctification at a women's group that gathered every week in her home beginning in the 1840s, the "Tuesday Meeting for the Promotion of Holiness." Soon, the Tuesday Meeting included men as well as women and attracted prominent Methodists such as the editor Nathan Bangs, Bishops Janes and Hamline, and other influential MEC officials, along with religious figures from other denominations. For more than three decades, Palmer maintained the leadership of these mixed gender gatherings, promoting sanctification through her so-called "parlor holiness." Palmer's reputation waxed as she spoke at churches and camp meetings throughout the North on the need for people to "lay it all on the altar" during an experiential crisis moment often referred to as the "second blessing," about which those thus affected were expected to give public witness. This stress on the importance of testifying to one's full consecration and surrender provided a new idiom for Methodists (and others) to reemphasize the doctrine of Christian perfection, and became the foundation for the later development of the "holiness movement." The Holiness movement grew out of, and was most influential within the Methodist family of churches, but eventually expanded to include other Christian traditions. Palmer's articulation of holiness tended to telescope the quest for perfection into a "shorter way" – an expectation that entire sanctification may be received soon after the new birth and almost on demand. This shortened process allowed the renewed stress on sanctification to fit easily into the revivalist temperament of the period, with its stress on volitional, punctiliar times of Christian commitment.[40]

In the years just preceding the Civil War, a struggle very similar to the one that resulted in the formation of the WMC took place again in the MEC, this time within the Genesee Annual Conference of western New York State. In 1851, B. T. Roberts, a Genesee Conference preacher, heard Phoebe Palmer speak on entire sanctification at a camp meeting, inspiring him to preach similarly. Soon, Roberts's energetic preaching caused his small church to grow dramatically – and his reputation, as well. Accordingly, Roberts's bishop decided to appoint him to a better-known congregation. When Roberts arrived in 1852 as the pastor of Niagara Street MEC, Buffalo's oldest and most prestigious – but staid

Figure 4. **Bishop Benjamin T. Roberts, the Free Methodist Church,** Methodist Library Image Collection, Drew University, Madison, New Jersey.

and declining – Methodist congregation, he learned that it was partly financed by annual pew fees, as were all of the Methodist churches in that city. As a committed revivalist, abolitionist, and proclaimer of entire sanctification, Roberts was concerned about the congregation's relatively formal services, tepid antislavery sentiments, and coolness toward holiness.[41]

Roberts agonized about many developments occurring in mid-century Methodism, all of which related to the MEC becoming more

upwardly mobile and desirous of greater status within American society. He saw evidence of a change in worship style that seemed to be
moving away from spontaneous, Spirit-led participation and toward an
emphasis on entertainment and performance – as indicated by organ
accompaniment, robed choirs, written liturgy, and elaborate buildings. (Pittsburgh boasted the first gothic-style Methodist church, built
in 1855.) He fretted over the lessened emphasis on spiritual accountability, as indicated by dwindling attendance at class meetings. Peter
Cartwright expressed the same concern at the same time, bemoaning
that "a great many worldly-minded, proud, fashionable members of our
Church, who merely have the name of Methodist, [are] pleading that
attendance on class-meetings should not be a test of membership in the
Church." Consequently, Cartwright warned, "the power of religion will
be lost in the Methodist Episcopal Church." Nonetheless, compulsory
class meeting attendance ended in the MECS in the 1860s and a bit later
in the North. Roberts worried, too, about the relaxation of strict behavioral standards regarding dress, jewelry, theater attendance, card playing, amusements, Sabbath observance, the use of tobacco and alcohol,
and membership in the Masonic order and other secret societies. Like
many others, Roberts was also bothered by the church's accommodation on slavery and the exclusion of laypeople in church government.
Most of all, he could not fathom why Methodist ministers permitted a
decline in revivalistic preaching for conversion and sanctification.[42] For
Roberts and the emerging holiness movement, all of these concessions
represented an ungodly desire for more influence and social esteem, a
capitulation to modern commercialized culture.[43]

But the precipitating flashpoint was the increasing use of pew
rents by urban congregations to finance elaborate church construction,
thereby (Roberts surmised) shutting out the poor. Roberts's agitation
against what he considered to be spiritual compromise had a strong
affect on many people – radicalizing some, but causing others to perceive him as divisive and fanatical. His preaching created such consternation that he and his other compatriots (nicknamed "Nazarites") were
expelled from the MEC – first by the Genesee Annual Conference and
then by the 1860 General Conference, which just happened to be meeting in Buffalo that year. After their ejection, the Nazarites established
the "Free" Methodist Church (FMC), so named because they advocated
"free pews, free grace, and free men" (i.e., no restriction on the applica-
bility of grace – especially to the poor and the marginalized – and with
an encouragement for all to receive the fullness of grace by experiencing
entire sanctification). Though never the largest holiness group, in many

ways the formation of the FMC represented the paradigmatic holiness denomination – and also displayed all three of the major divisive tensions plaguing nineteenth-century Methodism: the challenges to racism, to hierarchical power, and to the effects of increasing prosperity leading to conflict over what constituted true Methodist identity.[44]

The career of Matthew Simpson provides an interesting counterpoint to Roberts, representing the Methodist drift toward greater gentility and respectability. Born in small-town Ohio, Simpson traveled on the Methodist circuit for four years before becoming Professor and Vice President of Allegheny College in 1837 at age twenty-six, and then President of Indiana Asbury College (now DePauw) at age twenty-eight. After his election to the episcopate at forty-one, Simpson traveled widely, including four well-publicized trips to Europe, an excursion to the Holy Land, and another to Mexico. Ellen Simpson, the bishop's wife, enjoyed displaying the fine furniture, Parisian fashions, and bright bonnets she obtained from their travels.[45]

Bishop Simpson wanted Methodism to be seen as successful, cultured, and erudite. He wrote a three-volume *Cyclopaedia of Methodism*, because he believed that the denomination should have a learned constituency. A well-educated people demanded a well-educated ministry, so Simpson defended the Church's authorization of theological seminaries (such as Garrett Biblical Institute, of which he became president), much to the consternation of old-timers like Peter Cartwright who did not believe in seminary education. Simpson also asserted that Methodist church buildings ought to be "partly monumental" and a "source of great social refinement," because houses of God should be equal to the "grandest edifices of men." During the war, the bishop became a close and trusted associate to Lincoln, a sort of informal chaplain, and Lincoln reciprocated by favoring Simpson. After the assassination, Simpson gave an oft-cited, highly patriotic funeral oration in Springfield, extolling the president's noble virtues and godly character.[46]

In 1846, Cartwright condemned Lincoln as an "infidel"; by 1865, Simpson lauded him as a Christian hero. Arguably, Lincoln had not changed as much as Methodism, particularly in its relationship to the larger culture.[47]

AN UNOFFICIAL RELIGIOUS ESTABLISHMENT IN THE GILDED AGE

The Civil War served as a watershed in Methodist history as well as in national history. In relation to its influence in American society,

Methodism had arrived. President Ulysses S. Grant jested, in 1868, that the United States possessed "three great parties: the Republican, the Democratic, and the Methodist Church." Both Grant and Rutherford B. Hayes were postwar presidents closely associated with the MEC.[48] Bishop Simpson noted approvingly how a Supreme Court justice, the governor of Indiana, a senator from Iowa, the founders and presidents of scores of colleges and universities, many statewide legislators and judges, and the four Harper brothers – the proprietors of the largest publishing house in the country – were all Methodists. MEC and MECS leaders frequently paraded lists of prestigious politicians and businessmen connected with Methodism – some whose names graced Methodist universities, such as Drew, Vanderbilt, and Duke.[49]

African-American Methodists also desired to be viewed reputably within the larger society. Daniel Alexander Payne, the leading bishop of the AME for forty years, from 1852 until his death in 1893, stressed education in order "to improve the ministry" and thereby "to improve the people." He was also the first African-American president of a college (Wilberforce). In the worship life of African Americans, Payne accentuated "order" over "emotionalism." To him, typical African-American worship seemed uncivilized. Consequently, he tried to reform the style of music in AME churches by introducing trained choirs and instrumental accompaniment. The same emphasis on education and propriety motivated the ministry of Bishop J. W. Hood of the AMEZ.[50]

Some African-American Methodists disagreed with Payne. Within his own denomination, Payne's contemporary, Bishop Henry M. Turner, saw Payne's civilizing strategy as an accommodation to white privilege. In the light of the perpetuation of racial segregation, ostracism, and outright violence, Turner endorsed black nationalism, political resistance, and the value of black folk religion.[51] Similarly, Ida B. Wells, another conscientious AME, demanded action against the rash of lynchings that increased in the 1890s.[52]

Wells's activism was an example of the essential role of laypeople in the church, and especially laywomen. Women wanted to use their gifts in church but were often precluded from doing so by various constraints. Among white women, the deaconess movement – imported from German Methodism (and derivatively from Lutheranism) – was one way they chose to serve. After observing the selfless work deaconesses did in Germany, Bishop Simpson strongly supported the creation of deaconess institutions in the United States. Deaconesses soon carried out social ministry in hospitals, schools, and difficult urban settings. Especially notable was Lucy Rider Meyer, the 1885 founder of the Chicago Training

School (later to become part of Garrett Seminary). The deaconess movement received General Conference approval in 1888, becoming a socially acceptable route for middle class women to carry out their call.[53]

Another avenue of service for women (and men) was the temperance movement, and particularly the Woman's Christian Temperance Union (WCTU), established mostly by Methodists in 1874. Frances Willard, an amazing dynamo of an organizer, became president of the WCTU in 1879, a position she held for nineteen years. Under her leadership, the WCTU combined temperance with advocacy for women's suffrage and a wide range of other social issues (though Ida Wells accused Willard of neglecting the problem of race). Willard encouraged women to lobby, petition, publish, and preach.[54]

The drive for women to assume positions of pastoral leadership turned out to be a particularly long struggle throughout the nineteenth century and beyond. Phoebe Palmer urged women to be preachers, and B. T. Roberts insisted on the appropriateness of women's leadership in his 1891 book *Ordaining Women* (though the FMC did not support his position until after his death). In general, the smaller Methodist churches were ahead of Episcopal Methodism in this regard. Mary Wills became the first ordained woman of perhaps any denomination, but certainly of any Methodist denomination, when the Illinois Conference of the WMC ordained her in 1861.[55] Anna Oliver and Anna Howard Shaw tried to be ordained by the MEC, but were rebuffed. In fact, the MEC General Conference decided against women's ordination in 1880, a situation not resolved in favor of women pastors until 1956 (see Chapter 4); worse, all licenses to preach previously given to women were to be rescinded, a ruling that held until 1920. Shaw, who had earlier pastored a WMC congregation, finally received her ordination through the MPC in 1888. In 1889, Frances Willard published *Woman in the Pulpit* after she and other women were refused seating as lay delegates to the 1888 MEC General Conference; that same year, the UBC ordained Ella Niswanger, the first female graduate of what eventually became United Seminary. Ninety-seven UBC women were ordained by 1901.[56]

African-American women also broke ground as preachers, when Jarena Lee and, later, Zilpha Elaw, Julia Foote, and Harriet Felson Taylor became exhorters and itinerating proclaimers of the Gospel in the AME and AMEZ Churches. Foote later became the first AMEZ woman to become an ordained deacon, in 1894, and the second to become an elder, in 1900.[57]

The continued growth and organizational development of Methodism called for new institutionalization in the postwar era.[58] The evangelistic work of the MEC became more formalized with the establishment of the Church Extension Society in 1864 and the creation of a similar board in the MECS in 1882. Existing home missions expanded among Native Americans, Germans, and Latinos (under the leadership of Alejo Hernandez, for example) and new efforts started among Norwegian, Swedish, Italian, and Asian immigrants, especially among the Chinese and Japanese in San Francisco. The first ordained Japanese American Methodist, Kanichi Miyama, was converted to Christianity in 1877 and then ministered in California, Hawaii, and Japan. Foreign missions work multiplied, as well, in the late nineteenth century, in tandem with the proliferation of American commercial interests abroad. The Methodist denominations added new mission fields in Korea, Russia, India, the Congo, several Latin American countries (MEC and MECS), Japan (MEC, MECS, and MPC), South Africa (AME), Germany (EA and UBC), and Sierra Leone (UBC). Henry and Ella Appenzeller pioneered the efforts in Korea. James Thoburn and (later) William Taylor labored tirelessly in India, and both (at different times) became missionary bishops. Much of the work, though, was done by women, either as missionaries themselves (such as Clara Swain and Isabella Thoburn [James's sister] in India, and Mary Scranton, the founder of Ewha Women's University in Korea) or by women in the United States supporting mission endeavors through the various Women's Foreign Missionary societies established in each of the Methodist churches.[59]

Methodism became identified with American progress via educational programming directed toward all stages of human development, beginning with children in Sunday schools and then youth in Epworth Leagues, an umbrella ministry organization created in 1889. For the education of young adults, a new rush of Methodist college formation occurred in the late nineteenth century,[60] and theological seminaries rose up, too.[61]

Boston University School of Theology, the first Methodist seminary, also paved the way with new theological ideas. Borden Parker Bowne was the leading voice of Boston "Personalism" during his tenure there from 1876 to 1910. He held a progressive view of human anthropology and stressed the capacity of the human will and individual self-autonomous freedom. Bowne was also on guard against emotional aspects of religion and downplayed momentary experiences of divine grace. His confident liberalism became predominant at Boston and other seminaries by the turn of the twentieth century.[62]

John Heyl Vincent, an MEC elder who believed that education was the best strategy for religious change, encapsulated this late-nineteenth-century Methodist stress on progressive development. He agreed with Horace Bushnell that a child should be able to grow up never having to know that he or she was not a Christian. According to Vincent, "mental improvement" was to be preferred over revivalism – an outdated approach described by him as "the semblance of spirituality which is merely sentimentality." Vincent never had the chance for formal higher education himself, so he spent his life trying to provide learning opportunities for others in similar circumstances. As a leading proponent of Sunday schools, Vincent developed a "modern Sunday School" system by standardizing curriculum in the International Lesson Plans. Vincent's most notable achievement was the 1874 founding of the Chautauqua Assembly in southwestern New York. Originally planned as an interdenominational Sunday school training institute, Chautauqua soon modified to become a place for summer college-level courses and lectures held in an outdoor milieu, but deliberately distinguished from ordinary camp meetings by its intellectual content and atmosphere. Professors from major universities and seminaries, such as Borden Parker Bowne, were invited to speak. Everyday Methodists along with "eminent contemporaries," including several U.S. presidents, came to enjoy the bucolic surroundings. Vincent was elected to the episcopate in 1888. As a bishop, he promoted liberal thought, advanced liturgical regularity in Methodist worship ("the ceremonial side of religion"), and represented the MEC at several international ecumenical gatherings in Europe and elsewhere.[63]

All of these developments occurred incrementally, so they did not seem dramatic to the average congregant, who typically attended Sunday school, sang – along with traditional Charles Wesley hymns – the new gospel songs of Fanny Crosby, James Milton Black (from the MEC), and Elisha Hoffman (from the EA),[64] and supported missions financially. During the summer, Methodists still went to camp meeting, but, indicating a Gilded Age transformation, instead of being held in the rugged woods, as previously, these venerable religious mainstays were now situated (similar to Chautauqua) in vacation resort settings such as Ocean Grove and Ocean City (New Jersey), Martha's Vineyard (Massachusetts), Rehoboth Beach (Delaware), Round Lake (New York), Lakeside (Ohio), and Bay View (Michigan).[65] The standard late-nineteenth-century Methodist also comported himself or herself according to Victorian-era mores, including prohibitions against dancing, smoking, and drinking. In order to provide churches with a nonalcoholic alternative to communion wine, Dr. Thomas Welch, a devout teetotaling Methodist, created (in 1869) a grape beverage that would not ferment. The use of Welch's grape juice eventually became standard in Methodist worship.[66]

Another important Methodist adaptation began in 1867, when Rev. John Inskip and a group of Methodist pastors and laymen, mostly from the New York City area, founded the National Camp Meeting Association for the Promotion of Holiness. Unlike Chautauqua, the Association still encouraged revivals, but unlike traditional camp meetings, these revivals were geared specifically for the advancement of the experience of entire sanctification. At first, Bishop Simpson and other Methodist notables supported the large annual gatherings of the Association.[67]

POST-CIVIL WAR HOLINESS EMPHASES

In the 1880s and early '90s, "radical" holiness associations and conventions spun off of the National Camp Meeting Association and met throughout the rural Midwest and South. The preachers in these associations engendered controversy by their insistence that every Christian should experience entire sanctification as a "second definite work of grace" by the "baptism of the Holy Spirit" and accompanied by strict standards of behavior, plain dress, and enthusiastic manifestations, such as shouting, falling down, and divine healing. These manifestations were not too different from what had been standard early-nineteenth-century "Methodist usages" described by Peter Cartwright and others; nevertheless, in 1894, the MECS passed a resolution decrying the practices of the holiness radicals. Consequently, within a few years, various folks seceded or were forced out of the MECS (and the MEC), resulting in new holiness groups such as the Pilgrim Holiness Church, the Pentecostal Holiness Church, the Church of God (Anderson, Ind.), the Pillar of Fire, the Burning Bush, and the Missionary Church Association. Another related group was the Salvation Army, which came out of the British Methodist Church and began evangelistic efforts in the United States by 1880. Various already-existing denominations also drank deeply of holiness teaching during these years and became close allies with the Methodist-bred folk, including the Brethren in Christ, the Mennonite Brethren, the Evangelical Friends, the Seventh-Day Adventists, and the Christian and Missionary Alliance.[68]

Unlike the institutionalism characteristic of the Methodist majority, these more culturally marginalized holiness preachers – like Dow before them – became known for their eccentricities. Emblematic of such colorful holiness figures was Carry A. Nation, a contentious temperance crusader known for smashing saloons with her hatchet. Nation credited the Free Methodists in Kansas as her greatest supporters and the source of her spiritual inspiration.[69]

Holiness-related splits occurred during these years, as well, among both of the German Wesleyan groups. The 1889 split in the UBC, led by Bishop Milton Wright (father of Orville and Wilbur), centered on a controversy regarding the holiness antipathy toward membership in socially exclusive secret societies such as the Masons. Wright's group felt estranged from others in the UBC who wanted to allow for Masonic membership and who (Wright's followers claimed) unfairly modified the denomination's constitution in order to make the changes. Those who separated (Wright's faction) became known as the United Brethren in Christ (Old Constitution), a group that still continues as a small, stand-alone denomination.[70]

In the Evangelical Association, personal antagonisms and concerns over the amount of power held by bishops and denominational structures (once again similar to the authority issues that prompted the rise of the Republican Methodists, the MPC, and the WMC) led to an 1891 division resulting in the formation of the United Evangelical Church in 1894. The United Evangelical Church endorsed congregational polity and affirmed the representative role of laity as equal to that of clergy in the General Conference. Though both the EA and the United Evangelical Church taught about entire sanctification, the splinter church promoted the holiness doctrine more consistently and in distinctively Wesleyan language.[71]

In spite of the increasingly sectarian and schismatic extremism characteristic of much of the holiness movement in the 1880s and '90s, some holiness leaders stayed within the mainline Methodist denominations, most notably evangelists such as William Taylor, the MEC missionary bishop, Amanda Berry Smith, a "washerwoman" who preached all over the globe under the auspices of both the MEC and the AME Church, and – from the MECS – Henry Clay Morrison, the founder of Asbury Seminary, and Sam Jones, whose wry wit influenced Will Rogers and whose preaching prompted the building of a tabernacle in Nashville (Ryman Auditorium) that became the home of the Grand Ole Opry. Holiness influence persisted in the MEC and MECS through the continuation of holiness camp meetings, at holiness colleges such as Taylor and Asbury (founded by Methodists but not officially connected to the denominations); and through independent missionary efforts, which were loosely associated with MEC and MECS congregations and helped to establish a type of Methodism abroad that was heavily tinged with revivalist and holiness accents.[72]

In addition to holiness activity within the MEC and MECS, the breakaway holiness denominations (FMC, WMC, etc.) pressed ahead with their work. Holiness colleges connected with the smaller denominations sprang up during the late nineteenth century.[73] The splinter holiness groups also established their own home and foreign missions efforts; in one prominent instance, the Free Methodists sponsored the education and social work of Pandita Ramabai and her daughter, Hindu converts who returned to their native India to develop Christian ministry among destitute women and children.[74]

One more significant development occurred in the holiness movement when, in the early 1890s in California, MEC presiding elder Phineas Bresee encouraged evangelistic work among Asian Americans, became chairman of the board of the Methodist-affiliated University of Southern California, and also started preaching a series of holiness revivals throughout his district. Almost every church responded heartily to Bresee's emphasis on sanctification except Simpson MEC, a wealthy congregation that became, according to historian Timothy L. Smith, "a kind of symbol of Methodist aspirations for social eminence in southern California." When John Heyl Vincent became the officiating bishop of the Conference, he spoke against the "holiness cranks," promptly removed Bresee from the presiding eldership, and then appointed him to the Simpson Church, controlled by opponents of holiness revivalism. Frustrated after one year there, Bresee asked to be appointed to an evangelistic association, but the bishop refused; stymied, Bresee started (in 1895) an independent holiness congregation in Los Angeles especially dedicated to ministry with the poor and called "The Church of the Nazarene" because the name denoted "the toiling, lowly mission of Christ." Later, this congregation joined with others to form a larger organization with the same name, which eventually grew to become the largest holiness denomination.[75]

FIN-DE-SIÈCLE METHODISM

In terms of numbers and influence, mainline Methodism was in its heyday at the end of the nineteenth century; indeed, by 1900, Methodism could claim approximately 6 percent of the American population – its highest percentage ever.[76] One could argue that the mainstream Methodism of the MEC, MECS, AME, and AMEZ, represented by Lucy Meyer Rider, Borden Parker Bowne, and Bishops Simpson, Vincent, Payne, and Hood – a Methodism that identified closely with progress-oriented, nationalistic, and increasingly urbane American culture – won the day as the dominant expression of the Wesleyan tradition in industrial America; certainly that was true within much of the MEC and, to a lesser degree, within the MECS, and even within the AME and the AMEZ churches.

This mainline Methodism reveled at the denomination's emerging social clout. The election of William McKinley as president in 1896 heralded a moment of unparalleled prominence for Methodism in the halls of power. McKinley – who regularly attended Metropolitan MEC in Washington, DC, the "national church," – personified for many the widening of both American and Protestant global influence. A number of leading Methodists, such as AME pastor Archibald J. Carey, Sr. (who later became bishop), campaigned for McKinley. Since the results of the 1890 census determined that the western "frontier" had officially ended, it seemed fitting that aspirations for American (and Methodist) advancement – previously limited to "spreading scriptural Holiness across the continent" – now extended to territories beyond the North American landmass, to places such as Cuba, the Hawaiian Islands, and the Philippines. Methodists of all stripes gave McKinley nearly unqualified support for his pursuit of American exceptionalism and his expansionist exploits in the Spanish-American War. The EA church paper, for example, declared that "God is in this war.... The American nation is God's minister of justice." Many fin-de-siècle Methodists articulated the "white man's burden" of manifest destiny. And despite misgivings because of the implicit (and sometimes explicit) racism associated with the war, even the AME Church could not help but laud the potential for global evangelistic growth by the actions of this Methodist president. The century ended, then, with the hand in hand connection of American imperialism and Protestant foreign missions. Since Methodism was the largest Protestant denomination, this expansion seemed to solidify Methodist identification with American preeminence.[77]

Symbolizing the newfound status of the denomination, the MEC General Conference in 1892 decreed that the church should erect a college located in Washington, DC, at the center of American politics. Not to be outdone by Roman Catholics' similarly situated, newly established college in the nation's capital, named the Catholic University of America, the Methodists' new institution was christened *The American University.* This name needed no explanation, for in the minds of Methodists – and even in the view of many Americans of whatever denomination – Methodism equaled Americanism and vice versa.[78]

Meanwhile, in more obscure places like Olmitz, Iowa, Alexandria, Indiana, and Topeka, Kansas, radical holiness preachers in the late 1890s, such as Martin Wells Knapp, B. H. Irwin, Maria Woodworth-Etter, Charles Parham, and William Seymour, lambasted the formalism of the "new" Methodism, protested against the Eastern political establishment represented by McKinley, promoted a behavioral code that stood as an objection against the rise of commercialization, and fomented democratic dissent in economics, government, and religion. Many of the holiness folk supported William Jennings Bryan's brand of rural populism. (B. T. Roberts, for example, helped to organize the populist Farmers' Alliance. Some practiced interracial fellowship and encouraged the evangelistic preaching of both men and women.[79]

Most of the holiness radicals came from Methodist backgrounds. Martin Wells Knapp, for example, was an MEC pastor who helped to found the International Holiness Union and Prayer League in 1897 to promote worldwide revival work. The efforts of the Holiness Union resulted in brand-new city missions, rescue homes, foreign missions organizations (such as the Oriental Mission Society), and Bible colleges (such as God's Bible School) started by Knapp in Cincinnati in 1900). Irwin, a local elder in the WMC, preached a "third blessing" of "fire" and established the Fire-Baptized Holiness Church in 1895. The following year, some people among Irwin's biracial band of followers began to speak in unknown tongues, a religious practice soon appropriated by the newly forming Church of God (Cleveland, Tenn.) and a number of other groups that embraced Wesleyan theology. Woodworth-Etter, who affiliated with the UBC tradition, defied conventional practice as a woman who led evangelistic meetings for divine healing, some of which drew more than twenty thousand worshippers. Many holiness women evangelists followed in Woodworth-Etter's footsteps. Charles Parham, a MEC supply pastor, left his native denomination because he disagreed with the church hierarchy – as had O'Kelly, Dow, Snethen, Scott, and others before him. Parham's itinerant ministry resulted in his 1900 acceptance of the gift of speaking in tongues as the initial evidence of the baptism of the Holy Spirit. William Seymour experienced conversion to Christ at Simpson Chapel MEC in Indianapolis in 1895 and then became credentialed in 1900 as a minister under the more racially inclusive influence of the Evening Light Saints (a holiness sect that later merged into the Church of God [Anderson, Ind.], yet another group with Wesleyan theological roots). Within a few years, Seymour found himself as the unexpected leader of the multicultural Azusa Street revival.[80]

These turn-of-the-century holiness people expected a heartfelt sanctification experience, believed in supernatural healing, and looked forward to a transnational Holy Spirit revival. Indeed, the global revival they anticipated came to pass by the end of the twentieth century, as

90   *Douglas M. Strong*

the religious movement known as Pentecostalism – largely derived from
the holiness side of Methodism but very different from the mainstream
Methodism that prevailed in American society in the late 1800s and
early 1900s – eventually resulted in sweeping across the world

Notes

1   Peter Cartwright, *Autobiography of Peter Cartwright* (New York:
    Abingdon Press, 1956; original publication, 1856), 110–116; Robert
    Bray, *Peter Cartwright, Legendary Frontier Preacher* (Champaign, IL:
    University of Illinois Press, 2005).

2   Cartwright, *Autobiography*, 108ff.; Roger Finke and Rodney Stark,
    The Churching of America, 1776–2005 (New Brunswick, NJ:
    Rutgers University Press, 2005), 55–116; Russell E. Richey, ed.,
    Denominationalism (Nashville, TN: Abingdon Press, 1977), 178.

3   In sheer numbers, Roman Catholics overtook Methodists by the end
    of the nineteenth century (due to the large-scale immigration of Irish
    and German Catholics, beginning in the 1840s), but not in influence or
    demographic breadth. Finke and Stark, *The Churching of America*, 121;
    Diane Lobody, "That Language Might Be Given Me: Women's Experience
    in Early Methodism," in Russell Richey, Kenneth Rowe, and Jean Miller
    Schmidt, eds. *Perspectives on American Methodism* (Nashville, TN:
    Kingswood Books, 1993), 127–144.

4   Frederick A. Norwood, *The Story of American Methodism* (Nashville,
    TN: Abingdon Press, 1974), 154; Cartwright, *Autobiography*, 240; C.C.
    Goen, "The 'Methodist Age' in American Church History," *Religion in
    Life* 34 (1965): 562–572; Winthrop S. Hudson, "The Methodist Age in
    America," *Methodist History* 12 (April 1974): 3–15.

5   Lester Ruth, *A Little Heaven Below: Worship at Early Methodist
    Quarterly Meetings* (Nashville, TN: Kingswood Books, 2000); John
    B. Boles, *The Great Revival* (Lexington, KY: University of Kentucky
    Press, 1972); John Totten, *An Apology for Camp-Meetings* (New York:
    John C. Totten, 1810), cited in Russell E. Richey, Kenneth E. Rowe,
    and Jean Miller Schmidt, eds. *The Methodist Experience in America:
    A Sourcebook* (Nashville, TN: Abingdon Press, 2000), 166; Cartwright,
    Autobiography, 339.

6   William Taylor, *Seven Years' Street Preaching in San Francisco*
    (New York: Carleton and Porter, 1856); Norwood, *American Methodism*,
    145–163, 259–270; William R. Cannon, "Education, Publication,
    Benevolent Work, and Mission," in Emory Stevens Bucke, ed., *The
    History of American Methodism* (New York: Abingdon Press, 1964),
    I: 595; Charles W. Ferguson, *Methodists and the Making of America:
    Organizing to Beat the Devil* (Austin, TX: Eakin Press, 1983); Cartwright,
    Autobiography, 163.

7   J. Bruce Behney and Paul H. Eller, *The History of the Evangelical
    United Brethren Church* (Nashville, TN: Abingdon Press, 1979), 113–
    152; J. Steven O'Malley, *John Seybert and the Evangelical Heritage*

(Lexington, KY: Emeth Press, 2008); Norwood, *American Methodism*, 108–110, 114–115, 215–216.

8 H. V. Richardson, *Dark Salvation: The Story of Methodism as It Developed among Blacks in America* (Nashville, TN: Abingdon Press, 1976); Albert J. Raboteau, *Slave Religion: The "Invisible Institution" in the Antebellum South* (Oxford: Oxford University Press, 1978), 204– 207; Norwood, 171–174, 277.

9 Raboteau, *Slave Religion*, 177, 207, 212–288; Donald G. Mathews, *Slavery and Methodism* (Princeton, NJ: Princeton University Press, 1965), 66–67.

10 Cartwright, *Autobiography*, 331; Bray, *Peter Cartwright*, 206–212. Cartwright's biblical quote is from Romans 8.16.

11 Stephen J. Fleming, "John Wesley: A Methodist Foundation for the Restoration," *Religious Educator* 8:3 (2008): 131ff.; Cartwright, *Autobiography*, 225–228.

12 Cartwright, *Autobiography*, 43–45; Robert Baird, *Religion in America: Or an Account of the Origin, Relation to the State, and Present Condition of the Evangelical Churches in the United States: With Notices of the Unevangelical Denominations* (New York: Harper and Brothers, 1844); Robert Handy, *A Christian America: Protestant Hopes and Historical Realities* (New York: Oxford University Press, 1971); Richey, *Denominationalism*, 161–162, 164–168.

13 Finke and Stark, *Churching of America*, 57; John H. Wigger, *Taking Heaven by Storm: Methodism and the Rise of Popular Christianity* (New York: Oxford University Press, 1998), 21–47.

14 Anne M. Boylan, *Sunday School: The Formation of an American Institution, 1790–1880* (New Haven, CT: Yale University Press, 1988), 147–148; J. Steven O'Malley, "The Theological Heritage of Pietism," in O'Malley and Jason E. Vickers, eds., *Methodist and Pietist: Retrieving the Evangelical United Brethren Tradition* (Nashville, TN: Kingswood Books, 2011), 65. Some of the pre-1860 founded Methodist colleges that continue today (though not all are still connected to the denominations) include: Dickinson, Allegheny, Emory, Emory and Henry, Wofford, Centenary (Louisiana), Trinity (now Duke), Mount Union, Albion, Northwestern (Illinois), Genesee Wesleyan (now Syracuse), Illinois Wesleyan, Ohio Wesleyan, Kentucky Wesleyan, Tennessee Wesleyan, Iowa Wesleyan, Indiana Asbury (now DePauw), Cornell (Iowa), Central Methodist (Missouri), Baker, Willamette, Baldwin-Wallace (for the Germans in the MEC), Adrian (for the MPC), Wilberforce (for the AME), Otterbein (for the UBC), and Albright (for the EA).

15 William G. McLoughlin, *Cherokees and Missionaries, 1789–1839* (New Haven, CT: Yale University Press, 1984), 164, 168–169; Cannon, "Education, Publication," I: 586–95; Alfred Brunson, *A Western Pioneer; Or, Incidents in the Life and Times of Rev. Alfred Brunson* (n.p.: Hitchcock and Walden, 1879).

16 McLoughlin, *Cherokees and Missionaries*, 171, 175, 294–295, 314–315; Cannon, "Education, Publication," I: 594.

17 Dana Robert, *American Women in Mission* (Macon, GA: Mercer University Press, 1996); Jean Miller Schmidt, *Grace Sufficient: A*

History of Women in American Methodism, 1760–1939 (Nashville, TN: Abingdon Press, 1999), 151ff.; Ulrike Schuler, "The Practice of Mission and Evangelism: The Mission to Germany," in O'Malley and Vickers, eds., *Methodist and Pietist*, 168–169; Cannon, "Education, Publication," I: 595–598.

18 Cartwright, *Autobiography*, 110–116.

19 Douglas M. Strong, "The Eccentric Cosmopolite: Lorenzo Dow and Early Nineteenth Century Methodism," in Henry H. Knight III, ed., *From Aldersgate to Azusa Street: Wesleyan, Holiness, and Pentecostal Visions of the New Creation* (Eugene, OR: Pickwick Publishers, 2010), 78–89.

20 Alexander McCaine, *History and Mystery of Methodist Episcopacy* (Baltimore, MD: Richard J. Matchett, 1827); E. J. Drinkhouse, *History of Methodist Reform* (Baltimore, MD: Board of Publication of the Methodist Protestant Church, 1899); Douglas Chandler, "The Formation of the Methodist Protestant Church," in Bucke, *The History of American Methodism*, I: 636ff.; Nathan O. Hatch, *The Democratization of American Christianity* (New Haven, CT: Yale University Press, 1989).

21 Cartwright, *Autobiography*, 111, 246; Raboteau, *Slave Religion*, 145–148; Mathews, *Slavery and Methodism*, 142.

22 David Walker, *David Walker's Appeal to the Coloured Citizens of the World* (Baltimore, MD: Black Classic Press, 1993; original ed., 1830), 55–63; J. Gordon Melton, *A Will to Choose: The Origins of African American Methodism* (Lanham, MD: Rowman and Littlefield Publishers, 2007), 239–254; Mathews, *Slavery and Methodism*, 40–41.

23 Mathews, *Slavery and Methodism*, 113–176.

24 Mathews, *Slavery and Methodism*, 212–213, 221–224, 230–232; Douglas M. Strong, "Partners in Political Abolitionism: The Liberty Party and the Wesleyan Methodist Connection," *Methodist History* 23 (January 1985): 99–115; Strong, *Perfectionist Politics: Abolitionism and the Religious Tensions of American Democracy* (Syracuse, NY: Syracuse University Press, 1999), 88, 98–105, 129–131; Laura S. Haviland, *A Woman's Life-Work*, 4th ed. (Chicago, IL: Publishing Association of Friends, 1889).

25 Cartwright, *Autobiography*, 269–274; Mathews, *Slavery and Methodism*, 145–146, 240–282.

26 Mathews, *Slavery and Methodism*, 192–193.

27 Chandler, "Formation of the Methodist Protestant Church," I: 677–682. In the 1840s, some northern MPC congregations and even the entire Champlain District of the MPC went into the WMC.

28 Melton, *Will to Choose*, 174–182; Raboteau, *Slave Religion*, 175–177; Mathews, *Slavery and Methodism*, 62–87.

29 C. C. Goen, *Broken Churches, Broken Nation: Denominational Schisms and the Coming of the Civil War* (Macon, GA: Mercer University Press, 1985), 6, 140ff.; Cartwright, *Autobiography*, 111; Mathews, *Slavery and Methodism*, 207–208, 282; Strong, *Perfectionist Politics*, 44–57, 91ff.

30 MEC; MECS; MPC (northern); MPC (southern); AME; AMEZ; WMC, and the Free Methodist Church (established in 1860, discussed later in this chapter). This listing of eight "Methodist" denominations does not count the Methodist-leaning German-speaking Pietist groups – the UBC

and the EA, both of which had been established by the time of Asbury's death in 1816, or the African Union Church.

31 F. Vernon Aler, *Aler's History of Martinsburg and Berkeley County, West Virginia* (Hagerstown, MD: The Mail Publishing Co., 1888), 343–365.

32 There were, however, some proslavery members of the MEC and some pro-Union areas of the MECS, such as the Holston Conference in eastern Tennessee.

33 Roy P. Baker, ed., *Abraham Lincoln, The Collected Works* (1953), 7: 350–351, cited in Richey, Rowe, Schmidt, *Methodists in America: A Sourcebook*, vol. 2, 327.

34 William B. Gravely, *Gilbert Haven: Methodist Abolitionist* (Nashville, TN: Abingdon Press, 1973), 110ff.; and Gravely, "Hiram Revels Protests Racial Separation in the Methodist Episcopal Church," *Methodist History* 8 (1970): 13–20.

35 Charles Reagan Wilson, *Baptized in Blood: The Religion of the Lost Cause, 1865–1920* (Athens, GA: University of Georgia Press, 1980); Hunter Dickinson Farish, *The Circuit Rider Dismounts: A Social History of Southern Methodism, 1865–1900* (New York: DaCapo Press, 1969), 22–61.

36 Farish, *The Circuit Rider*, 62–73, 270–275, 305ff.

37 Dennis C. Dickerson, "Bishop Daniel A. Payne and the A.M.E. Mission to the 'Ransomed,'" in Knight, ed., *From Aldersgate to Azusa Street*, 129; Melton, *Will to Choose*, 266–277; Farish, *The Circuit Rider*, 81.

38 Othal Hawthorne Lakey, *The History of the CME Church*, rev. ed. (Memphis, TN: CME Publishing House, 1996), 733–734; Melton, *Will to Choose*, 277–278.

39 John L. Peters, *Christian Perfection and American Methodism* (Nashville, TN: Pierce and Washabaugh, 1956), 115–117; Melvin E. Dieter, *The Holiness Revival of the Nineteenth Century* (Metuchen, NJ: Scarecrow Press, 1980), 1–22.

40 Timothy L. Smith, *Revivalism and Social Reform* (Nashville, TN: Abingdon Press, 1957); Dieter, *Holiness Revival*, 22–45; Peters, *Christian Perfection*, 109–114.

41 Howard A. Snyder, *Populist Saints: B.T. and Ellen Roberts and the First Free Methodists* (Grand Rapids, MI: Eerdmans, 2006), 196ff.; Dieter, *Holiness Revival*, 42–46.

42 Snyder, *Populist Saints*, 218–264; Peters, *Christian Perfection*, 128–130; Cartwright, *Autobiography*, 336–337; Charles E. White, "The Decline of the Class Meeting," *Methodist History* 38:4 (July 2000): 258–267.

43 A. Gregory Schneider, *The Way of the Cross Leads Home* (Bloomington, IN: Indiana University Press, 1993); Robert D. Clark, *The Life of Matthew Simpson* (New York: Macmillan Publishers, 1956), 192.

44 Snyder, *Populist Saints*, 423–535.

45 George R. Crooks, *The Life of Bishop Matthew Simpson of the Methodist Episcopal Church* (New York: Harper and Brothers, 1891), 360; Clark, *Life of Matthew Simpson*, 190–191, 276.

46　Matthew Simpson, ed., *Cyclopedia of Methodism* (Philadelphia, PA: Louis H. Everts, 1880); Crooks, *Life of Matthew Simpson*, 376; Cartwright, *Autobiography*, 64–65.

47　Clark, *Life of Matthew Simpson*, 245–248; Bray, *Peter Cartwright*, 206–212, 259–260. During the war, even the aging Cartwright altered his view and spoke appreciatively about Lincoln.

48　Cited in Richard Carwardine, "Methodists, Politics, and the Coming of the Civil War," in John Wigger and Nathan Hatch, eds., *Methodism and the Shaping of American Culture* (Nashville, TN: Kingswood Books, 2001). Grant was raised as a Methodist. Lucy Webb Hayes, the president's wife, was a very active member of the MEC and was the president of the Women's Home Missionary Society WHMS (organized in 1880).

49　Clark, *Life of Matthew Simpson*, 191.

50　Daniel A. Payne, *History of the African Methodist Episcopal Church* (New York: Arno Press, 1969, reprint).

51　Dickerson, "Bishop Daniel A. Payne," 125–133.

52　Patricia A. Schechter, *Ida B. Wells-Barnett and American Reform* (Chapel Hill, NC: University of North Carolina Press, 2001).

53　Mary Agnes Dougherty, *My Calling to Fulfill: Deaconesses in the United Methodist Tradition* (New York: General Board of Global Ministries, 1997); Schmidt, *Grace Sufficient*, 154–161.

54　Ruth Bordin, *Frances Willard: A Biography* (Chapel Hill, NC: University of North Carolina Press, 1986).

55　Maxine Haines and Lee Haines, *Celebrate Our Daughters: One Hundred Fifty Years of Women's Wesleyan Ministry* (Indianapolis, IN: Wesleyan Publishing House, 2004).

56　Schmidt, *Grace Sufficient*, 104–112, 181–196; Paul Chilcote, "Women in the Pietist Heritage of Methodism," in O'Malley and Vickers, eds., *Methodist and Pietist*, 195–196.

57　William L. Andrews, *Sisters of the Spirit: Three Black Women's Autobiographies of the Nineteenth Century* (Bloomington, IN: Indiana University Press, 1986).

58　See Robert H. Wiebe, *The Search for Order, 1877–1920* (New York: Hill and Wang, 1967).

59　W. Richey Hogg, "The Missions of American Methodism," in Bucke, ed., *The History of American Methodism* III: 59–128; Schuler, in O'Malley and Vickers, eds., *Methodist and Pietist*, 168–169.

60　Methodist colleges formed after the Civil War include, in the MECS, Hendrix, Huntingdon, and Millsaps; in the MEC: Centenary (New Jersey), Ohio Northern, West Virginia Wesleyan, Kansas Wesleyan, Dakota Wesleyan, Puget Sound, Colorado (now University of Denver), and University of Southern California; in the AMEZ: Zion Wesley (now Livingston); in the MPC: Western Maryland (now McDaniel); in the EA: North Central; and in the UBC: Lebanon Valley.

61　The nineteenth-century Methodist seminaries were Boston, Garrett, Drew, Iliff, and Claremont (for the MEC), Vanderbilt and Duke (for the MECS), Westminster (now Wesley, for the MPC), Payne (for the AME

Church), Hood (for the AMEZ Church), Union (now United, for the UBC), and Evangelical (for the EA).

62 Francis J. McConnell, *Borden Parker Bowne* (New York: Abingdon Press, 1929); Douglas M. Strong, "Borden Parker Bowne and Henry Clay Morrison," in Knight, ed., *From Aldersgate to Azusa Street*, 297–306.

63 Leon Vincent, *John Heyl Vincent: A Biographical Sketch* (New York: Macmillan Publishers, 1925).

64 Edith Blumhofer, *Her Heart Can See: The Life and Hymns of Fanny J. Crosby* (Chicago, IL: University of Chicago Press, 2006). Some of the best known Methodist gospel songs, included, for Crosby: "Blessed Assurance" and "To God Be the Glory"; for Black: "When the Roll Is Called up Yonder"; and for Hoffman: "Are You Washed in the Blood?" and "Leaning on the Everlasting Arms."

65 Kenneth O. Brown, *Holy Ground: A Study of American Camp Meetings* (New York: Garland, 1992); Charles H. Lippy, "The Camp Meeting in Transition: The Character and Legacy of the Late Nineteenth Century," *Methodist History* 34:1 (October 1995): 3–17.

66 Jennifer Woodruff Tait, *The Poisoned Chalice: Eucharistic Grape Juice and Common-Sense Realism in Victorian Methodism* (Tuscaloosa, AL: University of Alabama Press, 2011).

67 George Hughes, *Days of Power in the Forest Temple* (Boston, MA: John Bent and Co., 1874); Charles E. Jones, *Perfectionist Persuasion: The Holiness Movement and American Methodism, 1867–1936* (Metuchen, NJ: Scarecrow Press, 1974), 16–46; Dieter, *Holiness Revival*, 79–110; Peters, *Christian Perfection*, 134–135.

68 Cartwright, *Autobiography*, 234, 337; Dieter, *Holiness Revival*, 13–15, 171–192, 207–228; Farish, *The Circuit Rider*, 74–75; Edward H. McKinley, *Marching to Glory: The History of the Salvation Army in the United States, 1880–1930* (Grand Rapids, MI: Eerdmans, 1995); William Kostlevy, *Holy Jumpers: Evangelicals and Radicals in Progressive Era America* (New York: Oxford University Press, 2010). There were also *new* groups that embraced holiness theology and experience but were not from Methodist roots, such as the Church of God in Christ and the Church of Christ (Holiness).

69 Snyder, *Populist Saints*, 737–738; Fran Grace, *Carry A. Nation: Retelling the Life* (Bloomington, IN: Indiana University Press, 2001), 97.

70 Behney and Eller, *History*, 225ff.; O'Malley and Vickers, eds., *Methodist and Pietist*, 68–70.

71 Behney and Eller, *History*, 283ff.; O'Malley and Vickers, eds., *Methodist and Pietist*, 70–72.

72 Estrelda Y. Alexander, "Amanda Berry Smith: Woman at the Intersections," in Knight, ed., *From Aldersgate to Azusa Street*, 158–166; Jones, *Perfectionist Persuasion*, 93–97; Dieter, *Holiness Revival*, 265.

73 The Holiness colleges founded in the late nineteenth century include, in the FMC: Roberts Wesleyan, Greenville, Spring Arbor, Seattle Pacific, and the Training School for Christian Workers (now Azusa Pacific); in the WMC: Houghton; and in the UBC (Old Constitution): Huntington.

74 Snyder, *Populist Saints*, 895–909.

75   Timothy L. Smith, *Called unto Holiness: The Story of the Nazarenes* (Kansas City, MO: Beacon Hill Press, 1962), 99–111; Dieter, *Holiness Revival*, 262–265; Jones, *Perfectionist Persuasion*, 90–119.

76   Finke and Stark, *The Churching of America*, 156ff., argue that the "market share" of church members held by Methodists began to decline in the late nineteenth century, but there is no evidence that Methodists perceived this declension until somewhat later in the twentieth century.

77   Dennis C. Dickerson, "Archibald J. Carey, Jr., African Methodism and the Public Square," in Knight, ed., *From Aldersgate to Azusa Street*, 318; Adna B. Leonard, "Prospective Mission Fields," *Gospel in All Lands* 19:8 (August 1898): 363–364, in Richey, Rowe, and Schmidt, *The Methodist Experience in America*, I: 455–456; Lawrence S. Little, *Disciples of Liberty: The African Methodist Episcopal Church in the Age of Imperialism, 1884–1916* (Knoxville, TN: University of Tennessee Press, 2000), 27–29, 94–97; *Evangelical Messenger* 51 (1898): 360, 372, cited in Behney and Eller, *History*, 306.

78   Mark Teasdale, "Pure American Evangelism: The Understanding and Practice of Evangelism in the Home Missions of the Methodist Episcopal Church, 1865–1920," Ph.D. diss., Southern Methodist University, 2010.

79   Snyder, *Populist Saints*, 744ff.; Joshua J. McMullen, "Bridging The Wesleyan-Pentecostal Divide," in Knight, *From Aldersgate to Azusa Street*, 185–226.

80   Jones, *Perfectionist Persuasion*, 90–119; Wayne E. Warner, *The Woman Evangelist: The Life and Times of Charismatic Evangelist Maria B. Woodworth-Etter* (Metuchen, NJ: Scarecrow Press, 1986), 202; Priscilla Pope-Levison, *Turn the Pulpit Loose: Two Centuries of American Women Evangelists* (New York: Macmillan Publishers, 2004), 97ff.; Donald W. Dayton, *The Theological Roots of Pentecostalism* (Peabody, MA: Hendrickson, 1993).

4 American Methodism in the Twentieth Century: Reform, Redefinition, and Renewal

WENDY J. DEICHMANN

At the start of the twentieth century American Methodism was on the rise, energetically multiplying robust programs of worship, evangelism, mission, education, and reform. Yet this family of denominations remained largely divided along cultural, theological, and institutional lines drawn in the nineteenth century. This chapter traces historical contours of three subgroups of American Methodism through roughly three periods of the twentieth century. The subgroups are defined as: 1) those that eventually merged to form The United Methodist Church, 2) the African Methodist Episcopal denominations, and 3) those that self-identified as holiness or Pentecostal.

The movement that brought together several denominations to form the first subgroup resulted from practical considerations, such as stewardship of resources, and theological convictions about Christian unity and witness. Before the end of the twentieth century, the Methodist Episcopal Church (MEC, 1784), the Church of the United Brethren in Christ (UBC, 1800), the Evangelical Association (EA, 1803), the Methodist Protestant Church (MPC, 1830), the Methodist Episcopal Church, South (MECS, 1844), and the United Evangelical Church (UEC, 1891) had worked their way through a series of compromises and mergers into one large body, The United Methodist Church (UMC, 1968). The new denomination had more than ten million members worldwide, exceeding twice the membership of the predecessor denominations in 1900. In the three decades following its founding, however, the UMC reversed this trajectory and by 2000 had lost more than two million members, numbering approximately eight and a half million, close to the 1940s level of the combined predecessor denominations.[1]

The second subgroup, consisting of African Methodist Episcopal (AME, 1816), African Methodist Episcopal Zion (AMEZ, 1821), and Colored (Christian after 1954) Methodist Episcopal (CME, 1870) churches, includes some of the earliest to define American Methodist traditions apart from what would later become known as the Methodist "mainline." They created and held resolutely to new institutions in which they were free to practice radical forms of social holiness they believed to be in keeping with true Methodist piety. Combining Methodist doctrine and polity with African-American values of racial equality and prophetic leadership in the context of a racially prejudiced and divided society, they aimed to nurture the faith and well-being of members and communities alongside evangelism and strenuous efforts for social justice. The African-American Methodist denominations more than quadrupled their collective membership in the twentieth century, from just fewer than one million to more than four million.[2]

The Wesleyan Methodists (WMC, 1843) and Free Methodists (FMC, 1860) also withdrew from the MEC in protest over matters of holiness, especially in relationship to their firm antislavery commitments. They constitute the earliest members of the third subgroup of American Methodism, which later grew to include the Pilgrim Holiness Church (1897) and the Church of the Nazarene (CON, 1908). Troubled by perceived inadequacies in MEC attitudes toward sanctification, the holiness denominations developed their own theologies and social practices in ways they judged most faithful to the Wesleyan tradition, including expectations for personal behavior, service, and worship. Initially, the Pentecostals that "came out" from both Methodist and holiness bodies beginning at the turn of the nineteenth to twentieth century differentiated themselves from holiness counterparts by the distinctive value they placed upon the practice of glossolalia, or speaking in tongues. The Pentecostal movement also became known for its literal Biblicism, emphasis on healing, ecstatic worship, and stringent standards of personal behavior and discipline. It spread rapidly, outpacing both holiness and Methodist adherents in growth not only in the United States, but across the world. The FMC and WMC alone more than tripled their membership in the United States in the twentieth century, from just more than 50,000 in 1925 to approximately 174,000 in 2000, and by 2001, the Church of the Nazarene reported more than 1,400,000 adherents.[3] By 1995 there were an estimated six million holiness adherents and more than ten million Pentecostals in the United States, and global Pentecostals numbered in the hundreds of millions.[4]

The first period to be considered in this chapter encompassed the first two and a half decades, through approximately 1925. This was a season characterized by mission and reform commitments largely inherited from previous centuries, and increasingly influenced by

Figure 5. **Procession at 1968 Uniting Conference,** General Commission on Archives and History, The United Methodist Church, Madison, New Jersey.

new philosophical and theological alignments that would change the nature and face of American Methodism. The second period featured a sequence of institutional mergers that created a large and structurally unified denomination of American Methodists, but with compromises that complicated its mission and ministry in subsequent decades. It entailed reunification of three long-divided branches of Methodism in 1939, unification of two German-American Pietist groups to form the Evangelical United Brethren Church (EUBC) in 1946, and the uniting of Methodists and EUBC to form The United Methodist Church in 1968. The third period, roughly 1975 through 2000, featured continuing differentiation between the major groups, reassessment of ministry and mission priorities, and new initiatives for both evangelism and renewal.

In addition to the qualities that set these three subgroups apart from one another, less visible distinctions and ideological divisions also cut across the American Methodist landscape throughout the century. Internal cultural and theological disputes over racism, gender roles, and popular social and political issues in church and society remained paramount. Increasingly, so did reinterpretations of the faith in the light

homosexuality
is not sin?

of emerging intellectual perspectives that spawned the Modernist and Fundamentalist debates across and between denominations. These developments deepened a chasm between so-called "liberal" and "conservative" American Methodists that appeared to intensify throughout the century.

While each Methodist-related denomination in its own way continued to hearken back to British Methodist historical roots, Pietism, and Wesleyan doctrine and practice, each also redefined this heritage within the larger currents of American culture as well as within distinct subcultural norms of its own, historically defined communities. By the end of the twentieth century, what had been popularized in the eighteenth century simply as an American Methodist mission to "reform the continent and spread scriptural holiness over these lands" had been reinterpreted through lenses of American revivalism, nationalism, post- and premillennialism, progressivism, conservatism, individualism, modernism, fundamentalism, the sexual revolution, civil and religious rights activism, pluralism, and globalism.

1900–1925: REFORM AND THEOLOGICAL REALIGNMENT

The vigorous American Methodist evangelistic and missionary thrust of the nineteenth century continued into the early twentieth, swelling church membership rolls as well as Methodist impact upon American society and beyond. In the United States, church membership growth as the result of itinerating preachers, revivals, class, prayer, and camp meetings had largely given way by 1900 to the influences of carefully orchestrated worship and prayer services; Sunday schools and Vacation Bible Schools; continuing and new mission initiatives; Chautauquas and extended Holiness Association Meetings. Evangelism and missions generally continued hand-in-hand notwithstanding ever changing methods of delivery.

In the opening decades of the century, American Methodists expressed their vital commitment to the mission of the church by not only making new converts, but also founding new annual, mission, and central conferences and schools, hospitals, and agencies to serve seemingly ever-growing memberships and missions. Within the first fifteen years of the century, the AME Church founded the Colored Deaconess Home in Virginia and the CME Church established Miles College in Alabama, Mississippi Theological and Industrial College, and the Harriett Holsey Normal and Industrial Institute in Georgia.[5] The MEC organized the

Mobile Conference, the Japanese Mission Conference, the Oklahoma-Nebraska Conference, the Puerto Rico Mission, the Mary J. Platt School for Spanish girls in Arizona, the Kimball School of Theology in Oregon, the Italian Mission Conference, and the California German Annual Conference. The EA added a second Annual Conference in Germany, established a mission in Hunan Province, China, that included multiple schools and hospitals, and established the Evangelical Theological Seminary in Reading, Penn. The MPC started its Baltimore-Washington Conference and Choctaw Mission Conference. The MECS opened the Lake Junaluska Assembly in North Carolina and organized the Latin District of its Florida Conference. Meanwhile, the UBC opened a school, hospital, and two orphanages in Sierra Leone, began a mission in Canton, China, that included two dispensaries, fourteen boarding schools, and thirty-eight churches and a Mission Conference. They also organized a Japan Mission Conference and mission work in Juana Dias, Puerto Rico, and a Mission Conference in the Philippines.[6]

Twentieth-century American Methodism inherited from founding leaders and from the century before it not only vigorous programs of evangelism, mission, and a proclivity to institution building, but also a deep-seated commitment to social holiness and social reform. Social holiness in Methodism and Pietism is most simply defined as the biblical injunction to love one's neighbor as oneself in practical ways. Social holiness was the doctrinal key and chief motivation behind vigorous Methodist and Pietist participation in the most influential social reform movement of the nineteenth century: antislavery. Post–Civil War, social holiness perspectives figured into Methodist participation in rebuilding the South and serving its most needy residents, as well as mission work in American cities. Next to evangelism, it was the main impetus shaping the nature of Methodist home and foreign missions activity in the twentieth century, including avid participation in the social gospel movement.

The social gospel movement in North America began as a grass-roots movement of laity and clergy in the 1860s in the aftermath of the Civil War. Freed from obsession with the issue of slavery and released from the restrictions of a warring homeland, American Christians resumed efforts inherited from Puritan forbears to build a Christian nation with Protestant values. Rampant social problems such as poverty, illiteracy, prostitution, poor sanitation, economic exploitation, lynching, liquor abuse, and civic corruption commanded the attention of Protestant crusades for social reconstruction and betterment. Advocates of a social gospel, including many Methodists, prodded the church and its networks of congregations to help alleviate the vast human need and suffering resulting from the concurrence of war's aftermath, subsequent sudden emancipation, and relocation of masses of former slaves, large-scale industrialization, rapid urbanization, and unprecedented levels of immigration.

AME pastor Reverdy Ransom (1861–1959) exemplified social gospel commitments in his founding of Chicago's Institutional Church and Social Settlement in 1900 to help meet the needs of Chicagoans and blacks who were migrating to the city.[7] Organized as a residential city mission, it featured an auditorium, dining room, kitchen, and gymnasium. Programs included men's and women's clubs, child care, concerts, classes, and lectures. Ransom's work embraced social activism such as mediation in labor disputes and addressing civic corruption in order to improve the social conditions of those with whom he ministered not only in Chicago, but later in Boston and New York. Ransom was an outspoken advocate for civil rights for African Americans and a leader in the formation of the National Association for the Advancement of Colored People. He became a bishop in the AME Church in 1924.

Members of African Methodist Episcopal denominations were especially responsive to the crises precipitated by the residual effects of slavery and racial discrimination. Outraged by the continuing scandals of lynching, segregation, and disenfranchisement, AME Sunday School teacher and journalist Ida B. Wells-Barnett became an outspoken and effective social gospeler and civil rights leader.[8] Other prominent social gospel Methodists included Woman's Christian Temperance Union (WCTU) President Frances E. Willard (MEC) of Chicago, Harry Ward and Frank Mason North (MEC) of New York City, Pastor Charles Albert Tindley (MEC) of Philadelphia, Edgar J. Helms (MEC) of Boston, Belle H. Bennett (MECS) of Kentucky, Bishop Alexander Walters (AMEZ), and William Bell (UBC) of Indiana. Social gospel commitments were institutionalized in denominational home missions societies and organizations such as the Methodist Federation for Social Service (1907), the Federal Council of Churches and Social Creed (1908), and the National Association for the Advancement of Colored People (1909).

Cultural changes in gender roles in the home, church, and society in this era factored significantly in the policy making and ministry of each Methodist body. For some, these changes inspired increased women's involvement, for others it meant stepped-up resistance to new roles for women. Women's leadership in denominational mission organizations had become well established in some denominations in the nineteenth century, often as a result of the fact that in many cultures, only women were allowed direct contact with indigenous women in the mission

From social work → to eventual becoming clergy women are getting plugged in to serve.

field. Methodist women's roles in the social gospel movement ranged from quiet, dedicated social work alongside other laity and pastors, to missionary service, and to advocacy for woman suffrage and full clergy rights for women. One such service-oriented role, that of the deaconess, was established as an office of ministry in the AMEZ Church in 1894, the UB in 1898, the MEC in 1888, the MECS and AME in 1902, the EA in 1903, and the MPC in 1908. By 1910, more than a thousand deaconesses were consecrated for service by the MEC alone.

Women's laity rights were granted during this period, but in some denominations only after a lengthy season of controversy and struggle. The AMEZ Church seated women as lay delegates in 1892 and the United Brethren did likewise the following year. In 1888, the MEC approved women to serve in the order of deaconess, but refused to seat five women who had been elected as delegates to General Conference, including Frances E. Willard, president of the influential WCTU. MEC permission for women to be seated as delegates was finally granted in 1904. The MECS eventually followed with a similar ruling in 1918, seating women as lay delegates for the first time in 1922.

The WMC, MPC, and the UBC precociously ordained and granted full clergy rights to women prior to the start of the twentieth century. The Illinois Conference of the WMC ordained Mary Wills in 1861, the Methodist Protestants ordained Maggie Elliot in 1877 and Anna Howard Shaw in 1888, and the United Brethren ordained Ella Niswonger in 1889. The AMEZ Church ordained Julia Foote as a deacon in 1894 and as an elder in 1900. Although Luther Lee and B. T. Roberts, founders of the Wesleyan (1843) and Free Methodist (1860) Churches, respectively, openly favored the ordination of women, it was not until 1891 that the WMC made a firm commitment to the ordination of women, and the FMC did the same two decades later in 1911. The CME Church waited until 1918 to grant women licensing and ordination rights as local preachers, deacons, and elders, and it extended full clergy rights in 1966. The General Conference of the AME Church began to ordain women in 1948. The MEC and MECS successfully resisted women's ordination until 1924 and 1930, respectively. With the EC and EUB denominations they continued to deny women full clergy rights throughout their organizational existence. This privilege was finally approved by their successor denomination, the Methodist Church, in 1956. Many, but not all Pentecostal denominations ordained women. By 1995, as many as 15 percent of ordained ministers in the Assemblies of God Church were women.[9]

When Victorian-era Methodist women felt called to serve in leadership beyond their traditionally designated feminine roles, they often made a compelling case that it was not only in the interest of social holiness, but also "home protection."[10] Thus, Methodist women continued to champion with a vengeance in the cause of temperance, especially through the WCTU, working in concert with likeminded men to combat "demon rum" and its production in the United States. In close association with the Anti-Saloon League, Methodist women and men alike engaged the educational and political processes of the nation in this campaign, with other crusaders successfully bringing about and then avidly supporting the Eighteenth Amendment in 1919. Methodists were among its chief advocates through the date of its repeal in 1933.[11]

Although historically holding in common a doctrinal commitment to holiness, Methodists were often far from agreement regarding practice of the gospel in relationship with one's neighbor, let alone larger social and political applications. After the Civil War, forms of literal Biblicism that had developed previously alongside and in support of slavery aligned with American premillennialist, fundamentalist, and holiness theologies under the rubric of a politicized form of Protestant "evangelicalism" in virulent opposition to theories of evolution, scholarly higher criticism, ecumenism, and social gospel-inclined elements of Protestantism.

Premillennialists devotedly awaited the second coming of Christ for inauguration of the kingdom of God on earth and perfection of society in lieu of joining postmillennialists working toward its creation in the here and now. The premillennialists' social agenda was primarily focused upon defeating within its own religious communities the "social sins ... of the theater, ball games, dancing, lipstick, cigarettes, and liquor" and so on. Ever fearful that social gospelers were prone to neglect individual salvation in favor of social salvation, premillennialists castigated them for allegedly substituting works-righteousness for saving grace.[12] Social gospelers returned the criticism, denigrating premillennialists for holding only to half the gospel, that which addressed personal salvation.

By the early twentieth century a rapidly growing number of Methodist, holiness, and Pentecostal bodies, especially in the South, had adopted premillennialist and literal Biblicist commitments and adapted these to their Wesleyan faith and heritage. Unlike the WMC and FMC departure from the MEC over slavery several decades earlier, at the turn of the century the new cause prompting the genesis of numerous holiness denominations from the MEC was a particular focus upon the experience of "second blessing" after conversion, also known as "entire sanctification." While many nineteenth-century Methodists had followed closely John Wesley's or Phoebe Palmer's teachings on this doctrine, it took on a new meaning decades later when combined with premillennialist opposition to the social reform, ecumenical, and scholarly sensibilities of established churches and leaders. In 1894, the MECS General Conference's staunch refusal to sanction this particular "holiness" reading of the Wesleyan doctrine of sanctification as normative outraged holiness partisans. They responded by founding new denominations in which the "second blessing" holiness teaching alongside literal Biblicist premillennial theology was indeed made normative. By 1900 twenty-three new holiness denominations were founded by up to 100,000 "come-outers" from MECS and MEC churches.[13] The Church of God in Christ denomination was founded in 1893, the Pilgrim Holiness Church (1897), and the Church of the Nazarene (1908) were subsequently formed through mergers of smaller groups.[14] By 1923, Asbury Theological Seminary was founded in Kentucky to help serve the growing need for theological education for holiness church leaders.

The Pentecostal movement was launched as a variation of holiness teaching with the unveiling of yet a "third blessing" in the life of the holiness Christian: speaking in tongues. Using a literal Biblicist reading of the Book of Acts, this third event was understood to serve as an individual's evidence of baptism by the Holy Spirit. This discovery is traced by adherents to December 31, 1900, when student Agnes N. Ozman spoke in tongues following a period of Bible study and holiness teaching and prayer with her holiness teacher, Charles Fox Parham, at his Bethel Bible School in Topeka, Kansas. Parham also instructed William Joseph Seymour, an African-American preacher credited with starting the three-year Azusa Street Revival in Los Angeles in 1906. This event marks the beginning of the modern Pentecostal movement, as many visitors returned home to advocate Pentecostal theology and practice, and to start new churches of their own.[15] Pentecostalism spread rapidly, much of its first three decades spent in active evangelization and creative theological differentiation between various Pentecostal leaders, congregations, and denominations.[16]

Notwithstanding the interracial character of the Azusa Street Revival, the American racial climate was not conducive to the formation of interracial organizations, especially in the South where the Pentecostal movement grew most rapidly. The prolific African-American Church of God in Christ ordained hundreds of white ministers who went on to form independent, white Pentecostal churches. By 1914 this growing network of white pastors formed the Assemblies of God, which soon became the largest Pentecostal group. By 1925, three more Pentecostal denominations succumbed to the pressures of Southern racial segregation. The Pentecostal Assemblies of the World lost its white ministers in 1925 to the new, all-white Pentecostal Ministerial Alliance, the Church of God segregated its black members into a separate General Assembly that lasted from 1926 to 1966, and the Pentecostal Holiness Church lost two African-American groups that chose to worship separately, the black Fire-Baptized Holiness Church (1908) and the Black Pentecostal Holiness Church in 1913.[17]

The twentieth century began on a high note with high hopes for many American Methodists. With Methodist President McKinley in the White House and widespread belief in historical progress and an imminent, earthly Kingdom of God, along with other Protestants, many anticipated and worked relentlessly for a "Christian century." In this season of optimism, the spirit of ecumenism and growing aspirations for church union emerged with unprecedented vigor among certain groups that realized they had much more in common than those things that set them apart. At the same time, chasms were deepening between literal Biblicists and the biblical scholars that embraced higher criticism; between premillennialists and postmillennialists; between Methodists who despised and actively opposed racism in all its forms, and Methodists who openly supported and practiced it even to the extent of fervent participation in the Ku Klux Klan. These differences led to further ideological and institutional realignments and deepened some of the divisions that already existed along racial lines. While also weathering the Great Depression, the advent of World War I and the emergence of the United States as a world power, American Methodists in the first two and a half decades of the twentieth century prepared for the next half century of ministry still divided. By 1925, negotiations were already under way that would redefine the contours of Methodist ecclesiastical structures, missions, and relationships between Wesleyan offspring and with the world beyond.

1926–1974: REORGANIZATION AND REDEFINITION

The largest group of Methodists at the start of the mid-century period was heavily occupied through much of the century with unification negotiations. As early as 1876, the MEC and MECS made commitments to improved relations, each body pledging "to honor the other as a legitimate heir of the [1784] Christmas Conference" and to send representatives to each other's General Conferences. A Joint Commission on Federation in 1898 made recommendations for cooperation in foreign missions and in publications. In 1905 the two denominations published a common catechism, hymnbook, and order of worship.[18] In 1908 the MEC and MPC exchanged delegations at their respective General Conferences, hoping to start a movement toward unification. Meanwhile, the CME and AMEZ churches explored merger possibilities in 1902,[19] and the MPC and UBC churches developed a plan of union that was adopted in 1914, but neither was brought to fruition.

It quickly became evident that the issue of race would be the largest challenge to resolve between the MEC and MECS. The MECS was determined that any unification would not include African-American Methodists or allow the northern majority of Methodists in the MEC controlling power. Many of the African-American former members of the MECS had transferred to the MEC, AME, and AMEZ Churches. By creating the CME Church in 1870, the MECS had successfully divested itself of blacks and was adamant that this state of affairs would continue despite the reality of more than 300,000 African-American members of the MEC. The MECS proposed a merger of all black Methodists into one African-American Methodist denomination, a suggestion that did not find sympathy in the African-American Methodist bodies. A Joint Commission on Federation between the MEC, MECS, and MPC in 1911 first proposed racially segregated quadrennial conferences and greater rights for laity in any merger. The themes of racially segregated administrative divisions and equal laity rights became major components of the following decades of negotiation. To this was added by 1920 the principle of jurisdictional regionalism that would protect "the southern (white) minority from domination by the northern majority." Although staunchly opposed by the vast majority of African-American MEC delegates and some northern representatives, the commitment to "the great cause ... of Methodist unity and union" was strong enough to gain approval by the General Conferences in all three bodies by 1936, and to effect their merger in 1939.[20]

Not everyone agreed to the merger. In 1940, the Southern Methodist Church was formed by MECS members in opposition, and in 1942 the Fundamental Methodist Church was founded by former MPC members. Others who disapproved transferred to alternate denominations. While the racially segregated model for the Methodist Church engendered bitter disappointment and regret among African Americans and some whites, it was accepted by many as an opportunity to build toward a better future. Members of the new African American Central Jurisdiction proceeded to elect their own bishops, serve as representatives of their jurisdiction in national leadership on boards and agencies of the Methodist

Church, produce their own newspaper (*The Central Christian Advocate*), and support black colleges and universities. Members of the Central Jurisdiction capitalized upon the connectionalism of their Methodist Church to promote, among other African-American Methodist values, the social holiness and social equality that they had often been denied. Meanwhile, from its beginning in 1939 until it was dismantled as a pre-condition of the merger with the EUB Church in 1968, persistent efforts were made to abolish the relic of Methodist institutional racism.[21] A Central Jurisdiction study commission formally recommended its elimination in 1956. It was officially dissolved in 1968, with all former Central Conference institutions merged with regional Conferences of the UMC by 1972.[22]

MPC women also suffered a setback in the compromises of 1939. For more than sixty years the MPC had ordained women into the ministry with full clergy rights. Merging with two of the Methodist bodies most resistant to women's ordination took its toll, and MPC women already ordained were forced to relinquish their full clergy rights in the MC. Meanwhile, the presidents of the three unifying denominations' women's home and foreign missions organizations worked closely together in advance of 1939 to organize what would become the Women's Division of Christian Service of the MC. Although denied ordination and clergy rights, MC women developed a formidable national ministry organization that delivered mission and education services across the church, extending its reach to join women's forces at the local church and national levels.[23]

While the MEC, MECS, and MPC negotiated their way to unification, the UBC and EC were doing likewise. The EC was formed in 1922 through a reunion of the Evangelical Association and the United Evangelical Church, healing a breach that occurred late in 1891. Committed to the principle of church unity, the UBC began to explore union possibilities with the Methodist Protestant and Congregational Churches in the first several years of the century, with the Reformed Church in the 1920s, and empowered its churches in Canada to merge with the Canadian Congregational Churches. In 1926 the EC and UBC began union conversations and by 1941 had developed a plan of union that was adopted by both denominations in 1946 to form the EUB Church. A significant compromise was struck between the UBC and the more culturally conservative EC to disallow licensing and ordination of women, a practice that the UBC had adopted fifty-seven years earlier.[24]

Unlike the MEC and MECS, the EC and UBC had no difficulty with racial issues in their negotiations. Both denominations had solidly opposed slavery and racial discrimination from their beginnings and were proactive in supporting integration and civil rights for all citizens.[25] Previously, their German language and agrarian cultural contexts had distinguished these groups from the other Methodists. Compelled by commitments to church unity and ecumenism, in 1948 the EUB Church became the first U.S. denomination to join the World Council of Churches.

Meanwhile, the entrenched racial situation in the United States that gave rise to separate African-American Methodist denominations in the first place was not conducive to the existence of interracial communities, let alone merger conversations between white and black Methodists. African Americans across Methodist traditions shared a common black experience, community ethic, and worship preferences that in effect also set them apart from white counterparts. This reality in an environment that was commonly hostile to both equal rights and interracial collaboration contributed to continuing denominational alignment along racial lines. It also helped to foster the radical social and civil rights commitments of African-American Methodists throughout the century. AME civil rights activists included A. Philip Randolph; Rosa Parks; Sadie T. M. Alexander; Archibald Carey, Jr.; Oliver Brown; and J. A. De Laine.[26] Along with AME Bishop Ransom and Ida B. Wells-Barnett, AMEZ Bishop Alexander Walters was a key player in the formation of the NAACP. CME civil rights leaders included attorney Donald Hollowell and Student Nonviolent Coordinating Committee leader Ruby Doris Smith Robinson. Other Methodist civil rights activists included the influential James Farmer and James Lawson.

By mid-century, uniting American Methodists were not only sorting out details of mergers, but also rethinking and restructuring their approach to missions and evangelism. Missions and evangelism had been operating hand in hand as Methodist mainstays in previous generations and so they continued to function together in the African-American Methodist, holiness, and Pentecostal denominations throughout the twentieth century. In the late 1920s and early 1930s, some Methodists were calling into question traditional approaches to missions, in particular the association of missions with evangelism. Too often, it was observed, missions' efforts were characterized by Western imperialism, Christian hypocrisy, and manipulative conversion techniques.[27] By 1939, the Uniting Conference of the MC was prepared to arrange a new structure for evangelism separate from the work of missions. The new denomination created a General Commission on Evangelism to address the "low ebb" of "the spiritual life of multitudes of Church members" as well as the large number of unchurched in the United States. In 1948, the Committee was restructured to oversee both membership and evangelism. Its goal was "to undertake the evangelization of America" and "the Christianization of the social order."[28] The following year, the Foundation for Evangelism was incorporated to raise funds for MC evangelism, signaling another step toward the differentiation of the more "spiritual" work of evangelism apart from more practical, service-oriented missions.

Meanwhile, under leadership deeply committed to the social gospel, the Methodist Federation for Social Service (MFSS) spoke out regarding situations thought to defy the principles of the Methodist Social Creed. Harry Ward, Bishop Francis McConnell, and Winifred Chappell publicly took positions along both labor union and socialist lines, which prompted a strong reaction by MEC social and theological conservatives. While the 1932 General Conference had supportively declared, "the present industrial order is unchristian, unethical and anti-social," by 1936 the denomination was split by political debate over these issues and the General Conference, voted to remove the Social Creed from its *Book of Discipline*. It was reinstated in revised form by action of the 1939 Uniting Conference but by 1952, the MC General Conference broke ties with the MFSS because of perceptions of objectionable social and political activities.[29] Renamed in 1948 the Methodist Federation for Social Action (MFSA), the agency continued as a separate entity, with a significant number of sympathetic, socially "progressive" Methodists as members and in its leadership.

American Methodism placed a renewed emphasis on academic scholarship and theological education mid-century, with the CME founding Phillips School of Theology in 1950, followed by the EUB Church's merger of Evangelical School of Theology (Penn.) and Bonebrake Seminary (Ohio) into United Theological Seminary in Dayton, Ohio, in 1954; the MC founding of Methodist Theological School in Ohio (1957), St. Paul School of Theology, Wesley Theological Seminary (formerly MPC), and participation in the creation of the Interdenominational Theological Center (including 1883 Gammon) in 1958. In 1956 the MC established as normative the requirement for degreed seminary education as a precondition for ordination, and in 1968 created the Ministerial Education Fund (MEF) to support the UMC schools charged with educating ministerial candidates. The growing emphasis on graduate theological education at Methodist schools further estranged those who opposed higher criticism and the nature of social ethics taught at the denominational schools.

By 1966 a Plan of Union had been adopted by the EUB and the MC. The Uniting Conference occurred in 1968, forming The United Methodist Church and adopting a resolution for "The Cause of Christian Unity."[30] In this era, Methodists John R. Mott, Charles Parlin, and Bishop G. Bromley Oxnam helped to found the World Council of Churches, and Methodists offered strong leadership as well in the Federal Council of Churches. In 1951 the World Methodist Council was formed with Methodist Elmer T. Clark serving as general secretary. The MC and EUB Churches had both joined the Consultation on Church Union (COCU), begun in 1962, and by 1964 the MC had established a Committee on Ecumenical Affairs, which was continued in the UMC as part of the General Board of Global Ministries.[31]

While the uniting Methodists focused upon merger, African-American Methodist denominations maintained their own organizations and commitments to ministry, mission, and civil rights activism. Alongside other African Americans, they were key players in bringing about community and national legislative changes, building upon the radical holiness traditions of John Wesley and Richard Allen. Meanwhile, the holiness and Pentecostal denominations continued to strengthen their capacity for mission and evangelism not only in the United States, but throughout the world.

1975–2000: REASSESSMENT AND RENEWAL

In the final quarter of the twentieth century, the UMC settled into its new organizational structure, which included both old and new elements. In addition to establishing separate general boards and agencies to manage finance, education, evangelism, ministry, and mission, new agencies and caucuses were generated to oversee implementation of hard-won racial, gender, and ecumenical priorities. The Central Jurisdiction finally dismantled, the denomination created a Commission on Religion and Race to monitor racial equality. At the same time, African-American United Methodists founded Black Methodists for Church Renewal to ensure continuing dialogue and mission fulfillment, and to hold the denomination accountable for progress in supporting ministry by and with African Americans. Following a Pan-Methodist dialogue between the UM, AME, AMEZ, and CME churches in 1979, a Commission on Pan-Methodist Cooperation was formed in 1985, and a Pan-Methodist Commission on Union in 1998.

Ecumenical commitments continued in the final decades of the century with UMC continuing participation in the Consultation on Church

Union (COCU), formation of a General Commission on Christian Unity and Interreligious Concerns (GCCUIC) in 1980, new dialogue between the UMC and the Evangelical Lutheran Church of America in 1977, and dialogue with the Episcopalians for eucharistic fellowship in the 1990s. In 1999 the UMC consulted with representatives from American Holiness denominations regarding historical, theological, and practical matters and explored possible next steps for continuing a dialogue.[32]

Racial, ethnic, gender, and sexual orientation diversification of leadership was a central focus in the UMC in the last quarter of the century, featuring resistance and support by opposing factions. The UMC formalized its commitment to women in leadership by forming the United Methodist Women (UMW) as a subset of the Women's Division of the General Board of Global Ministries, and through the General Commission on the Status and Role of Women (GCSRW), begun in 1976. The same year women celebrated the seating of ten women as clergy delegates to General Conference. The first female UMC bishop, Marjorie Matthews, was elected in 1980, and Bishops Leontine Kelly and Judith Craig followed in 1984. The AME Church elected Bishop Vashti McKenzie in 2000.

The subject of homosexuality became the source of widespread, virulent controversy in the UMC in the late twentieth century. Prohibitory language was added in 1972 to the denomination's *Book of Discipline* followed by an Affirmation Caucus founded to advocate for full clergy and laity rights for gay and lesbian persons in 1975, and Reconciling Congregations in 1984 (incorporated in 1990, changed to Reconciling Ministries Network in 2000). A Houston Declaration by opposed clergy responded against allowing homosexual practices in 1987, and a Committee to Study Homosexuality was formed by General Conference in 1988, which continued for the next two quadrennia.

While in the last decades of the twentieth century the UMC was poised to celebrate many of its own hard-won accomplishments in the areas of race, gender, diversity, and church unity, the denomination was also faced with the reality that it was declining rapidly in membership. From 1970 to 2000, the UMC lost more than two million members, or 20 percent of its adherents, while the average age of its members was steadily increasing, accelerating the rate of decline. Grassroots efforts to stem the tide of decline and bring about renewal in its place demonstrated the wide range of value-laden ideologies represented in the UMC, as well as the deep commitments to the same body by a wide theological range of adherents. Denominational officials gradually accepted the difficulties of downsizing, pondering possible remedies and inevitabilities.

Meanwhile, each racial, ethnic, gender, sexuality, and theological group, caucus, and program asserted the unique solutions it could offer for authentic renewal. The socially conservative, "evangelical" Good News caucus was founded in 1967 and the Foundation for Theological Education and charismatic Aldersgate Renewal Ministries were organized in 1977. The Walk to Emmaus was begun in 1978, The Mission Society in 1984, Disciple Bible Study in 1987, Good News's Renew (for women) in 1989, the Good News Memphis Declaration in 1992, the Reimagining Conference in 1993, and the Confessing Movement in 1995.

The most visible divisions that remained in the UMC by century's end concerned unresolved theological, social, and political differences between parties that included laity, pastors, agency executives, and bishops. Arguments over sexuality and other social and political issues became the chief focus of congregations, annual conferences, and General Conferences, threatening to divide the denomination down the middle between opposing sides. Behind the disputes were competing theories of the proper role and interpretation of the Bible, United Methodist doctrine, and discipline.

These and similar issues were also addressed by African-American Methodists and holiness and Pentecostal denominations, but in ways suited to their traditions and values. Though not unscathed by arguments about biblical interpretation, gender, sex, and sexuality, the African-American Methodist churches kept their public focus in more traditional ways upon ministry, mission, and traditional social justice challenges. African-American Methodists experienced substantial growth throughout the century primarily in the United States, but also in Canada and Africa. Holiness and Pentecostal churches tended to maintain conservative social perspectives influenced by literal Biblicist interpretations regarding sexuality and family relationships and structures. Though widely diversified with regard to fine points of doctrine, their characteristic foci throughout the twentieth century continued to be charismatic worship and unrelenting evangelism. In the twentieth century, the holiness and Pentecostal denominations spread across the earth, and became one of the largest, global branches of Christianity alongside Roman Catholicism and other forms of Protestantism.

As the UMC approached the end of the twentieth century, leaders committed to the denomination's renewal observed that it lacked an updated mission statement that could bridge theological differences and unify its mission and ministries. In 2000 the UMC adopted a simple mission statement: "The mission of the church is to make disciples of Jesus Christ." In 2004, the phrase was added, "for the transformation of the world." In the subsequent five years, the UMC added 4.4 million members in Africa, Europe, and Asia, resuming its earlier growth pattern and registering more than twelve million members by 2009. What was American Methodism at the start of the twentieth century became a multiracial, multicultural, and global church by the start of the twenty-first century, with untold numbers of Methodist, holiness, and Pentecostal adherents and their influence throughout the world.

[handwritten annotation: pretty cool. (started out as a little of franc) how small.]

Notes

1 Russell E. Richey, Kenneth E. Rowe, and Jean Miller Schmidt, *The Methodist Experience in America: A Sourcebook*, vol. 2 (Nashville, TN: Abingdon, 2000), 22; and http://www.gcah.org/site/c.ghKJIoPHIoE/b.3828783/.

2 C. Eric Lincoln and Lawrence H. Mamiya, *The Black Church in the African American Experience* (Durham, NC: Duke University Press, 1990), 65, and Eileen W. Lindner, ed., *Yearbook of American & Canadian Churches 2000* (Nashville, TN: Abingdon Press, 2000), 336, 341 (CD-ROM).

3 E. O. Watson, ed., *Yearbook of American and Canadian Churches 1924–5* (Baltimore, MD: J. E. Stolmann, 1925), 397; and Lindner, ed., *Yearbook of American & Canadian Churches 2000*, 345, 351. For Church of the Nazarene Growth, see Annual Statistics from the General Secretary's Reports, http://nazarene.org/files/docs/statisticsannual/.pdf.

4 Vinson Synan, *The Holiness and Pentecostal Tradition: Charismatic Movements in the Twentieth Century* (Grand Rapids, MI: Eerdmans, 1997), 206, 286.

5 Hawthorne Lakey, *The History of the CME Church* (Memphis, TN: CME Publishing House, 1985), 338–339.

6 Rex D. Matthews, *Timetables of History for Students of Methodism* (Nashville, TN: Abingdon Press, 2007), 149–167.

7 Ralph E. Luker, *The Social Gospel in Black and White: American Racial Reform, 1885–1912* (Chapel Hill, NC: The University of North Carolina Press, 1991), 173–174.

8 Luker, *Social Gospel*, 92–95, 233, 261, 265.

9 Synan, 190.

10 Jean Miller Schmidt, *Grace Sufficient: A History of Women in American Methodism, 1760–1939* (Nashville, TN: Abingdon Press, 1999), 157.

11 Russell E. Richey, Kenneth E. Rowe and Jean Miller Schmidt, eds. *The Methodist Experience in America: A History*, vol. 1 (Nashville, TN, Abingdon Press, 2010), 338.

12 Synan, *Holiness and Pentecostal Tradition*, 46–47.

13 Ibid., 40–43.

14 Ibid., 48–49.

15 Ibid., 90–91, 93, 97.

16 Ibid., 195.

17 Ibid., 170–183.

18 Richey, Rowe and Schmidt, *The Methodist Experience*, I: 363.

19 Lakey, *History of CME Church*, 350–352.

20 Harry V. Richardson, *Dark Salvation: The Story of Methodism as it developed among Blacks in America*, (Garden City, NY: Anchor Press/ Doubleday, 1976), 272; Richey, Rowe and Schmidt, *The Methodist Experience*, 1: 363–437.

21 Richey, Rowe and Schmidt, *The Methodist Experience*, 1: 388–391.

22 Richardson, *Dark Salvation*, 280–281.

23 Richey, Rowe and Schmidt, *The Methodist Experience*, 1: 398–399.

24 Kenneth W. Krueger, ed., *The History of the Evangelical United Brethren Church* (Nashville, TN: Abingdon Press, 1979), 360; Schmidt, *Grace Sufficient*, 284.

25 Wendy J. Deichmann, "'True Holiness' as Social Practice in the Evangelical and United Brethren Traditions: A Legacy for Successor Denominations" in J. Steven O'Malley and Jason E. Vickers, eds., *Methodist and Pietist: Retrieving the Evangelical United Brethren Tradition* (Nashville, TN: Kingswood Books, 2011), 182, 185–188; and Richey, Rowe and Schmidt, *The Methodist Experience*, 1: 397.

26 Dennis C. Dickerson, "The Wesleyan Witness in the U.S. Civil Rights Movement: The Allen Legacy against 20th Century American Apartheid," www.divinity.duke.edu/oxford/docs/2007papers/2007–3Dickerson.pdf.

27 Richey, Rowe, and Schmidt, *The Methodist Experience*, 1: 298.

28 Wendy J. Deichmann, "Mission Becomes Institution: The Example of United Methodism" in Alan G. Padgett, ed., *The Mission of the Church in Methodist Perspective* (Lewiston, NY: The Edwin Mellen Press, 1992), 78–80.

29 Richey, Rowe and Schmidt, *The Methodist Experience*, 1: 326, 334, 421–422.

30 Ibid., 1: 428.

31 Ibid., 1: 423–425.

32 Ibid., 1: 539–542.

Part II

The Religious Culture of American Methodism

5   Revivalism and Preaching

MICHAEL K. TURNER

In this chapter, the relationship between Methodism and revivalism is explored. From the time of its founding in eighteenth-century England until the middle of the nineteenth century, Methodism was intimately tied to the work of revivalism, or the generation of mass religious conversions and excitement through embracing unorthodox methodologies. It was through utilization and innovation of traditional revival formats that Methodism was able to grow into one of the largest religious denominations in the United States. Curiously, despite the numeric success that they helped bring about, Methodist groups in the late nineteenth century largely abandoned the revival methodologies of the earlier period. This abandonment indicated that the Methodists of the late nineteenth and early twentieth centuries had entered into a new era of social respectability that had little use for "unseemly" revivals. But, the embrace and abandonment of religious enthusiasm and revivalism also revealed that, fundamentally, American Methodism of the nineteenth and early twentieth centuries was deeply pragmatic, displaying a willingness to shift with changing cultural needs.

REVIVALISM AND THE WESLEYAN REVIVALS

The eighteenth-century Methodist movement in England was committed to the work of religious revival. The early Methodists could be understood as a movement that was willing to use untraditional techniques to bring about mass religious conversions. This, in fact, was a mission clearly stated by John Wesley, who taught that the primary work of the Methodists was to create and renew Christians. When instructing the Methodist preachers, John Wesley informed them that their primary responsibility was to bring the Christian message to those not being reached by traditional means. He wrote, "You have nothing to do but save souls. Therefore spend and be spent in this work; and go always, not only to those who want you, but to those who want you most."[1]

Wesley's commitment to the work of saving souls led to his embracing of unorthodox methods of outreach. Wesley did not believe that his preaching should be limited to the parish setting, as was conventional in eighteenth-century England. Pushed by his friend George Whitefield, John Wesley began preaching to outdoor crowds at first in Bristol and, eventually, throughout England. Wesley saw this practice as beneficial because it allowed him to reach out to persons who had little interest in churches.[2] Indeed, Wesley became enamored with the effectiveness of open-air revivals. He and the other early Methodist preachers frequently spoke in front of large crowds in the center of the marketplace, in barns, near mines, and in other open-air locations. These events allowed an opportunity to speak to the unchurched and host an attendance that exceeded the normal capacities of a church.[3]

The unorthodox means of evangelizing produced an unexpected consequence. Attendees at the open-air revivals frequently displayed a very visceral reaction to the preacher's message. At almost every one of these worship events participants cried, laughed, fainted, or exhibited other outward displays of emotions. While Wesley was not entirely comfortable with these physical reactions present at the revivals, he permitted them among the Methodists because he believed they were a legitimate manifestation of the Holy Spirit. Wesley believed that these experiences were exaggerated or false, at times. On the topic of religious fits, Wesley insisted that he neither forwarded nor hindered them. However, he believed that genuine physical responses to the Holy Spirit did, in fact, occur. According to Wesley, the "Spirit of God, sharply convicting the soul of sin, may occasion the bodily strength to fail."[4] He become convinced that the religious excitement or enthusiasm present was a legitimate work of God by his reading of Jonathan Edward's *Faithful Narrative of the Surprising Work of God in Northampton, Massachusetts*, which gave a vivid account of similar actions occurring in North America.

Still, Wesley believed that there was a fine line between true manifestations of the Holy Spirit and religious enthusiasm. In his *Complete English Dictionary*, Wesley referred to enthusiasm as "religious madness."[5] He believed that the lens of scripture and clear reason could be used to determine whether religious emotion and the religious claims it sometimes produced were sanctioned by the Holy Spirit or misguided.[6]

Despite the crowds and excitement produced by the association of Methodism with outbreaks of emotion, Wesley was clear that it should be tempered for the sake of legitimate religion. In pursuing this goal, he was intent on making sure that his preachers communicated sound doctrine. He utilized the Methodist Conferences as a time to vet and instruct preachers. Wesley also was intent on making sure that the preachers did not view highly emotional worship as the pinnacle of Methodism. He encouraged and expected his preachers to possess minds that were informed by voracious reading and that followed traditional methodologies whenever possible. At the 1744 Conference, Wesley instructed his ministers to avoid field preaching when suitable parish or house settings were available. He cautioned, "we never preach *without* doors when we can with any conveniency preaching *within*."[7] He further instructed his preachers to always preach with clear, even voices. In a letter to Sarah Mallett he wrote, "Never scream. Never speak above the natural pitch of your voice; it is disgustful to the hearers.... It is offering God murder for sacrifice."[8] Similarly, Wesley discouraged congregations from excessive religious excitement. In his instructions for congregational singing he implored participants in Methodist worship to temper the excitement they demonstrated in worship. Wesley wrote, "Above all, sing *spiritually*. Have an eye to God in every word you sing ... attend strictly to the sense of what you sing; and see that your heart is not carried away with the sound, but offered to God continually."[9]

Wesley was concerned about any Methodist preacher whose chief goal was to inspire religious frenzy. Regardless, there was little doubt that the frenzy of these open-air revivals and the excitement associated with Methodist worship did a great deal to help swell the number of Methodist societies in England.

REVIVALISM IN EARLY AMERICAN METHODISM

The growth and identity of early American Methodism was also intimately linked to its participation in revivalism and religious enthusiasm. Like the English Methodists, the early American Methodists preachers were passionately committed to the work of revival. Their goal was to bring about the largest number of Christian conversions possible. Andrew Manship argued that this was the defining trait of American Methodism. He wrote, "May the Methodist Episcopal Church ever remember she is a *revival Church!*"[10] The published and unpublished journals of Methodist itinerant preachers were littered with references to charge's being in the "flame of revival" or there being large scale regional revivals.[11] This point was clearly articulated by Methodist preacher Thomas Ware when he wrote, "a single motive, to serve God and save souls, has actuated the body of Methodist preachers from the beginning."[12]

The American Methodists were more utilitarian in their attitudes toward revival and enthusiasm than their English counterparts. The English Methodists were led by an extremely well-educated Anglican priest who was willing to set limits on the methodologies and extremes of the preachers and worshippers. The American Methodists lacked a similar guiding ideology. In fact, their primary leader was the largely self-educated, Francis Asbury, who historian Frank Baker aptly described as an ever-pragmatic "ecclesiastical Darwinist."[13] Unlike Wesley, Asbury had little use for high-church liturgy. Asbury and the early Methodists were willing to believe that results, measured by emotional intensity and numerical gains, were evidence enough that God sanctioned revival and worship methodologies.

So, the Methodist leadership in America was not concerned with the visceral displays of religion that took place in Society meetings. In fact, these outbreaks of emotion were normative among the very first Methodists in North America. For many Methodists, the chief purpose of worship was experiencing spiritual rapture, or "getting happy."[14] To the leadership, the ecstatic nature of worship was a sign that it was effective. Early American Methodist worship was decisively evangelical and revivalist; this meant that it was focused around inspiring religious conversions in those who were in attendance. Physical exercises and outbreaks of emotion were signs that this goal had been accomplished.

The highly ecstatic nature of early American Methodist worship was rooted in a number of different factors. All of early Methodist worship was highly participatory. Lay participants frequently offered testimonies of their own conversion experiences in excited tones. It was also not uncommon for religious seekers to be called upon to speak, as if to be invited into the frenzy of worship. According to William Burke, "The practice then among the Methodists was to call upon all the seekers of religion to pray in public at the prayer meeting."[15]

Not only were lay members expected to participate and offer testimonies, they were often given leadership roles. Methodist societies were generally organized into classes of around twelve persons. While a traveling preacher periodically visited a society, a mature Christian known as a class leader was charged with leading the worship activities. Licensed exhorters were also common spokespersons at the meetings. The licensed exhorters were laypersons with other fulltime employment that were sanctioned by the Methodist Episcopal Church (MEC) to speak publically. Unlike the traveling preachers, the exhorters' messages normally did not focus on specific biblical passages; instead, they often offered a basic evangelical message focused on repentance or an accounting of their own call to conversion.

The inclusivity of early American Methodism also contributed to its ecstatic nature. It was not uncommon for a mixture of different races and genders to be present at early society meetings. Early on, women and African Americans frequently became class leaders or licensed exhorters. The integrated nature of the meetings further contributed to the emotional atmosphere, as they provided for an opportunity for the already emotional worship of early Methodism to come into direct contact and enter into a syncretistic relationship with an African-American worldview still deeply rooted in the West African traditional religions. In West African traditional religions spirit possession, magic, divination, and other supernatural feats were common beliefs.[16]

Finally, Methodist preaching was interested in generating visible signs of effectiveness. In the early Methodist worldview, the call to conversion or sanctification was genuine only if it was physically experienced. John Emory said in his sermon before the British Methodist Conference, "The gospel which is not *felt* ... is not the gospel of Christ."[17] The most popular Methodist preachers were those who were accomplished in invoking this feeling in listeners. Thomas Ware wrote, "People love the preacher who makes them feel."[18] Indeed, the preachers measured success and failure by the physical displays of emotion present at sermons. Recalling the events of a preaching excursion, Freeborn Garrettson wrote, "We had a wonderful display of the power of the Lord. After ... my discourse, the young people hung around each other, crying for mercy."[19] Preaching was considered successful if it produced visible, religious experiences in attendees.

In order to optimize its effectiveness, Methodist preaching in early America developed distinctive traits. First, it was almost always extemporaneous. Wesley encouraged the use of the extemporaneous method among the English Methodist preachers. Similarly, in the early days of American Methodism it was frowned upon for a preacher to utilize a manuscript in delivering sermons. Davis W. Clark remarked that this made it a very challenging task to compile a volume of sermons. He wrote, "Our preaching, from the origin of Methodism, having been for the most part extemporaneous, few preachers have written and preserved manuscript sermons enough to form a volume."[20] The rationale with extemporaneous prayers was that it was considered to be more powerful than manuscript preaching or "sermon reading," as it was often called. The American Methodists believed that manuscript preaching was too programmed and, perhaps most importantly, too subdued to be

Figure 6. **Methodist Camp Meeting (1836),** Methodist Library Image Collection, Drew University, Madison, New Jersey.

effective. Effective preaching was enthusiastic and fiery. Abel Stevens insisted, "One fact let him be assured of; namely, that whatever uniform and respectable character his manuscript preaching may have, the *maximum* power of preaching can never be attained by the sermon-reader."[21] This *"maximum* power" generated by extemporaneous preaching usually, for the Americans, also meant loud intonations. The practice was particularly well suited to large worship environments like the camp meeting, as a loud volume was necessary in order for the preacher's voice to reach the entire audience.

Beyond being given extemporaneously, early American Methodist sermons were also well known for their simplicity. The early preachers were mostly uneducated and their sermons stayed focus on providing listeners with a primer on how to achieve salvation. Prominent Methodist preacher and historian Abel Stevens contended that the basic discourse of early American preaching was focused on the "essential doctrines of grace." He wrote,

> Seldom did the man who was inquiring "What shall I do to be saved?" hear a Methodist preacher, without bearing away with him the precise answer. The lost condition of the soul by nature, repentance toward God, faith toward our Lord Jesus Christ, justification, sanctification, the witness of the Spirit – such truths seemed to make up the alphabet out of which the very syllabification of their discourse was formed.[22]

While simple, vivid imagery was often utilized to optimize the effectiveness. Edward Dromgoole believed that the only way to effectively bring about conversions was by exploring the intricacies of the human heart. In his estimate, the most effective way to do this was by rousing the imagination. He writes,

> It is through material and animated pictures of Good and Evil, Virtue and Vice, Heaven and Hell, and all those other awful and momentous topics which religious affords ... the judgment must be informed, and the passions moved in order to do lasting good.[23]

The ecstatic nature of Methodist worship and preaching in early America made it a natural fit for the revivals of the nineteenth century. While the MEC enjoyed some initial, limited numerical growth after organizing into a religious denomination during the Christmas Conference of 1784, the most substantial growth occurred after 1800. In 1800, there were just fewer than 65,000 members of the MEC in the United States, but by 1830 the total number was in excess of 478,000.[24] Within twenty years, that membership total almost tripled. This meant that nearly one of every fifteen Americans belonged to a Methodist church.[25] This remarkable growth was largely propelled by the Methodist participation in revivals of the early national period.

The MEC experienced great success in gaining converts from the western population that was expanding in the early nineteenth century. In the years immediately prior to the American Revolution, many Anglo-Americans began to immigrate to the area west of the Appalachian Mountains in search of cheap, fertile land. This westward migration was made possible by the discovery of the Cumberland Gap, which provided a flat trail to Tennessee and Kentucky, and the establishment of military roads by the British during the French and Indian War, which provided access to the areas surrounding the Ohio River.

The MEC was one of the very first religious bodies to attempt to gain a substantial presence in the southern and midwestern regions of the new nation. Methodism's success in these western regions was partially the product of its practical, effective system of itinerancy. This system of itinerant ministry dictated that preachers were assigned to specific geographic regions or circuits to serve. This system was an enormously beneficial system for increasing the geographic outreach of the denomination. Immediately following the 1784 Christmas Conference, the Methodists began to establish circuits in areas throughout the South and Midwest. While the Methodists were not initially successful in gaining a large number of followers in these western territories, they were active and deliberate. The Methodist organized a sizable number of circuits and held at least eighteen annual conferences between 1788 and 1800.[26]

The great turning point for the denomination's numeric growth occurred around the year 1800. In that year, the western phase of what historians have termed the "Second Great Awakening" started. These nineteenth-century revivals were different from the revivals of the previous century. They, firstly, were infamous for outbreaks of religious enthusiasm that exceeded in the temperament and extremity of those earlier revivals. The later revivals were also more geographically widespread and longer in duration. The revivals made inroads into the southern, midwestern, and northeastern regions of the young nation and spanned the first several decades of the century. Jesse Lee wrote, "the Methodist connection hardly ever knew such a time of general revival of religion through the whole of the circuits, as they had about the latter part of the year 1800."[27]

Finally, the revivals of the nineteenth century innovated many of the methodologies utilized by previous revivals to reach prospective converts. The most infamous and, perhaps, the most successful of these methods was that of the camp meeting. Seemingly based off the open-air preaching model popular during the revivals of the eighteenth century, camp meetings were multiple-day revival meetings (the number of days varied a great deal) generally held in a specifically prepared wilderness area, though Charles Finney would adapt the camp meeting format to suit urban areas in the middle decades of the nineteenth century.

The first camp meeting is credited to the joint efforts of James M'Gready and the brothers John and William McGee. In 1796, James M'Gready became the pastor of three small Presbyterian churches in Logan County, Kentucky. Following in the tradition of Scottish Presbyterian seasonal revivals, or "Holy Fairs," M'Gready began holding multiple-day worship events. Essentially, the congregations met together from Friday to Sunday. These protracted meetings featured preaching and hymn singing on Friday and concluded with communion services on Sunday afternoon. M'Gready held one of these services at his Red River Church in June 1800. He invited the brothers John and William M'Gee to officiate with him. While William was a fellow Presbyterian, John was a Methodist who was notorious for generating religious excitement at worship events. Supposedly, John's preaching caused the congregations to erupt into religious frenzy. The next month an even more spectacular series of outdoor religious services were held at Gasper River Church, constituting the first camp meeting. In the following months, camp meetings were held in other areas of the West.[28]

The most important camp meeting was held in Cane Ridge, Kentucky, from August 6 to August 12, 1801. According to estimates from those present at the event, the Cane Ridge Revival attracted between twenty and thirty thousand people. The success of the revival was traced to a variety of factors. Attendees were drawn from multiple religious groups. While the event was not well attended by Baptists, who were "confined pretty much to their own people," Methodists and Presbyterians attended in large numbers.[29] Presbyterian Minister Barton W. Stone, who organized the event, also made effective use of advertising. He sent announcements of the event to Methodist and Presbyterian fellowships throughout the Cane Ridge region.

The success of Cane Ridge inspired the Methodists to begin organizing and utilizing camp meeting revivals as a tool for evangelizing in the West. The Methodist preacher Peter Cartwright wrote that it was from Cane Ridge that "our camp-meetings took their rise."[30] In fact, no religious group was as strongly associated with the camp meetings as the Methodists.

The Methodists were attracted to the camp meetings for at least two distinct reasons. One reason that the camp meetings proved to be so popular with the Methodists was because of their familiarity with the events. The enthusiastic worship of the camp meetings was similar to, and partially inspired by, the society worship prevalent among the Methodists. The camp meetings also bore a number of similarities with the quarterly meeting format that was already being utilized by various Methodist denominations. The quarterly meetings, a practice adapted from the English Methodists, were originally designed as business meetings for circuits. Over time, these meetings developed into public worship events. By the end of eighteenth century, the quarterly meetings were multiple-day meetings characterized by highly emotional worship that resembled the camp meeting format.[31]

A second reason that camp meetings were attractive to Methodists was because they were effective in helping grow the denomination. The large revivals brought thousands of converts to the fledgling denomination. While the Methodists never officially institutionalized the practice of camp meetings, they did allow the presiding elders and traveling preachers to call them.[32] The leader of the MEC, Bishop Francis Asbury, mentioned them with incredible frequency in his journal; he listed four hundred for the year 1811 alone.[33] He also made a great effort to attend as many as possible. Other traveling preachers, as well as the major Methodist periodicals, such as the *Methodist Magazine,* also gave accounts of camp meetings with incredible frequency.

The camp meetings led by the Methodists and other religious groups were even more emotional than the English Methodist open-air revivals or the typical American Methodist worship. Highly visible displays of emotion were regular features of the camp meetings. Attendees frequently broke into fits of shouting or crying. Fainting also occurred with great frequency. At the Cane Ridge Revival, James Finley recounted seeing a mass of hundreds of persons falling to the ground simultaneously. He wrote, "The noise was like the roar of Niagara.... At one time I saw at least five hundred swept down in a moment as if a battery of a thousand guns had been opened upon them, and then immediately followed shrieks and shouts that rent the very heavens."[34]

The camp meetings also became commonly associated with more extreme examples of religious emotionalism. As some participants in the revivals were undergoing a religious conversion or simply caught up in the excitement of the revival, they barked like animals. Rolling exercises were also common; these were when a person was "cast down in a violent manner, doubled with the head and feet together, and rolled over and over like a wheel."[35] The most notorious example of religious enthusiasm was the jerks. Jerks were probably the most common action to take place. They developed slowly; for instance, the forearm might begin to twitch, this twitching eventually spread until every muscle joined in the spasmodic twitching.

Every feature of the camp meeting was designed to elicit an emotional reaction. This included the camp meeting's basic layout. The focal point of every camp meeting was the pulpit. It was an enclosed space that was elevated several feet from the ground. Directly in front of the pulpit was an area known as the mourners' bench or anxious seat. Seekers who expected to have a religious conversion were instructed to sit in these particular seats. This area was, thus, notorious for intense emotional reactions. There were also two sections of seats made of planks of wood that were used as seating for the event. At most revivals, women sat on one side of the divide, while men sat on the other. Slaves were normally relegated to the back of the event, where a black preacher led the service.[36] While the segregation of sexes and races was designed to prevent irreligious behavior, it also succeeded in putting converts into situations where they felt comfortable and, hence, were less reserved.

Despite the fact that camp meetings were "popular," they were subject to a great deal of criticism from both insiders and outsiders.

The most common critique levied against the camp meetings was that of religious enthusiasm, or excess emotionalism. Outsiders considered the displays of emotion present at the event barbaric, unnatural, and vulgar. Some critics even felt that the revivals left the many young women in attendance in a vulnerable situation. An author writing under the pseudonym "Frances Trollope" criticized the camp meeting preachers for lechery and encouraging physical displays of emotions. She wrote,

> above a hundred persons, nearly all females came forward, uttering howlings and groans so terrible that I shall never cease to shudder when I recall them…. Many of these wretched creature were beautiful young females. The preachers moved among them, at once exciting and soothing their agonies…. I saw the insidious lips approach the cheeks of the unhappy girls.[37]

Trollope further speculated that the religious frenzy created by the preachers had a monetary motivation. Sarcastically, she wrote, "before our departure we learned hat [sic] a very *satisfactory* collection had been made by the preachers, for Bible, Tracts, and *all other religious purposes.*"[38]

The social dimension of the camp meetings also was widely attacked by both internal, as well as external, critics. One of the reasons that camp meetings were so successful was that they provided enormous entertainment and social value. In the South and Midwest, where people often lived far apart from one another, the camp meetings established makeshift "Cities of God" that temporarily provided community. Hence, the revivals were social gatherings or "religious retreats" held shortly after the fall harvest. In the Northeast and mid-Atlantic, the revivals provided a social escape from industrial labor.[39] Because of this social appeal, the camp meetings were attended in large numbers, from both the religious and irreligious persons in a given community. Thus, camp meetings were places where behavioral lapses occurred. Some individuals used the events as a time to show off the latest fashions. Prostitutes and liquor dispensers often attended the revivals, as well.[40] William Puddefoot, a frequent attendee of camp meetings, wrote, "Many were there, like myself, out of curiosity and for amusement; some for downright sin. Whisky in flasks and in hidden places in the woods was plentiful and cheap."[41] The events were also fairly notorious for providing a space for people to make romantic connections. In a letter reflecting on the enjoyable time she had at a camp meeting, an Alabama girl wrote that she made "many boy friends."[42]

The camp meeting methods were also routinely criticized in Christian theological circles for perverting proper liturgical form. John Nevin, professor of theology at the German Reformed Theological Seminary in Mercersburg, Pennsylvania, made this point forcibly in his 1843 book *The Anxious Bench*.[43] Responding to the growing presence of the camp meetings in the German immigrant churches in North America, Nevin contended that the revival format constituted a distinct religious form that was harmful to true religion. He wrote, "The truth is, this system, as we have said, has a life and spirit of its own.... A false theory of religion is involved in it, which cannot fail to work itself out and make itself felt, in many hurtful results, wherever it gains footing in the Church." According to Nevin, the liturgical form of camp meetings and similar revival settings stood in opposition to genuine religious instruction. Nevin insisted, "The spirit of the Anxious Bench is at war with the spirit of the Catechism."[44]

Particularly the concern with emotional frenzy and irreligious behavior encouraged some religious leaders to handle camp meetings with caution. Dubbing their meetings "General Camp Meetings," the earliest Methodist camp meetings were often held in conjunction with the Presbyterians.[45] Worried about the emotional frenzy associated with the meetings, the Presbyterians generally stopped their involvement with them. In fact, the controversy over the meetings contributed to the formation of the Cumberland Presbyterian Church. The first Cumberland Presbyterians were from the prorevivalists who had left or been expelled from the Presbyterian Church in the United States of America.

Ever pragmatic, the majority of the Methodists were willing to accept camp meetings as a legitimate work of God because the events produced converts. Some Methodists rationalized that the negative criticisms levied against the meetings were exaggerations. One supporter, writing under the pseudonym Theophilus Armenius, rationalized that the critics of the meetings were either irreligious themselves or overly educated "professors" who "took advantage of every circumstance, and exaggerated every unfavourable occurrence to such a degree as to give a false and dreadful colouring."[46] In a similar way, some accounts of camp meetings emphasize the appropriate decorum that was practiced at them. *The Weekly Recorder* noted that an 1818 camp meeting in the Philadelphia Conference was "that (with the exception of a few individuals) the whole of the vast concourse of people behaved themselves with the utmost propriety."[47]

One of the great intellectual leaders of the MEC, Nathan Bangs, argued in favor of the meetings. He contended that the similar physical and emotional reactions could be read about in the Bible, as well as the revivals of Jonathan Edwards and John Wesley. Most importantly, these meetings were acceptable because they brought about the conversion of many sinners. Though, Bangs was willing to concede that camp meetings were not perfect events. He wrote, "there must have been some disorder, some mingling of human passions not sanctified by grace, and some words and gesticulations not in accordance with strict religious decorum."[48]

THE DECLINE OF REVIVALISM
IN AMERICAN METHODISM

By the middle decades of the nineteenth century, the connection of Methodism to revivalism and religious enthusiasm was beginning to wane. The denomination that was regarded by many as the quintessential revival denomination largely abandoned camp meetings and the raucous church revivals that had characterized its first century of existence. The transition of attitudes about revivalism was very much rooted in Methodism's attempts to respond to shifting cultural needs. For many Methodists, the enthusiasm prevalent in the early nineteenth century was a pragmatic necessity for a different age. The current age called for new methodologies and responses in order to optimize outreach and meet the needs of the people.

In these years, American society was undergoing some distinctive transformations. In the Northeast, the emergence of merchant capitalism led to a fairly radical geographic redistribution. Between 1830 and 1920, hundreds of small and large cities emerged. While the South and West lacked the emergence of many large urban areas, small towns became commonplace in this time. For example, by 1850 there were more than 130 small towns containing between 500 and 2,500 persons in the South.[49]

With the increasing urban nature of American society, the needs and demands put on Methodist churches and preachers changed. In these new urban areas the large downtown churches emerged. In order to meet the needs of these new, populous churches many Methodist bodies moved away from appointing pastors to large circuits. Instead, preachers were often assigned to smaller charges or a station, which was a charge consisting of one church.

These increasingly populous and wealthy churches had little use for the rugged, revival-minded preachers. Raucous revivalism was associated more and more with a previous age. More and more, camp meetings became the providence of rural, less well-educated preachers, sometimes referred to as "camp meeting men."[50] The attendance at camp meetings failed to reach the numbers it did in the early nineteenth century, as well. No longer did thousands attend these events. W. G. Miller preached at a camp meeting in 1853 at Lake Butte des Morts in eastern Wisconsin and reported that the "attendance was good, there being ten tents on the ground, there were fifty conversions."[51] Similarly, quarterly meetings ceased being held with the same regularity and when they were held they ceased being worship events, largely because of sparse attendance. B. W. Gorham reflected, "Our modern Quarterly Meetings, where indeed we continue to have Quarterly Meetings at all, usually call together but two of us, the P. Elder and the Pastor."[52] "Old-fashioned" church revivals were semiregular occurrences at rural and some city churches. Generally, these events were small, more formal, and more subdued than the revivals of the earlier periods.

These new congregations demanded powerful, yet eloquent, ministers. Ministers should not be concerned with generating emotional upheaval in parishioners. The early-nineteenth-century insistence on generating visceral, emotional reactions during worship was a sign of the "simple lives" lived by the early preachers. Bishop Francis McConnell argued that, in the modern age, responses to the gospel message might be more subdued. He insisted, "There are Methodists who at one end of the line identify conversion with great emotional upheaval, just as there are those at the other end of the line who think of it as nothing more than signing a card in the Sunday school, or shaking hands with the minister in response to an invitation to join the church."[53]

Indeed, the new ideal was for a minister to develop a "sympathetic voice," or the ability to intuit the individual needs of parishioners. Matthew Simpson insisted that ministers should use even tones and emotional warmth in their preaching. He contended, "The minister should pour forth truth from a warm and sympathetic heart, for the personal benefit and edification of his congregation, and to touch and elevate the aspirations of every individual."[54]

Gone were the loud, vivid sermons of early American Methodism. Instead, these simple, conversion-centered sermons were increasingly replaced with more nuanced, thematic discourses. Manuscript preaching became more popular in the late nineteenth and early twentieth centuries as well. This practice was already emerging by the 1860s. In 1866,

George Brown lamented, "The Methodists ... have now, in many places, readers of sermons in their pulpits, instead of preachers."[55] While prominent church leaders like Matthew Simpson initially openly discouraged manuscript preaching, the practice gradually became more tolerated in the denomination.[56] In an 1842 article, Rev. Daniel Wheeler admitted, "manuscript reading has a good supply of honorable examples" among the most esteemed preachers of the day.[57] Another observer admitted that the "written sermon ought to have more thought expressed in better language" than an extemporaneous discourse.[58]

The need for more polished preachers who could relate to their increasingly well-educated urban audiences created a demand for more formal theological education. In the late decades of the nineteenth century, a number of theological schools were founded in the United States, including Methodist General Biblical Institute (1850) in Massachusetts, Drew Theological Seminary (1867) in New Jersey, Garrett Theological Seminary (1853) in Illinois, and Vanderbilt University (1875) in Tennessee. While theological education was enormously controversial in Methodist circles, it became more commonplace for preachers by the end of the nineteenth century.

Naturally, the introduction of formal education and the shift of pulpit focus away from conversion were controversial. Rev. John M'Ferrin insisted that many of the great Methodist preachers were "self-made men." He warned, "Woe to the Methodist Church should the day ever come when college training and a regular course in theological seminary shall be deemed essential prerequisites to an entrance upon the work of the ministry!"[59] Rev. Andrew Manship insisted that the old ways of being a Methodist preacher, which meant the methods of the early nineteenth century, were superior to the new. He wrote,

> I may be considered an *old fogy* but when I hear persons calling for *alterations in Methodism, especially in the cities* ... it is deeply impressed upon my mind to inquire modestly, is there not "a more excellent way?" I think so ... let us preach Christ and him crucified, attend prayer meetings and camp meetings, ... and labour constantly for revivals of religions, not recognising "the spirit of the age" as a controlling influence.[60]

Despite the controversy, theological education became a prominent feature of Methodism in the twentieth century, and the camp meeting style of revivalism ceased being a major factor in the denomination, though its purpose was picked up by the holiness revivals of the late nineteenth century.[61]

By the middle of the twentieth century, the word "revival" was used principally in Methodist circles to refer to either localized revivals designed for the renewal of present congregants or to refer to reclamation movements centered on the revival of emphases within the various Methodist denominations. With the 1969 introduction of *The Common Lectionary* (an adaptation of the Roman Catholic Lectionary) by the United Methodist Church, debates transitioned from being focused on the tension between manuscript and extempore preaching to being focused on whether thematic or exegetical preaching was more appropriate.[62]

The twentieth-century changes in revival and worship techniques should not be viewed as an abandonment of Methodism's core identity. Much as the nineteenth-century revival methodologies were developed as an attempt to address the shifting cultural needs of a geographically diffused population (and later a northeastern culture adjusting to new modes of labor), the twentieth-century move away from these methods was the result of Methodism attempting to respond to new cultural needs. This is the greatest weakness and strength of Methodism, its willingness to adapt to shifting cultural needs.

Notes

1 *Minutes of the Methodist Conference* (London: John Mason, 1862), 1: 494, 496.
2 Richard P. Heitzenrater, "John Wesley's Principles and Practice of Preaching," *Methodist History* 37 (1999), 90.
3 Ibid., 91.
4 John Telford, ed. *The Letters of John Wesley*, 8 vols. (London: Epworth Press,1931), 2:24. The letter was from March 5, 1744.
5 John Wesley, *The Complete English Dictionary, Explaining most of the Hard Words which are found in the Best English Writers* (1777), quoted in David Hempton, *Methodism: Empire of the Spirit* (New Haven, CT: Yale University Press, 2005), 37.
6 Hempton, *Methodism,*37.
7 *Minutes of the Methodist Conferences*, 1: 23, quoted in Richard Heitzenrater, *Wesley and the People Called Methodists* (Nashville, TN: Abingdon Press, 1995), 149.
8 John Telford, ed. *The Letters of John Wesley* (1931), 8:190, quoted in Heitzenrater, "John Wesley's Principles and Practice of Preaching," 97–98. The letter was from December 15, 1789. Wesley citation.
9 John Wesley, *The Works of the Reverend John Wesley, A.M.*, edited by John Emory (n. p.: J. Collard, 1831), 609.
10 Andrew Manship, *Thirteen Years' Experience in the Itinerancy* (Philadelphia, PA: Higgins & Perkinpine, 1856), 357.

11 W. G. Miller, *Thirty Years in the Itinerancy* (Milwaukee, WI: I. L. Hausen and Co., 1875), 265.

12 Thomas Ware, *Sketches of the Life and Travels of Rev. Thomas Ware* (New York: T. Mason and G. Lane, 1842), 244.

13 Frank Baker, *From Wesley to Asbury; Studies in American Methodism* (Durham, NC: Duke University Press, 1976), 120.

14 Lester Ruth, ed., *Early Methodist Life and Spirituality: A Reader* (Nashville, TN: Kingswood Books, 2005), 162.

15 William Burke, "Autobiography of William Burke," in *Sketches of Western Methodism: Biographical, Historical, and Miscellaneous,* edited by James B. Finley, (Cincinnati, OH: R. P. Thompson, 1854), 25.

16 Dee Andrews, *The Methodists and Revolutionary America, 1760–1800: The Shaping of an Evangelical Culture* (Princeton, NJ: Princeton University Press, 2000), 81.

17 John Emory, "The Substance of a Sermon Preached in Liverpool, on the 30th of July, 1820 before the Conference of the Ministers late in Connexion with the Rev. John Wesley," *The Wesleyan-Methodist Magazine* (1822), 89.

18 Ware, *Rev. Thomas Ware,* 175.

19 Nathan Bangs, *The Life of the Rev. Freeborn Garrettson: Compiled from his Printed and Manuscript Journals* (New York: O. Lane and C. B. Tippett, 1845), 97.

20 Davis W. Clark, *The Methodist Episcopal Pulpit: A Collection of Original Sermons from Living Ministers of the M.E. Church* (New York: Lane & Tippett, 1848), 5.

21 Abel Stevens, "The Preaching Required by the Times," *The National Magazine* 4 (1854), 411.

22 Abel Stevens, *Essays on the Preaching Required by the Times and the Best Methods of Obtaining it* (New York: Carlton and Phillips, 1855), 121–122.

23 "The Art of Preaching" (Edward Dromgoole papers), 5–9, quoted in Ruth, 199.

24 Hempton, *Methodism,* 212.

25 Nathan Hatch, "The Puzzle of American Methodism," *Church History* 63 (1994), 11.

26 *Minutes of the Annual Conference of the Methodist Episcopal Church for the Years 1773–1828* (New York: T Mason & G. Lane, 1840), 1: 29–89.

27 Jesse Lee, *A Short History of the Methodists in the United States of America* (Baltimore, MD: Magill & Clime, 1810), 273.

28 John Boles, *The Great Revival: Beginnings of the Bible Belt* (Lexington, KY: University Press of Kentucky, 1996), 52–55.

29 Theoilus Armenius, "Account of the Rise and Progress of the Work of God in the Western Country, pt. 1," *The Methodist Magazine* 2 (1819), 186.

30 Peter Cartwright, *The Autobiography of Peter Cartwright* (New York: Carlton & Porter, 1856), 34.

31 Lester Ruth, *A Little Heaven Below: Worship at Early Methodist Quarterly Meetings* (Nashville, TN: Kingswood Books, 2000).

32   Lee, *Short History of Methodists*, 362.

33   Dickson D. Bruce, Jr., *And They All Sang Hallelujah: Plain-Folk Camp Meeting Religion, 1800–1840* (Knoxville, TN: University of Tennessee Press, 1974), 52.

34   James B. Finley, *Autobiography of the Reverend James B. Finley*, W. P. Strickland, ed. (Cincinnati, OH: Hitchcock & Walden, 1853), 165–170.

35   Richard M'Nemar, *The Kentucky Revival: Or, a Short History of the Late Outpouring of the Spirit of God in the Western States of America* (New York: Edward O. Jenkin, 1846), 61.

36   Bruce, *They All Sang Hallelujah*, 71–80.

37   Frances Milton Trollope, *Domestic Manners of the Americans* (London: Whittaker, Treacher, & Co., 1832), 143–144.

38   Ibid., 146.

39   Paul E. Johnson, *A Shopkeeper's Millennium: Society and Revivals in Rochester, New York, 1815–1837* (New York: Hill and Wang, 1978), 3–14.

40   Bruce, *They All Sang Hellelujah* 56.

41   William George Puddefoot, *Leaves from the Log of a Sky Pilot* (Boston, MA: The Pilgrim Press, 1915), 70.

42   Charles A. Johnson, *The Frontier Camp Meeting: Religion's Harvest Time* (Dallas, TX: Southern Methodist University Press, 1955), 210.

43   This book was revised and expanded in 1844.

44   John Williamson Nevin, *The Anxious Bench* (Chambersburg, PA: Weekly Messenger, 1843), 55–56.

45   Nathan Bangs, *History of the Methodist Episcopal Church*, 4 vols. (New York: G. Lane and C. B. Tippett, 1845), 2: 107–110.

46   Theophilus Armenius, "Account of the Rise and Progress of the Work of God in the Western Country, pt. 3," *The Methodist Magazine* 2 (1819), 274.

47   "Methodist Camp Meeting," *The Weekly Recorder* 5 (1818), 59.

48   Bangs, *History of the Methodist Episcopal Church*, 2:113.

49   Donald B. Doddand Wyndle S. Dodd, eds., *Historical Statistics of the South, 1790–1970* (Tuscaloosa, AL: University of Alabama Press, 1973); see also E. Brooks Holifield, *The Gentlemen Theologians: American Theology in Southern Culture, 1795–1860* (Durham, NC: Duke University Press, 1978), 6.

50   Jacob Young, *Autobiography of a Pioneer; or, the Nativity, Experience, Travels, and Ministerial Labors of Rev. Jacob Young* (Cincinnati, OH: Cranston and Curtis, 1857), 300.

51   W. G. Miller, *Thirty Years in the Itinerancy* (Milwaukee: WI: Hausen and Co., 1875), 166.

52   B. F. Gorham, *The Camp Meeting Manual* (Boston, MA: H. V. Degen, 1854), 37.

53   Francis J. McConnell, *The Essentials of Methodism* (New York: Methodist Book Concern, 1916), 12, 16.

54   Matthew Simpson, *Lectures on Preaching* (New York: Phillips and Hunt, 1879), 304.

55   George Brown, *Recollections of Itinerant Life* (Cincinnati, OH: R. W. Carroll & Co., 1866), 451.

56   Simpson, *Lectures an Preaching,* 170.
57   David H. Wheeler, "Changes in Methodist Preaching," *The Homiletic Review* 7 (1842), 342.
58   "Our Itinerancy," *Methodist Review* 18 (1866), 216.
59   John B. M'Ferrin, *Semi-Centennial Discourse* (Nashville, TN: Publishing House of the M. E. Church, South, 1882), 13–14.
60   Manship, *Thirteen Years Experience,* 358.
61   Marvin Deiter, *The Holiness Revivals of the Nineteenth Century* (New York: Scarecrow Press, 1996).
62   James F. White, "Methodist Worship" in Russell E. Richey, Kenneth E. Rowe, and Jean Miller Schmidt, eds., *Perspectives on American Methodism: Interpretive Essays* (Nashville, TN: Kingswood Books, 1993), 478.

6 Sacraments and Life-Cycle Rituals

KAREN B. WESTERFIELD TUCKER

HISTORICAL AND RITUAL FOUNDATIONS

Methodist denominations in the United States all trace their liturgical roots to a dual inheritance given by John Wesley to the "people called Methodist" in North America. On the one hand, Wesley commended an informal, flexible, "heart-warming" style of worship that regularly consisted of extemporary and spontaneous prayers, Scripture reading, singing, and preaching and/or exhortation, to which might be added personal testimonies of spiritual experience and a collection of monies for the poor. On the other hand, he bequeathed a more formal style, with liturgies and set prayers for Sunday worship, the Lord's Supper, infant and adult baptism, weddings, funerals, and ordination supplied in his abridgement of the Church of England's *Book of Common Prayer* (1662) published as *The Sunday Service of the Methodists in North America* (1784).[1] Many Methodists in North America were already acquainted with both of these liturgical styles before the *Sunday Service* was officially adopted at the founding of the Methodist Episcopal Church (MEC) in December 1784. The informal style arrived with the first Methodist immigrants in the 1760s, shaping services for Sundays and other days of the week as well as for special occasions such as funerals and the characteristically Methodist watch nights and love feasts – all of which could be led by the unordained. Familiarity with the more formal approach came from attendance at the Lord's Supper, baptism, and the solemnization of marriage rites held in the Anglican parish church because prior to 1784 the leadership of such services was by Wesley's decree (and sometimes by civil law) not permitted to the lay preachers. However, some preachers, such as Robert Strawbridge of Maryland and certain participants at the 1779 Conference held in Fluvanna County, Virginia, ignored Wesley's restriction and took up a sacramental role, improvising services for the sacraments that might draw upon ritual language from the *Book of Common Prayer*.[2] Thus, from the beginnings of denominational

Methodism/Wesleyanism in the United States, model ritual texts and patterns were available for the two sacraments and for several life transitions. Although the *Sunday Service* would undergo significant revision in 1792 at the hands of MEC redactors, the sacramental and life-cycle rites still retained strong affinities with their Anglican origins and would continue to do so in a few denominations even into the twenty-first century.

From the 1780s to the early twentieth century, the number of denominations claiming a Wesleyan/Methodist heritage increased, with new denominations sometimes emerging as the result of disputes over worship praxis (for example, the concern raised by some that a formal worship style necessarily yielded dry formalism; an informal style best invited the working of the Holy Spirit). The ritual repertoire within all of these denominations also changed over time. Inherited ritual texts were modified by addition and/or subtraction or by complete overhaul – and worship in the informal, unscripted style was adjusted – in response to shifts in theological, liturgical, cultural, sociological, and psychological understandings. New texts and practices were developed to fill in perceived gaps. Because no Methodist or Wesleyan denomination mandated the use of all liturgical resources authorized by a General Conference or equivalent body, a variety of practices existed (and exists) within a denomination and also across the denominations; however, liturgical freedom did not extend to engagement in practices that violated the fundamental articles of faith or constitution, nor was interference allowed in rites that had the status of statutory law (for example, the "Reception of Covenant Members" in the Wesleyan Church).[3] Pastors and congregations were (and are) at liberty to use the authorized texts verbatim, modify existing texts, borrow from other resources, or create something new. Thus, although many congregations would be familiar with all or part of the authorized liturgies for the sacraments and the life cycle, examination of the authorized material tells only part of the story of actual American Methodist worship praxis. Yet because congregational worship leaders within a denomination would all have access to their particular authorized, common texts, the liturgies contained in the denominational Rituals or Books of Worship will be the main sources here.

Across the several Wesleyan/Methodist denominations, five generally experienced life events found ritual expression: birth, adolescence, marriage, sickness, and dying/death;[4] each of these life events will be explored below. Christians have often used the language of "new birth" as a spiritual life event in association with baptism, so under the category of "birth" the sacrament of baptism will be examined – and along with it the Lord's Supper, which may be regarded as a baptismal remembrance.

BIRTH

Physical Birth

A rite related to physical birth was included in the 1662 *Book of Common Prayer* with focus on the safe delivery of the mother and not directly on the newborn's passage into the world. Without explanation Wesley omitted this "Thanksgiving of Women after Child-Birth, commonly called the Churching of Women" in his 1784 revision of the Prayer Book. Only in the late twentieth century did Methodists – and just two denominations – introduce thanksgiving rites acknowledging the birth of a child, though in 1945 the Methodist Church (MC) had provided in its *Book of Worship* a solitary prayer "After the Birth of a Child," which was placed, quite remarkably, in a collection of prayers under the heading of "The Ministry to the Sick."[5] The rite in the 1992 *United Methodist Book of Worship* addressed the social reality that families were not constituted solely by parental procreation in its "Order of Thanksgiving for the Birth or Adoption of a Child," which supplied prayers of thanksgiving and intercession for the newborn, the mother, the adopted, and the entire family. The instructions (rubrics) at the beginning of the rite made it explicit that this order was not an equivalent or substitute for baptism, and it was to be used prior to the baptism of a child or in cases where an already-baptized child was introduced to a new congregation.[6] An "Order of Thanksgiving for the Birth or Adopting of a Child" produced earlier in 1984 by the African Methodist Episcopal Church (AME) was not so clear in its relationship to baptism. The introductory rubrics specify that the service is "not intended to discourage infant baptism," yet they go on to state that the child must be presented by a member of the congregation if the parent(s) are not members. The first part of the Order consists of thanksgiving prayers for the newly born or adopted, but then the rite continues with the giving of a name to the child (accompanied with the laying on of hands), the congregation's promise to nurture the child in the faith, and the entry of the child's name into the Roll of Preparatory Members – actions usually associated with baptismal rites.[7] These two late-twentieth-century rites demonstrate the complexity of separating birth as a distinct event common to all people from the Christian sacrament of baptism (or a rite of infant dedication), particularly because infant baptism is regarded by many Christians – and even non-Christians – as a *de facto* birth rite (and right) celebrated within the broader American culture.

Baptism in Relation to Spiritual Birth

The separation of the rite of infant baptism from a rite connected with physical birth was not the only theological and liturgical problem for Methodists/Wesleyans as pertains to "birth" rites. Perhaps the greater challenge has been interpreting the relationship between water baptism (for all ages) and a spiritual "new birth," a connection complicated by John Wesley's own writings.

The Inheritance from Wesley

Regarding the subjects of baptism, Wesley never wavered: infants, children, and professing adults were all proper recipients of baptism, though in the case of youngsters he preferred that parents answer the prebaptismal questions rather than a godparent. Of the two modes – dipping (immersion) and pouring – specified in the 1662 Prayer Book, Wesley early in his ministry favored dipping in imitation of the early church's practice, but by mid-career was indifferent to mode and even considered the sprinkling of water permissible. On the matter of Wesley's views of the baptismal rite and its effects, especially regeneration ("being born anew"), it is much more difficult to assess his overall position. As an Anglican priest, Wesley was principally concerned that recipients of infant baptism (the dominant practice in his day) come to a full assurance of salvation in their faith journey and demonstrate faith's visible fruits. His sermons and other writings that address baptism and the "new birth," when taken together, articulate historic Anglican teachings as well as an evangelical concern for a subjective experience of faith, resulting in an apparent tension. Wesley agreed with his Church that infants receiving the sacrament of baptism were at the same time born again; the outward, material sign accompanied the inward, God-bestowed spiritual grace.[8] Yet Wesley observed that some persons who claimed the new birth of their infant baptism had lost the "principle of grace" because of unrepentant sinful acts. In Wesley's mind, these persons needed to be "born again" a second time by a conscious experience of saving grace in order to receive the "circumcision of the heart."[9] Thus, two spiritual births were necessary for most persons – a sacramental and objective one via ritual baptism and an experiential and subjective one by a "heart-warming" encounter with Christ through the power of the Holy Spirit. Although these two new births can be connected – the second birth may be viewed as a recovery of the grace received in the first – Wesley never specifically qualifies their relationship.

To complicate the issue even further: in the *Sunday Service*'s infant baptism rite, as in the adult rite, Wesley (or perhaps Thomas Coke) deleted or modified the Prayer Book's references to regeneration after the imposition of water while keeping the references before, suggesting a possibility, but not a certainty, of a sacramental new birth. Wesley would have conceded that it was possible for an adult initiand not to be born again in baptism in situations where the individual had not fully repented and believed in the gospel (hence placing an obstacle in the way of the reception of grace) or when the individual had accepted God's pardoning grace prior to the baptismal rite.[10] Perhaps the adjustment to the rites arose from a concern to avoid any understanding of the sacrament's effect *ex opere operato*: God's promise of regeneration could be acknowledged prior to the imposition of water, but to speak of it afterward might emphasize the rite itself or human agency over the workings of God. Whatever the reason, references to regeneration were further reduced when in 1786 Wesley republished the *Sunday Service*; the language of the 1786 version was largely maintained when the MEC did its own revision of the *Sunday Service* in 1792. The ambiguities of Wesley's literary repository relative to the "new birth" have generated different readings by later interpreters, resulting in multiple understandings and ritual expressions within the Methodist/Wesleyan family.

Wesleyan and Methodist Developments and Divergences
Internal and external issues shaped the development of spiritual birth theologies and practices for the different denominations over the course of more than two centuries.[11] All the denominations, from their origins to the beginning of the twenty-first century, kept rites for both infant and adult baptism but with varying degrees of connection over successive revisions to the language of Wesley's texts. In response to debates within the denominations on such subjects as ritual formalism, the sacrament's efficacy *ex opere operato*, sin (original, inherited and actual), and/or the necessity of a personal appropriation and profession of faith, references to baptismal regeneration gradually fell out of the rites for infants; the AME retained the language the longest by preserving the 1792 MEC form until the 1950s. A similar, though slower, decline occurred with regeneration language in the adult rites, because many Methodists and Wesleyans, with Wesley, considered a baptismal rebirth possible when accompanied by honest repentance and faith. Serious discussion about baptism's regenerational capacity for infants and adults again came to the fore in the late twentieth century when the United Methodist Church (UMC) introduced its first authorized service of Baptismal Covenant intended for all ages, which, in the introduction, stated that through baptism, "We are incorporated into God's mighty acts of salvation and

given new birth through water and the Spirit."[12] Questions about baptismal regeneration continue to press Methodists and Wesleyans engaging in bilateral and multilateral ecumenical dialogues, and establishing covenant agreements with other denominations when the partner churches claim the gift of new birth to be an essential characteristic of baptism as a sacrament.

That all the denominations maintained authorized baptismal rites for infants and young children was not an indicator of actual practice. Because of what was read as Wesley's particular emphasis on the second new birth, some Methodist pastors and laity, even in the early nineteenth century, preferred that the practice of baptism follow conversion and profession of faith, and so withheld the rite from infants. At the same time, the practice of infant baptism was often vehemently defended against critical believer Baptists (for example, Baptists and Campbellites/Disciples of Christ) by using arguments for the antiquity and longevity of the practice (for example, Jesus's welcoming of little children, cf. Mark 10:14 and cognates; and the baptism of households, cf. Acts 16:15), baptism's supervention of circumcision, and the dominical warrant (Matthew 28:19, "all nations" being inclusive of the very young). Denominational leaders particularly of the episcopal Methodisms provided literature, legislation, and other encouragements to inspire parents to bring their children to the font. One action taken by the MEC beginning in 1844 and adopted by the Methodist Episcopal Church, South (MECS) at its founding was, in provisions for the "Instruction of Children" in their respective *Disciplines*, to encourage preachers to invite parents to "dedicate" their children in baptism;[13] the concept of dedication was already present in the Methodist Protestant Church's (MPC) initial infant baptism rite (for example, "thou hast made it our privilege to dedicate our children to thy service"[14]). In the first half of the twentieth century, the holiness churches started to make explicit what had become implicit in their infant baptism practice and hinted at in the baptismal formulations of other denominations: They produced a rite of infant dedication that stood alongside – and sometimes was a "dry" parallel – to the infant baptism rite. The Church of the Nazarene (CN) introduced a dedication rite in 1936, which soon was more widely used than the baptism service. The CN's 1972 *Manual* demonstrates how, in effect, dedication and baptism were often conceptually conflated: under the heading "The Sacrament of Baptism" appears a single rite with the subheading "The Dedication or Baptism of Children."[15] The Free Methodist Church's (FMC) infant baptism rite of 1974 was similarly conflated:

If the parents wish this to be a dedication ceremony, the pastor shall substitute the statement of baptism with the following words: "We, your pastor and your parents, dedicate you, *Name*, to God and the service of his kingdom, in the name of the Father, and the Son, and the Holy Spirit. Amen." [When dedicating, water shall not be used.][16]

In 1985, the FMC introduced a separate Service of Infant Dedication to stand beside the infant baptism rite;[17] and in the twenty-first century, the CN provided two dedication rites, with one specified for use by a single parent or guardian.[18]

The terminology of "dedication" was only the beginning of a redefinition of the meaning and purpose of the rite in some denominations, which was still further nuanced in the first decades of the twentieth century by the Bushnellian language of nurture and moral formation, and by a liberal theology that downplayed the notion of original sin in favor of a human positivism, including (at the most extreme) an assertion that even prior to baptism "all children are members of the kingdom of God and therefore graciously entitled to Baptism."[19] The baptism rite for these churches had, in effect, ceased to be objective and sacramental and instead had become subjective and even Pelagian. But by the 1940s, moves started to be made (especially in the MC and eventually the UMC) toward the formulation of infant rites where baptism was understood to be: a means of grace and new birth with the accompanying meanings of covenant; adoption, initiation, and incorporation into the Church; and (through the influence of the Liturgical Movement) participation in the paschal mystery of Christ's death and resurrection. The creation of the UMC in 1968 brought the practices of infant dedication (from the Evangelical United Brethren) and infant baptism (MC) head to head; both practices were permitted to coexist until authorized UMC rites were produced – without the option of dedication.

At the beginning of the twenty-first century, the connections between physical birth, spiritual birth, baptism, and church membership still puzzled Methodists and Wesleyans, with ecumenical texts such as the World Council of Churches' convergence document *Baptism, Eucharist and Ministry* and its derivatives influencing theological reflection.[20] Writers among the holiness traditions had proposed to their constituencies a reconsideration of the burgeoning practice of infant dedication in an attempt to draw closer to their Wesleyan roots, other Methodist kin, and the larger Church,[21] but such reorientation was slow to be embraced by pastors and congregations precisely because the problem of the two new births had not yet been resolved. Even as such discussions continued on the objective and subjective aspects of new birth, Methodist and Wesleyans were confronted with a related dilemma: the relationship of the Lord's Supper to baptism in light of John Wesley's use of the terminology "converting ordinance" in regard to the eucharistic event.

The Lord's Supper in Relation to Baptism

Wesley gave priority to the Lord's Supper as one of the means of grace ordained by Christ himself, and encouraged the early Methodists to engage in "constant communion" while singing hymns, especially selections from the 166 texts in the *Hymns on the Lord's Supper* (1745).[22] In the late 1730s, Wesley's insistence that the sacrament was a means of grace gave rise to controversy at Fetter Lane in London where a religious society gathered comprising Methodist and Moravian participants. When the Moravian Philip Henry Mother taught in the society that the sacrament should be limited to those who had full assurance of faith, Wesley countered that the Supper could be a converting ordinance for persons with some degree of faith – namely, those baptized in infancy who had not yet become believers in a full sense, in other words, who lacked the second "new birth." Through the sacrament God would convey the preventing (prevenient), justifying, or sanctifying grace most needed for the communicant's spiritual situation.[23] The rift between Moravian and Methodist was irreparable, and the Methodists in 1740 established their own society, one with rules directing that adherents were to receive the sacrament in the Anglican parish church or elsewhere every week.[24]

On account of his esteem for the rite and its practice, Wesley's revision to The Order for the Administration of the Lord's Supper in the 1784 *Sunday Service* was a conservative one. There were no major changes except for the removal of the Nicene Creed to avoid the use of two creeds in a single liturgical event, because Morning Prayer (with the Apostles' Creed) typically preceded the order for communion. Wesley made no alteration to the eucharistic invitation (that was preserved by most American denominations, even into the twenty-first century[25]), which was virtually a paraphrase of the last question in the 1662 Prayer Book's Catechism used for baptized persons preparing for the rite of Confirmation:

Quest. What is required of them who come to the Lord's Supper?

Answ. To examine themselves, whether they repent them truly of their former sins, stedfastly purposing to lead a new life; have a lively faith in God's mercy through Christ, with a thankful remembrance of his death; and be in charity with all men.

Ye that do truly and earnestly repent of your sins, and are in love and charity with your neighbours, and intend to lead a new life, following the commandments of God, and walking from henceforth in his holy ways; Draw near with faith, and take this holy Sacrament to your comfort; and make your humble confession to Almighty God, meekly kneeling upon your knees.

The invitation to the Supper thus assumed that communicants would have been baptized, though the *Sunday Service* lacked explicit rubrics instructing such, and so the inherent linkage between baptism and the invitation was quickly lost.

In a letter dated September 10, 1784, that was sent to America with the *Sunday Service*, Wesley advised "the elders to administer the supper of the Lord on every Lord's day,[26] thereby connecting the Lord's Supper with the Lord's day, but also conceding that such would only be possible in locations where itinerating elders (presbyters) were present. There is evidence that for a time and in some cities during the early nineteenth century that MEC ministers clustered in a "station" were able to provide the sacrament weekly; from 1830 it was legislated that MPC stations always were to receive at least once a month.[27] More often Methodists received the sacrament in conjunction with quarterly meetings that ensured reception minimally four times a year.[28] The quarterly custom came to be interpreted as a maximum in many denominations; an exception was during and after periods of sacramental revival (for example, the MECS in the late 1800s), which resulted in the codification of a more frequent (at least monthly) practice. Whether practiced quarterly or more often, Methodists/Wesleyans maintained a desire to receive the sacrament and regarded it as a precious time with their God: noted the CN in 1919, "of the obligation to partake of the privileges of this Sacrament, as often as we may be providentially permitted, there can be no doubt."[29] The Liturgical and Ecumenical Movements of the twentieth century inspired many Methodist/Wesleyan congregations to receive communion – now termed the eucharist – weekly; the UMC's Services of Word and Table authorized in 1984 assumed structurally the normativity of the Lord's Supper on the Lord's Day even though the sacrament might not be observed.[30] The Liturgical Movement in particular advocated a stronger linkage between baptism and eucharist theologically and practically, and in the UMC this resulted in a rubric encouraging the giving of communion immediately after the baptism of adults and children.[31] Yet at the same time this placed in tension a practice introduced in the twentieth century in many Methodist congregations across the denominations – the "open table."

As noted earlier, most Methodist/Wesleyan denominations kept the invitation to the table inherited from Wesley, though without acknowledging its implicit baptismal associations. Yet all of the denominations assumed in their official documents the classical and Anglican sequence of baptism before Supper (for example, in the Articles of Religion or equivalent), while recognizing as an exception that the Spirit's working on the heart might bring an individual to the table before the font. Casual admission (even of the baptized) usually was not practiced, because through to the late nineteenth century some of the denominations required from congregation members as well as visitors (from other Methodist/Wesleyan congregations or Protestant denominations) the presentation of a ticket or a token indicating spiritual seriousness prior to admission to the table. Starting in the early twentieth century, several factors from different theological directions precipitated the shift toward access to the table without preconditions: liberal theological emphases on the social gospel, an optimistic view of the human condition, and the values of democracy; evangelical stress on conversion, which was aided by a decontextualizing of Wesley's use of the term "converting ordinance"; and a rising interest in Christian "cordiality" and "hospitality." Post-modern pluralism and relativism that accentuate the experience of the individual reinforced (perhaps unconsciously) a denomination's desire to offer an open table. As a result, in the early twenty-first century, the relation between baptism and the Lord's Supper was largely undefined or unclear across the different denominations.[32]

ADOLESCENCE

Among the various life transitions, the passage from childhood to adulthood is the least represented in churchly rites. The rite of Confirmation came to function as an adolescent rite for profession of faith by the early Middle Ages, though originally in the early church it was the postbaptismal anointing/laying on of hands by the bishop in the unified event of water bath–laying on of hands/anointing–eucharist. The 1549, 1552, and 1662 versions of the *Book of Common Prayer* included Confirmation, though not without debate from various factions, especially the Puritan wing, within the Church of England. Because of theological concerns about the rite and its purpose, the decline in the practice of the rite during his time, and the association of the rite with episcopal administration, Wesley did not include Confirmation in his *Sunday Service*. American Methodists/ Wesleyans thus did not inherit this or any other "adolescent" rite, and only in 1964 did one of the Methodist/Wesleyan denominations (the MC) approve a rite explicitly entitled "confirmation," though for some time "membership rites" existed in order for those baptized in infancy to become "full" members.[33] The UMC kept the practice of Confirmation (administered by elders [presbyters]) in its 1992 *Book of Worship*, which was defined within the ritual text as a renewal of the covenant made at baptism, an acknowledgement of God's present work in the person's life, and an affirmation of commitment to Christ's holy Church.[34]

In the period preceding the publication of the UMC's *Book of Worship*, a draft text was produced for an adolescent rite common in Hispanic communities – the Quinceañera for a girl celebrating her fifteenth birthday – though in the published book only a prayer was included.[35] Given the tendency of Christian teens to adopt cultural (and sometimes unhealthy) rites of passage in the absence of churchly ones, theologically, socially, and psychologically appropriate adolescent rites are a needed addition to the Methodist/Wesleyan ritual repertoire.

WEDDINGS

Just as affinities exist between Wesley's revision of the Lord's Supper liturgy and many twenty-first-century Methodist/Wesleyan communion rites (thereby ritually linking even in a partial way the Methodist family diachronically with its past and synchronically with its present), so too do linguistic and structural connections remain with most marriage rites. However, theological and cultural shifts over two centuries related to gender roles, the place of the family, understandings of marriage (and divorce), and marriage restrictions or laws produced several notable deletions from and additions to Wesley's text, some shared across the denominations. Of course, weddings are not unique to Methodist/Wesleyan communities, so the performance of nuptials was also decorated with local and ethnic traditional customs as well as with emerging cultural innovations (for example, unity candles in the late twentieth century).

Explicit regulations regarding marriage to a non-Christian or to a non-practicing Christian found in American Methodism's first decades gradually softened or disappeared in most cases.[36] The several Sunday reading of the "banns" – a public notification requesting information about possible impediments to an upcoming marriage – indicated in Wesley's rite and its 1792 MEC revision, and also the final reading of the banns given at the wedding to the congregation ("if any man can show any just cause why they may not lawfully be joined together") and to the couple ("if you know any impediment why you may not be lawfully joined"), were eventually dropped in many denominational rites because of the couple's procurement of a civil marriage license. Neither the banns nor the request for the revealing of impediments was entirely displaced in all rites, however: In the early twenty-first century, the banns rubric remained in AME and FMC rites, and the final request regarding impediments persisted in AME and African Methodist Episcopal Zion Church texts.[37]

The classic western purposes of marriage (procreation, avoidance of sexual sin, companionship) taken from the Prayer Book into Wesley's 1784 rite were omitted in 1792. What remained – and continued in all of the denominations into the twenty-first century – was language describing marriage as an "honorable estate instituted of God," which signified the "mystical union" (cf. Ephesians 5:32) between Christ and his Church. Marriage was not to be entered into "unadvisedly," but rather "reverently, discreetly, and in the fear of God." In an alternate ritual form produced by the UMC that was designed as complete service of worship with the celebration of the Eucharist, the marital covenant was also defined in relation to the covenant of baptism; the marital union was to be understood as an outgrowth of union with Christ himself.[38]

Notable changes in the rite from 1784 onward occurred as the result of cultural pressures. Although Wesley had excluded the giving away of the bride and the use of a bridal ring (historically part of the dowry), both returned to revised wedding texts likely after the practices had already been widely taken up. Not without controversy, the MEC in 1864 deleted "obey" from the woman's vow ("Wilt thou obey him, serve him, love, honor and keep him ... "), and other denominations that had inherited the word, after debate, followed suit in their own time. Further concern that the equality of the couple be expressed ritually resulted in double ring ceremonies and, in some denominational texts, the elimination of the "giving away" or the reappropriation of that action as a presentation or blessing of each individual by the respective family.

In the second half of the twentieth century, a few denominations put forward prayers and services for wedding anniversaries and for the reaffirmation or renewal of marriage vows, intended both to celebrate and to shore up the institution.[39] Denominational and public response was mixed to an experimental set of "Rituals with the Divorced" published by the UMC in 1976, resulting in the inclusion only of a prayer and several suggested scripture readings for "Ministry with Persons going through Divorce" in the section on "Healing Services and Prayers" in the 1992 *Book of Worship*.[40]

SICKNESS

The *Sunday Service* included a prayer and selected scripture verses in a section on the "Communion of the Sick" (which vanished in the 1792 revision),[41] but no special rites. Indeed, none were really needed because the American Methodists had already for improvised their practices for decades and continued to do so over the next generations, taking seriously the scriptural injunction (cf. James 5:14–16) to offer the "prayer of faith" over the sick.[42] Thus, the MPC was unique by its inclusion from 1830 to 1877 of directions for the visitation of the sick that were intended to guide clergy and laity in their administration of "instruction, conviction, support, consolation, or encouragement" as each situation required.[43] These directions were removed when practice in many of the denominations shifted away from regarding sickness as an opportunity to expose sin's consequences and focused instead on the patient's psychological need to receive comfort and support in order to promote the restoration of health. This change is evident in the prayers recorded in the section on "Ministry to the Sick" in the MC's 1945 *Book of Worship* that petition the "Great Physician" to grant "heavenly healing."[44] Improvisation remained the principal means of providing rituals for the pastoral care of the sick in the twenty-first century, though print resources were available for use in cases such as Alzheimer's disease and pregnancy loss, and for corporate worship services addressing all facets of healing.[45]

DYING AND DEATH

From the end of the eighteenth century to the beginning of the twenty-first, Methodists and Wesleyans accompanied the dying and commended the newly deceased to God with scripture readings, prayer, and song. Bedside rituals with the dying were informal, though all or part of a formal Lord's Supper liturgy might be used. Impromptu prayer and song sometimes accompanied the preparation of the body for the grave in the days before professional funeral homes took up the task that once belonged to female relatives. Testimonies, eulogies, and the reading of an obituary might join scripture, prayer, and song at the wake or visitation held during the day or night prior to the funeral service and burial. All of this was unscripted, though local congregations established "traditions" for the practices chosen and the sequencing of ritual components.

The Order for the Burial of the Dead in the *Sunday Service* was, thanks to Wesley's deletions, essentially a graveside version of the Prayer Book's service for church and cemetery, which nonetheless provided form and content for a practice in which the Methodist laity had long been engaged. The service consisted of scriptural and other sentences, the reading of Psalm 90 and 1 Corinthians 15:20–58, a Kyrie eleison, the Lord's Prayer, a concluding collect, and a benediction. This inherited scheme of scripture sentences and readings, prayer, and the saying of the Lord's Prayer provided a foundation for denominationally published funeral rituals to which were eventually added other elements such as congregational song, a sermon/homily, a eulogy, the reading of an obituary, and a creed or affirmation of faith. A prayer of committal, which Wesley removed, was restored first by the MECS in 1858 using the formulation in the Protestant Episcopal Church's 1789 *Book of Common Prayer*; other Methodist/Wesleyan denominations missing the committal subsequently made a similar move. Although other alterations and substitutions were made to Wesley's text, some of the specific components received from Wesley survived to the twenty-first century (for example, the concluding collect "O Merciful God, the Father of our Lord Jesus Christ, who is the resurrection and the life"),[46] albeit with some modification. The choices of scripture readings and the content of the printed prayers were adjusted over the course of two centuries as theological and societal views of death and of the relationship between the living and the dead changed. By the twentieth century, certain denominations provided liturgies and prayers for different situations (for example, the death of a child and sudden death) and acknowledged by rubric that the rites of death could occur in one or more locations (for example, family house, hospital, church, funeral home chapel, mausoleum, crematorium, cemetery, or other preferred spaces).

Of all the rites pertaining to death in the Methodist/Wesleyan family, the UMC's Services of Death and Resurrection alone explicitly connected the dying and rising of baptism (cf. Romans 6:4–5) with the death of the baptized and his/her anticipated resurrection, and invited a final sharing of the eucharist in the presence of the deceased.[47] The rite thus connected the beginning and the end of the life cycle while helping to usher the loved one to a new – and eternal – life.

Notes

1 John Wesley, *The Sunday Service of the Methodists in North America* (London: Strahan, 1784). For a facsimile edition with an introduction,

notes, and commentary, see James F. White, ed., *John Wesley's Prayer Book* (Akron, OH: OSL Publications, 1991).

2   See Karen B. Westerfield Tucker, *American Methodist Worship* (New York: Oxford University Press, 2001), 93, 119.

3   The Wesleyan Church, *The Discipline of the Wesleyan Church* (Indianapolis: Wesleyan Publishing House, 2008), 175.

4   For detailed accounting of these rites across American Methodism, see the various chapters in Westerfield Tucker, *American Methodist Worship*.

5   The Methodist Church, *The Book of Worship for Church and Home. With Orders for the Administration of the Sacraments and Other Rites and Ceremonies According to the Use of the Methodist Church* (Nashville, TN: The Methodist Publishing House, 1945), 514.

6   The United Methodist Church, *The United Methodist Book of Worship* (Nashville, TN: The United Methodist Publishing House, 1992), 585–587.

7   The African Methodist Episcopal Church, *The Book of Worship of the African Methodist Episcopal Church* (Nashville, TN: The A.M.E. Sunday School Union, 1984), 56–58.

8   Compare the Twenty-seventh Anglican Article of Religion ("Of Baptism") with Wesley's revision of the same as Methodist Article Seventeen. For the Methodist Article, see James F. White, ed., *John Wesley's Prayer Book*, facsimile, 312. See also John Wesley's sermons "The Means of Grace, 2.1, 3, *The Works of John Wesley*, vol. 1, edited by Albert C. Outler (Nashville, TN: Abingdon Press, 1984), 381–382, and "The New Birth," 4.1–2, *The Works of John Wesley*, vol. 2, edited by Albert C. Outler (Nashville, TN: Abingdon Press, 1985), 196–197.

9   See John Wesley, "A Treatise on Baptism," 2.1; 4.2,10, *The Works of John Wesley*, vol. 10, ed. Thomas Jackson (London: Wesleyan Conference Office, 1872; reprint), 190–191, 193, 198; and also John Wesley's sermons "The Circumcision of the Heart," "The Almost Christian," "The Marks of New Birth," "The Great Privilege of Those That Are Born of God," "The New Birth," and "On Sin in Believers."

10   Cf. Wesley, "The New Birth," 4.2, *The Works of John Wesley*, 2: 197.

11   In addition to Westerfield Tucker, *American Methodist Worship*, see Gayle Carlton Felton, *This Gift of Water* (Nashville, TN: Abingdon Press, 1992).

12   The United Methodist Church, *The Book of Services* (Nashville, TN: The United Methodist Publishing House, 1984), 54.

13   The Methodist Episcopal Church, *The Doctrines and Discipline of the Methodist Episcopal Church* (New York: G. Lane and C. B. Tippett, 1844), Chap. I, Section 16.5, 67; and The Methodist Episcopal Church, South, *The Doctrines and Discipline of the Methodist Episcopal Church, South* (Louisville, KY: John Early, 1846, 1851), Chap. 3, Section 3.5, 75.

14   The Methodist Protestant Church, *Constitution and Discipline of the Methodist Protestant Church* (Baltimore, MD: John J. Harrod, 1830), 83.

15   Church of the Nazarene, *Manual* (Kansas City: Nazarene Publishing House, 1972), ¶687, 307–308. On the history of Nazarene practice and

theology, see Stan Ingersol, "Christian Baptism and the Early Nazarenes: The Sources That Shaped a Pluralistic Baptismal Tradition" *Wesleyan Theological Journal* 25.2 (Fall 1990), 24–38; and Jeffrey H. Knapp, "Throwing the Baby Out with the Font Water: The Development of Baptismal Practice in the Church of the Nazarene," *Worship* 76.3 (May 2002), 225–244.

16   The Free Methodist Church, *The Book of Discipline, 1974* (Winona Lake, IN: The Free Methodist Publishing House, 1975), 29. See also the AME conflation noted above at footnote 7.

17   The Free Methodist Church, *The Book of Discipline, 1985* (Winona Lake, IN: Free Methodist Publishing House, 1986), ¶901.2, 224–226; cf. The Free Methodist Church of North America, *The Book of Discipline 2007* (Winona Lake, IN: Free Methodist Publishing House, 2008), ¶8020, 212–213, where the service appears under the general heading "Baptism."

18   The Church of the Nazarene, *Manual 2009–2013* (Kansas City, MO: Nazarene Publishing House, 2009), ¶800.4, 244–245.

19   The Methodist Episcopal Church, *Doctrines and Discipline of the Methodist Episcopal Church* (New York: Methodist Book Concern, 1932), "The Order for the Baptism of Children," ¶513, 505.

20   *Baptism, Eucharist and Ministry*, Faith and Order Paper No. 111 (Geneva: World Council of Churches, 1982), esp. B2–13; and, for example, *One Baptism: Towards Mutual Recognition*, Faith and Order Paper No. 210 (Geneva: World Council of Churches, 2011).

21   See for example, Rob L. Staples, *Outward Sign and Inward Grace* (Kansas City, MO: Beacon Hill Press of Kansas City, 1991), 161–200; Knapp, "Throwing the Baby Out with the Font Water," and Brian D. Walrath and Robert H. Woods, "Free Methodist Worship in America: A Historical-Critical Analysis," *Wesleyan Theological Journal* 40.1 (2005), 208–228.

22   See John Wesley's sermons "The Means of Grace," *The Works of John Wesley*, vol. 1 (1984), 378–397, and "The Duty of Constant Communion," *The Works of John Wesley*, vol. 3, ed. Albert C. Outler (Nashville, TN: Abingdon Press, 1986), 428–439; and John Wesley and Charles Wesley, *Hymns on the Lord's Supper* (Bristol: Felix Farley, 1745; reprint Madison, NJ: The Charles Wesley Society, 1995). For book-length studies of the eucharistic hymns, see J. Ernest Rattenbury, *The Eucharistic Hymns of John and Charles Wesley* (London: Epworth Press, 1948; reprint Akron, OH: OSL Publications, 2006); and Daniel B. Stevick, *The Altar's Fire* (Peterborough: Epworth Press, 2004).

23   John Wesley, Journal entries for June 26–28, 1740, *The Works of John Wesley*, vol. 19, edited by Richard P. Heitzenrater and W. Reginald Ward (Nashville, TN: Abingdon Press, 1990), 158–159. On the role the *Hymns on the Lord's Supper* played in the controversies with Molther and other Moravians, see Karen B. Westerfield Tucker, "Polemic against Stillness in the *Hymns on the Lord's Supper*," *Bulletin of the John Rylands University Library of Manchester* 88.2 (2006), 101–119.

24   "Directions given to the Band Societies," *The Works of John Wesley*, vol. 9, edited by Rupert E. Davies (Nashville, TN: Abingdon Press, 1989), 79.

25   For example, The African Methodist Episcopal Church, *The Book of Worship*, 27; The United Methodist Church, *The United Methodist Book of Worship* (1992), 44; The African Methodist Episcopal Zion Church, *The Bicentennial Book of Worship of the African Methodist Episcopal Zion Church* (Charlotte, NC: A.M.E. Zion Publishing House, 1996), 15; The Free Methodist Church of North America, *The Book of Discipline 2007* (2008), ¶8110; and The Wesleyan Church, *The Discipline of the Wesleyan Church* (Indianapolis: Wesleyan Publishing House, 2008), ¶¶5615 and 5635.

26   John Telford, ed., *The Letters of the Rev. John Wesley, A.M.*, 8 vols. (London: Epworth Press, 1931), Letter to "Our Brethren in America," 7:238–239.

27   See Lester Ruth, "Urban Itinerancy: 'Stational' Liturgy in Early American Methodism" *Studia Liturgica* 32.2 (2002), 222–239; and The Methodist Protestant Church, *Constitution and Discipline* (1830), 81.

28   For the place of the Lord's Supper at the quarterly meeting and the relation of the Supper to the love feast, see Lester Ruth, *A Little Heaven Below: Worship at Early Methodist Quarterly Meetings* (Nashville, TN: Kingswood Books, 2000). See the reference to the quarterly sacrament in Christian Methodist Episcopal Church, *The Book of Discipline of the Christian Methodist Episcopal Church* (2006), ¶300.1, 80.

29   Church of the Nazarene, *Manual of the History, Doctrine, Government, and Ritual of the Church of the Nazarene* (Kansas City, MO: Nazarene Publishing House, 1919), 23–24.

30   The United Methodist Church, *The United Methodist Book of Worship*, 13–39.

31   The United Methodist Church, *The United Methodist Book of Worship*, 94.

32   The UMC's official statement on the Lord's Supper, "This Holy Mystery," tries to hold together both the traditional sequence of baptism to eucharist and the open table. See The United Methodist Church, *The Book of Resolutions of the United Methodist Church 2008* (Nashville, TN: The United Methodist Publishing House, 2008), ¶8014, 961–1008.

33   The Methodist Church, *The Book of Worship for Church and Home* (1964, 1965), 12–13.

34   The United Methodist Church, *The United Methodist Book of Worship*, 87.

35   The United Methodist Church, *The United Methodist Book of Worship*, 534. The drafted text of the Quinceañera rite appeared in the revision committee's discussion documents at their February 1991 meeting.

36   An exception: the CN expected any "contemplated union" to be in accord with "scriptural requirements." See The Church of the Nazarene, *Manual 2009-2013* (2009), ¶35, 51.

37   The African Methodist Episcopal Church, *Book of Worship*, 59, 63; The African Methodist Episcopal Zion Church, *Bicentennial Book of Worship*, 29; and The Free Methodist Church of North America, *The Book of Discipline 2007* (2008), ¶8200, 224.

38   The United Methodist Church, *The United Methodist Book of Worship*, 116–127.

39 The Methodist Church, *Book of Worship* (1964, 1965), 227; The African Methodist Episcopal Church, *Book of Worship*, 67–71; The African Methodist Episcopal Zion Church, *Bicentennial Book of Worship*, 33–36; and The United Methodist Church, *The United Methodist Book of Worship*, 135–138.

40 *Ritual in a New Day: An Invitation* (Nashville, TN: Abingdon Press, 1976), 74–96; and The United Methodist Church, *The United Methodist Book of Worship*, 626.

41 Two centuries after the Sunday Service, the 1984 AME *Book of Worship* introduced a specific service for communion in the home (38–39).

42 The Church of the Nazarene, *Manual 2009–2013*, ¶18, 36.

43 The Methodist Protestant Church, *Constitution and Discipline* (1830), 90–92.

44 The Methodist Church, *Book of Worship* (1945), 511; see also The Methodist Church, *Book of Worship* (1964, 1965), 233–236.

45 The African Methodist Episcopal Zion Church, *Bicentennial Book of Worship*, 124–125; The United Methodist Church, *The United Methodist Book of Worship*, 613–629.

46 E.g., The African Methodist Episcopal Church, *Book of Worship*, 73; and The Free Methodist Church of North America, *The Book of Discipline 2007* (2008), ¶8310, 230.

47 The United Methodist Church, *The United Methodist Book of Worship*, 139–171.

7 Discipline and Polity

DOUGLAS M. KOSKELA

In any discussion of Methodist polity, it is very likely that one will at some point encounter the following quotation from John Wesley:

> What is the end of all *ecclesiastical order*? Is it not to bring souls from the power of Satan to God? And to build them up in his fear and love? *Order*, then, is so far valuable as it answers these ends; and if it answers them not it is nothing worth.[1]

The apparent ubiquity of this statement is quite appropriate, as it captures the deeply missional orientation of the people called Methodists. For Wesley, a church's patterns of organization and authority – that is, its polity – must be oriented toward the church's mission. As Methodism made its way across the Atlantic to America, gradually evolving from a movement into a church (and before long into many churches), the same concern for mission would continue to guide its organizational patterns. While American Methodists' understanding of their mission would be subject both to disagreement and to development over the years, the basic conviction that polity should reflect and support that mission remained intact.[2]

The aim of this chapter is to explore the essential shape of ecclesiastical order in the Methodist churches in America. At the outset, it is worth offering some reflections on terminology. The word "discipline" is used in at least three distinct but overlapping ways in ecclesiological reflection. First, in the narrowest sense, it can refer to the particular practices and protocols for dealing with some sort of moral or spiritual failure in the church. Second, the term is used by many denominations to refer to the manual outlining of their official doctrines, structures, and practices of order: "The Book of Discipline," or often informally, "The Discipline." Third, "discipline" can be used more broadly to refer to the various commitments and practices by which a community of faith seeks to fulfill its calling. In the context of American Methodism and for the purposes of the present chapter, the third use of the term is primary. While discipline in this broader sense will inevitably involve the other two uses of the term, its scope extends well beyond them. When one recognizes that discipline comprises much more than a book of rules and much more than a way of dealing with problem clergy or lay members, one begins to get a sense of the Methodist conception of discipline. It is thus generally a positive term, capturing the distinct means by which Methodists hold each other accountable in their response to God's grace and their pursuit of holiness.

"Polity" refers generally to the delineation of organization and authority in an institution. Church polity thus typically addresses such matters as church governance structures, relationships among congregations, ordination, the calling or appointment of ministers, membership, sacramental order, and the like. Though it would be something of an oversimplification, one could reasonably describe polity as related to the church as an *institution* and discipline as related to the church as a *community* – they offer distinct angles of vision into the one reality of the church. To address polity and discipline together, then, is to reveal something significant about the ways that Methodists in America have shaped their lives together. For Methodists, the structures and practices of polity *are* structures and practices of discipline. The institutional forms that have naturally and necessarily developed over the course of Methodism's corporate life exist to sustain and nourish a community of faith living out its vocation. For example, one of the key aspects of Methodist polity addressed shortly, conference, can readily be understood as a form of discipline in the sense we have described. Moreover, the structure of Methodist discipline par excellence, the class meeting, was crafted with sharp attentiveness to issues of authority and social dynamics (the very stuff of polity).

There is one more term that is essential to understanding discipline and polity in a Methodist key, connectionalism. In discussions of American religious history, connectionalism is often used broadly to identify episcopal or presbyterial polities in distinction from congregational or free-church polities.[4] In the context of Methodism, however, the term has a more precise meaning. It refers to a commitment among members to share spiritual, missional, organizational, and financial responsibility with each other. During Wesley's life, "the connexion" referred to the network of itinerant preachers that he cultivated (and occasionally to the network of societies in which they ministered as well).[5] Wesley not only supported and closely examined each of these preachers, but he also developed an extensive practical system for supporting their material needs. When Methodism emerged on the American continent, this connectional vision was received even more favorably than it was in Britain (particularly after Wesley's death).[6] Though its expressions have evolved, that sense of mutual commitment and accountability have continued to characterize American Methodist ecclesiology. There is a hint of irony in the recognition that Methodism, which historian Nathan O. Hatch famously called "quintessentially American,"[7] has been marked so profoundly by connectionalism. In a land that has valued self-sufficiency and autonomy, Methodists have embraced an ecclesiological principle that acknowledges mutual dependence. As Russell E. Richey suggests, "connectionalism has been a Wesleyan precept, an ecclesial vision, a missional principle, a covenantal commitment, an ethic of equity and proportionality, a tactical stratagem, an elastic and evolving standard, a theology in praxis." Connectionalism is thus not so much a structure within Methodist polity as it is the guiding vision that gives shape to Methodist polity.

In what follows, we will explore four key aspects of American Methodist discipline and polity: conference, episcopacy, itinerant ministry, and class meetings (or similar small-group accountability structures). While all four are perhaps most naturally considered structures, they can and should be conceived as practices as well. They are meant to be engaged in an active posture of mutual support and accountability, which is fitting in an ecclesial tradition that formally frames its organization in terms of discipline. Furthermore, as we shall see in the course of our discussion, each of these structures appears across the pan-Methodist landscape in America. They are characteristic not only of the United Methodist Church (UMC) and its predecessors, but also of African-American Methodist churches and of Wesleyan Holiness churches. Thus, we will explore representative examples from these various churches as we proceed. Finally, each of these aspects of Methodist discipline serves as an expression of that particular brand of connectionalism that lies at the heart of the Methodist ecclesiological vision. While these four elements certainly do not represent an exhaustive account of Methodist polity, the loss of any of them would diminish something of the distinctly Methodist way of living in ecclesial connection.

CONFERENCE

In his monumental late-nineteenth-century work *A Constitutional History of American Episcopal Methodism*, John J. Tigert suggested that there are two essential features of Methodist polity: episcopacy and conference. "These two factors," he wrote, "are constitutional or elemental in the government of Methodism. The system itself changes as either of these elements changes or is variously combined with the other: the disappearance of either is the destruction of the system."[9] As one can detect even in Tigert's phrasing, the relationship between the two elements has been the source of significant debate. For example, it is likely no accident that he, writing from the perspective of the Methodist Episcopal Church, South (MECS), listed the episcopacy ("a superintending and appointing power") first and described the conference as "a consulting body." Indeed, the relative power of the bishops and of the General Conference in particular has been one of the more significant issues in American Methodist polity. We will consider both of these elements, beginning with conference.

The practice of conferencing in Methodism began with John Wesley himself, who gathered a number of hand-selected preachers together beginning in 1744 to deliberate on crucial questions that had arisen in the movement. Throughout Wesley's life, formal authority in the connection rested with Wesley himself and the conferences served in an advisory capacity. In 1785, Wesley wrote: "A Conference while I live is 'the preachers whom I *invite* to confer with me.' ... No contentious persons shall for the future meet in any Conference."[10] As many American Methodists can attest, that reality would change in more than one respect across the Atlantic.

Methodist conferences in America came to reflect the republican ethos of the surrounding political culture.[11] Rather than serving as an advisory council as Wesley's conferences had, American Methodist conferences embodied a legislative function beginning with the 1784 "Christmas conference" that formally constituted the Methodist Episcopal Church (MEC). One crucial step in this regard was taken when Francis Asbury refused to accept the role of superintendent (the office that would later be known as bishop) unless the conference elected him – even though Wesley had already designated Asbury and Thomas Coke as his chosen superintendents. John Wigger notes that Asbury had two reasons for requesting election. First, it located his authority as superintendent in the will of the conference rather than Wesley's designation, thus precluding Wesley from recalling or replacing him. Second, Asbury recognized the importance of elections in ascribing authority in American society.[12] While he would be quite comfortable employing the power the preachers had ascribed to him, he understood the significance of formalizing the role that the conference played.

The political functions of conferences would continue to be developed and refined over the succeeding decades. But it is important to recognize that they were not merely legislative bodies. Russell E. Richey offers a rich description of the other aspects of American Methodist conferencing, particularly in the early years:

> The political function of conference, though vital, was, as we have seen, only one of its several dimensions.... It measured time and defined space. It established social boundaries, particularly among the preachers. It functioned politically, providing order and structure to the movement. Conference even gave, even if only implicitly, ecclesial expression to Methodism and fostered Methodist spirituality.[13]

Regarding the last of those dimensions, it is notable that conferences (particularly, but not exclusively, the quarterly meeting) were often an occasion for preaching and spiritual revival.[14] Gradually, the administrative and political functions of conference would move the spiritual dimension aside, leaving some to wonder if there is any remnant of it left in contemporary conferences.[15] The question is worth asking in many quarters of Methodism, though one should not neglect the example of the Wesleyan Holiness denominations. In the Free Methodist Church (FMC), for instance, both annual and general conferences continue to be understood as opportunities for worship, fellowship, and testimony as well as administrative business.[16]

There are two challenges in speaking generally about the various forms of conference in American Methodism. First, the particular structures and their respective aims and responsibilities have evolved over time. Second, at any given point in time, the exact arrangement of conference structures varies across the American Methodist churches. Still, essentially all Methodist ecclesial bodies have remained committed to conferencing at three levels: churchwide (General Conference or General Assembly), regional (annual conferences or district assemblies), and local (quarterly meetings, charge conferences, or their equivalents). In some Methodist churches, there is also a regional layer between the General Conference and the annual conferences, such as the jurisdictional conferences in the UMC[17] or the episcopal districts in the African Methodist Episcopal Zion Church (AMEZ).[18]

The General Conference is the primary locus of authority in essentially all American Methodist churches. In the UMC, for example, Frank notes,

> The General Conference comprised of these delegates from annual conferences is the only body in the UMC with legislative powers over the connection as a whole. It defines and fixes the powers of all

other units, including the bishops, clergy, laity, annual conferences, and 'connectional enterprises of the Church' in missions, education, and other ministries (¶ 16).[19]

Though the Restrictive Rules of 1808 limited somewhat the powers of the General Conference, there is no office or body with greater authority than the General Conference. A similar authority is held by the General Conference (or General Assembly) of the other American Methodist churches as well. The language of the *Manual* of the Church of the Nazarene (CN) exemplifies the sort of language used in parallel manuals throughout the American Wesleyan ecclesial landscape: "The General Assembly is the supreme doctrine-formulating, lawmaking, and elective authority of the Church of the Nazarene, subject to the provisions of the church Constitution."[20] The General Conference of almost all American Methodist denominations meets quadrennially, making each gathering (at least potentially) a significant event in the history of that church. (One exception is the Church of God, Anderson, Indiana, whose General Assembly meets annually and does not claim ecclesiastical authority over Church of God congregations.[21] However, while this community is deeply informed by Wesleyan theology and typically considered a Wesleyan holiness church, its congregational polity renders it at best a borderline representative of American Methodist ecclesiology.) The combination of authority and infrequency renders General Conference an occasion unlike any other. In the words of Robert L. Wilson and Steve Harper, "the gathering can be described as a combination of a revival meeting, a class reunion, political convention, and county fair. Elements of all are present."[22] What began in 1792 as a gathering of all the itinerant preachers transitioned in 1808 to a delegated conference, to which each annual conference would send its elected representative elders. Lay members were eventually included as well, and now the General Conference of the various American Methodist churches comprises an equal number of clergy delegates and lay delegates from the annual conferences.

Annual conferences in Methodism have both a temporal dimension and a spatial dimension. The term refers to the yearly gathering of clergy and laypeople in a particular geographic region as well as to the region represented by that yearly gathering. Membership of Methodist pastors resides in the annual conference rather than in a local congregation, and annual conferences oversee the process of preparation and eventually ordination for ministerial candidates. Though bishops generally have authority to appoint pastors, the annual conference is the locus of the appointment process – the elders of a given annual conference are appointed to the churches of that annual conference. In most cases, a bishop presides at an annual conference gathering. The purview of a bishop may be one (as is typical in the case of the UMC) or more (as in the case of the AMEZ or FMC) annual conferences. For the ongoing business of the conference throughout the year – that is, between annual conference gatherings – a bishop (UMC) or conference superintendent (FMC) provides primary leadership in that conference. While the General Conference is the primary legislative body for American Methodist churches, there is a significant sense in which the annual conference is the fundamental unit of American Methodism. The decisions made by that body consistently have a direct and significant impact on the ministers and congregations within it.[23]

Conferencing has also been an important part of Methodist practice at the local level. In early American Methodism, the quarterly meeting was a gathering of ministers, lay leaders, and many other lay members of a particular circuit. There was a revivalist energy to early quarterly meetings, which were often held in conjunction with camp meetings.[24] As circuits slowly transitioned to station churches in the nineteenth century, quarterly meetings gradually gave way to congregational meetings (now typically known as charge conferences).[25] Richey pinpoints this as a significant marker of broader changes in American Methodism: "The reality was that the territorial, conferencing character of local Methodism had long since yielded to congregation and building. Program and even polity oriented attention away from land to edifice. Methodist space had become more interior than exterior."[26] Despite these changes, there are still indicators of the distinctly Methodist form of connectionalism in the practices of local conferencing. In the UMC, for example, the fact that the district superintendent presides at the charge conference suggests that local conferencing is not a purely congregational matter. Furthermore, that district superintendent serves as an extension of episcopal oversight,[27] which represents another crucial dimension of Methodist polity. To that dimension we now turn.

EPISCOPACY

The ecclesiological status of the episcopacy in American Methodism is a complex matter. As Tigert noted, a superintending and appointing power has always been part of Methodist church structure in America. Yet the particular form of superintendence has varied across time and even across regions. Furthermore, distinctly theological reflection on the office has often been moved to the margins by pragmatic concerns. This can be seen even in the irregular origin of the episcopacy (and indeed the ordained ministry as a whole) in American Methodism. When the Anglican priest John Wesley took upon himself the prerogatives of a bishop in ordaining elders and setting Coke apart as a superintendent for American Methodists, he had a theological justification in hand for an act that was dictated by necessity.[28] But the hesitation with which Wesley undertook this action signaled the ecclesiological defensiveness of Methodists in later generations.[29] Methodists have followed Wesley's conviction that bishops are not a third order of ministry but rather a functional office of oversight for the church.[30] There has also been terminological variation in the title of the office: Wesley was quite surprised when the title of bishop (rather than his designated title of superintendent) was employed by the MEC a few years after the formation of that body. While the term general superintendent is still used in the CN and the Wesleyan Church (WC), the term bishop is most commonly used in American Methodist churches. Bishops in some churches (such as the UMC) serve life terms, while bishops or superintendents in other churches (such as the FMC) serve four-year terms.[31]

The formal powers of the superintending office have remained remarkably consistent on the whole – particularly presiding at conferences, appointing pastors, and ordaining new elders. (While the decision regarding who will be ordained rests entirely with the annual conference, the bishops actually perform the ordination.) Still, there has been considerable variation of the powers of the episcopacy in relation to the conferences. Two historical episodes proved to be especially significant in this regard. The first involved a challenge to the episcopal power of appointment. At the first General Conference of the MEC in 1792, a presiding elder named James O'Kelly proposed that preachers who felt "injured" by their appointment might have the right to appeal that appointment to the annual conference. Despite the considerable debate on the conference floor, the proposal was soundly defeated and the bishop's power of appointment was reinforced.[32] The second episode involved the authority of the bishops in relation to that of the General Conference. At the 1844 MEC General Conference, the center of debate was Bishop James O. Andrew, who had inherited slaves by marriage after his 1832 election to the episcopal office. A proposal was made to suspend Andrew, supported by the northern delegates who argued that the bishops were entirely accountable to the General Conference. That body, they contended, held the authority to remove a bishop at its discretion – without formal charges or a trial. Southern delegates argued in response that the episcopacy was a coordinate branch of church government and that the

General Conference did not have the authority to summarily remove a bishop without due process. The motion to suspend Andrew was passed, triggering the series of events that would divide the MEC into the MEC and MECS. While bishops in the MECS would retain significantly more authority than their counterparts in the MEC during the years of division, the decision of the 1844 General Conference limiting episcopal authority was an indicator of the future of American Methodism.[33]

There has also been a pattern of gradual localization of the Methodist episcopacy over the course of its history in America. The vision of "itinerant general superintendency" was modeled in the early MEC by Francis Asbury, who insisted that bishops must continually travel to fulfill their apostolic vocation.[34] Asbury refused to localize the episcopacy and moved among all of the annual conferences during his entire tenure as bishop. The 1808 Restrictive Rules of the MEC prohibited the General Conference from eliminating the plan of itinerant general superintendency. However, it was not long before Asbury's vision of itinerating bishops began to give way to regionalization. Indeed, given his status as the paradigm of the Methodist bishop, it is striking to notice how few have followed his particular example of itinerating.[35] One significant step was taken in 1816, when the MEC bishops began to divide the duties of presiding at the various annual conferences, departing from the prior pattern in which all of the bishops attended all of the annual conferences. Eight years later, the work of the bishops was grouped regionally, with some bishops presiding at the northern and eastern conferences and others presiding at the southern and western conferences.[36] Perhaps the most dramatic marker in this pattern of episcopal regionalization was the creation of jurisdictional conferences in the 1939 formation of the Methodist Church (MC). This not only limited bishops' service to a particular jurisdiction; it also shifted the election of bishops in the MC from the General Conference to the jurisdictional conferences.[37] It is debatable whether the plan of itinerant general superintendency – theoretically protected by the Restrictive Rules – has been retained in practice in any recognizable sense. Still, one could certainly argue that the Wesleyan Holiness Churches, most of which elect bishops or general superintendents in General Conference or General Assembly, have been more concerned to resist episcopal localization than the UMC or its predecessors.

ITINERANT MINISTRY

Asbury did not limit his vision of itinerancy to bishops; he insisted that all preachers in the connection be constantly on the move. To this day, the itinerant system is one of the defining features of Methodist ecclesiology. Ministers are formally appointed to their pastoral charges each year at their annual conference, and the reading of appointments at the end of conference sessions is a longstanding ritual in American Methodism. There are both practical and theological reasons for the itinerant system, many of which were espoused by Wesley himself. In practical terms, Wesley was convinced that itinerancy enabled the movement of preachers where they were most needed, helped to maintain theological unity throughout the connection, and prevented the spiritual stagnation that can set in when a preacher is in one location for too long.[38] The itinerant system that Asbury refined in America demonstrated the same practical advantages. It proved remarkably flexible and efficient in directing resources toward America's rapidly expanding frontier.[39] It provided a check against theological fragmentation of the connection, particularly along regional lines.[40] Like Wesley, Asbury was also convinced that the system helped to prevent spiritual stagnation. As he and Coke wrote in their annotated 1798 *Discipline*: "next to the grace of God, there is nothing *like this* [itinerant ministry] for keeping the whole body alive from the centre to the circumference."[41] The system also enabled substantial mentoring of younger preachers by experienced circuit riders with whom they traveled.[42]

The pragmatic advantages were not, however, the only reason that Methodist leadership embraced the principle of itinerancy. There was also a theological rationale for asking ministers to undertake such a demanding way of life. The first dimension of this theological vision involved obedience and the conforming of one's will to God's will. Itinerancy reflects an understanding of ministry in which God calls and sends, and one's response is not subject to considerations of convenience or preference. The itinerant system served as a tangible expression of obedience to God's calling and sending of those who would proclaim the gospel.[43] Second, the constant motion of itinerancy was a symbolic expression of the movement one experiences along the way of salvation. A preacher's travel through and among circuits embodied the highs and lows of the spiritual journey.[44] Finally, the itinerant ministry offered a visible expression of the distinctly Methodist form of connectional ecclesiology. Setting aside ambitions for wealth, comfort, and deep roots in a particular locale, Methodist preachers depended on each other for their own practical and spiritual needs.[45]

One might understandably ask what remains of the principle of itinerancy in contemporary American Methodism. While the appointment system remains formally in place, there have been considerable changes in the nature of itinerancy in essentially all branches of Methodism. Pastors are often reappointed to the same charge for many years and even decades, particularly in large urban or suburban congregations. The appointment process in many quarters of American Methodism now involves significant interaction between the bishop's representatives (the district superintendent or conference-level appointment committee) and the congregation. In many pastoral charges, housing allowances are replacing traditional parsonages. The ability of pastors to move is often limited by health issues, the employment of a spouse, or other considerations.[46] While many of these issues reflect longstanding tension points in the itinerancy, there is no question that the practical realities of ministry have changed along with American society.[47] Such a recognition does not require one to conclude, however, that the principle of itinerancy has been abandoned in Methodism. While the pragmatic considerations that so motivated Wesley and Asbury may not apply as directly in the contemporary setting, the theological convictions that undergird the itinerant system remain as relevant as ever. Indeed, the continuing embrace of itinerancy in Methodism reflects a theology of ministry that emphasizes submission of the will, dynamism in the Christian journey, and interdependence.

THE CLASS MEETING

The theological emphases that make sense of the itinerant system also help us to understand a crucial structure for early Methodist laity, the class meeting. This was another aspect of British Methodism under Wesley that came to hold a central place in America. John Wigger suggests that "the fundamental building block of American Methodism was the class meeting."[48] In their annotated 1798 *Discipline*, Coke and Asbury offered a similar assessment: "through the grace of God our classes form the pillars of our work, and ... are in a considerable degree our universities for the ministry."[49] It was here that members met weekly under the oversight of a class leader to support, encourage, and press each other on the way of salvation. The care with which class meetings were structured – the diligent use of time, close examination of members' spiritual lives, and careful scrutiny of class leaders' effectiveness – demonstrates how discipline and polity coalesced in American Methodism. Furthermore, there was a remarkable synergy between the itinerant ministry and the class meetings.[50] While a traveling preacher would only occasionally be present at any one location, class leaders provided crucial ministerial oversight that helped to sustain the connection.

Indeed, the capacity to identify and develop lay leaders to serve in such crucial roles was a hallmark of Methodist discipline.[51]

It might appear strange, however, to include class meetings in a contemporary discussion of essential practices of Methodist discipline and polity given the decline of those meetings in the middle of the nineteenth century. The gradual settling of the itinerant ministry coincided with a diminished role for lay leadership in many sectors of American Methodism. Furthermore, class meetings began to seem distasteful to a membership that increasingly valued privacy and aspired to upward mobility.[52] Still, the story of the class meeting is not exhausted by a narrative of rise and decline. Wesleyan holiness churches continued to champion the vital role of class meetings after they had fallen out of favor in mainline Methodism. For example, Free Methodist Bishop Wilson T. Hogue suggested in 1907 that "revival of the class-meeting and the revival of Methodism in spiritual life and power, and as an evangelizing agency, are also equally inseparable."[53] Moreover, a significant role for class leaders and class meetings has persisted to this day in African-American Methodist churches. One finds, for instance, sections on class leaders in the AME, AMEZ, and CME *Disciplines*. That office was also restored to the UMC *Discipline* in 1988 after a half-century absence.[54] The UMC action coincided with a revival of sorts of small-group accountability structures in that body, most notably in the Covenant Discipleship groups. The crucial point to be discerned in these developments is that a viable means of mutual accountability is deeply needed in contemporary congregations. The small-group structure that was so fundamental to Methodist identity holds tremendous promise – perhaps with appropriate adjustments for a fresh context – for meeting that need.

DISCIPLINE AND POLITY SUNDERED?

The foregoing discussion has explored numerous transitions in conference, episcopacy, itinerancy, and the class meeting. These transitions may be interpreted by some as signaling the gradual erosion of discipline in American Methodist polity. Other developments, such as the expanding bureaucracy of general boards and agencies and the increasing professionalization of the ministry, might seem to bolster that suggestion.[55] Yet I would argue that discipline still reflects the appropriate mode in which to understand Methodist polity, even if the particular shape of these structures evolves with the times. The organization of ecclesial life in American Methodism still aims to serve the mission God has given the church and to foster faithful response to God's calling. The theological vision underlying that organization calls for submission of the will to God, dynamic movement along the way of salvation, and interdependence within the community of faith. As we have seen, that theological vision has not been displaced by the changing forms of order in the life of the church. The Methodist patterns of conference, episcopacy, itinerancy, and class meetings presume that mutual accountability is necessary to sustain the faithful pursuit of these ends. In that light, polity in American Methodism might well be understood, for all of its tensions and shortcomings, as a means of grace.

Notes

1   John Wesley, "Letter to John Smith" (June 25, 1746), in *The Works of John Wesley*, Volume 26: Letters II: 1740–1755, edited by Frank Baker (Nashville, TN: Abingdon Press, 1982), 206.

2   For a helpful discussion of this conviction in the context of the United Methodist Church, see Robert L. Wilson and Steve Harper, *Faith and Form: A Unity of Theology & Polity in the United Methodist Tradition* (Grand Rapids, MI: Francis Asbury Press, 1988), 198–203.

3   See the illuminating treatment of this emphasis in Thomas Edward Frank, *Polity, Practice, and the Mission of the United Methodist Church* (Nashville, TN: Abingdon Press, 2006), 46–54.

4   Russell E. Richey, "Introduction," in *Connectionalism: Ecclesiology, Mission, and Identity*, edited by Russell E. Richey, Dennis M. Campbell, and William B. Lawrence (Nashville, TN: Abingdon Press, 1997), 1.

5   Richard P. Heitzenrater, "Connectionalism and Itinerancy: Wesleyan Principles and Practice," in Richey et al., eds., *Connectionalism*, 30.

6   David Hempton, *Methodism: Empire of the Spirit* (New Haven, CT: Yale University Press, 2005), 128–129.

7   Nathan O. Hatch, "The Puzzle of American Methodism," in *Methodism and the Shaping of American Culture*, edited by Nathan O. Hatch and John H. Wigger (Nashville, TN: Kingswood Books, 2001), 36.

8   Richey, "Introduction," 3.

9   Jno. J. Tigert, *A Constitutional History of American Episcopal Methodism* (Nashville, TN: Publishing House of the M. E. Church, South, 1894), 15.

10 John Wesley, "Letter to Thomas Wride" (July 8, 1785), in *The Letters of the Rev. John Wesley, A.M.*, Volume 12, edited by John Telford (London: Epworth Press, 1931), 279.

11 Frank, *Polity, Practice, and the Mission of the United Methodist Church*, 118–119.

12 John Wigger, *American Saint: Francis Asbury & the Methodists* (New York: Oxford University Press, 2009), 144.

13 Russell E. Richey, *Early American Methodism* (Bloomington, IN: Indiana University Press, 1991), 71.

14 Russell E. Richey, *The Methodist Conference in America: A History* (Nashville, TN: Kingswood Books, 1996), 13–14.

15 Richey, *The Methodist Conference in America*, 199.

16 This is even reflected in the Free Methodist *Book of Discipline*, which states that the annual conference "ensures that pastors and congregations are counseled and encouraged." Free Methodist Church of North America, 2007 *Book of Discipline* (Indianapolis, IN: Free Methodist Publishing House, 2008), ¶ 5000.

17 *The Book of Discipline of the United Methodist Church* (Nashville, TN: The United Methodist Publishing House, 2008), Part V, Chapter Four, Section II.

18 *The Book of Discipline of the African Methodist Episcopal Zion Church* (Charlotte, NC: A.M.E. Zion Publishing House, 2008), Part III, Chapter IV.

19 Frank, *Polity, Practice, and the Mission of the United Methodist Church*, 120.

20 *Manual of the Church of the Nazarene, 2009–2013* (Kansas City, MO: Nazarene Publishing House, 2009), Part IV, Chapter III, Section A, ¶ 300.

21 *Constitution and Bylaws of the General Assembly of the Church of God, Anderson* (Anderson, IN: Church of God Ministries, 2010), Article III.

22 Wilson and Harper, *Faith and Form*, 100.

23 Wilson and Harper, *Faith and Form*, 111.

24 Richey, *The Methodist Conference in America*, 59–61.

25 Richey, *The Methodist Conference in America*, 116, and Frank, *Polity, Practice, and the Mission of the United Methodist Church*, 136.

26 Richey, *The Methodist Conference in America*, 162–163.

27 Frank, *Polity, Practice, and the Mission of the United Methodist Church*, 249.

28 See the discussion of this series of events in James E. Kirby, *The Episcopacy in American Methodism* (Nashville, TN: Kingswood Books, 2000), 25–37.

29 I engage this issue with reference to the notion of apostolicity in Douglas M. Koskela, "'But Who Laid Hands on Him? Apostolicity and Methodist Ecclesiology," *Pro Ecclesia* (2011), 28–42.

30 The African Methodist Episcopal (AME) Church has affirmed this quite clearly – see *African Methodist Episcopal Church Polity*, edited by Harold I. Bearden (Nashville, TN: AMEC Sunday School Union, 1984), 168.

31 Kirby notes that, in the discussions leading to the 1968 formation of the United Methodist Church, the Evangelical United Brethren proposal for four-year terms for bishops was quickly rejected by the Methodist Church. See James E. Kirby, "Episcopacy and Ordination," in *Methodist and Pietist: Retrieving the Evangelical United Brethren Tradition*, edited by J. Steven O'Malley and Jason E. Vickers (Nashville, TN: Kingswood Books, 2011), 145–146.

32 Kirby, *The Episcopacy in American Methodism*, 56–57.

33 See the discussion of the 1844 General Conference and its implications for polity in Kirby, *The Episcopacy in American Methodism*, 127–144.

34 John Wigger offers a helpful treatment of this theme as reflected in Asbury's famous valedictory address in *American Saint*, 388–390.

35   Russell E. Richey and Thomas Edward Frank, *Episcopacy in the Methodist Tradition: Perspectives and Proposals* (2004), 65–66.

36   Kirby, *The Episcopacy in American Methodism*, 102.

37   The various issues this raised for the episcopacy are addressed in Kirby, *The Episcopacy in American Methodism*, 221–238.

38   Heitzenrater, "Connectionalism and Itinerancy," 31–34.

39   John H. Wigger, *Taking Heaven by Storm: Methodism and the Rise of Popular Christianity in America* (Urbana, IL: University of Illinois Press, 1998), 22; and Russell E. Richey with Dennis M. Campbell and William B. Lawrence, *Marks of Methodism: Theology in Ecclesial Practice* (Nashville, TN: Abingdon Press, 2005), 48.

40   Thomas Coke and Francis Asbury, *The Doctrines and Disciplines of the Methodist Episcopal Church, in America* (1798), excerpted in Russell E. Richey, Kenneth E. Rowe, and Jean Miller Schmidt, eds., *The Methodist Experience in America: A Sourcebook, Volume II* (Nashville, TN: Abingdon Press, 2000), 124.

41   Coke and Asbury, *Doctrines and Disciplines*, excerpted in *The Methodist Experience in America: A Sourcebook*, 125.

42   Wigger, *Taking Heaven by Storm*, 71.

43   Dennis M. Campbell, *The Yoke of Obedience: The Meaning of Ordination in Methodism* (Nashville, TN: Abingdon Press, 1988), 57.

44   See the illuminating discussion in Richey, Campbell, and Lawrence, *Marks of Methodism*, 51.

45   Richey, Campbell, and Lawrence, *Marks of Methodism*, 51.

46   See the discussion of these and other transitions in the itinerancy in Richey, Campbell, and Lawrence, *Marks of Methodism*, 54–57.

47   Wigger addresses the particular challenges marriage posed to the itinerant ministry in *Taking Heaven by Storm*, 64–71.

48   Wigger, *Taking Heaven by Storm*, 80.

49   Coke and Asbury, Doctrines and Disciplines, excerpted in *The Methodist Experience in America: A Sourcebook*, 133.

50   Wigger, *Taking Heaven by Storm*, 82.

51   David Lowes Watson, "Class Leaders and Class Meetings: Recovering a Methodist Tradition for a Changing Church," in *Doctrines and Discipline*, edited by Dennis M. Campbell, William B. Lawrence, and Russell E. Richey (Nashville, TN: Abingdon Press, 1999), 258–260.

52   Wigger, *Taking Heaven by Storm*, 87 and 194.

53   Wilson T. Hogue, *The Class-Meeting as a Means of Grace* (Chicago, IL: W. B. Rose, 1907), 73.

54   Watson, "Class Leaders and Class Meetings," 256–257.

55   Richey explores many of these developments in *The Methodist Conference in America*, 159–174.

8 Clergy

E. BROOKS HOLIFIELD

Sometime before the end of 1766, three immigrant lay preachers and one determined immigrant lay woman introduced the Methodist movement to America. In the next eight years John Wesley sent eight more lay preachers, and two others came on their own initiative. By 1784, Methodist preachers sitting in "conference" recognized 157 additional preachers either by placing them "on trial" or "admitting" them to the fellowship of preachers to proclaim the gospel and spread holiness throughout America. Almost all of these 170 preachers were, by the standards of the Church of England, laity.[1]

In 1784, Wesley "set apart" three English preachers, designating one a "superintendent," as missionaries to transform American itinerants into ordained ministers. In December, on three separate days, the three men, aided by a German Reformed pastor, ordained Francis Asbury as a deacon, an elder, and a superintendent, and then they and Asbury ordained twelve (possibly thirteen) other preachers, first as deacons, then as elders. This "Christmas conference" established the Methodist Episcopal Church (MEC) with its own ministers, separate from the Church of England, though of the 266 Methodist preachers active eight years later, only seventy eight had received ordination and sacramental authority. The denomination, led partly by ordained and partly by nonordained preachers, found that questions of clerical authority produced continuing tensions.[2]

Authority has not been the only issue to engender tensions among Methodist preachers. They have had to overcome recurring disagreements about the itinerancy, education, economic class, social reform, political activity, race and ethnicity, gender, theology, regional and national differences, relationships with laity, and the power and status of conferences. The tensions produced new Methodist denominations, some permanent and others temporary, but most ministers learned to live with their differences, and they have continued to assume leadership in congregations, denominational boards, theological seminaries, foreign missions, colleges, counseling centers, hospitals, prison and military chaplaincies, social reform, work with the hungry and homeless, humanitarian relief organizations, group homes for children and the elderly, spiritual retreat centers, evangelistic organizations, ecumenical agencies, international associations, youth ministries, publishing companies, denominational newspaper offices, theological authorship, and foundations. By the late twentieth century the variety itself had become a source of minor tensions; in 1976, the United Methodist Church (UMC) asked that "special appointments" be clarified.[3]

Methodist diversity makes generalization difficult. The American story began with the lay mission, which issued in the MEC (1784). The largest denomination is now the UMC (1968), formed by a union of The Methodist Church (MC) (1939) and the Evangelical United Brethren (EUB) (1946). By 2005 it had 45,148 ordained pastors and 6,600 "local pastors." Other sizable existing groups include the Wesleyan Methodist Church (1843) and the Free Methodist Church (FMC) (1860) along with three historically black denominations, the African Methodist Episcopal Church (AME) (1816), the African Methodist Episcopal Church, Zion (AMEZ) (1821), and the Christian Methodist Episcopal Church (CME) (1870). But at least nineteen other Methodist denominations have existed in America, and that number does not include such holiness churches as the Salvation Army (1865), the Church of the Nazarene (1908), and others that have Methodist roots. The array is, in part, a reflection of the tensions.[4]

CLERICAL AUTHORITY

Asbury insisted, and the recently arrived Thomas Coke apparently concurred, that the preachers at the 1784 conference elect them as superintendents, meaning that Wesley's appointment of them functioned like a nomination. The superintendents soon became "bishops," charged with making appointments, visiting and presiding at conferences, disciplining preachers, and ordaining. In 1786, the preachers defied Wesley, who wanted to appoint the third superintendent, and insisted on the right of election. By 1792, some preachers defied even Asbury, and one of them, James O'Kelly of Virginia, insisted at the General Conference that preachers should be able to appeal to a district conference if they received an unwanted appointment to a "circuit," the geographical grouping of congregations and classes to which a designated preacher regularly traveled. After the conference rejected his proposal, O'Kelly led dissidents in forming the Republican Methodist Church (1792). A pamphlet war over the relative authority of bishops and conferences lasted for the next decade, but by the nineteenth century bishops in the largest Methodist denominations could wield authoritarian power. As late as the 1950s, they "read the appointments" to anxious pastors only on the final day of annual conference. But by the late 1960s they engaged in far more negotiation with both pastors and churches, and they also became to a greater degree pastors to their pastors.[5]

The office of "presiding elder" (later, district superintendent) proved almost equally contentious. First clearly defined in the conference minutes of 1789, the office designated the elders, initially the first group Asbury and his colleagues ordained, who administered the sacraments for nonordained preachers and oversaw the preachers within "districts," regions larger than circuits but smaller than conferences. The disputed question was whether bishops should appoint them or conferences elect them. The larger Methodist bodies decided for appointment, which has remained the most frequent practice, but the decision engendered tensions.

Underlying such issues were questions about the preachers' authority. Everyone agreed that the ultimate source of authority was a divine call to promote the gospel of Jesus Christ and to help diffuse holiness through the land, but authority also had human dimensions. The bishops, for example, ordained preachers as elders and deacons. The eldership was the highest order, carrying the authority to preach, administer the sacraments, receive appointments to the circuits, and join with bishops in ordaining new ministers. The 1784 conference determined, however, that no one could be ordained an elder unless first elected to membership by the conference. Was it then election or ordination that conferred this authority? Some nonordained traveling preachers could belong to a conference; after 1792, the presiding elder administered the sacraments for them. Others could be ordained and then surrender their conference membership but without losing their orders and sacramental privileges. Ordination became the standard practice in the nineteenth century, but numerous preachers claimed that their authority rested in a divine call and their success in attracting converts. The Methodists had a problem with authority.[6]

The issue found further expression in the debate over deacons. The earliest bishops, at Wesley's behest, ordained deacons who served for a time before becoming elders. Their ordination gave them authority to preach, assist the elder at Holy Communion, baptize, and care for the sick and poor. The order was a stepping stone to ordination as an elder. To reformers of the 1820s, who also questioned the authority of both bishops and elders, a subordinate diaconate seemed undemocratic, and when they formed the breakaway Methodist Protestant Church in 1830, they dropped the office, as did the FMC and the EUB.[7]

The main body of Methodists, including the three black denominations, continued the diaconate, but in 1964 a committee of the MC proposed to redefine it as an office, not an order, though it still would lead to elder's orders. The issue troubled the new UMC at the time of its formation in 1968, but it deferred the question until 1976, when it decided to keep the traditional diaconal "order" but add an "office" of diaconal ministry to recognize full time lay church workers. In 1996, the UMC made the diaconal "order" permanent, charged with a ministry of word and service but lacking the authority to officiate at the Holy Communion. In 2008, deacons received the authority to officiate under conditions set by the bishop, but normally they had authority only to assist the elder. At each stage, the changes generated disagreement, and no resolution promises universal assent.[8]

Other tensions marked the practice of itinerancy, the system in which bishops appointed preachers to circuits. At first the bishops normally rotated them to new circuits every year, but by 1804 some could stay two years. Usually riding on horseback, the itinerants traveled hundreds of miles, usually in pairs, often in rugged territory, preaching, administering the sacraments, and working with lay leaders who oversaw local "class meetings" of the faithful. Methodists viewed the itinerating ministry as the "grand peculiarity" of their system, but by 1844 they recognized that it had almost imperceptibly changed into a system in which even itinerant preachers served not a circuit but a local congregation – or "station" – for a period of years and then moved to another one. In the late nineteenth century the possible length of appointment expanded. Even now parish ministers still accept periodic reassignments, with tenure of varying lengths. Itinerancy now means service by ordained members of annual conferences who are willing to move wherever bishops and superintendents determine. Some complain that the largest churches can keep their pastors as long as they want, but one reason for this is that the itinerancy has, in many conferences, become a seniority system in which successful younger pastors move gradually upward into larger local churches. In 2010, however, 64 percent of the congregations in the UMC had fewer than 175 members. The WC and FMC had smaller congregations; the three black denominations reported, on average, larger ones.[9]

As the itinerancy changed, it became more difficult to distinguish the ordained itinerant in full "conference connection" from "local pastors" who still functioned as lay preachers but often remained in one place. Wesley had valued such persons, and in America the office could designate 1) nonordained persons intending to become ordained itinerants, 2) nonordained preachers who remained in one location, and 3) ordained preachers who withdrew from the traveling ministry but retained their orders and could still preach and administer sacraments. By 1812, the church had 2,000 local preachers compared with 700 itinerants, and the MEC was permitting African Americans to be ordained as local deacons. By 1816, as many as 821 of the 1,616 itinerating preachers received into the conferences during the previous thirty-two years "located," or left the itinerancy to settle in one place. The local preachers, later named "local pastors," had less status than the traveling elders, and they also lacked the authority to administer sacraments or hold conference membership. Reformers of the 1820s left the denomination in part because these lay preachers, along with other laity, had no conference vote. This was one issue behind the formation of the MPC.[10]

By the early twentieth century, the Methodist Episcopal Church, South (MECS) permitted some nonordained "supply pastors" to administer the sacraments in their own congregations, and the assembly that merged the MEC, the MECS, and the MPC into The Methodist Church in 1939 followed this precedent, but by 1948 the denomination removed the right of these local pastors to administer Holy Communion. Attuned to fresh ecumenical currents, ministers in the MC began to worry that they had undervalued ordination, and in 1968 the UMC decided that no one should officiate at Communion without it, and the AME, AMEZ, and CME have the same policy. The decision, made at a time when many of the young were calling for "power to the people," generated a backlash. By 1976, in an atmosphere of suspicion toward "clericalism" and a growing reliance on nonordained local pastors in small rural churches, the UMC – but not the African-American denominations – allowed bishops to authorize the local pastors to officiate under restricted circumstances. Between 1985 and 2005, the number of local pastors increased while the number of elders fell slightly. By 2010, ordained deacons normally assisted the elder at the sacrament, but UMC bishops could also grant them sacramental rights if they served a local parish. In the UMC, sacramental authority, in effect, flowed from the appointment of a bishop and not from ordination, a practice that elicited less than universal satisfaction.

Far more controversial was the question of whether the church had the authority to ordain women as pastors. A few women had served as nonordained traveling preachers under Wesley in England, and between 1784 and 1845 at least twenty-two women preached for the MEC and the African Methodists. By the 1840s, however, as Methodists gained social respectability, they excluded women from the pulpit, though Wesleyan denominations less regardful of fashion either licensed women ministers (the United Brethren [1800] in 1851 and the FMC in 1874) or ordained them (the Wesleyan Methodist Church in 1864). The early Holiness churches accepted women as elders, though some would later withdraw that right because of fundamentalist influence. By the 1880s, calls for the ordination of women generated intense debate, typified by Frances Willard's *Woman in the Pulpit* (1888), and when Anna Oliver and Anna Howard Shaw in New England sought ordination and membership in the MEC in 1880, the bishop defied the conference and refused to ordain them. Shaw received orders in the MPC in 1880, which were rescinded in 1884, though in 1889 the denomination voted to ordain women. The AME and AMEZ denominations ordained women by 1894. Not until 1956 did the MC ordain Maud K. Jensen, but by 1994 the UMC had more ordained women (3,003) than any denomination except the Salvation Army. The changes reflected the force of women's rights movements in the larger society, an emphasis on the authority of religious experience, and a growing disinclination to equate biblical authority with biblical literalism.[11]

The most polarizing issue after 1980 was whether to ordain noncelibate gay and lesbian Methodists as pastors. In 1987 a UMC church court in New Hampshire defrocked a local pastor for being openly lesbian. The UMC voted in 2004 to uphold a ban on noncelibate homosexual pastors, and the Judicial Council upheld the 2005 denial of clerical rights to another lesbian pastor, but at meetings of the UMC General Conference proponents of gay rights continued to insist on ordination. At times the issue appeared to have the potential to split the denomination. In 2011, no Methodist denomination permitted the ordination of gay and lesbian applicants.

POPULIST OR PROFESSIONAL

Disagreements about education produced other tensions. Almost none of the first and second generation preachers had more than a common school education. Wesley recommended a school, and the early first *Discipline* urged conscientious reading, but the preachers rejected any call for educational requirements. Thomas Ware expressed the consensus: "Grace, rather than human learning, qualifies a man to preach."

It was a matter of pride that Methodist preachers "never rubbed their backs against the walls of a college."[12]

The result was a populist style of preaching that repudiated learned sermons in favor of impassioned, extemporaneous, emotional, witty, anecdotal exhortations to escape the fires of damnation and obtain a heavenly bliss. The preaching at Methodist camp meetings, one of the primary showpieces for clerical rhetorical skills, often produced fainting, shouting, weeping, and physical jerking. Critics saw Methodist preachers as noisy, uncouth babblers who reported miracles, prophecies, revelatory dreams, and visions. Some preachers reveled in the criticism: "We could not, many of us," said the Illinois preacher Peter Cartwright, "conjugate a verb or parse a sentence, and murdered the king's English almost every lick."[13]

Because they appealed initially to a social class that was itself largely uneducated, the unschooled Methodist preachers had stunning success in gathering converts. Cartwright boasted that "the illiterate Methodist preachers actually set the world on fire" while the educated clerical gentlemen of some other denominations "were still lighting their matches." In 1773, the Methodists claimed 1,160 members; by 1828 they counted 420,618. By 1855, Methodist ordained and local preachers constituted 40 percent of the preachers in America.[14]

Their numerical success enabled them to disregard appeals for a formally educated clergy. The view that the Methodist proportion of members declined after 1850 partly because the denomination opened seminaries cannot explain why the proportional decline began long before many preachers began to receive theological, or even collegiate, education. In 1886, a teacher at Wofford College in South Carolina complained that a man could become an MECS itinerant without the ability to "write a complex sentence or understand it when written." In 1926 the MECS reported that only 4 percent of its preachers in the rural South had graduated from both a college and a seminary. In the northern MEC, only half the preachers in 1920 had a high school education and only an eighth had college and seminary training. Eighty percent of the rural southern preachers in the AME churches and 85 percent in the CME churches had only a high school education or less.[15]

As early as 1816, however, Methodists had a company of "gentlemen theologians" who pushed for higher educational standards. Embarrassed by the "inefficiency" of many of the preachers, the MEC General Conference in 1816 told the bishops to prepare a two-year, and then a four-year, course of study and to require tutored reading as a preparation

Figure 7. **Peter Cartwright, the Methodist Episcopal Church,** Methodist Library Image Collection, Drew University, Madison, New Jersey.

for full connection. By 1848, every MEC conference imposed the requirement. The next step was to build colleges and encourage candidates for ministry to enroll. Between 1830 and 1861, the MEC founded thirty-four permanent colleges, several of which later became universities, and ministers taught in the classrooms and assumed the presidency of these schools. College-educated preachers sometimes underwent hazing from critics, designated at the time as "Croakers," but Methodist membership was moving into a different social class, and a more educated laity demanded more educated ministers.[16]

The next step, the creation of theological seminaries, proved difficult. The majority resisted fiercely, but John Dempster, a presiding elder in the Oneida Conference, generated support in 1839 for a New England Biblical Institute that in 1867 became Boston Theological Seminary. Eventually the UMC supported thirteen seminaries, the AME three, the CME one, the AME, Zion two, the FMC six, and the Wesleyan Methodist Church one. But in none of these denominations did all pastors graduate from a seminary. At its founding in 1939 the MC made a seminary degree the requirement for admission into full connection in an annual conference, but nonordained local pastors occupied 43 percent of that denomination's pulpits, and in 1958 the number of its seminary educated ministers dropped to 22 percent. In 2003, in the UMC local pastors without a standard seminary education still served 25 percent of the congregations, and in some regions of the South and Midwest half the UMC pastors lacked a seminary degree. The percentage with no seminary degree was higher in other Methodist denominations.[17]

Despite strong antiintellectual currents, Methodist clergy invested considerable effort to establish newspapers and journals. The early MEC had one national newspaper and six regional papers. *The Christian Advocate*, edited by Nathan Bangs in New York in the mid-nineteenth century, had a circulation rivaling any commercial newspaper, and Benjamin Tanner made the *Christian Recorder* (1852) the most important religious newspaper in the black churches. In 1818, preachers in the MEC revived earlier journals to establish the *Methodist Magazine*, dedicated to promoting more rational faith. By 1841, the *Methodist Quarterly Review* and the *Quarterly Review of the Methodist Episcopal Church, South* (1847) competed with the best denominational and national quarterlies. The *AME Church Review* (1884) became the standard bearer in black Methodism. When the UMC tried to revive the *Quarterly Review* in 1980 it lasted twenty-five years but finally failed for lack of subscriptions, though a few clergy are now attempting an online *Methodist Review*.

Methodist ministers proved, moreover, to be prolific theological authors. They have shared no singular theological position. They have disagreed about holiness, divided along liberal and conservative lines, and advanced theologies ranging from Wesleyan traditionalism, Fundamentalism, and holiness theologies to Personalism, evangelical liberalism, Neo-Orthodoxy, Process theology, Liberation theologies, black and Womanist theology, feminist theology, and theologies that accented the formative power of narrative, especially the biblical narratives. In 1969, however, 63 percent of UMC clergy found the ministry confused and uncertain about theological issues; a symbol of their division was that 40 percent believed that Jesus Christ was the sole means of salvation while 60 percent questioned that belief. The 1970s brought increased conservatism, though rarely of a Fundamentalist variety. In any event, the Methodists have produced scores of theologians and a variety of theological positions.[18]

Even advocates of an educated ministry have sometimes criticized the idea of a "professional" ministry. In the nineteenth century, the term "professional" meant simply "educated," usually designating graduation from a seminary, but some Methodists have always had reservations about the term. Without necessarily advocating a populist view, some have argued that ministry is not a "helping profession" but rather a form of discipleship to Jesus that stands in tension with a society that enshrines professional values. Other Methodists, however, have insisted that educated "professionals" are ideally "reflective practitioners" who can draw on theology, tradition, and the arts and sciences in order to interpret the contexts in which they minister, and that the clergy need more professionalism, not less.[19]

ETHNICALLY INCLUSIVE OR EXCLUSIVE

The color line long divided Methodist clergy, and early African Americans faced unremitting discrimination. The earliest Methodists attracted African-American adherents and admitted them to their class meetings and worship services. Such preachers as Harry Hosier, who traveled with Asbury, Henry Evans in North Carolina, Richard Allen in Pennsylvania, Daniel Coker in Maryland, and the female lay preacher Jarena Lee in Pennsylvania attracted both black and white hearers in the early nineteenth century, and the MEC ordained some of them as local deacons. In 1810, Coker listed eight ordained black Methodists and eleven local preachers, surely an incomplete listing. Slave preachers were especially in demand among the southern slaves, who preferred them to white preachers. They mediated between African and white cultures and between slaves and their masters. They transmitted Methodist doctrines in a manner, as Allen noted, that the least educated could understand.[20]

They encountered discrimination at every turn; in 1800, the MEC declined to ordain African Americans as elders or grant them conference membership. After continued humiliations, black ministers led between 1813 and 1870 in forming five African-American Methodist denominations, three of which grew rapidly after the Civil War as blacks migrated from white-controlled Methodist churches. In 1864, moreover, the MEC established separate annual conferences for African Americans that lasted until late in the twentieth century.[21]

Regardless of denomination, the agenda for most of the black ministers was to preach the gospel, support benevolent causes, underwrite education, and encourage foreign missions, especially to Africa and the Caribbean islands. The ministers also became, as W. E. B. Dubois observed, the leaders of the black community. During Reconstruction, some ran for political office, accepted government appointments, and organized voters for the Republican Party. The end of Reconstruction in 1877 brought an end to the political side of such dual careers, but the leadership continued. By 1900, for example, with preachers taking the lead, the AME formed thirty-two schools and colleges, the AMEZ eight, and the CME five. In some southern counties during the 1920s, the clergy in 75 percent of the black churches, mainly Methodists and Baptists, oversaw the provision of food, clothing, and money to help members and others in the community.[22]

By the end of the twentieth century, black ministers served in 6,200 AME, 3,125 AMEZ, 3,069 CME churches, and more than 2,400 UMC congregations. The color line was beginning to crack. The MECS, for example, had accepted reunion with the MEC in 1939 only if the reunited denomination (the MC) organized its black annual conferences into a segregated Central Jurisdiction. This organization went out of existence, officially, in 1966, and gradually black and white clergy in the UMC joined the same annual conferences. In 1965, some clergy began to explore the possibility of uniting the three historic black denominations and the UMC, but the discussions have produced no mergers.

Other ethnic tensions have divided the clergy. From the early nineteenth century, when German immigrant preachers and laity formed the United Brethren in Christ (1800) and the Evangelical Association (1803), which later merged as the EUB Church (1946), linguistic and cultural differences strained the Wesleyan movement, and as other German immigrants joined the MEC, it established in 1864 separate German conferences. It had already created a separate Indian Mission Conference (1844). The early missionaries to the Indians were whites, and the few Native American preachers had to fight for their languages and traditions, but by the mid-twentieth century Native American clergy predominated as the largest group, the Oklahoma Native American Conference. Missionaries from the MECS formed a Hispanic annual conference in 1885, which in 1939 joined with others to form the Rio Grande Conference, with largely Hispanic pastors. Similar conferences emerged among Swedes (1877), Norwegians (1880), Danes (1880), and later Japanese (1940) and Chinese (1945). Eventually most of these merged into larger groups, and in 1968 the largest, the UMC, mandated that its boards and agencies have Native-American, African-American, Hispanic-American, and Asian-American representatives. Korean Americans formed a Methodist Church in Alaska in 1903, and by 1996 more than 500 Korean-American pastors served Methodist churches. Racial and ethnic tensions among Methodist clergy have by no means evaporated, but the trajectory in most of the Methodist denominations is toward greater degrees of inclusivity.

INDIVIDUAL SALVATION OR SOCIAL REFORM

Early American Methodist preachers were revivalists, intent on saving souls. They also saw themselves, however, as advocates of a doctrine of holiness with social implications, and during the Revolutionary War some of the preachers promoted a pacifist witness. Most, however, tried to avoid social and political questions, arguing that their loyalty was to a heavenly kingdom, but social conditions drew them into social activism.[23]

In 1784, the first annual conference required that members and ministers free their slaves, but reactions from southern laity compelled the conference to recommend delay despite its "deepest abhorrence" of slavery. By the 1830s, Methodist preachers fragmented into pro- and antislavery factions, and the preachers led in the formation of separate northern and southern churches in 1844. Antislavery also prompted the formation of the Wesleyan Methodist Church (1843) and the FMC (1860), though the latter division also reflected tensions about social class, holiness doctrine, the equality of ministers and lay persons, and free pews. By the end of the 1840s, a few prominent preachers in the MEC agitated to abolish slavery while a few prominent ministers in the MECS reached in favor of slavery and wrote influential biblical defenses of it. No other social issue has divided the clergy to the same extent.

By the 1840s ministers began to vote in large numbers (prior to that time many viewed voting as too "partisan"), and some worked in political campaigns or even stood for political office. One prominent preacher announced that all political questions had a connection with morality and religion. Methodist ministers involved themselves in Indian rights and were opposed to the Mexican War. They served as chaplains on both sides in the Civil War. Many promoted restrictions on immigration both before and after that war.[24]

Even more poured their social energies into the temperance and pro- hibitionist cause, though AME preachers, especially, continued their political activism during Reconstruction in the South. CME pastors, on the other hand, stood somewhat aloof from political questions, a tendency that brought conflict with AME ministers. With the ending of Reconstruction, ministers in both churches battled against alcohol, as did the preachers in other Methodist denominations. By 1908, one minister announced that the MEC was a "temperance society," and as late as 1928, Methodist preachers opposed the presidential candidacy of Alfred E. Smith, partly because he was Catholic but primarily because he wanted to revoke the Eighteenth Amendment (1918). Throughout most of the twentieth century, candidates for ordination had to take a pledge not to drink or smoke and the Methodist denominations still officially view abstinence from alcohol and tobacco as a witness to the gospel's concern for human well-being. In 1969, 70 percent of younger ministers in the UMC, and even more UMC ministers over fifty five, considered it wrong for clergy to drink alcohol, though those percentages have probably fallen.[25]

Methodist pastors, however, have had social aims beyond opposition to drinking, dancing, theater going, and card playing; most of these prohibitions disappeared gradually in the twentieth century. Although most sympathized with the managing and owning classes during the labor unrest of the late nineteenth century, other pastors proclaimed a social creed that condemned the exploitation of laboring people, especially of children. The MEC bishop Francis J. McConnell helped make the steel strike of 1914 an occasion for national reform. Nineteenth-century preachers publicized the dangers of militarism, sought justice for workers, responded to the plight of immigrants, and built "institutional churches" that provided material help and education for the poor in their neighborhoods. In the early twentieth century, many supported the Social Gospel, an effort to apply the teachings of Christ to social problems and attain a more just society.

During the Civil Rights movement, black Methodist pastors led movements from sit-ins to boycotts, and some helped form such organizations as the National Association for the Advancement of Colored People (1909) and the Southern Christian Leadership Conference (1957). The majority of black ministers were not activists, but a large minority, joined by a smaller minority of white pastors, took immense risks. During the 1950s, the majority of white preachers in the South remained silent or supported racial segregation, though a small minority of white southern pastors courageously opposed the racism of their communities. Many of them lost their pulpits, and most bishops remained silent.

In the 1980s, Methodist ministers began to disagree sharply about homosexuality; the majority determined that the church should treat gays and lesbians as people of sacred worth but opposed homosexual practice and demands for gay marriages on the grounds that homosexuality conflicted with biblical mandates. In the UMC, even "holy union" ceremonies, something short of marriage, brought church trials and expulsion from the ministry. Every other Methodist denomination prohibited clerical participation in same-sex marriage or holy union ceremonies.

The tensions between individual and social ministries altered missionary work. From the sending of Melville Cox to Liberia in 1833 to the present, Methodists pursued foreign missions. The black denominations sent large numbers to African and the Caribbean; the MEC and MECS added Asian countries to the list. The original goal was the conversion of individuals, but soon the missionaries began to concentrate also on education, medical work, and humanitarian assistance. By 2010, more than 40 percent of the missionaries in the UMC came from outside the United States, and UMC missionaries served in sixty countries. By then, they had passed leadership to indigenous pastors and laity. The mission continued its social and educational work, but after the opening of the former Soviet Bloc in the 1990s, the UMC resumed the work of church formation, seeking both social justice and individual salvation.[26]

One result of the social debates was the division of pastors, especially in the UMC, into caucuses to support African Americans, women, Hispanics, Asians, and gays and lesbians within the church. For some, the caucus, rather than the conference, became the place for sharing with like-minded colleagues. In 1969, a majority of UMC pastors thought that the ministry should try to influence the power structures of American society, and 37 percent thought that social service could offer a better opportunity than parish ministry for Christian service. Beginning in the mid-1980s, however, the term "holistic piety" – indicating a balance between social reform and individual piety – began to appear in clerical speech, and the parish came back into favor as the primary site for ministry.[27]

DECLINE

Have Methodist clergy lost authority in American society? In 1969, most UMC clergy believed that their profession carried less prestige than it did fifty years earlier. The reasons were multiple. Certain professions, like social work and psychological counseling, have assumed functions that once belonged to pastors. Certainly no Methodist clergy have the national political clout that Matthew Simpson held in the nineteenth century. They are not presidents, as they once were, of state universities, and they rarely hold the presidency of the best liberal arts colleges. Few exercise state political influence in the way that James Cannon did in Virginia in the 1920s. They lack the influence in Washington that G. Bromley Oxnam held in the 1950s. In the 1980s, the so-called Religious Right – which included relatively few Methodist pastors – attracted more public attention. When UMC bishops spoke on atomic warfare, they received less national attention than Catholic bishops speaking on the same topic.[28]

Yet as the leaders of local churches pastors still have considerable authority. Despite the theologies of lay ministry that began to appear in the 1940s, nationwide surveys show that laity still expect pastors to do most of the "ministry" in their churches and they see themselves more as passive spectators or volunteers following the lead of clerics. The decline in membership in some Methodist denominations, including some of the smaller conservative denominations, has diminished pastoral outreach, but Methodist preachers still have occasion each week to address millions of Christians from the pulpit, and despite the tensions and conflicts, the most skillful preachers and pastors make a real difference, sometimes a life-changing difference, for individuals and local communities.[29]

Notes

1   Frank Baker, "The Status of Methodist Preachers in America, 1769–1791," in *Rethinking Methodist History*, edited by Russell E. Richey and Kenneth E. Rowe (Nashville, TN: Kingswood Books, 1985), 32.

2   W. W. Sweet, *The Methodists: A Collection of Source Materials 1783–1840* (Chicago, IL: University of Chicago Press, 1946), 40.

3   Richard P. Heitzenrater, "A Critical Analysis of Ministry Studies Since 1948," in *Perspectives on American Methodism*, edited by Russell E. Richey, Kenneth E. Rowe, and Jean Miller Schmidt (Nashville, TN: Kingswood Books, 1993), 438.

4   Michelle Fugate, *Final Survey Findings*, http://www/gbhem.org (2007); Arthur C. Piepkorn, *Profiles in Belief: The Religious Bodies of the United States, Volume II, Protestant Denominations* (New York: Harper and Row, 1978), 533–625.

5   James O'Kelly, "The Author's Apology for Protesting against the Methodist Episcopal Government," in *The Methodist Experience in America: A Sourcebook*, edited by Russell E. Richey, Kenneth E. Rowe, and Jean Miller Schmidt (Nashville, TN: Abingdon Press, 2000), 113–115.

6   Heitzenrater, "Critical Analysis," in *Perspectives*, 435.

7   Nolan B. Harmon, "Deacon," in *The Encyclopedia of World Methodism*, vol. 2, edited by Nolan B. Harmon (Nashville, TN: United Methodist Publishing House, 1974), 640.

8   Heitzenrater, "Critical Analysis," in *Perspectives*, 435, 439; and Kenneth Rowe, "Deacon," in *Historical Dictionary of Methodism*, 2nd ed., edited by Charles Yrigoyen, Jr., and Susan E. Warrick (Lanham, MD: Scarecrow Press, 2005), 88.

9   E. Dale Dunlop, "The United Methodist System of Itinerant Ministry," in *Rethinking*, 14; and Russell Richey, *The Methodist Conference in America: A History* (Nashville, TN: Kingswood Books, 1996), 115.

10 Richey, *The Methodist Conference*, 86; Dunlop, "United Methodist System of Itinerant Ministry," in *Rethinking*, 13; and Heitzenrater, "Critical Analysis," in *Perspectives*, 435.

11 E. Brooks Holifield, *God's Ambassadors* (Grand Rapids, MI: Eerdmans, 2007), 13, 60, 93, 121–122, 127–128, 176–177, 262–264; and Catherine A. Brekus, "Female Evangelism in the Early Methodist Movements, 1784–1845," in *Methodism and the Shaping of American Culture*, edited by Nathan O. Hatch and John Wigger (Nashville, TN: Kingswood Books, 2001), 135–173.

12 Paul N. Garber, *The Methodist Ministry 1959* (Nashville, TN: Department of Ministerial Education of the Methodist Church, 1959) 12; John Wigger, "Fighting Bees: Methodist Itinerants and the Dynamics of Methodist Growth, 1770–1820," in *Methodism and the Shaping*, 120; and W. J. Sassnet, "The Pulpit," *Quarterly Review of the Methodist Episcopal Church, South 4* (1852), 565.

13 Peter Cartwright, *Autobiography of Peter Cartwright* (New York: Abingdon Press, 1956), 64; and Nathan Hatch, *The Democratization of American Christianity* (New Haven, CT: Yale University Press, 1989), 81–112, 133–141.

14 Cartwright, *Autobiography*, 79; *Minutes of the Annual Conferences of the Methodist Episcopal Church 1773–1828*, vol. 1 (1840), 5, 572; and Holifield, *God's Ambassadors*, 113.

15 Roger Finke and Rodney Stark, *The Churching of America 1776–1990* (Brunswick, NJ: Rutgers University Press, 1992), 146–47, 154; "An Episcopal Address," *Nashville Christian Advocate 88* (24 June 1927), 774–775; Richey, *Methodist Conference*, 12; and Edmund S. Brunner, *Church Life in the Rural South* (New York: George H. Doran, 1923), 89.

16 Garber, *Methodist Ministry 1959*, 15.

17 Garber, *Methodist Ministry*, 39; and Patricia M. Y. Chang, *Assessing the Clergy Supply in the 21st Century* (Durham, NC: Duke University Press, 2004), 8.

18 Murray H. Leffer, *Changing Expectations and Ethics in the Professional Ministry* (Evanston, IL: Garrett Theological Seminary, 1969), 146–47; and Holifield, *God's Ambassadors*, 322.

19 Stanley Hauerwas and William H. Willimon, *Resident Aliens* (Nashville, TN: Abingdon Press, 1989), 121; William H. Willimon, *The Theology and Practice of Ordained Ministry* (Nashville, TN: Abingdon Press, 2002), 14; and Jackson W. Carroll, "The Professional Model of Ministry: Is It Worth Saving?," *Theological Education 21* (1985), 7–48.

20 Cited in Richey, *The Methodist Conference*, 56.

21 Richey, *The Methodist Conference*, 56, 148.

22 Lawrence N. Jones, "The Black Churches: A New Agenda," in *African American Religious History A Documentary Witness*, edited by Milton G. Sernett (Durham, NC: Duke University Press, 1999), 580, 581; William E. Montgomery, *Under Their Own Vine and Fig Tree* (Baton Rouge, LA: Louisiana State University Press, 1993), 308, 322; W. E. B. DuBois, *The Negro Church* (Walnut Creek: Alta Mira, 1903, reprint 2003), 6; and Brunner, *Church Life*, 88.

23 Cynthia Lynn Lyerly, *Methodism and the Southern Mind, 1770–1810* (New York: Oxford University Press, 1998), 20.

24 Richard Carwardine, "Methodist Ministers and the Second Party System," in *Rethinking Methodist History*, 138; Richard J. Carwardine, "Methodists, Politics, and the Coming of the American Civil War," in *Methodism and the Shaping*, 309–342.

25 C. H. Phillips, *The History of the Colored Methodist Episcopal Church in America* (Jackson, TN: Publishing House of the C.M.E. Church, 1989), 171, 137; and Murray H. Leffer, *Changing*, 43.

26 Dana L. Robert, "Missions," in *Historical Dictionary of Methodism*, 212–213.

27 Leffer, *Changing*, 104.

28 Leffer, *Changing*, 169.

29 Holifield, *God's Ambassadors*, 272.

9 Laity

JENNIFER L. WOODRUFF TAIT

It is ironic that a movement that began as a disciplined lay religious order within the Church of England is now one of the most clerical of American churches. United Methodists are not the only modern denomination to struggle with how, and in what ways, laity should be in ministry. But the Methodist history of transformation from society to church – and failure to develop a full articulated theology of ordination in the process – continues to trouble the current church.[1] EUB and Methodist Protestant witnesses have further complicated this history, sometimes in ways that have yet to be fully digested by "United" Methodism.[2] And African Americans, both inside and outside the UMC, have found the issues of clergy and laity power strongly complicated as well by issues of racial power.[3]

Four main themes characterize the historical place of the laity in American Methodism. One is the continued agitation for, and eventual achievement of, lay representation as delegates to Annual and General Conference structures. The second is the movement of the locus of lay ministry from class meeting and circuit leadership to the benevolent and fellowship societies of the church, especially following the 1872 Methodist Episcopal Church's (MEC) decision that brought many of these societies under the control of General Conference (GC) in the name of greater centralization and professionalization. The third is the perceived tension from at least the mid-nineteenth century, seen initially in the protest and departure of the holiness movement but continuing to manifest itself in present-day caucus struggles, between what Riley Case has termed establishment/"official" and populist/"unofficial" Methodism – the latter seen as being more responsive to lay concerns.[4] And the last is the degree to which the story of women's ministry is the story of lay ministry because for many decades in most parts of the Methodist/EUB tradition it was the only avenue of ministry for women to choose.

LAY REPRESENTATION

Before the late eighteenth century, the vast majority of Methodists both in Britain and America were laity, even when they were preachers. Wesley, in contrast to some parts of the Anglican tradition, viewed preaching as a ministry open to the unordained.[5] (This fact always comes as a surprise to my students in United Methodist History, who tend to take Wesley's arguments about who was called to preach – including his approval of women in this role – as arguments about who was, or should be, ordained to sacramental administration.) Methodist laypeople brought the Methodist message to America in the 1760s and began to spread it throughout the eastern part of the continent, and ordinations only began in a regular fashion (as opposed to Strawbridge's irregular one) at the formation of the MEC in 1784.[6] This included the ordination of those who were already acknowledged leaders and preachers in the growing movement, such as Francis Asbury. It also included battles over whether African Americans seeking ordination would be granted similar rights and in what relationship they would stand to Caucasian clergy, battles that eventually produced the AME, AMEZ, and African Union churches.[7]

This dynamic produced a sense that, though ordination was necessary for the sacraments, for reasons often imperfectly grasped by American Methodists then and now, conference membership in a "missionary order of preachers" subject to deployment by the movement's leaders was the original, and in some sense primary, relationship.[8] It was only natural that, as conferences grew in size and power, those in church leadership who were not among the members of that missionary order wanted a place in the decision making. While the O'Kelly schism of 1792 and the early-nineteenth-century defection of the Reformed Methodists were largely schisms of preachers, not laity, the seeds of the protest against power being centralized in the bishop and conference is seen in those debates.[9] In the 1820s, agitation erupted further into proposals that local (non-itinerating or "located") preachers and laymen be represented in annual and general conferences, and that presiding elders (today's district superintendents) be elected by annual conferences rather than appointed by the bishop. These suggestions were rejected by the 1828 MEC GC, and in many cases those who had made them were expelled from the MEC's ministry and membership. The "union societies" of reformers who had coalesced around these ideas began to meet in general conventions and, in 1830, formed themselves into the Methodist Protestant Church (MPC), governed by a president, not a bishop; committees made pastoral appointments that were confirmed by the annual conference. Caucasian laymen were granted equal representation with itinerant preachers in the conferences of the new denomination, though local preachers and African Americans were not so lucky.[10] Laywomen began to be elected to MPC annual conferences in the 1880s and received the right to be elected as lay delegates to the GC in 1892 (this conference also included the MPC's first female *clergy* delegate, Eugenia St. John).[11] The African Unionists, a breakaway African Methodist denomination from the MEC formed in 1813 by a group of African-American laity, rejected the episcopacy along similar lines as the MPC, adopted a more congregational polity, and provided a strong role for (male) laity as governing elders of congregations, with the right to ordain clergy and license preachers.[12]

The United Brethren Church (UBC) gave a weaker voice to higher levels of the church hierarchy in its emerging polity. This polity is summarized by Russell Richey, Ken Rowe, and Jean Miller Schmidt as "term episcopacy, elective presiding elders ... appointment of preachers by committee (not by bishop), a congregational locus for ministerial identity, loosely structured and voluntary class meetings, and a general wariness about hierarchy and centralization."[13] In fact, the loose nature of UBC polity was one reason given by Asbury for not considering more seriously Otterbein's overtures toward possible merger; it also hampered overtures between the UBC and the Evangelical Association (EA).[14] There was a heavy percentage of laity among early UBC leadership. Tyron Inbody has described them as stressing "church government of the people, suspicion of the clergy, and the rights of the laity. Ultimate power lay in the hands of the people."[15] However, the UBC did not adopt the idea of lay representation in annual conferences until 1872, and in GC until 1889. The EA followed suit in its 1903 Annual Conference (AC) and again in its 1907 GC.[16] Laywomen were accepted as UBC GC delegates in 1893, the first GC after the one that had approved women's ordination. The Evangelicals never allowed laywomen representation in conferences (annual or general) throughout their history until the 1946 merger between the Evangelical Church (EC) and the UBC.[17]

By the late 1800s, the transformation from society to church made many roles obsolete such as class leaders that had previously given outlets for lay ministry in the MEC and MEC South (MECS) – a point that will be discussed further. Agitation grew once again in those denominations for lay representation:

> Methodist laity who participated actively in the commercial, political, and social life of their communities, states, and countries

chafed at their exclusion from church governance, particularly as conferences made financial decisions for which lay purses would care or addressed themselves to matters of war and policy about which laity had keen concern.[18]

Laymen were seated in both general and annual conferences of the MECS in 1870. In the MEC, petitions to this effect began in the 1850s, but were repeatedly rejected until, as opinion turned, a referendum on amending the constitution succeeded after the 1868 GC. Laymen were first seated in the MEC GC in 1872 ("Who, after all, could protest the inclusion of governors, senators, cabinet members, and leading industrialists?" note the authors of *MEA*), but they did not gain annual conference representation until the 1939 merger.[19] Not until the merger, in fact, did any branch but the MPC experience equal representation of clergy and laity in both general and annual conferences, and this was not required by the United Methodist Church's (UMC) Constitution until 1976.[20]

The fight for women's ability to be seated as lay delegates was particularly bitter in the MEC due to the championship of the opposing view by James M. Buckley, influential editor of the New York *Christian Advocate* and general foe of innovations in Methodism. Buckley protested against Frances Willard speaking at the 1880 GC despite the fact that she brought greetings on behalf of the Methodist-supported Woman's Christian Temperance Union (WCTU); he also protested in 1888 when five conferences elected women as lay delegates, and vividly led the successful fight not to seat them.[21] The right was eventually granted in 1900 and the first laywoman delegates were elected and seated in 1904.[22] The MECS was the last of the UMC's predecessor denominations to seat woman delegates (not counting the EC's refusal to consider the matter at all), which they did in 1920, following a successful advocacy campaign by Belle Harris Bennett, a leading voice in southern Methodism and the president of the Woman's Home Missionary Society (WHMS) as well as the first woman ever to address an MECS GC.[23]

LAY MINISTRY

American Methodists inherited the system of "accountable discipleship" in bands, classes, and societies from Wesley, and for some time made eager use of it in their new context.[24] Lester Ruth argues,

Early Methodists zealously dedicated time, energy, and resources to the development of structures that cultivated a unified, holy fellowship. In contrast to later forms of denominational structure, there were virtually no early Methodist programs or activities that did not relate directly to creation of community and its spiritual vitality in worship and evangelism. While traveling preachers cultivated this type of community in conference, laypeople correspondingly cultivated it in society and class meetings.[25]

Crucial to making the system work was the class leader, who not only supervised the weekly meeting, but visited and prayed with class members in their homes. Ruth notes that "an average Methodist received most of her or his spiritual direction and pastoral care from the class leader, not the ever-traveling itinerant preacher."[26] While many class leaders were men, it was also an accepted avenue for "mothers in Israel" to exercise leadership gifts. The class leader would lead out in testimony at the weekly meetings as well as examine and counsel the members about their spiritual walk.[27] Through the class meeting and its issuance of quarterly tickets, control was also exerted over who would be admitted to the love feast and Lord's Supper when these occurred, usually at the quarterly meeting when the presiding elder visited.[28] Class leadership was thus a powerful role and was held, at its best, by spiritually disciplined and mature laity exercising their pastoral gifts.[29]

Other roles encouraged upon lay men and women included prayer, exhortation, and testimony in both "closed" and public worship services; leading family worship within the home; visitation of the sick; and many other roles of public responsibility, as Karen Westerfield Tucker notes:

> Exhorters, men and women who by design did not directly interpret Scripture, held forth at prayer meetings with spiritual encouragements and admonitions. Precentors and song leaders lined out and directed congregational singing. Stewards registered marriages and baptisms, collected and arranged for the distribution of alms that had been offered for the poor at the Communion service, and provided bread and drink for the Lord's supper and the love feast.... Except for the sacraments, weddings, and funerals, any service of worship and prayer could, in principle, be led by the laity.[30]

There were also a number of licensed lay preachers, the predecessors of today's local pastors. While they did not itinerate, they were frequently used to supply circuits and preaching stations that would otherwise have been without ministerial leadership, provoking debates that still echo in the current UMC regarding their ability, or lack of same, to administer the sacraments in their pastoral charges despite their unordained status (African-American Methodists, on the other hand, have not granted this right to the unordained).[31]

While even early class leaders struggled to discipline their members,[32] the whole system began to break down by the mid-nineteenth century (though less so in African-American Methodism). David Lowes Watson attributes this to two causes. The first was the superseding of the "disciplined religiousness" of the class meeting by the "unrestrained democratic spirit of the American Revolution," which led to the class meeting becoming only one of many ways to share religious experience. The second was the "increasingly dominant role of the clergy, not only in congregations, as circuit riding gave way to stationed appointments ... but also in the wider church, as Methodism moved toward an ethos of corporate governance rather than pastoral oversight. Preaching and organization became the primary modes of pastoring, rendering class leaders and class meetings optional and ultimately marginal."[33]

In the stationed, upwardly mobile and respectably middle-class churches of the later nineteenth century – and in the benevolent societies and organizations that surrounded, assisted, and deployed the resources of these congregations – different models of lay ministry, and different roles for laity, emerged. In the more ornate and cultured worship services that developed, laity might find themselves serving as "choristers, instrumentalists, lay readers, acolytes, and ushers," as well as assisting in the distribution of the Communion elements.[34] African-American Methodists developed the role of the stewardess, who prepared the altar and the Communion elements and vessels for worship and often dressed in white to perform this role.[35] Sunday schools had been growing since the 1820s; their mission shifted as the century wore on from public education to catechesis, and increasingly to Christian nurture of both children and adults.[36] With their growth, and with the growth of missionary societies for both men and women, came a shift in emphasis:

> The vibrant Sunday Schools, Bible classes, and missionary societies had ... increasingly crowded the class meeting, absorbing some of the latter's formation and nurturing functions but not its probationary and disciplining responsibilities. The old lay offices – class leaders, stewards, and local preachers – suffered similarly, remaining official roles but seeing the local church's imagination captured by Sunday School superintendents, trustees, and missionary secretaries.[37]

Large enrollments and vast numbers of age-graded classes provided increased opportunities for teachers and helpers in the system – both men and women, though Sunday school superintendents were usually male.[38] Laity took worship roles in the Sunday school, especially in its prominent opening and closing exercises.[39] Within the African-American Methodist tradition, besides the official roles of lay leadership in worship there was often room for an unofficial but acknowledged "elder (usually, but not invariably, a senior woman) [who] regulated the spiritual temperature of the service."[40]

Local chapters of organizations for service and fellowship also arose. Women were active in the Woman's Home and Foreign Missionary Societies founded from the late 1860s through the early 1890s in all the predecessor UMC denominations, the Ladies' and Pastors' Christian Union (a group organized for benevolent work in the MEC in 1868), and the WCTU (which was not officially Methodist, but counted prominent Methodists such as Frances Willard and Annie Wittenmyer among its leaders).[41] Lay men had opportunities beginning in the 1880s to join one of many brotherhoods: the Wesley Brotherhood, the Oxford Brotherhood, the Charles Wesley Brotherhood, the St. James Brotherhood, the Methodist Club, the Methodist Men's Meeting, the Methodist Men's Mutual Aid Society, and the Brotherhood of St. Paul. Their activities have been described as "a cross between the Catholic Knights of Columbus and a Methodist men's Bible class ... with snazzy regalia, colorful badges and sashes, inspiring ritual, and snappy mottoes."[42] (Methodist men were also active in several interdenominational brotherhoods.) In 1898, the MEC brotherhoods merged into one single brotherhood, which in 1908 was made an official organization of the church. Both the UBC and the EA also founded official brotherhoods in 1909 and 1930, respectively.[43] At the same time, youth organizations arose: the Epworth League in the MEC (1889) and MECS (1890); the Young People's Alliance in the EA (1891); and the Young People's Union in the UBC (1893).[44] In all these cases laity, "no longer needing to fill in during the pastor's absence ... were increasingly organized into distinctive ministries of their own aimed at supplementing the work of the pastor."[45]

Increasingly, too, there was a trend for these societies and organizations to become centralized under the corporate governance of denominational hierarchies. In the MEC, this trend is seen most clearly in 1872, when GC decreed that the boards of the Missionary Society, the Tract Society, the Sunday School Union, and other benevolent societies loosely associated with the church's work were to be directly elected by GC.[46] (This was also the first GC of the MEC to seat laymen as delegates, and the connection was not accidental.)[47] In the early twentieth century, GC reorganized the boards it already controlled and began to assume oversight of new organizations: the Epworth League, the Brotherhoods, the new Methodist Federation for Social Service, and others. In 1912, the Laymen's Missionary Movement (LMM) – a society focused on efficient operation of denominational boards and agencies as well as on promoting benevolent giving – proposed what was called the "New Financial Plan." This consisted of unified apportioned giving from local churches, overseen and organized by yet another new board, the General Conference Commission on Finance.[48] Methodists now belonged, William King argues, "to an ecclesiastical corporation, which sought to promote church unity by means of the responsiveness of its executive agencies to the religious ideals of the whole constituency."[49] Eventually a Board of Lay Activities was formed in both MEC and MECS, and manuals were published guiding young laity as to their place in the whole scheme (and sometimes designed to be presented to them on the occasion of their joining the church).[50]

Similar organizations continued to emerge, such as the Methodist Minute Men, a missional fundraising organization drawn from the ranks of the LMM and the MEC and MECS Brotherhoods. Testimonies to the work of this organization at the 1919 Centenary Celebration of Methodist Missions, in which they played a prominent role, included such remarks as "In this largest age the world has ever seen, the laymen have come to the largest place they have ever occupied" and "The laymen were mighty powers in the early days of Methodism and we had rather slipped a cog and got out of sight and were leaving the work to the ministers and the women. It is time now that we men get back to our job and see about taking this world for Jesus Christ."[51] In later years the organization of Methodist Men (now United Methodist Men) continued this advocacy.[52]

Tension remains today over which of these conceptions of lay ministry – pastoral oversight connected to accountability structures, or supplemental distinctive ministries reporting to a denominational hierarchy – represents the best way forward, or if there is a way the two can merge. Simply calling modern small groups "class meetings" is not enough. If class leaders are going to exist again in a meaningful way, David Lowes Watson argues, "they must be given church-wide authority to complement the administrative and programmatic roles already assigned to laity in our polity.... Making it just another organizational option will not suffice."[53] There is room, also, for thinking whether the call to preach always represents a call to ordination, or whether there is room to envision a revitalized role for the "extraordinary call" of the preaching laity, perhaps through an expansion of the existing lay speaker program.[54] Jesse Lyman Hurlbut may have been overstating his case when he remarked in 1902 that "Methodism was the first organization in modern times to call for the abilities of laymen in religious work, and especially in preaching the gospel.... No layman had ever prayed in public [for a thousand years] until the Methodist revival," but he was correct in seizing on lay preaching as central to early Methodist work.[55]

LAY CONCERNS

As the nineteenth century wore on, the perception grew that Methodism was becoming a more middle-class, settled, prominent, and respectable church. In the eyes of some, this was a welcome development, proving the vitality of the Methodist message.[56] In the eyes of others, it spelled decline.[57]

Phoebe Palmer's Tuesday Meetings for the Promotion of Holiness, which began in the 1850s, were originally welcomed by many Methodists, both laity and clergy. Palmer was certainly one of the most influential lay Methodists of the nineteenth century, and the movement she birthed provided ample space for leadership and testimony by laity of both genders.[58] But tensions were evident in the 1860 defection/expulsion of the Free Methodists, who were concerned both that Methodism had lost its heart for the underprivileged and that it had lost its commitment to Wesleyan theology.[59] Postwar mainline Methodism, both MEC and MECS, grew less friendly to those who, in the words of Kirby, Richey, and Rowe, persisted in thinking that

> Methodism needed recommitment to holiness, revivalism, a rural style, and a gospel for the poor, not improvements expressive of bourgeoisification that catered to the church's social elite and its locally and nationally powerful. They experienced denominational centralization, development, the urban tilt, formalization, culture, and progress as pushing Methodism beyond the limits of genuine Wesleyanism and as abandoning the church's old landmarks.[60]

Those who identified themselves under the growing banner of the holiness movement and who organized the National Camp Meeting for the Promotion of Holiness in 1867 also grew less friendly to bourgeois Methodism.[61] Similar trends also troubled the UBC, who proposed in the 1880s a controversial change to their constitution that would allow people to join the UBC while maintaining membership in secret societies, a combination heretofore forbidden. Case notes that this tension was largely between "rural Brethren and city Brethren, and between populist Brethren and those who argued that openness to secret societies would make their church available to persons of prestige."[62]

Eventually, many who identified themselves with the holiness cause left episcopal Methodism by the early 1900s, leading to the formation of the Church of the Nazarene, the Pilgrim Holiness Church, and the Church of God (Anderson) as well as many smaller groups.[63] The UBC split in 1889 into the group that would eventually join with the Methodists and the UBC (Old Constitution), which still exists and considers itself the true heir of the United Brethren message.[64] This tension was also seen, though without the same ecclesiastical fissures, in the battles between AME bishop (after 1852) Daniel Payne and many AME laity who resented his emphases on formal education, rigorous ordination examinations, and trained choirs, and his attempts to drive excess emotionalism from AME worship.[65] Such laity argued that he, in the words of one Baltimore congregation, "kept too fine a carpet."[66]

One former holiness adherent has commented that "the Holiness movement is what the laity did when the clergy took the church from them." While it is certainly true that clergy were among those leaving and laity were among those staying, many who took leadership in these new denominations – preaching, evangelizing, organizing churches, running social service programs – were laity, and in some cases they were laity who were fed up with clergy. (One excellent example is one of the smaller and more radical bodies, the Metropolitan Holiness Association, which began life as a group of devout youth at the Western Avenue MEC in Chicago and leapt into churchhood, and out of bourgeois Methodism, under the leadership of class leader Edwin Harvey.)[67] Much holiness (and later Pentecostal) leadership, in fact, was exercised by lay women – some who could not achieve credentialing from their denominations, some who did not seek it, and some who (like Alma White, Lela McConnell, and Aimee Semple McPherson) created their own ecclesiastical organizations to gain it.[68]

But not everyone who was sympathetic with holiness aims, whether clergy or laity, ended up leaving the MEC and MECS. And suspicions about the direction Methodism was going remained among those who stayed. On the one hand there was what Case has described as

> establishment Methodism ... the Methodism of tall steeples, rented pews, robed choirs, General Conferences, denominational journals, colleges, and bishops. It was Methodism becoming institutionalized,

with authority focusing more and more in bishops, presiding elders, conferences, and (later) committees and agencies ... one best filtered and controlled by those with education and experience.[69]

On the other hand Case places a "populist" strand of

log cabins, moral crusades, circuit preachers, revivals, camp meetings, prayer bands, and indigenous Methodist gospel music ... an 'unmediated' Christianity, one not needing to be filtered by educated clergy or annual conferences.... Its authority derived not from the *Book of Discipline* or the blessing of bishops, but from the anointing of the Spirit and appeal to the power of primitive Methodism.[70]

One can argue – and many have – whether Case's characterization is entirely fair. It stands in a long tradition of Methodist "croaking" dating back at least as far as Peter Cartwright.[71] What is undeniably true is that Case's paradigm remains a powerful explanatory one in the minds of many modern United Methodist laity. As Thomas Frank puts it: "The national body is the 'They' or 'Them' of 'bloated bureaucracy' that has lost touch with 'Us' – 'the silent majority.'"[72] Case himself, who is ordained, uses the paradigm to interpret the rise of the twentieth-century Good News evangelical caucus. While Good News has considerable clergy involvement, it has positioned itself as a champion of lay rights and lay beliefs over against the institutional hierarchy, and works through a magazine edited and written in great part by laity.[73] Other renewal movements which sprang up in the post-1960s UMC, including Aldersgate Renewal Ministries, the Lay Witness Mission, and the Walk to Emmaus, often foregrounded lay testimony and made explicit space for lay leadership, sometimes explicitly as a critique of clergy influence but more often as an implicit desire to empower modern United Methodists with some of what tradition had granted them in the beginning.[74]

Others have rooted the tension between establishment and populist segments of the church in the more congregational, decentralized, and democratic nature of UBC polity: "The local church [for Asbury] was an expression of the conference, whereas Otterbein began with the local congregation and built up from there."[75] William Abraham explicitly contrasts the way in which EUB's formed and appropriated their doctrines in the context of their ecclesiology with the way in which he thinks Albert Outler and other architects of post-1968 United Methodism were "deeply alienated from the corporate faith of their communities."[76] The growing tendency in modern UMC polity is to focus on the local congregation as opposed to the annual conference, a trend troubling to many from the Methodist side, which is directly traceable to EUB influence.[77] Because the EUB was, on the whole, more theologically conservative than the Methodist Church, these two lay-emphasizing strands of DNA – UBC and Holiness – may in fact be mutually and subconsciously reinforcing each other in the modern UMC.

LAY WOMEN

For some generations following the establishment of both the Methodist and EUB strands of the tradition, ordained ministry was not a vocation open to women called to leadership. The MPC and the UBC were the forerunners in this. Although the process was not without hiccups, the MPC ordained Anna Howard Shaw in 1880 and authorized women's ordination on a more general basis in 1892. The UBC authorized ordinations and ordained Ella Niswonger – who was also the first graduate of the denomination's seminary, Union Biblical Seminary (now United) – in 1889. (Both branches of the UBC continued to ordain women after the 1889 split.)[78] The MEC approved local ordinations in the 1920s, but it was not until 1956 that women were allowed to become members of the MC annual conference with pension and appointment rights – a restoration for MPC women ministers in the denomination, who had possessed full membership in conference until the 1939 merger.[79] UBC women, who had lost the official right to ordination in their 1946 merger with the EA –though annual conferences in fact continued to ordain them – gained full clergy rights in the 1968 merger with the MC.[80] Among African-American Methodists, the AMEZ was first in its ordination of Julia Foote as deacon (1894) and elder (1900); women in the AME were not ordained until 1948 and in the CME in 1954.[81]

Some women pursued local preachers' licenses, and in some cases these were granted, although the MEC was later to retract the privilege – Maggie Newton van Cott and Anna Oliver (who later failed in her bid for ordination) were among the most prominent examples in the MEC.[82] The first formal UBC license was considered to be that given to Lydia Sexton in 1851, and Paul Chilcote comments "even after the 1857 GC action that prohibited such licenses for women, the requisite annual renewals seem to have been easy for her to obtain."[83] Sexton later became a prison chaplain.[84] Union Biblical Seminary admitted women beginning in 1875, and this action began to create a "circle of educated women who could move fluidly into leadership roles" in the UBC, whether they sought credentialing or not.[85] Credentialing was also sought by African-American Methodist women; Jarena Lee and Amanda

Smith were among the most famous, but large numbers of women in these traditions continued to preach and exhort throughout the nineteenth century despite repeated denials by their General Conferences of petitions for licensing and ordination.[86] The AME granted exhorter's licenses in 1884, forty years after the first petition on the issue (though they forbade licensed women from taking pastorates).[87]

In the 1880s within the MEC another avenue for women's ministry arose, spearheaded by the work of Lucy Rider Myer, who founded a training school for women in Chicago in 1885 that soon became the Chicago Deaconess Home.[88] Myer's early deaconess work focused on assisting the immigrant poor of Chicago. In 1888, the MEC GC explicitly endorsed her work and described the duties of deaconesses as "to minister to the poor, visit the sick, pray with the dying, care for the orphan, seek the wandering, comfort the sorrowing, save the sinning, and, relinquishing wholly all other pursuits, devote themselves in a general way to such forms of Christian labor as may be suited to their abilities."[89]

Deaconesses were laywomen, but they were consecrated for their role in a service drawn from the early church worship order called the "Apostolic Constitutions."[90] Women called to this life could pursue a vocation as a nurse deaconess or a missionary deaconess. They wore distinctive uniforms, took no salaries, and generally lived in sisterhoods in deaconess homes where they received room and board and a monthly allowance.[91] (This led to accusations of them being "Protestant nuns," although their defenders pointed out that they "took no vows and were free to leave the work at any time).[92] If they worked in a church setting they "had liberty to conduct worship, especially with children and youth, or to hold prayer meetings. Those who were trained musicians prepared choirs for the sanctuary."[93] In addition, if they obtained a license to preach (after 1920 when these began to be granted again in the MEC) they could work as a "pastor deaconess," which was "virtually a local church pastor usually in the mission field."[94] The movement's leadership grew increasingly (if controversially) sympathetic with the claims of the Social Gospel and four deaconesses were charter members of the Methodist Federation for Social Service (MFSS) at its founding in 1908.[95] Deaconess work was launched in the UBC (1897), MECS (1902), EA (1903), and MPC (1908), and adopted by African-American denominations as well – though the AME was careful to circumscribe the role as subservient to male supervision and approval.[96] It remains an avenue for lay female ministry in today's UMC, and in 2004, the office of Home Missioner was added to give a corresponding role to lay men who felt a similar call.⁹⁷ The UMC also experimented with a lay diaconate for both genders from 1976–1996, which was meant to affirm a calling to full-time ministries of service in various specialized roles including music ministry, youth and children's ministry, and business administration.⁹⁸

Despite the prominence of the struggles for lay representation, licensing, and ordination, and despite the social and intellectual leadership of deaconesses, one of the most common avenues of ministry for lay women in the late nineteenth century was involvement in one of the home or foreign missionary societies that had recently arisen. MEC women founded a foreign missionary society in 1869 and a home missionary society in 1880; corresponding dates for the MECS were 1878/1886 and the MPC 1879/1893. The UBC in 1875 and the EA in 1893 each founded one society that began as a foreign missionary society and later expanded its work to include home missions.⁹⁹ In each case these societies published periodicals, which reached into churches all over the connection, and supported single female missionaries around the globe. Their leaders "traveled, spoke, corresponded, promoted, and wrote for the magazine" as well as established networks of local chapters that fostered women's involvement and leadership skills across the denomination. Often these leaders were prominent among those elected as lay delegates to conferences when this right was granted.¹⁰⁰ They also fought on a fairly regular basis with the men's missionary boards that wanted tighter control of the women's activities and (especially) their money.¹⁰¹ This was particularly evident in the EA, where the Women's Missionary Society worked in a dependent relationship to the Board of Missions.¹⁰² In the AME, the women who achieved high status in the denominational missionary societies were often the wives of bishops or (in local chapters) of clergymen.¹⁰³

In 1921, the MEC founded an auxiliary organization to the Women's Foreign Missionary Society and Woman's Home Missionary Society for working women. This was the Wesleyan Service Guild, which was a "self-conscious and intentional effort on a large scale to meet the needs of business and professional women," including the scheduling of evening meetings.¹⁰⁴ While the other Methodist denominations did not found similar groups, upon merger in 1939 the WFMS and WHMS of the three predecessor groups merged into one organization – the Woman's Division of Christian Service, working under the auspices of the Board of Missions but with a great deal of autonomy – and the Wesleyan Service Guild was retained as an auxiliary.¹⁰⁵ All these groups were particularly active in struggles for racial reconciliation and the ending of racist laws and structures in society and in the MC's own segregated Central

Jurisdiction; in this endeavor they also cooperated with women from the African-American Methodist denominations.[106] During this time – especially after a 1964 decision that transferred missionary supervision to other parts of the Board of Missions – the emphasis changed from one of missionary support to one of fellowship, spiritual development, and education about the mission work of the MC.[107]

The 1968 merger with the EUB (which had similar missions organizations but no working women's auxiliary) did not immediately change this structure, but in 1972 when the Board of Missions became the Board of Global Ministries the Women's Division decided to end the separation of employed women and homemakers and created one organization, the United Methodist Women (UMW).[108] While the vast majority of local UMW members, at least in smaller and more rural churches, tend to be conservative, concerns on the part of laywomen involved with Good News about the perceived liberalism of the Women's Division hierarchy and its published resources, as well as the feminist bent of the UMC's Commission on the Status and Role of Women (founded in 1972), led to the establishment by Good News of an alternative women's organization, RENEW.[109]

The appeal of the UMW as an avenue of ministry for laywomen today seems to be shrinking. This may be because other avenues of ministry for United Methodist women, including the ordained ministry, have grown, and because society as a whole holds more possibilities out to women, however contested, for spiritual and vocational fulfillment. The elimination of a separate group for working women, while well-meant, may have decreased the attractiveness of the group to professional women (it certainly seems, anecdotally, to have decreased the number of evening and weekend meetings). Nevertheless – as I have known intuitively ever since I served a church where the UMW leadership refused to give the senior pastor the keys to the church's silver cabinet – it remains an important avenue for many lay women to exercise power alongside of, and in opposition to, the ordained hierarchy of the church.

CONCLUSION

In a recent book, Thomas Edward Frank argues that Methodism in the twentieth century is returning to its roots as a lay movement in four major ways. Laity "have the majority role in the oversight of the connection" due to their considerable presence in general agencies and annual conference staffs, program units, and committees, including "oversight roles once designated or assumed for bishops"; laity "have a growing role in assessing candidates for ordained ministry" due to their presence on AC Boards of Ordained Ministry; laity "serve as pastors" as either full-time or part-time local preachers; and due to the large number of retired clergy who do not attend conference regularly, laity "dominate annual conferences" in both oversight and educational roles.[110] Laity have, Frank maintains,

> campaigned for these expanded political rights for generations, com-plaining vigorously about a clergy-dominated church.... The next step, coming soon, will be full constitutional voting and delegate rights for all clergy members whether or not they are ordained. Or alternatively, some will propose that all pastors be ordained elders under norms of professional education and formation considerably less than currently expected.[111]

Either way, he thinks, the covenant fellowship of itinerant elders is in trouble.

Methodism, despite being tightly controlled at the top by an ordained Anglican priest, certainly began as a lay movement. From the moment it became a church, tensions between those in the itinerant covenant and the large numbers who make the wheels of Methodism turn as laity on the outside of that covenant have not abated. Proposals before the 2012 GC indicated that the tensions will continue, and that they may someday be resolved in some of the ways Frank fears. Two questions remain for the modern UMC: Is he right about the coming apocalypse? And is he right to fear it?

Notes

1   William Lawrence, "Has Our Theology of Ordained Ministry Changed?" in *Questions for the Twenty-First Century Church*, edited by Russell Richey, William Lawrence, and Dennis Campbell (Nashville, TN: Abingdon Press, 1999), 151–167; and Richard P. Heitzenrater, "A Critical Analysis of the Ministry Studies Since 1948," in *Perspectives on American Methodism*, edited by Russell Richey, Kenneth Rowe, and Jean Miller Schmidt (Nashville, TN: Kingswood Books, 1993), 431–447.

2   Lawrence, "Theology," 157–159; *Methodist and Pietist*, edited by J. Steven O'Malley and Jason E. Vickers (Nashville, TN: Kingswood Books, 2011), especially James E. Kirby, "Episcopacy and Ordination," 139–148.

3   In what follows I use the actual term "African-American Methodists" to refer to the historically black Methodist denominations (AME, AMEZ, CME, African Union) unless otherwise stated.

4   Riley Case, *Evangelical and Methodist* (Nashville, TN: Abingdon Press, 2004), 13–23.

5   Thomas Edward Frank, "What Is the Common Discipline for Local Churches?" in *Questions for the Twenty-First Century Church*, 222–225.

6   Russell Richey, Kenneth Rowe, and Jean Miller Schmidt, *The Methodist Experience in America* (Nashville, TN: Abingdon Press, 2010), 9–52. Hereafter *MEA*.

7   Will Gravely, "African Methodisms and the Rise of Black Denomination-alism," in *Perspectives*, 108–126; Doris Andrews, "The African Methodists of Philadelphia, 1794–1802," in *Perspectives*, 145–155.

8   I owe the term to Frank, *Questions for the Twenty-First Century Church*, 224.

9   *MEA*, 68–71, 142–143.

10 *MEA*, 164–174; and Jean Miller Schmidt, *Grace Sufficient: A History of Women in American Methodism 1760–1939* (Nashville, TN: Abingdon Press, 1999), 224.

11 *MEA*, 281–282.

12 Grant Shockley, *Heritage and Hope: The African-American Presence in United Methodism* (Nashville, TN: Abingdon Press, 1991), 32; Gravely, 121.

13 *MEA*, 146.

14 Scott Kisker, "Martin Boehm, Philip William Otterbein, and the UBC," in *Methodist and Pietist*, 31–36; and Tyron Inbody, "Doctrine and Theology in the Church of the UBC," in *Methodist and Pietist*, 85–87.

15 Inbody, "Doctrine and Theology," 85.

16 *MEA*, 229.

17 *MEA*, 282–283; Schmidt, *Grace Sufficient*, 231.

18 *MEA*, 225–226.

19 *MEA*, 226–229, 383–384.

20 *MEA*, 384; Thomas Edward Frank, *Polity, Practice, and the Mission of the UMC, Revised Edition* (Nashville, TN: Abingdon Press, 2006), 219.

21 *MEA*, 278–281, Schmidt, *Grace Sufficient*, 213–214, 219–221.

22 *MEA*, 282.

23 *MEA*, 282–283.

24 For the best description of the system and its implications see David Lowes Watson, *The Early Methodist Class Meeting* (Nashville, TN: Discipleship Resources, 1985), 93–145.

25 Lester Ruth, *Early Methodist Life and Spirituality* (Nashville, TN: Kingswood Books, 2005), 258–259.

26 Ruth, *Early Methodist Life*, 258–259.

27 Ruth, *Early Methodist Life*, 259–260.

28 Karen Westerfield Tucker, *American Methodist Worship* (New York: Oxford University Press, 2001), 61, 63, 71–73, 144–145; and Ruth, *Early Methodist Life*, 277.

29 Examples abound in Ruth, *Early Methodist Life*, 266–285.

30 Westerfield Tucker, *American Methodist Worship*, 224–238, 262–263.

31 Westerfield Tucker, *American Methodist Workshop*, 264–267.

32 Ruth, *Early Methodist Life*, 275–285.

33 David Lowes Watson, "Class Leaders and Class Meetings: Recovering a Methodist Tradition for a Changing Church," *Doctrines and Discipline* (1999), 254.

34 Westerfield Tucker, *American Methodist Worship*, 263.
35 Westerfield Tucker, *American Methodist Worship*, 263.
36 *MEA*, 119–123, 248–251.
37 *MEA*, 248–249; Westerfield Tucker, *American Methodist Worship*, 26.
38 *MEA*, 250.
39 *MEA*, 250; Westerfield Tucker, *American Methodist Workshop*, 26–29.
40 Kenneth Cracknell and Susan White, *An Introduction to World Methodism* (Cambridge: Cambridge University Press, 2005), 201.
41 *MEA* 234–241; Schmidt, *Grace Sufficient*, 152–158.
42 *MEA*, 284.
43 *MEA*, 284–285.
44 *MEA*, 285.
45 *MEA*, 285.
46 William McGuire King, "Denominational Modernization and Religious Identity: The Case of the MEC," in *Perspectives*, 344–345.
47 King, "Case of the MEC," 349.
48 King, "Case of the MEC," 351–352.
49 King, "Case of the MEC," 353.
50 Two good examples: Jesse Lyman Hurlbut, *Our Church: What Methodists Believe, and How They Work* (New York: Eaton and Mains, 1902); and Charles Selecman, *The Methodist Primer* (Nashville, TN: Tidings, 1955). For the Board of Lay Activities, see *Manual of Lay Activities* (1922); and *Methodist Primer*, 67.
51 Speeches by J. H. Martin and Francis Baldwin, "Layman's and Minute Men's Rally, July 4, 1919," 1117, 1131. Special Collections, United Methodist Commission on Archives and History, Drew University, Madison, NJ. Cited by Christopher Anderson, "The Methodist Minute Man: Early 20th Century Expression of American Manhood," unpublished paper delivered to the American Society of Church History, January 2012.
52 *Methodist Primer*, 67; http://www.gcumm.org/ (accessed February 16, 2012).
53 Watson, "Class Leaders," 259. See also Watson, *The Early Methodist Class Meeting*, 148–152.
54 Watson, "Class Leaders," 261–262.
55 Hurlbut, *Our Church*, 132.
56 *MEA*, 113–114.
57 A. Gregory Schneider, "Connectionalism Versus Holiness: Contrasting Bases of Identity for Leaders of Late-Nineteenth-Century Methodism," in *Doctrines and Discipline* (UMAC 3), edited by Dennis Campbell, William Lawrence, and Russell Richey (Nashville, TN: Abingdon Press, 1999), 131–157; Melvin Dieter, *The Holiness Revival of the Nineteenth Century* (Lanham, MD: Scarecrow Press, 1996), 79–128, 171–233; *MEA*, 223–224.
58 *MEA*, 128–133; Dieter, *Holiness Revival*, 13–77.
59 Dieter, *Holiness Revival*, 45–46; Case, *Evangelical and Methodist*, 16.
60 *MEA*, 223.
61 *MEA*, 224; Dieter, *Holiness Revival*, 81–115.
62 Case, *Evangelical and Methodist*, 17.
63 Dieter, *Holiness Revival*, 255–265.

64 Case, *Evangelical and Methodist*, 17; http://ub.org/about/history/ (accessed February 16, 2012).

65 James Campbell, *Songs of Zion: The AME Church in the United States and South Africa* (Chapel Hill, NC: The University of North Carolina Press, 1998), 37–43.

66 Campbell, *Songs of Zion*, 43.

67 William Kostlevy, *Holy Jumpers: Evangelicals and Radicals in Progressive Era America* (New York: Oxford University Press, 2010), 41–53; and Schneider, "Connectionalism Versus Holiness," 150–152.

68 Susie Stanley, *Holy Boldness: Women Preachers' Autobiographies* (Knoxville, TN: University of Tennessee Press, 2002); and Edith Blumhofer, *Aimee Semple McPherson: Everybody's Sister* (Grand Rapids, MI: Eerdmans, 1993).

69 Case, *Evangelical and Methodist*, 14.

70 Case, *Evangelical and Methodist*, 14.

71 *MEA*, 139–140; Jennifer L. Woodruff Tait, "'Everything Arose Just as the Occasion Offered:' Defining Methodist Identity through the History of Methodist Polity," in *American Denominational History*, edited by Keith Harper (Tuscaloosa, AL: University of Alabama Press, 2008), 98–99.

72 Frank, *Polity* (revised ed.), 135.

73 Case, *Evangelical and Methodist*, 269–288; *MEA* 502–507, 515–516; http://goodnewsmag.org/about/, http://goodnewsmag.org/support-good-news/, http://goodnewsmag.org/category/magazine/jan-feb-2012-magazine/ (accessed February 16, 2012).

74 *MEA*, 506; and *Any Old Bush Will Do: An Account of the Methodist Lay Witness Mission Movement*, edited by Carolyn Lawrence (Lima, OH: Express Press 2003).

75 Inbody, "Doctrine and Theology," 89.

76 William Abraham, "The EUB Tradition and the Future of United Methodism," in *Methodist and Pietist*, 221–222.

77 Inbody, 9; Russell Richey, "Are the Local Church and Denominational Bureaucracy Twins?" in *UMAC 4*, 232–241; Thomas Edward Frank, "What Is the Common Discipline for Local Churches?" in *UMAC 4*, 29–220; Frank, *Polity* (revised ed.), 131–138, 173–179.

78 *MEA*, 245; Paul Chilcote, "Women in the Pietist Heritage of Methodism," in *Methodist and Pietist*, 195–196.

79 Schmidt, *Grace Sufficient*, 281.

80 *MEA*, 348, 402; Chilcote, "Women in the Pietist Heritage," 196; Schmidt, 284.

81 Barbara Brown Zikmund, "The Ordination Movement," in *Encyclopedia of Women and Religion in North America, Vol. II* (Bloomington, IN: Indiana University Press, 2006), 946.

82 *MEA*, 242–244; Schmidt, *Grace Sufficient*, 181–185, 192.

83 Chilcote, "Women in the Pietist Heritage," 194; Schmidt, *Grace Sufficient*, 109–111.

84 Schmidt, *Grace Sufficient*, 111.

85 Chilcote, "Women in the Pietist Heritage," 194.

86 Schmidt, *Grace Sufficient*, 103–104, 144–147; Campbell, *Songs of Zion*, 48–51.

87 Schmidt, *Grace Sufficient*, 332; Campbell, *Songs of Zion*, 52; Nellie McKay, "Nineteenth Century Black Women's Spiritual Autobiographies: Religious Faith and Self-Empowerment," *Perspectives*, 178–191; William Andrews, ed., *Sisters of the Spirit: Three Black Women's Autobiographies of the Nineteenth Century* (Bloomington, IN: Indiana University Press, 1986).

88 Schmidt, *Grace Sufficient*, 197–199.

89 Schmidt, *Grace Sufficient*, 200–201.

90 Westerfield Tucker, *American Methodist Worship*, 268.

91 Schmidt, *Grace Sufficient*, 203–204.

92 Schmidt, *Grace Sufficient*, 210–211.

93 Westerfield Tucker, *American Methodist Worship*, 268.

94 Westerfield Tucker, *American Methodist Worship*, 268.

95 Schmidt, *Grace Sufficient*, 208.

96 Schmidt, *Grace Sufficient*, 208–209; Chilcote, "Women in the Pietist Heritage," 201; Westerfield Tucker, *American Methodist Worship*, 236, 268; Campbell, *Songs of Zion*, 52–53.

97 http://new.gbgm-umc.org/about/us/mp/deaconess-homemissioner/ (accessed February 16, 2012).

98 Thomas Edward Frank, *Polity, Practice, and the Mission of the UMC* (Nashville, TN: Abingdon Press, 1997), 180–182 (cited from the older edition of Frank due to the elimination of this office in 1996); Westerfield Tucker, *American Methodist Workshop*, 269; Lawrence, "Has Our Theology of Ordained Ministry Changed?" 151–155.

99 *MEA*, 236; Chilcote, "Women in the Pietist Heritage," 197–202; Schmidt, *Grace Sufficient*, 158–174.

100 *MEA*, 238; Schmidt, *Grace Sufficient*, 163–164, 174–178.

101 *MEA*, 237–240.

102 *MEA*, 239; Chilcote, "Women in the Pietist Heritage," 199–200.

103 Campbell, *Songs of Zion*, 94–95.

104 Schmidt, *Grace Sufficient*, 270.

105 Schmidt, *Grace Sufficient*, 270–272, 284–286.

106 Schmidt, *Grace Sufficient*, 275–280, 287–290; Alice Knotts, *Fellowship of Love: Methodist Women Changing American Racial Attitudes, 1920–1968* (Nashville, TN: Kingswood Books, 1996); Task Group on the History of the Central Jurisdiction Women's Organization, *To a Higher Glory: The Growth and Development of Black Women Organized for Mission in the Methodist Church 1940–1968* (1980).

107 Schmidt, *Grace Sufficient*, 290–291.

108 Schmidt, *Grace Sufficient*, 291–292; *MEA* 462–467.

109 *MEA*, 466–467; 504; http://www.renewnetwork.org/ (accessed February 16, 2012).

110 Thomas Edward Frank, "Minutes of Several Conversations Between Russell E. Richey and Thomas Edward Frank, as Recorded in an Imaginary Exchange of Letters," in *The Renewal of United Methodism: Mission, Ministry, and Connectionalism: Essays in Honor of Russell E. Richey*, edited by Rex Matthews(Nashville, TN: General Board of Higher Education and Ministry, 2012), 162–163.

111 Frank, "Minutes," 164. See also Frank, *Polity*, revised ed., 219–220.

10 Asceticism

MAURA JANE FARRELLY

At 6:30 on a cold Sunday morning in November 1989, Mike Sawyer, a
Master of Divinity student at Asbury Theological Seminary in Wilmore,
Kentucky, set out to walk the twelve miles that lay between the room he
shared with his wife and two sons and the church he had been assigned
to serve in the Bowling Green District of the United Methodist Church.
Sawyer had made the journey many times before, and he had found the
solitude that he usually encountered on the walk to be an ideal opportunity to "try to listen to God." Sawyer did not expect to be able to
listen to God on this particular Sunday morning, however. He had left
his home carrying a sign that bore the title of the sermon he planned
to deliver at his church later that day, and the young Methodist minister fully expected that his message would not be popular with the people he passed on his peregrination through the rolling hills of central
Kentucky.

Sawyer's message was that "Tobacco Kills." The first person he
encountered was a young woman who made her opinion known to him
by raising her arm as she drove by in her truck and gesturing confidently
with the middle finger on her left hand. The second person did not pass
Sawyer until he was nearly six miles into his journey; that individual
drove by the young preacher without incident, but then turned around
about a quarter of a mile down the road and proceeded to charge after
him at a high rate of speed. "Are you sure about that?" the beefy driver
reportedly yelled, as Mike Sawyer threw himself into a ditch, avoiding the front grill of his interlocutor's 4 x 4 by the smallest of margins. "Yes," the earnest divinity student shouted back. "It killed my dad
when I was eleven!"

The reception Sawyer received at his church after he preached his
sermon was less aggressive, but no less angry. He had chosen to focus on
a passage from the Book of James: *Behold the farmer waiteth patiently
for the precious fruit of the earth.* "Are *you* waiting patiently for a precious fruit?" Sawyer asked his congregants. "Or are you wasting this

precious soil that God gave you to plant a killer, instead of a life food for the body to live on?" It was a rhetorical question that Methodists in Hart County, Kentucky, had absolutely no interest in pondering. Rather than consider the Christian merits of planting corn and wheat instead of tobacco, Mike Sawyer's congregants elected to remove him from his post six days after he delivered his sermon.

"You must realize that tobacco pays your salary," one of his congregants reportedly told Sawyer in an attempt to explain the decision to fire him. "Tobacco is not as harmful as riding in a vehicle," another insisted, while a third informed him that "everyone is stopping by my business, upset at your sermon." It was that third point that had proven to be the most salient factor in the congregation's decision to look for another minister. Mike Sawyer's message was offensive – and as such, it could not be tolerated.

Sawyer says the superintendent in charge of the Bowling Green District told him he should have waited at least three years before criticizing the livelihood of the Methodists he served. That way, Sawyer's congregants would have had time to get to know him and – presumably – be less offended by his naïve enthusiasm.[1] Two and a half centuries earlier, Methodism had begun in England and North America with exuberant itinerates who stood outside taverns and accused the owners of "murder[ing] His Majesty's subjects wholesale" when they sold "drams or spirituous liquors" to "sheep" who had "sunken lower than the majority of beasts that are destined to perish," by consuming alcohol.[2] The faith of John and Charles Wesley had come a long way, however, since the days when Methodists believed they were obliged to be offensive in defense of asceticism.

It is tempting to dismiss this incident as merely being about economics. In 1989, after all – fifteen years before Congress finally voted to remove federal price supports for tobacco – nearly 70 percent of the farmers in Kentucky were growing the "stinking weed," and tobacco, alone, was responsible for more than 40 percent of the state's overall crop values. Hay – the second-largest commodity – accounted for just 20 percent of the crop values in the so-called Bluegrass State, making Kentucky more dependent by far on tobacco revenue than any other state in the country.[3]

But although economics were certainly at play in Hart County when Mike Sawyer was informed that he would no longer be pastoring to Methodists there, the fact remains that until recently, Methodists have had a somewhat inconsistent relationship with tobacco. Liquor, dancing, jewelry, gambling, theater going, horse racing, cock fighting, and card playing were all solid components of Methodist asceticism from the very beginning; early Methodists shunned these "wordly amusements" as diversions that distracted the faithful from the path that Jesus had laid out for them and made it impossible for individuals to attain the kind of self-mastery that the followers of John and Charles Wesley believed was essential to any communion with Christ.[4] Tobacco, however, was for many years unproblematic for Methodists – and even when some church leaders in the mid-nineteenth century did begin to identify smoking and chewing as troublesome habits, most conferences were still unmoved to formally condemn the plant.

The fact that tobacco defined the economic and social relations in many of the colonies and states where Methodism first took root does not, in and of itself, explain the hesitancy of early Methodists to incorporate tobacco usage into their understanding of asceticism. After all, when they avoided theaters and taverns – and exhorted their neighbors to do the same – early Methodists defiantly set themselves apart from the culture that dominated the region where they first took root in North America. Although Methodism would not remain a southern phenomenon for long, its origins in the territory that would one day become the United States were solidly southern – as were many of the amusements that Methodists stood so staunchly against. South Carolina Congressman William J. Grayson emphasized this fact when he fondly recalled the "deep drinking, hard swearing and practical joking" that the Revolutionary War veterans he knew in his childhood were "addicted to." Anyone who suggested that the men were not "model gentlemen" because of their behavior was sorely mistaken. Indeed, Grayson insisted that the vets were the very embodiment of the southern value system, because drinking and swearing – even when they occurred on the Sabbath – were "not incompatible with the character of a man of honour."[5]

In contrast, Methodists insisted that even seemingly "innocent, elevated, and healthy" amusements like dancing were "impure and heathenish" and "incompatible with the purity and refinements of civilized Christian society."[6] In 1829, Stith Mead, a native of Virginia who was brought to Methodism through his friendship with Francis Asbury, recalled with a mixture of embarrassment and condemnation that his Anglican father had made him learn the arts of *Dancing and Fencing.* In a book that he published for all the world to see, Mead insisted that his father had to "call for the rod of correction, before I would move in a dancing attitude," as if to assure his readers that he had been a Methodist in his heart, long before he had been exposed to the words

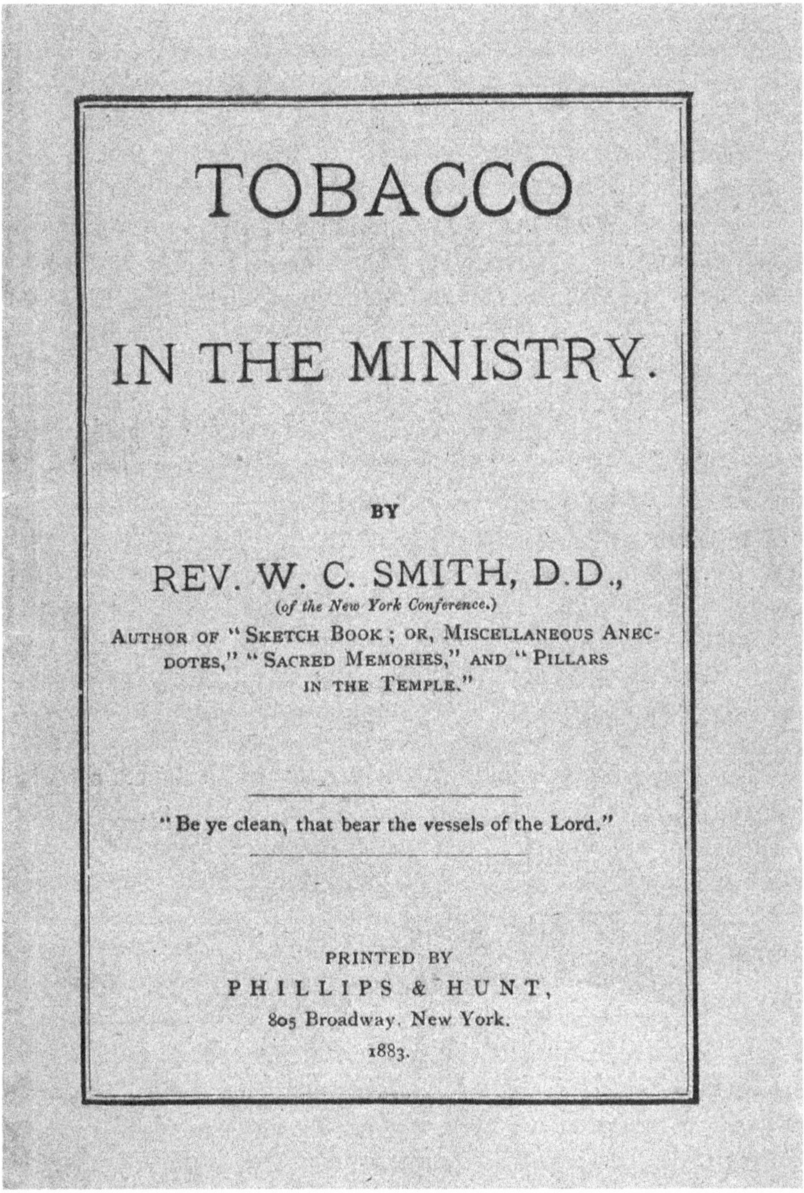

TOBACCO

IN THE MINISTRY.

BY

REV. W. C. SMITH, D.D.,

(of the New York Conference.)

AUTHOR OF "SKETCH BOOK; OR, MISCELLANEOUS ANEC-
DOTES," "SACRED MEMORIES," AND "PILLARS
IN THE TEMPLE."

"Be ye clean, that bear the vessels of the Lord."

PRINTED BY

PHILLIPS & HUNT,

805 Broadway. New York.

1883.

Figure 8. **Cover from anti-tobacco pamphlet (1883)**, Methodist Library Pamphlet Collection, Drew University, Madison, New Jersey.

and ideas of John Wesley. No doubt Mead's father, William – a prominent Episcopal vestryman and Revolutionary War veteran who, like the
vets William Grayson recalled, probably engaged in quite a variety of
worldly amusements – was none too pleased to learn that his son was
judging him in such a public forum.[7]

But if their judgmental words alienated people, then that was just
one more roadblock that Satan had set up for early Methodists in their
efforts to bring their friends and neighbors to Christ. "Be not conformed
to either the wisdom ... or the fashions of 'the age,'" John Wesley warned
his follows in 1786. "You are called to show by the whole tenor of your
life and conversion that you are 'renewed in the sprit of your mind.'"[8]
It was not an easy challenge for anyone to meet, and in 1790, when he
came upon a tavern in eastern Tennessee after traveling for days with
a "nervous headache" an "inflammation of the throat," and an "unset-
tled stomach" that reminded him of the illness that had "terminated
the life of my grandfather," even the great Methodist itinerant Francis
Asbury was tempted to spend the night. But he knew that the innkeeper
earned £300 a year by distilling whiskey, and so Asbury continued on
to Virginia.[9]

Methodists could not pretend that liquor, gambling, dancing, and
ostentatious dress were not sinful amusements capable of "disgusting
people against their proper employments." To do so would be to abandon their obligations to God and consign their neighbors to a "gilded
and flowery way to ruin."[10] Methodists *had* to judge their friends, family, and neighbors when it came to worldly amusements, and if the price
for that judgment was ridicule – or sometimes even death threats, as the
reverend Freeborn Garrettson discovered in the 1780s when an angry
woman showed up at his camp meeting, prepared to shoot him with not
just one, but two pistols – then so be it.[11]

Smoking and chewing were different, though. Granted, few Methodist
preachers ever formally advocated the use of tobacco (unless one considers modeling a habit to be an actual endorsement of it), and beginning
in the 1840s, some Methodists did rail against tobacco usage, calling it a
"filthy lust of the flesh" that defiled the body – an "exquisitely wrought
machine," according to John Wesley – and violated the divine order to
keep God's temple clean.[12] "Free" and "Wesleyan" Methodists, as participants in the holiness movement that took off in the mid-nineteenth
century and emphasized the possibility of "Christian perfection," were
particularly ardent opponents of the use of tobacco.[13] But not until 1920
did the Methodist Episcopal Church – the largest group of Methodists
in the United States at the time – finally incorporate a statement on

tobacco into its Book of Discipline, calling the "habitual use" of the plant a "practice out of harmony with the best Christian influence."[14] Four years later, William Preston Few, the president of a tiny North Carolina college that was under the auspices of the Methodist Episcopal Church, South, convinced James B. Duke to use his tobacco fortune to endow the college and, in so doing, create one of the greatest universities in the Methodist system of higher education.[15] Explaining his decision to endow the college, the father of the "little white slaver" recalled the commitment of his own father, Washington Duke, to the tenets of Methodism, announcing "if I amount to anything in this world, I owe it to my daddy and the Methodist Church."[16]

Undoubtedly, the opposition to his antitobacco message that Mike Sawyer encountered among Methodists in Hart County, Kentucky, was rooted in the county's economic dependence on tobacco production. But to let the analysis stop there would be to do a disservice to Methodism's historical commitment to asceticism – and to ignore changes that took place within the Methodist movement throughout the nineteenth and early twentieth centuries, changes that had a profound impact on the Methodist understanding of self-discipline.

Early Methodists were not slaves to conformity; they willingly opposed many popular amusements, even when their asceticism made them decidedly unpopular in their communities. But when the faith moved from marginal to mainstream, becoming the second-largest Protestant denomination in the United States, many Methodists learned to compromise. The opposition that Mike Sawyer encountered in the 1980s and the criticism of his lack of decorum implied in his firing point to the transformation of an approach to Christianity that began in the 1730s with two brothers from England who were ridiculed by their peers at Christ Church, Oxford, for their disciplined, uncompromising, and "methodical" understanding of the individual's obligation in Christ. This transformation resulted in a veritable splintering of the Methodist movement, causing many modern-day theologians to remark on the "bewildering spectrum of doctrinal diversity" that can be called "Methodist."[17]

The opposition that Sawyer encountered in Reagan- and Bush-era Kentucky also harks back to the tactics that early antitobacco reformers utilized – tactics that linked tobacco to slavery and, in so doing, undermined the crusade against tobacco by muddying it with deep cultural divisions that already existed within the Methodist community. Finally, the unwillingness of Mike Sawyer's congregants to challenge tobacco's economic and habitual role in their community – sixty-five years after church leaders had incorporated a condemnation of its use into the Methodist Book of Discipline – testifies to the powerfully addictive qualities of the stinking weed.

Methodist asceticism was, for a time, quite extreme. In the early years of the faith's development, Methodists distinguished themselves from other evangelicals by embracing a theology that gave an almost radical degree of responsibility to the individual to use his or her reason to discern the will of God. In the eighteenth century, Baptists and Presbyterians were still professing (or, by the end of the century, *clinging*) to a predestinarian theology that was meant to protect believers from the kind of "slippery slope" corruption that had characterized the sixteenth-century Catholic Church and had led to the Protestant Reformation. For those who took their inspiration from the writings of John Calvin, the individual played no real role in his salvation. For those who subscribed to the free-will tenets of John Wesley, however, the individual had the freedom to accept or reject the salvation that God offered in Christ.[18]

Wesley insisted that his "Arminian" theology denied neither the reality of Original Sin nor the imperative of Justification by Faith. He did, however, deny that grace was irresistible, and unlike John Calvin, he maintained that grace was available to everyone, not just the elect. Wesley agreed with Calvin that the decision to offer grace was God's alone to make. He believed, however, that the individual had a responsibility to accept the grace that had been bestowed upon him by God. Acceptance of grace was not a one-time endeavor; the individual could choose to give up the grace his reason had compelled him to accept by not living a life in faith. Men and women were obliged, therefore, to bring God into their lives wholly, permanently, and diligently – working at all times not to "fall from grace" and lose the salvation that they had, at one time, chosen to accept.[19]

Asceticism was the foundation of spiritual diligence. It was not what saved the individual; that way of thinking smacked of popery. Rather, it was what kept him saved. By accepting the grace of God, men and women were rendered capable of adopting the ascetic lifestyle, and by adopting the ascetic lifestyle, then, Christians achieved a degree of self-discipline that allowed them to keep Christ in their hearts even as they were forced to live in a fallen world. John Wesley had many terms to describe the state people were in once they had accepted the discipline that a true, Christian life demanded: "full sanctification," "pure love," and "Christian perfection" were the terms he most commonly used. But he also occasionally referred to this state as a "second blessing," implying to some Methodists that the ability to lead an ascetic life was a gift from God that was in some way different from the initial salvation that the individual chose to accept.[20]

True Christians could embrace the ascetic lifestyle, because their love of God trumped everything. "When the eye of our mind is singly fixed on God," John Wesley wrote in the late 1760s, "we are then simple of heart." Inspired by the writings of the thirteenth-century Catholic monk Thomas á Kempis, Wesley taught that those who loved God with all their "soul," "body," and "substance" would be able to resist worldly distractions and desires. When Christians had "one design in all we speak or do, and one desire ruling all our tempers," they would seek just one kind amusement – that is, "the enjoyment of God in time and in eternity."[21]

Although it was the acceptance of God's grace that enabled the individual to embrace asceticism – and asceticism, then, helped the individual hold on to the grace he had accepted – early Methodists did not hesitate to preach the merits of asceticism to those who had not yet accepted God into their hearts. In the winter of 1740, while he was spending the night at an inn along the coast of South Carolina, the proto-Methodist itinerant George Whitefield saw fit to join a group of people who "met together to divert themselves with country dances" on New Year's Day. "At my first entrance, I endeavored to shew the folly of such entertainments," Whitefield wrote in his diary. Targeting one woman in particular, he worked to "convince her how well-pleased the devil was at every step she took." Although the dynamic preacher did convince the fiddler to briefly "lay aside his instrument" and listen to the Word of the Lord, "after I had gone to bed," Whitefield wrote, "I heard their music and dancing resume."[22]

The closest George Whitefield ever came to a condemnation of tobacco, however, was his private assertion in 1739 that of all the groups he encountered, he was most likely to convert the Scotch-Irish in Virginia, because "they raise little or no tobacco, but things that are useful for common life."[23] Alas, Whitefield did not elaborate on this idea, privately or in public. We are left, therefore, with no understanding of why it is that he believed tobacco was not useful – in spite of the fact that it was actually being used as currency at the time in Maryland, Virginia, and North Carolina.[24] We also do not know the nature of the connection he saw between conversion and the growing of agricultural products that were useful in some way.

The first prominent person in eighteenth-century America to suggest that the use of tobacco might be morally dubious was Dr. Benjamin

Rush, a Presbyterian physician from Philadelphia. Rush was undoubtedly aware of studies coming out of London that linked the use of snuff to nasal cancer when he published his *Observations Upon the Influence of the Habitual Use of Tobacco Upon Health, Morals, and Property* in 1798. Unlike his English colleague, John Hill, however, Dr. Rush did not confine his concerns about tobacco just to its poisonous effects on the body. "The use of tobacco, more especially in smoking, disposes to idleness, and idleness has been considered as the root of evil," he wrote. Tobacco was "connected to the neglect of cleanliness," and smoking was offensive to people who did not participate in the habit. "To smoke in company ... is a breach of good manners," Rush insisted, and "manners may be considered as the outpost of virtue."[25]

Lawmakers in nearby Lancaster, Pennsylvania, eventually embraced Rush's opinion of pipes and cigars, voting in 1818 to outlaw smoking on all public streets. The officials expressed no concerns about the use of snuff or chewing tobacco, however, and Alderman John Passmore was actually the first person fined for violating the smoking ban. He became the town's mayor less than five months later.[26]

Rush's pronouncements aside, tobacco – particularly when it was not smoked – was unproblematic for most Americans during the first four decades of the nineteenth century. Indeed, many physicians during this period believed that tobacco could alleviate the discomfort and symptoms of a wide variety of ailments, including hernias, asthma, and edema.[27] This mistaken sense of tobacco's medicinal qualities worked against the demonization of the weed, not just among Presbyterians like the ones Benjamin Rush worshipped with, but also among staunchly ascetic Christians like the early Methodists, who believed that disorders of the body made it difficult for the individual to receive the salvation of God. Illnesses hindered sick bodies from loving God, according to John Wesley, and while prayer was always the most appropriate way to deal with illness, true Christians should not hesitate to use "medicines" to heal themselves. Wesley himself advised his followers to heal their sick bodies with tar water, radish juice, marigolds, and – occasionally – "Spanish snuff."[28]

Beginning in the late 1830s, a growing number of physicians in the United States did start to question the prevailing medical wisdom on tobacco. Many protestant ministers, Methodists among them, proved more than willing to add their moral indignation to the chorus of criticism.[29] Not all Methodists, however, were inclined to criticize the weed. Many – lay and clerical alike – chose to refrain not only from condemning tobacco but also from giving it up. In fact, the problem of "puffing preachers" – as *Time* Magazine so gleefully put it in 1935 – was an issue that many conferences were still addressing years after the Methodist Episcopal Church had adopted a condemnation of tobacco usage into its Book of Discipline.[30]

By the 1870s and 1880s, the "tobacco issue" had come to epitomize the transformation of American Methodism – and specifically the disappointment that some Methodists felt when confronting this transformation. Most of the Methodists who insisted that tobacco usage was ungodly fell into the "holiness" camp, and their primary concerns with tobacco were that it sullied the body – that is, God's temple – and that it worked against human freedom, which was a pillar of Methodist theology. "There are but very few forms of bondage so galling as that of the tobacco consumer," the Reverend Albert Sims wrote in 1878, in a book that he hoped would convince his fellow Methodists who were addicted to tobacco to give it up. "Are tobacco smokers and chewers free?" he asked rhetorically. "Verily not.... How many of them often make the said confession, 'I would give up the habit if *I could*.' Is this Gospel freedom?"[31]

Sims was a preacher in the East Ontario Conference of the Free Methodist Church, a break-away denomination within Methodism that was started in upstate New York in 1860 by a group of preachers and laypeople who felt the leadership of the Methodist Episcopal Church had abandoned some of the teachings of John Wesley.[32] "There has always been a tendency in the Church, considered as an earthly institution, toward backsliding," Bishop Wilson Thomas Hogue wrote in his less-than-objective *History of the Free Methodist Church in North America* in 1915. The Methodist Episcopal Church had "abandoned the 'heroic ideals of the elder time,'" according to Hogue, and embraced the idea that "we are sanctified wholly the moment we are justified, and are neither more nor less holy to the day of our death."[33] Individuals, in other words, could not fall from grace once they had been sanctified; that was how Free Methodists understood Methodist Episcopal theology. There was no need, therefore, for people who subscribed to such a theology to embrace an ascetic lifestyle. Certainly by 1908, when the New York Conference of the Methodist Episcopal Church adopted a resolution "to repeal the old anti-amusement rule of the Church forbidding dancing, card-playing, and certain other amusements of society folk," asceticism no longer seemed to be a necessary component of some Methodists' identity.[34]

When the New York Conference voted to repeal the church's "old" rule on the "amusements of society folk," there were more than four million Methodists in the United States, not counting the Methodists who fell into the "holiness" camp. Scholars believe that the number of people who attended Methodist worship services but did not actually belong to the Church may have been four times higher, and if this estimate is correct, it means that at the turn of the twentieth century, more than one-fifth of the people in the United States were listening to a Methodist preacher when they went to church on Sunday mornings.[35]

This ascendency did not happen overnight. Methodist numbers had been exploding in the United States since the 1840s and 1850s. By 1906, when the U.S. Census Bureau took its first "Survey of Religious Bodies," even New England – the cradle of Congregationalism – had a formidable Methodist element, particularly in Connecticut.[36] No longer a faith that was practiced primarily by the poor and uneducated on the margins of society, Methodism had become "respectable" – the belief system of factory owners, college professors, and career politicians. The discipline that defined the faith had proven to be a solid foundation for financial success, and in the words of one scholar, "not all congregants remained comfortable with the radical faith and the social opprobrium initially associated with American Methodism."[37]

Many Methodists, in other words, wanted to belong. They no longer had a burning desire to be obnoxious – and while they continued to reject many of the luxuries associated with industrialization and America's economic expansion, they did feel comfortable expressing a taste for some of the finer things in life. This change in orientation was evident among Methodists as early as the 1820s, when the New York Conference of the Methodist Episcopal Church elected to put a carpeted altar into the John Street Church in New York City. That decision alienated quite a few people in the congregation, but as time wore on – and with the help of clerical leaders like Nathan Bangs, who desperately wanted his faith to achieve some degree of respectability in the United States – Methodism gradually became less militantly ascetic than it had been in the eighteenth century.[38]

This transitional period in American Methodism – roughly 1830 to 1870, when Methodists founded thirty colleges in nineteen states, and Americans elected their first Methodist president, James K. Polk – coincided with the period when the medical community in the United States and Europe was finally starting to understand that tobacco usage could be dangerous.[39] In spite of these medical concerns, chewing tobacco and snuff remained popular habits among "rough" and "fashionable" Americans alike, and few, if any conferences within the Methodist Episcopal Church or the Methodist Episcopal Church, South, ever took the step of universally condemning the use of tobacco. This failure to fully condemn tobacco at a time when the weed's physical dangers were being discovered by doctors and its moral perils were being emphasized by leaders of the holiness movement testifies to the connection between the rise of Methodist respectability and the decline of Methodist asceticism.

To be fair, some conferences did have individual members who pressed the issue. Several of the men who belonged to the Rock River Conference in DeKalb, Illinois, for example, wanted to "discountenance, both by precept and example" the use of tobacco among conference members in 1862. Unlike Albert Sims, these men did not appeal to the free-will theology of Methodism when making their case. Their problem with tobacco was not that it restricted human freedom, but that it was a gateway drug. "The fact has already been incontrovertibly established that there is a close alliance between this habit [i.e., tobacco] and the habit of using strong drink," they argued. The men proposed "that every man addicted to the habit, asking admission to the conference, be requested to free himself from it." Their resolution failed, however, and the following year, there was no mention of tobacco at the conference's annual meeting.[40]

When W. W. Shaw and W. D. Fero presented the Hudson Conference in New York with a resolution in 1873 that would have required "all members of the Conference to refrain wholly from [tobacco's] influence" and "all candidates for admission" to "pledge entire abstinence from this injurious superfluity," the response they received from their colleagues was surprisingly un-Christian. "The Conference laughed heartily over the expression 'injurious superfluity," the *New York Times* reported. The Reverend Abiathar Osbon, an "inveterate tobacco chewer" from Poughkeepsie, attacked the resolution and accused its authors of "base back-biting and slandering." After a series of "countermotions were hurled at the chair from all sides of the room," the resolution was referred to a special committee – where it subsequently died.[41]

In Georgia, the reaction against any criticism of tobacco was even more vociferous. When a handful of clergymen in Macon proposed that the younger members of their conference abstain from the use of tobacco in 1872, one minister after another stood up to testify to the health benefits associated with the plant. One man claimed that using tobacco had helped him to keep his teeth. He knew this because "feeling a call to bear testimony against the use of the weed, he had quit it, and lost a tooth by the operation." Another minister insisted that chewing tobacco and "not expectorating as usual, but taking the juice into the stomach" had helped him with his "distemper." At the age of eighty three, he was still healthy enough to wake up every morning and "bless the precocious plant – tobacco."[42]

In the South, any possibility of a crusade against tobacco may have been stymied early on by the involvement of ardent abolitionists like William Lloyd Garrison and Lyman Beecher in the burgeoning antitobacco movement. In August 1841, while following his friends Thomas Parnell Beach and Ezekial Rogers to an abolitionist conference in New Hampshire, Garrison was "alarmed at seeing *smoke* issue from their chaise-top." He "cried out to them that their chaise was afire," but as he did so, he was "more than suspicious ... that it was something worse than that." Garrison suspected that "the *smoke* came from friend Rogers' mouth," and as it turned out, he was right. When the group stopped to water their horses, William Lloyd Garrison gave Ezekial Rogers "a faithful admonition ... that he, an *abolitionist*, on his way to an *anti-slavery* convention, should desecrate his *anti-slavery* mouth ... with a stupefying tobacco weed."[43]

In the decades that followed the Civil War, some conferences in the North, South, and West did take steps to bar ministers from using tobacco, though they said nothing about the habit among the laity, and the bans on smoking and chewing that they initiated among the clergy seem to have been only moderately successful. In September 1899, the Reverend D. B. Holt created a "sensation" in Newport, Kentucky, when he claimed to have "personal knowledge" that several ministers in the area "openly ignored" their "sacred vows" and used tobacco. Thomas Hanford followed Holt's allegations with his own assertion that he knew of "twenty or thirty members of the conference present whom he could name who used tobacco." That number amounted to about two-thirds of the people present at the meeting. Only one man came forward to admit that he was a smoker, however – J. F. Deal, a "young divine" from the town of Fire Brick. "I use it for medical purposes, and I could not stop if I wanted to," he told the gathering. "If you don't like it, I can get out [of the ministry.] I propose to use tobacco just the same."[44]

Deal seemed to confirm the assertions made by Free Methodists like Albert Sims that tobacco violated human freedom and, in so doing, hindered the ability of the individual to choose to receive and keep the grace of God. It is not known whether Sims ever heard the story of his contemporary, the Reverend W. P. Watkins of Waterloo, Iowa – but if he did, he was undoubtedly devastated by the news. In the fall of 1873, Watkins "was made temporarily insane" by "the combined effects of anxiety about his wife, who was dangerously sick, and efforts to give up the use of tobacco, to which he had long been a devotee." Unable to handle the pressures, Watkins apparently "went out and drown[ed] himself" in the Cedar River.[45] Such was the power that tobacco had over the will of the individual.

"So fearfully enslaving is the habit that its victims, when deprived of the weed for a while, will do almost anything to get a quid or pipeful of tobacco," Albert Sims proclaimed, before telling his readers a story about a man in England who was "sentenced to three months imprisonment for skinning a living small terrier dog" so that he could use "the skin for a tobacco-pouch!!!" Sims claimed to "know an excellent clergyman who assured me that he had sometimes wept like a child when putting a quid of tobacco in his mouth." The minister wept from the "sense of his degradation and bondage to this filthy habit."

The problem, Sims insisted, was that Methodists who smoked and chewed "commonly say there is nothing in sacred writ against the indulgence of the weed." For that reason, the minister produced a book that was "purposely written from a scriptural stand-point," so as to show his readers that God did not, in fact, have no opinion on the subject. But much like the abolitionists who worked hard to show that the Bible condemned slavery in spite of Christ's failure to say anything specific about the institution, Albert Sims had to get a bit creative with the Scripture he quoted in order to make his case.

Sims reminded his readers of Paul's words in Ephesians about the importance of "redeeming the time," before calculating that the typical tobacco user, smoking three pipes a day at twenty minutes a piece, would have wasted an entire year of his life after smoking for two dozen years. He invoked the injunction against killing in Exodus to convince men that they put their mortal souls in danger when they elected to smoke. "It is admitted by the most competent authorities on medicine that tobacco contains a strong, very strong poison," Sims informed his readers. "Such is the rankness of the poison of tobacco, that even to *sleep* with an inveterate smoker is dangerous." Drawing upon Exodus again – and specifically God's order to "have no other gods before me" – Albert Sims insisted "the pipe in the greatest number of cases becomes a god." When users found themselves "under any cross of affliction, instead of looking to God for support, the pipe or the twist is applied to with quadruple earnestness." Recalling a minister he once met in Vermont, Sims told of the man's habit of getting up in the middle of the night just to smoke a pipe. "Is this not idolitary?" he asked his readers pointedly.[46] His words, however, had little effect on Methodists who were not a part of the holiness movement.

Sims continued to speak and write on the subject of tobacco for many years, becoming a widely recognized expert on the subject and publishing an updated treatise on the dangers of the weed in 1894.[47] After 1900, however, his eschatology became increasingly premillennial, and Sims turned his anger away from tobacco and toward the dangers of the trade union movement, which he believed was linked to the coming of the Antichrist.[48]

Nevertheless, Sims did live to see a Methodist lawmaker on the other side of the Detroit River enact a law in 1909 that – in theory – restricted the ability of cigarette manufacturers to add foreign ingredients to their product. Michigan governor Fred M. Warner was adopted at the age of three by devout Methodists in Farmington, and his commitment to the Church was revealed by his donation of four stained-glass windows to the First Methodist Episcopal Church there. His effort to halt the sale of so-called "adulterated cigarettes," however, seems to have been part of a lifetime commitment to consumer advocacy, rather than any latent Wesleyan asceticism.[49] His concern was not that Michigan's citizens were smoking tobacco, but that they were *not* smoking tobacco, because their cigarettes had been corrupted with fillers.

Today, Mike Sawyer is no longer a Methodist pastor. His last interview for a position with the Church was in 1991, when he met with a pastor in Waco, Texas, to discuss a job as an outreach coordinator. Then, as now, Sawyer was deeply involved in the antitobacco crusade that he launched on that cold November morning in 1989. "My church just isn't ready for you," the pastor reportedly told him, before recommending that Sawyer look for a job in a part of the country where tobacco was not grown.

Looking back on the experience of delivering his antitobacco sermon to Methodists in Hardyville, Kentucky, Sawyer insists that he could not have done otherwise. "I couldn't hide the message," he says. "It was do or die. I just didn't have a clue as to the depths of the retaliation I would receive."

He still gets emotional when he thinks about the sermon and the reaction it engendered among his congregants. He is convinced that "a real revival could have broken out there" if the Methodists he was speaking to had been willing to "open their hearts and receive" the message that God was conveying to them. But he believes that the men and women who heard him were not receptive to God's message because many Methodists today do not see their church as a leader on ascetic issues. While the Book of Discipline discourages the use of tobacco,

"Christian men," Sawyer says, "have become wimps, depending upon the government to make anti-smoking laws, when the Church could be a real force behind this."

"The Bible says you gotta be content with nothing," Sawyer notes, before insisting that a "spirit of contentment" has taken over the United Methodist Church. Methodist leaders today, he says, are too willing to compromise, so as not to offend the powerful and influential members of the communities they serve. "If we were really doing God's business, we wouldn't be all that fashionable," Sawyer proclaims – in words that might have warmed John Wesley's heart.[50]

Notes

1   Michael E. Sawyer, "Preaching on Tobacco Road," *Tobacco Control* 4 (1998), 438–440.
2   Sermon 50, "The Use of Money," §I.4, Works, 2:271.
3   William M. Snell, "The Volatile and Uncertain Outlook for Tobacco in Kentucky," in *The Frontier of the Future: How Kentucky Will Live, Learn, and Work*, edited by Michael T. Childress et al., (Kentucky Long-Term Policy Research Center, 1996), 155–156.
4   Cynthia Lynn Lyerly, *Methodism and the Southern Mind, 1770–1810* (New York: Oxford University Press, 1998), 38–41.
5   William J. Grayson, "The Character of a Gentleman," *Southern Quarterly Review* 7 (January, 1853), 58; Bertram Wyatt-Brown, *Southern Honor: Ethics and Behavior in the Old South* (New York: Oxford University Press, 1982), 23–24; Richard Briggs Stott, *Jolly Fellows: Male Milieus in Nineteenth-Century America* (Baltimore, MD: Johns Hopkins University Press, 2009), 9–10.
6   John G. Jones, *An Appeal to All Christians, Especially the Members of the Methodist Episcopal Church, Against the Practice of Social Dancing* (St. Louis, MO: P. M. Pinckard, 1867), 4.
7   Stith Mead, *A Short Account of the Experience and Labors of the Rev. Stith Mead, Preacher of the Gospel and an Elder in the Methodist Episcopal Church, Written by Himself* (Lynchburg, VA: Stith Mead, 1829), 32; William Wallace Bennett, *Memorials of Methodism in Virginia* (Richmond, VA: William Wallace Bennett, 1871), 301.
8   Sermon 80, "On Friendship with the World," §I.1, Works, 3:127.
9   Quoted in John Wigger, *American Saint: Francis Asbury and the Methodists* (New York: Oxford University Press, 2009), 187–188, 211. Asbury, like most early Methodists, was opposed to liquor, rather than alcohol in general. In fact, Asbury was known to use wine – claret in particular – to deal with his stomach ailments.
10 Jones, *An Appeal to All Christians*, 4, 6; "Gambling," *Southern Christian Advocate*, July 22, 1837.
11 Freeborn Garrettson, *The Experience and Travels of Freeborn Garrettson in North America* (Philadelphia, PA: Parry Hall, 1791), 112.

12   Albert Sims, *The Sin of Tobacco: Smoking and Chewing, Together with an Effective Cure for these Habits* (Toronto: A. Sims, 1878), 5; Sermon 80, "The Good Steward," §I.4, Works, 2:285.

13   Randall Stephens, *The Fire Spreads: Holiness and Pentecostalism in the American South* (Cambridge, MA: Harvard University Press, 2008), 68–69, 171.

14   *Doctrines and Discipline of the Methodist Episcopal Church, 1920* (New York: J. Emory and B. Waugh, 1920), 71; "Religion: Puffing Preachers," *Time Magazine*, April 8, 1935, 12.

15   Supporters of Duke University are fond of pointing out that the Duke family made its initial fortune off of electricity, rather than tobacco – suggesting that the money that went to Trinity College was untainted by the moral ambiguity of the cigarette industry that James B. Duke not only prospered from, but actually created. See Robert Franklin Durden, *Lasting Legacy of the Carolinas: The Duke Endowment, 1924–1994* (Durham, NC: Duke University Press, 1998), 1–28.

16   Howard C. Wilkinson, "Sam's Creek Revisited," *The Duke Divinity School Review* 31(1966), 3–4; Cassandra Tate, *Cigarette Wars: The Triumph of 'The Little White Slaver'* (New York: Oxford University Press, 1999), 11–17. The term "little white slaver" as a synonym for "cigarette" was first used publicly by Henry Ford in his self-published *The Case against the Little White Slavery* (Detroit, MI: H. Ford, 1914).

17   E. Brooks Holifield, *Health and Medicine in the Methodist Tradition: Journey toward Wholeness* (New York: Crossroad, 1986), 4.

18   Cynthia Lyerly, *Methodism and the Southern Mind* (New York: Oxford University Press, 2006), 28–29; John Boles, *The Great Revival, 1787–1805: The Origins of the Southern Evangelical Mind* (Lexington, KY: University Press of Kentucky, 1972), 138; Donald Matthews, *Religion in the Old South* (Chicago, IL: University of Chicago Press, 1977), 31–34.

19   Holifield, *Health and Medicine*, 17; Kenneth Wilson, *Methodist Theology* (2011), 61, 63.

20   Laurence Wood, "Pentecostal Sanctification in Wesley and Early Methodism," *Wesleyan Theological Journal* 34(1999), 24–63. For a different point of view on the importance of a "second blessing" to John Wesley, see Randy Maddox, "Wesley's Understanding of Christian Perfection," *Wesleyan Theological Journal* 34 (1999), 78–110.

21   Sermon 80, "The Witness of Our Own Spirit," §13, Works, 1:307; and "Plain Account of Christian Perfection," in *The Works of John Wesley, A.M., Sometime Fellow of Lincoln College, Oxford*, edited by Thomas Jackson (London: Wesleyan Methodist Book Room, 1872), 11:366–246.

22   Quoted in Ann Wagner, *Adversaries of Dance: From the Puritans to the Present* (Champagne, IL: University of Illinois Press, 1997), 85. Whitefield was a member of the "Holy Club" that John and Charles Wesley founded at Oxford, serving as its leader for a time when the brothers were in the North American colonies. Like the Wesleys, Whitefield grounded his theology in the idea of affection, and he believed that faith restored the individual's love of God. He never embraced the Wesleys' Arminianism,

however, retaining a commitment to the doctrine of predestination until his death. Many modern scholars, therefore, refer to him as a "Calvinist Methodist." See Randy L. Maddox, "Theology of John and Charles Wesley," in *T&T Clark Companion to Methodism*, edited by Charles Yrigoyen, Jr. (London: T&T Clark, 2010), 20–35; Harry S. Stout, *The Divine Dramatist: George Whitefield and the Rise of Modern Evangelicalism* (Grand Rapids, MI: Eerdmans, 1991), esp. 16–29.

23   George Whitefield, *Journals (1737–1741)*, edited by William V. Davis (Gainesville, FL: Scholars' Facsimiles and Reprints, 1969), 387.

24   Alvin Rabushka, *Taxation in Colonial America* (Princeton, NJ: Princeton University Press, 2008), 233–235.

25   Benjamin Rush, "Observations upon the Influence of the Habitual Use of Tobacco upon Health, Morals, and Property," in *Essays, Literary, Moral, and Philosophical* (Philadelphia: Thomas and William Bradford, 1798), 267; John Hill, *Cautions Against the Immoderate Use of Snuff: Founded on the Known Qualities of the Tobacco Plant and the Effects It Must Produce When This Way Taken into the Body* (London: R. Baldwin and J. Jackson, 1761).

26   F. R. Diffenderfer, "Secretary's Report," *Historical Papers and Addresses of the Lancaster County Historical Society* (Lancaster, PA: Lancaster County Historical Society, 1899), 4:114–115.

27   R. B. Walker, "Medical Aspects of Tobacco Smoking and the Anti-Tobacco Movement in Britain in the Nineteenth Century," *Medical History* 24 (1980), 391.

28   Holifield, *Health and Medicine*, 22; John Wesley, *Primitive Physik; Or, an Easy and Natural Method of Curing Most Diseases* (London: W. Strahan, 1761), 37, 100.

29   For examples of Protestants who began to question the medical merits of tobacco, see William A. Alcott, *The Use of Tobacco: Its Physical, Moral, and Intellectual Effects on the Human System* (New York: Bela Marsh, 1836); Orin Fowler, *A Disquisition on the Evils of Using Tobacco* (Boston, MA: William Peirce, 1835); Edward Hitchcock, "Lecture IV: Alcoholic and Narcotic Substances as articles of common use," *Dyspesy Forstalled & Resisted* (Boston, MA: J. C. & C. Adams and Company, 1830), 130–177; George Trask, *Thoughts and Stories on Tobacco for American Lads* (Boston, MA: G. Trask, 1860).

30   "Religion: Puffing Preachers," *Time*, April 8th, 1935, 12.

31   Sims, *The Sin of Tobacco*, 7.

32   Donald W. Dayton, *Discovering an Evangelical Heritage* (New York: Harper & Row, 1976), 102; Wilson Thomas Hogue, *History of the Free Methodist Church in North America* (Chicago, IL: Free Methodist Publishing House, 1915), 2:162, 1:5. Early Free Methodists insisted that they were not secessionists – that they had formed the new denomination only after they were excluded from their local conference of the Methodist Episcopal Church.

33   Hogue, *History of the Free Methodist Church*, 1:11, 13.

34   "Methodist Laymen in Favor of Dancing," *New York Times*, April 4th, 1908.

35 David Hempton, *Methodism: Empire of the Spirit* (New Haven, CT: Yale University Press, 2005), 212, 202.

36 Richard D. Shiels, "The Methodist Invasion of Congregational New England," in *Methodism and the Shaping of American Culture*, edited by Nathan O. Hatch and John H. Wigger (Nashville, TN: Kingswood Books, 2001), 267–268; "United States Census of Religious Bodies, State File, 1906, Excel File," *The Association of Religion Data Archives*, November 15 2011, http://www.thearda.com/Archive/Files/Descriptions/1906CENSST.asp.

37 William R. Sutton, "'To Extract Poison from the Blessings of God's Providence': Producerist Respectability and Methodist Suspicions of Capitalistic Change in the Early Republic," in *Methodism and the Shaping of American Culture*, 232.

38 Ibid., 236; Nathan O. Hatch, *The Democratization of American Christianity* (New Haven, CT: Yale University Press, 1989), 201–205.

39 Walker, "Medical Aspects of Tobacco Smoking," 394–396.

40 "Minutes from the Rock River Annual Conference, 1862," 32,39; and "1863," 27. Inventory of the First United Methodist Church, DeKalb, IL. Regional History Center, Northern Illinois University. RC 24, Box 4, Folders 29, 26.

41 "Amusements and Tobacco: The Discussion in the Methodist Conference at Hudson on Saturday," *New York Times*, April 7, 1873.

42 "A Methodist Conference on Tobacco," *Georgia Weekly Telegraph and Georgia Journal & Messenger*, April 23, 1872.

43 Quoted in Wendell Phillips Garrison and Francis Jackson Garrison, *William Lloyd Garrison, 1805–1879, The Story of His Life, Told By His Children* (New York: Century Company, 1889), 3:22.

44 "Clergymen Who Use Tobacco; Sensational Charges at M.E. Conference," *New York Times*, September 10, 1899.

45 *Daily Evening Bulletin* (San Francisco, CA), September 19, 1873.

46 Sims, *The Sin of Tobacco*, 7–9, 3, 10–11, 16, 18, 45–46.

47 Nehemiah Asa Hunt, *Tobacco Manual* (Portland, ME: Brown Thurston & Company, 1888), 72; Rob Cunningham, *Smoke and Mirrors: The Canadian Tobacco War* (Ottawa: International Development Research Center, 1996), 32; Albert Sims, *The Common Use of Tobacco: Condemned by Physicians, Experience, Common Sense, and the Bible* (Toronto: W. Lightfoot & Son, 1894).

48 Albert Sims, *A Bible Portrait of Satan's Last Dread Counterfeit: The Dragon, the Antichrist and the False Prophet* (Toronto: A. Sims, 1928); Robert C. Fuller, *Naming the Antichrist: The History of an American Obsession* (New York: Oxford University Press, 1995), 151; William Kostlevy, *Holy Jumpers: Evangelicals and Radicals in Progressive Era America* (New York: Oxford University Press, 2010), 174.

49 E. A. Armstrong, *Minutes of the Michigan Annual Conference of the Methodist Episcopal Church* (Charlotte, MI: Michigan Annual Conference, 1905), 487; Jean M. Fox, *Fred M. Warner: Progressive Governor* (Farmington Hills, MI: Farmington Hill Historical Commission, 1988).

50 Mike Sawyer, phone interview with author, November 21, 2011.

11 Healing

CANDY GUNTHER BROWN

Beginning with John Wesley, there is a long tradition of Methodists expecting God to heal through prayer as well as through medical means. The idea that God provides for physical healing developed as a corollary to a view that God redeems humans from the consequences of the fall to sin. Early Methodists saw no conflict between medical and divine healing; the offer of both constituted a draw for poor people who needed healing. From the mid-nineteenth through the mid-twentieth centuries, a rift developed between those Methodists who envisioned divine healing as a fruit of entire sanctification rooted in the Atonement and those who questioned God's will for physical healing or turned their attention to caring for the sick through medical means. Leaders in the late-twentieth-century charismatic movement reenvisioned divine and medical healing as twin aspects of God's redemptive work in the world.

John Wesley had a life-long interest in physical healing. One reason may be that Wesley himself suffered a variety of physical infirmities – from nose bleeds to consumption (tuberculosis), many of which are detailed in the pages of his journals. Wesley traced all illness to the Fall; he understood salvation as restoration of a good created order that included health. If, as Wesley taught, the Christian receives a "new birth," or justification, and "perfect love," or entire sanctification, by divine grace rather than by human effort, it logically follows that God might similarly heal the body without the requirement of human effort. Wesley himself did not fully develop a theology of physical healing as a counterpart to spiritual sanctification, both of which are made available in the present life by the Atonement (based on Isaiah 53:5: "by his stripes we are healed"), but later divine healing advocates did make this logic explicit.[1]

Wesley believed that God heals through both medicine and prayer. His basic position was that "God has more than one method of healing either the soul or the body." As a seventeen-year-old student at Oxford, Wesley began to read books on "anatomy and physic," a reading practice he continued throughout his lifetime. As Wesley started to visit parishioners, he found many of them in poor physical health. Frustrated by the limited help available from physicians – whose remedies were both harsh (such as bleeding and purging) and expensive – in 1746 Wesley himself began to offer free medical consultations. He opened medical dispensaries in several English cities for much the same reasons that he became involved in educational and poor relief efforts – because he had compassion for the needs of the common people and had a view that there is "no holiness but social holiness."[2]

In 1747, Wesley published the first edition of a medical textbook, *Primitive Physick; Or, An Easy and Natural Method of Curing Most Diseases,* that was destined to go through several dozen British and American editions by the end of the nineteenth century. The text consists of a combination of common sense advice (such as cold water for drinking and bathing, fresh air, exercise, and a tranquil mind), and simple, low-cost remedies drawn from conventional and folk medical wisdom – the lines between which were not at all clear in the eighteenth century. Wesley was criticized by contemporary physicians, as well as modern scholars, for including ineffectual and some apparently "magic" treatments – such as powdered toad, a live puppy on the belly, breathing into a hole in the ground, or use of a yellow flower to treat jaundice – a prescription that seems to express the metaphysical doctrine of "signatures." It is important to note, however, that many contemporary physicians and apothecaries prescribed similar medicines. Most of Wesley's remedies have been evaluated as harmless if not beneficial – and the same could not be said of many conventional medical regimens of his era. Wesley advocated an empirical trial-and-error approach to the treatment of chronic conditions, experimenting with one inexpensive remedy at a time and observing the results. For acute diseases, Wesley urged people to seek a "physician who fears God." The preface to the *Primitive Physick* also commended readers to, "above all, add to the rest (for it is not labour lost) that old, unfashionable medicine, prayer." This injunction was not merely an obligatory gesture to faith – Wesley really expected prayers to be effective in healing the sick.[3]

Wesley's *Journal* and the *Arminian Magazine* include numerous accounts of divine healing through prayer – of conditions ranging from toothaches to cancer. On the one hand, Wesley guarded against supernatural claims that appeared to confirm charges of Methodist "enthusiasm." For example, he chastised certain followers who "imagined themselves to be endued with a power of working miracles, of healing the sick by a word or a touch, of restoring sight to the blind; yea, even of raising the dead" – but whose characters he mistrusted. On the other hand, Wesley believed that God did heal miraculously through his own and other people's prayers. For instance, he recounted an instance in which a traveling companion became ill and a physician pronounced that he did not expect him to live until morning. Wesley "went to him, but his pulse was gone. He had been speechless and senseless for some time. A few of us immediately joined in prayer: (I relate the naked fact). Before we had done, his sense and his speech returned. Now, he that will account for this by natural causes has my free leave: But I choose to say, 'This is the power of God.'" The unexpected and rapid nature of the recovery – and its coincidence with the time of prayer – led Wesley to attribute it to supernatural intervention. Wesley similarly evaluated the efficacy of prayers by others whom he respected. Of one Bridget Bostock – an elderly British Methodist woman who had a reputation for healing through prayer (as well as using "a little liquor of a red complexion" and "fasting spittle" to anoint the sick) – Wesley concluded that he "found no room to doubt" the genuineness of her healings.[4]

Wesley also recounted his own personal experiences as a recipient of apparent divine healings. He attested to having been "preternaturally restored more than ten times." For instance,

> What I here aver is the naked fact. Let every one account for it as he sees good. My horse was exceeding lame; and my head ached much. I thought, cannot God heal man or beast by means or without? Immediately my weariness and headache ceased, and my horse's lameness in the same instant. But what does all this prove? Only that I believe God now hears and answers prayer, even beyond the ordinary course of nature.

It is significant that Wesley did not reject the use of medical means, but he did believe that God could heal with or without means. On another occasion, Wesley became ill, took medicine, and then prayed for healing; when the condition recurred, "a thought came into my head, 'Why do I not apply to God in the beginning rather than the end of an illness?' I did so, and found immediate relief; so that I needed no further medicine." Wesley would it seems have been quite willing to take additional medicine had it been needed, but praying first had removed the necessity. Wesley wrote to his brother Charles that he did not want to resort first to "ordinary means" based on a false sense that "it is our duty to try them." To the contrary, "all our lives and all God's dealing with us have been extraordinary from the beginning. We have reason therefore to expect that which has been to be again." Based on past experiences of apparent divine interventions, Wesley considered it reasonable to expect God to continue to provide needed help in extraordinary ways.[5]

The appeal of early Methodism to poor people was indeed greatly enhanced by the practical help offered through both ordinary and extraordinary means. Many converts lived in impoverished farming, mining, or fishing villages in Britain or in African-American slave communities in the United States and suffered ill health that was exacerbated by poor working conditions and inadequate nutrition. These are people who had practical needs for healing, as well as longing for spiritual succor. Moreover, the supernaturalist strain of Methodism appealed to common people who embraced the worlds of folklore, magic, and conjure that were increasingly rejected by the educated classes. Those who converted to Methodism were already accustomed to seeking help with physical needs from nonphysical sources.[6]

The itinerant preachers commissioned by Wesley followed his lead in combining healing with proclamation of the gospel. Wesley forbade itinerants from pursuing trades, including the sale of "pills, drops or balsams," but itinerants did use the *Primitive Physick* to provide unpaid medical treatments as well as praying for healing and reporting miraculous cures. A spiritual approach to healing seemed particularly in order when the cause of an affliction appeared to be demonic. For instance, one George Lukyns had long suffered from seizures, and he himself claimed to be possessed by seven devils; witnesses attested to Lukyns's good character and sincerity, noting that his affliction had prevented him from working for an income. A group of seven clergymen (four of whom were Methodists) prayed for Lukyns's deliverance – provoking dramatic convulsions, blasphemies spoken in several male and female voices, and Latin speech – although Lukyns was illiterate. The exorcism was apparently successful, leading to Lukyns's recovery. Such instances, which are abundant in the early Methodist literature, suggest that Methodism spread through a combination of natural and supernatural approaches to meeting people's needs.[7]

After Wesley's death in 1791, the themes of entire sanctification and divine healing became less prominent as an increasingly respectable Methodist movement took root in America. Many Methodists adopted a view of suffering common in Reformed churches – that God sent physical sickness as a trial of faith or chastisement to produce spiritual sanctification – a view that discouraged concern for physical healing. For instance, Joanna Baily (1801–1833) of Poughkepsie was eulogized for patiently enduring sickness during the last two months of her life: a "trying season by which her faith was tested, and it proved as gold tried in the fire." A few days before her death, Baily professed the "blessing of perfect love," which she experienced the day before her departure as "ecstasy: 'This,' said she, 'is the happiest day I ever saw.'" Likewise, "nearly six years of almost unexampled suffering" was credited with producing the "holy life and triumphant death" of Reverend Professor Bascom of Kentucky. Despite such correlations of physical affliction with spiritual sanctity, Wesley's *Primitive Physick* remained popular throughout the nineteenth century, and the practice of praying for healing never disappeared. When American bishop Francis Asbury (1745–1816) became seriously ill, people prayed passionately for his recovery – without prefacing their prayers "if it be thy will." The itinerant evangelist Freeborn Garrettson (1752–1827) reported praying for his "dangerously ill" brother and "instantly the disorder turned." The autobiography of itinerant Billy Hibbard (1798–1844) contains a number of divine-healing claims, including an account of a woman being raised from the dead.[8]

Healing was likewise a significant concern for many in the early African Methodist Episcopal (AME) church. AME founder Richard Allen included a record of black people ministering to sick and dying white people during the Philadelphia yellow fever epidemic of 1793. A number of AME women joined predominantly female praying and singing bands that often prayed for healing of the sick. A participant in one such band, Rebecca Cox Jackson (1795–1871), was a free African-American evangelist raised in Philadelphia's Bethel AME Church who claimed that many for whom she prayed recovered – including an elderly blind woman who allegedly received her sight. As the AME leadership sought respectability by the 1830s, they denounced the bands in which Jackson and other women had practiced healing, and Jackson herself moved on to join the Shakers.[9]

Secessionist groups such as the Primitive Methodists (PM) gained adherents along the American frontier in part by preserving an emphasis on healing for several decades longer than did most leaders in the Methodist Episcopal Church (MEC). Hugh Bourne (1772–1852), editor of the *Primitive Methodist Magazine*, used the journal to recount healing experiences – as when in 1810 a poor woman villager told him that she had been growing progressively sicker despite four years of medical treatment; "she then prayed and pleaded with the Lord ... till she was instantaneously healed." Elizabeth Smith (1805–1836), a PM preacher, was well known for demonstrating healing gifts as she prayed for sick people in their cottages. In like fashion, Betsy Tomlinson, a Forest (or Magic) Methodist preacher, gained assurance of her call to preach by healing experiences such as this one: "I did not send for the doctor. I thought when Christ was applied unto in the days of his flesh either for body or soul, he did for them whatever they had need of; and while I was looking to him ... I felt, in the twinkling of an eye, that all the fever was gone, and all my pain had ceased. I was quite restored to health." For Tomlinson, physical healing provided evidence that God had heard her plea for the healing of the soul as well as the body, thereby validating her apparent divine calling.[10]

By the 1860s, as the economic standing of early secessionist groups improved, their distinctiveness from other Methodists diminished, as did an emphasis on divine healing. Yet, other splinter groups arose in their place – such as the Free Methodist Church of North America (FMC) formed in 1860 under the leadership of Benjamin Titus Roberts (1823–1893). As part of its critique of MEC worldliness, the FMC reaffirmed the doctrines of entire sanctification and divine healing. Other promoters of sanctification and healing left the MEC for groups such as the Pilgrim Holiness and Wesleyan Methodist churches. It is not coincidental that Charles Parham, one of the founders of Pentecostalism, was a former Methodist. Holiness denominations that formed in the early twentieth century, notably the Church of the Nazarene, initially included divine healing as an article of faith.[11]

Within the MEC, renewed concern for entire sanctification in the 1830s provided a theological foundation for a subsequent renewal of interest in divine healing by some leaders of the holiness movement of the 1870s. Through her well-known Tuesday Meetings for the Promotion of Holiness in New York, Phoebe Palmer (1807–1874) popularized a modified version of Wesley's doctrine of perfect love. According to Palmer's altar theology, the Christian must first decide to consecrate oneself entirely to Christ, by figuratively laying one's "all upon the altar." One knows that the blessing of sanctification has been received by "naked faith" in a "naked promise" of the Bible; one need not wait for the Holy Spirit to give "witness" to sanctification through an emotional experience. Finally, the sanctified Christian must testify publicly or risk losing the blessing through disobedience to a biblical command. This morphology of sanctification was applied by late-nineteenth-century "faith cure" advocates to healing. By this model, the Christian in need of healing must consecrate oneself to Christ, receive healing based on the Bible's promise, and testify to having been healed – and begin acting as if one has in fact been healed – without waiting for an experience of the disappearance of physical symptoms.[12]

Only a minority of those who joined the holiness movement advocated the practice of divine healing – and only a subset of these held tightly to the faith-cure model. The Methodist layman Ethan O. Allen (1813–1903) has been called the "Father of Divine Healing" for promoting the idea that as God redeems Christians from the spiritual consequences of sin through entire sanctification, sanctified Christians are also redeemed from the physical consequences of sin through divine healing. In 1846, Allen persuaded a group of Methodist class leaders to pray for him – and attested to experiencing both sanctification and healing from consumption (tuberculosis) simultaneously. Allen spent the remainder of his life as a full-time itinerant healing evangelist. He usually prayed for sick people one-on-one in their homes – often devoting several days to prayer and fasting for one person – but he also prayed for the sick in faith cure homes and at camp meetings as these developed an emphasis on healing. Allen believed that much sickness was demonic in origin, and he often cast out evil spirits before praying for healing. Allen was also one of the first well-known divine-healing practitioners to reject the use of medical means as indicating a lack of faith in God to heal.[13]

Among those who experienced healing through Allen's prayers was a free black woman and AME church member (who later joined the Advent Christian Church) Sarah Ann Freman Mix (1832–1884). After experiencing relief from consumption, Mix spent the next seven years (until she ultimately died from a recurrence of consumption) as the first known African American and first full-time female healing evangelist. Like Allen, Mix advised against the use of medical means on the grounds that it might prevent one from placing complete trust in God to heal. Mix often visited the sick in their homes to pray, laid hands on the sick, and anointed them with oil (based, for instance, on James 5). Mix also prayed at a distance for those who requested prayers by postal mail; it was in this manner that Carrie Judd Montgomery (1858–1946) reportedly recovered from a long-term disability that had resulted from a fall, and went on to become a leader in the holiness and Pentecostal movements – as well as a model for the holiness healing evangelist Maria Beulah Woodworth-Etter (1844–1924). Woodworth-Etter, whose itinerant ministry was sponsored by the United Brethren, MEC, and Churches of God, preached salvation, sanctification, and healing to crowds of as many as 25,000 people. She was known for her brusque tactics – including physically hitting diseased body parts to combat the demon spirits behind afflictions – and for her rejection of medicine, because the Bible "nowhere commands the use of medicine with prayer and faith." Mix's example similarly influenced a number of African-American women. For instance, Amanda Berry Smith (1837–1915) was an African-American

Figure 9. **Amanda Berry Smith,** Methodist Library Image Collection, Drew University, Madison, New Jersey.

holiness evangelist who attested that "the Lord was my physician" and refrained from the use of medicine, instead resorting to prayer when she or others needed healing.[14]

By the mid-nineteenth century, the apparent complementarity of medical and divine healing had seemed to unravel – as some Methodist and holiness leaders prayed for healing but renounced medical means as contrary to faith, and as others argued that prayer for healing apart from medical means should be rejected as presumption and superstition. A number of influential holiness leaders who had attended Phoebe Palmer's Tuesday meetings – for instance, the Episcopalian Charles

Cullis (1833–1892) and the Presbyterian William E. Boardman (1810–1886) – came to promote both sanctification and divine healing as provisions of the Atonement at holiness camp meetings. John S. Inskip (1816–1884), president of the National Camp Meeting Association for the Promotion of Holiness, became convinced of the divine healing message after experiencing healing through Cullis's prayers.[15]

Not every holiness leader who practiced divine healing utterly rejected medical means, but the two approaches were increasingly held in tension. Cullis, who was by profession a homeopathic physician, insisted that he would "by no means disparage the use of medicines. The matter stands to me as one of privilege. You can take remedies, or you can take the Great Physician himself to be your healer, without medicine. There can be no condemnation to the one using medicine; you can certainly ask God's blessing upon the means used; but there is a better way, and that is, the communion that brings blessing and healing upon body and soul." Boardman, a leader of the Keswick Holiness movement and founder of the Association for Holding Union Holiness Conventions, promoted healing through his book *"The Lord that Healeth Thee" (Jehovah-Rophi)* (1881), writing that "I am glad of this opportunity to take rank with the fanatics who believe in God's method of curing people, and who think that the scriptures mean just what they say in declaring that 'the prayer of faith shall save the sick, and the Lord shall raise him up.' [James 5:15]." In cofounding (with Elizabeth Baxter) the Bethshan Healing Home in London, Boardman discouraged the use of medical means by those who committed to trust God for healing.[16]

Reacting against this antimedical position, James Monroe Buckley, the editor of the U.S. *Methodist Christian Advocate* from 1880 to 1912, waged a concerted campaign against divine healing. In an 1875 address to Methodist ministers in New York, Buckley called "faith healing" an "excrescence on Christianity, a kind of quackery of faith" that degraded "the holy faith to the level of the superstitions of Paganism." Buckley published a number of articles in the *Christian Advocate* that characterized divine healing as "a very superficial and unwarranted interpretation of Scripture" and as an "absurdity." Writing a book-length repudiation of divine healing (classed alongside Christian Science) in 1892, Buckley charged that claiming prayer results in healing "seriously diminishes the influence of Christianity by subjecting it to a test which it cannot endure. It diverts attention from the moral and spiritual transformation which Christianity professes to work, a transformation which wherever made manifests its divinity, so that none who behold it need any other proof that it is of God." Buckley avoided the danger of the apparent failure of Christian prayer by redefining "proof" of the truth of Christianity in nonfalsifiable terms, as unquantifiable moral and spiritual changes, rather than as verifiable answers to prayer.[17]

Buckley became a key promoter of the hospital movement – motivated not simply by compassion for the sick, but more basically by a desire to offer a scientifically advanced alternative to the presumed superstition and magic of faith healing. The hospital movement had roots in early Methodism. As early as 1787, Methodists had organized "Strangers' Friend Societies" to assist "poor, sick, friendless strangers," and a Methodist hospital was built in Ireland in 1790. It was not, however, until the late nineteenth century that Methodists had accumulated sufficient financial means and institutional stability to construct a significant number of hospitals. A Methodist Episcopal General Hospital was founded in Brooklyn, New York, in 1881. During the next fifty years, Methodists built fifty-nine U.S. hospitals as well as dozens of missionary hospitals overseas, providing many services free of charge to the poor.[18]

Alongside the building of modern hospitals, the deaconess movement provided institutional support for Methodist women to care for the sick and to minister to other practical needs of the urban poor. Wesley himself had encouraged women to become official visitors of the sick, based on the model of Phoebe the deaconess (Romans 16:1–2). German and Swiss Methodists were at the forefront of developing the deaconess movement in the last quarter of the nineteenth century, training women to serve as nurses in hospitals and homes; the movement quickly spread to the United States and other countries. In 1885, Lucy Rider Meyer founded a deaconesses training school in Chicago, and similar schools soon opened in other U.S. cities. By the end of the nineteenth century, at least 600 women were recognized as deaconesses.[19]

For the first half of the twentieth century, a rift divided Methodists who promoted healing through prayer from those who worked to advance healing by means of modern medicine. There were individuals who sought to integrate the two approaches, sometimes in novel ways. For instance, in the post-World War I era the English Methodist Leslie Weatherhead advocated the integration of the new fields of depth psychology and psychosomatic medicine with prayer. It was not, however, until the ecumenical Charismatic renewals of the 1960s to 1970s that a large-scale rapprochement between medical and divine healing occurred. At the helm of this new movement were two American evangelists with Methodist roots – Oral Roberts (1918–2009) and Kathryn Kuhlman (1907–1976).[20]

Roberts grew up in the MECS and, in 1947, began itinerating as a tent-meeting evangelist for the Pentecostal Holiness Church. By 1951, the majority of people who attended his crusades belonged to Methodist or other mainstream denominations. Roberts attracted larger and still more diverse audiences after he began to use television in 1954. In 1968, Roberts joined the United Methodist Church and was ordained as an elder. In the early years of Roberts's evangelistic career, he preached extensively on healing and did not hesitate to cast out demons from the pulpit. Over time, his approach shifted to a softer message of financial prosperity and "seed faith" giving, which better corresponded to the felt needs of his increasingly middle-class audiences. Another key to reaching the Methodist and American cultural mainstreams was Roberts's concerted efforts to bridge the gap between prayer and medicine. Symbolic of this approach, Roberts built the City of Faith Medical and Research Center in Tulsa, Oklahoma (opened in 1981 but closed in 1989 as a financial failure), where, he claimed, the "healing streams of prayer and medicine must merge." The premise – not far from what Wesley had envisioned two centuries earlier – was that God heals through both prayer and medicine, and the most effective strategy is to combine the best of both approaches.[21]

Alongside Roberts, Kathryn Kuhlman played a pivotal role in reconciling divine and medical models of healing. The daughter of Methodist and Baptist parents, Kuhlman captivated ecumenical audiences who sometimes traveled thousands of miles to attend her "miracle services." Beginning in 1947, people began to report experiencing healing in her services while she preached about the Holy Spirit or delivered "words of knowledge" concerning God's will to heal particular individuals at that time – without her laying hands on the sick to pray for them. From the mid-1960s until her death, Kuhlman regularly attracted overflow crowds of thousands in Pittsburgh, Los Angeles, and other cities across the United States and Canada.[22]

Unlike evangelists who urged the sick to "claim" healing by faith, regardless of physical symptoms, or who discouraged the sick from seeking medical attention, Kuhlman insisted that medical evidence back every healing report. Kuhlman invited medical doctors to attend her services and frequently called upon them to evaluate healing claims. Kuhlman produced over four thousand radio and five hundred television broadcasts, many of which featured healing testimonials – in every case confirmed by medical professionals. Kuhlman insisted on still more exacting standards for those cases she publicized in print. Emulating criteria established by the Roman Catholic Lourdes Medical

Bureau, Kuhlman published only those cases for which the following criteria could be shown: First, the disease or injury had been medically diagnosed as resulting from an organic or structural problem, involving more than the unexplained failure of a body part to function. Second, the healing had to have occurred rapidly, involving changes that could not easily be explained as psychosomatic. Third, the patient's primary physician had to verify the healing. Fourth, the healing had to have occurred long enough in the past that it could not readily be diagnosed as remission. Kuhlman's book trilogy, *I Believe in Miracles* (1962), *God Can Do It Again* (1969), and *Nothing Is Impossible with God* (1974), consists of a total of sixty carefully selected healing testimonials, each of which is supported by before-and-after medical documentation.[23]

Kuhlman's book series builds upon a Methodist tradition that envisions sanctification of the soul and healing of the body as complementary. The typical testimonial describes a spiritual transformation that accompanied physical healing, drawing not only the person healed, but also family and friends into a deeper relationship with God. For example, Gilbert Strackbein had long been antagonistic to religion before his wife, Arlene – who attended the local Methodist church without her husband – was diagnosed with multiple sclerosis. Gilbert began searching for God as Arlene's condition worsened: "In the beginning I was thinking only of Arlene's healing. But the more I read the Bible I realized that it also contained the answer to my own personal needs." After months of such spiritual searching, Gilbert reported, his wife was physically healed during a Kuhlman service. "It would seem that Arlene's healing should have been the climax of our lives," reported Gilbert, "but instead, it has been only the beginning." After being "baptized" in the Holy Spirit, Gilbert began leading his family in nightly devotions and, together with Arlene, taught a Sunday school class at their Methodist church. Like many others who attested to divine healing in Kuhlman's miracle services, for the Strackbeins healing of the body and the soul seemed to go hand in hand. Such a claim did not, for those influenced by Kuhlman, require a simultaneous rejection of modern medicine. Rather, after doctors had done all they could to facilitate healing, medical evidence became a tool for validating claims that God can heal with or without medical means.[24]

In the early twenty-first century, American Methodists express a range of views on healing. Most affirm that healing is a valid goal – rather than urging the sick to resign themselves to sickness as productive of sanctity. Many seek healing primarily through modern medicine. Methodist hospitals dot the American landscape, thanks in no small part to generous financial gifts from Methodist church members. For one among many comparable examples, Nebraska's Methodist Hospital Foundation, an affiliate of the state's Methodist Health System, raises and distributes funds to support excellence in health-care education and delivery; a Charitable Care program assists patients unable to pay for needed health-care services – a legacy of Wesley's own particular concern for the health-care needs of the poor.[25]

Those Methodists influenced by the Charismatic movement generally accept modern medicine but also pray expecting that God can heal either through or apart from medical means. Prayer for healing may occur during church services or pastoral visits or through participation in ecumenical conferences and parachurch ministries. Methodists are, for instance, active in volunteering with one of more than two thousand "healing rooms" affiliated with the International Association of Healing Rooms, or IAHR, headquartered in Spokane, Washington. For example, John and Pat Milner, directors of IAHR healing rooms in West Chester, Pennsylvania, began their "quest for 'more of God'" at a "large Methodist Church in Northern Delaware," where they started a healing ministry before joining the IAHR movement. In the IAHR model, two or three lay Christians drawn from a variety of local churches pray one-on-one for healing in private rooms. Leaders encourage the sick to follow up with their doctors, while also affirming that God can heal through prayer alone. Such an approach hearkens back to Wesley's understanding that God has more than one method of redeeming the body as well as the soul, and that no God-given method should be rejected.[26]

Notes

1   E. Brooks Holifield, *Health and Medicine in the Methodist Tradition: Journey Toward Wholeness* (New York: Crossroads Publishing Company, 1986), 13–14, 29; John Wesley, *A Plain Account of Christian Perfection* (London: Epworth Press, 1991), 7–8; Henry D. Rack, "Doctors, Demons and Early Methodist Healing," in *The Church and Healing: Papers Read at the Twentieth Summer Meeting and the Twenty-First Winter Meeting of the Ecclesiastical History Society*, edited by W. J. Sheils (Oxford: Basil Blackwell, 1982), 151; Robert Bruce Mullin, *Miracles and the Modern Religious Imagination* (New Haven, CT: Yale University Press, 1996), 90; Donald W. Dayton, *Theological Roots of Pentecostalism* (Grand Rapids, MI: Francis Asbury, 1987), 119; Amanda Porterfield, *Healing in the History of Christianity* (New York: Oxford University Press, 2005), 167.

2   John Wesley, February 16, 1757, *The Works of the Reverend John Wesley* (1831), 3:621, quoted in Holifield, *Health and Medicine*, 28; Wesley to

Vincent Perronet, 1748, in Wesley, *The Letters of the Reverend John Wesley*, edited by John Telford, 8 vols. (London: Epworth, 1931), 2:307, quoted in Rack, "Doctors, Demons," 139; Wesley, *Complete Works of John Wesley*, 14 vols. 3rd ed. (Albany, OR: CD-ROM, Ages Digital Library, Ages Software: 1997), 14:321; Candy Gunther Brown, "'Faith Working through Love': The Wesleyan Revivals and Social Transformation – Considerations for the Contemporary Filipino Church," *Phronesis* (January 1997): 5–20.

3   Holifield, *Health and Medicine*, 30, 34, 49; Rack, "Doctors, Demons," 143, 144; Samuel J. Rogal, "Pills for the Poor: John Wesley's *Primitive Physick*," *Yale Journal of Biology and Medicine* 51.1 (January-February, 1978): 81–90; Keith Thomas, *Religion and the Decline of Magic* (New York: Scribner, 1971), 224, 265; G. Dock, "The 'Primitive Physic' of Rev. John Wesley," *Journal of American Medical Association* 64 (1915): 629– 638; John Wesley, *Primitive Physick; Or, An Easy and Natural Method of Curing Most Diseases* (Bristol: 1759), xviii.

4   Paul Gale Chappell, *The Divine Healing Movement in America* (Ph.D. diss., Drew University, 1983), 89; John Wesley, *Complete Works of John Wesley*, vol. 5, *Sermons*, "The Nature of Enthusiasm," and vol. 1, *Journal*, 15 December 1741, quoted in James Robinson, *Divine Healing, the Formative Years, 1830–1890: Theological Roots in the Transatlantic World* (Eugene, OR: Pickwick, 2011), 113–114; Wesley, *Journal*, 8:156– 157, quoted in Rack, "Doctors, Demons," 142.

5   Wesley, *Complete Works*, vol. 9, *Letters*, "A Letter to the Right Reverend the Lord Bishop of Gloucester," and Luke Tyerman, *The Life and Times of John Wesley, M.A., Founder of the Methodists* (1872), 261–262, quoted in Robinson, *Divine Healing*, 114, 115; Wesley, *Journal*, 4:187–188, quoted in Rack, "Doctors, Demons," 145.

6   Rack, "Doctors, Demons," 151; Kenneth Stanley Inglis, *Churches and the Working Classes in Victorian England* (London: Routledge & K. Paul, 1963), 32; Holifield, *Health and Medicine*, 39.

7   John Wesley, *Letters*, 5:288, quoted in Rack, "Doctor, Demons," 146; Rack, "Doctors, Demons," 147–148.

8   Candy Gunther Brown, *The Word in the World: Evangelical Writing, Publishing, and Reading in America, 1789–1880* (Chapel Hill, NC: University of North Carolina Press, 2004), 90–92; Holifield, *Health and Medicine*, 73; CA 7.28 (February 19, 1833): 4; Jon Butler, *Awash in a Sea of Faith: Christianizing the American People* (Cambridge, MA: Harvard University Press, 1990), 236; John H. Wigger, *American Saint: Francis Asbury and the Methodists* (New York: Oxford University Press, 2009), 305; John H. Wigger, *Taking Heaven by Storm: Methodism and the Rise of Popular Christianity in America* (New York: Oxford University Press, 1998), 106–107.

9   Holifield, *Health and Medicine*, 50; Robinson, *Divine Healing*, 125– 126; Wigger, *Taking Heaven by Storm*, 122–123; James Craig Holte, *The Conversion Experience in America: A Sourcebook on Religious Conversion Autobiography* (New York: Greenwood, 1992), 119; Jean McMahon Humez, *Gifts of Power: The Writings of Rebecca*

Jackson, Black Visionary, Shaker Eldress (Amherst, MA: University of Massachusetts Press, 1981), 312.

10 W. Reginald Ward, *Religion and Society in England, 1790–1850* (New York: Schocken, 1972), 79; Hugh Bourne, *The Journal of Hugh Bourne, American Mission, 1844–1846*, edited by John Thomas Wilkinson (East Ardsley, England: Micro Methods, 1952), 74; Robinson, *Divine Healing*, 119–120; Deborah M. Valenze, *Prophetic Sons and Daughters: Female Preaching and Popular Religion in Industrial England* (Princeton, NJ: Princeton University Press, 1985), 26.

11 Inglis, *Churches and the Working Classes*, 32; Robinson, *Divine Healing*, 135–136; Holifield, *Health and Medicine*, 41; Chappell, "Divine Healing Movement," 363.

12 Phoebe Palmer, *The Way of Holiness: With Notes by the Way; Being a Narrative of Religious Experience Resulting from a Determination to be a Bible Christian* (New York: Palmer & Hughes, 1867), 43, 60, 105.

13 Chappell, "Divine Healing Movement," 88; Holifield, *Health and Medicine*, 39.

14 Chappell, "Divine Healing Movement," 92, 229; Robinson, *Divine Healing*, 128, 129; Rosemary D. Gooden, introduction to Mrs. Edward [Sarah Ann Freman] Mix, *Faith Cures and Answers to Prayers* (original ed.,1882; Syracuse, NY: Syracuse University Press, 2002), xi, xxii–xxiii, xxxii, lvi, lviv, lv; Candy Gunther Brown, "Maria Woodworth-Etter," in *Encyclopedia of Religious Revivals in America*, ed. Michael J. McClymond (Westport, CT: Greenwood, 2007), 471–472; Maria Beulah Woodworth-Etter, *Signs and Wonders God Wrought in the Ministry for Forty Years* (New Kensington, PA: Whitaker 1997), 188.

15 Holifield, *Health and Medicine*, 28.

16 Charles Cullis, *The Seventeenth Report of the Consumptives' Home: And Other Institutions Connected with a Work of Faith, to September 30, 1881* (Boston, MA: Willard Tract Repository, 1881), 28; William E. Boardman, *"The Lord that Healeth Thee" (Johovah-Rophi)* (London: Morgan & Scott, 1881), 138; Gooden, introduction to Mix, *Faith Cures*, xxiv; Chappell, "Divine Healing Movement," 80.

17 Holifield, *Health and Medicine*, 40; James Monroe Buckley, *An Address on Supposed Miracles Delivered Monday, September 20, 1875, before the New York Ministers' Meeting of the M. E. Church* (New York: Hurd & Houghton, 1875), 23, 26, 45; Chappell, "Divine Healing Movement," 159–160; James Monroe Buckley, *Faith-Healing, Christian Science, and Kindred Phenomena* (New York: Century Company, 1892), 46.

18 Holifield, *Health and Medicine*, 53–54, 55.

19 Holifield, *Health and Medicine*, 23–24; Candy Gunther Brown, "Prophetic Daughter: Mary Fletcher's Narrative and Women's Religious and Social Experiences in Eighteenth-Century British Methodism," *Eighteenth-Century Women* 3 (2003): 77–98.

20 Holifield, *Health and Medicine*, 41–42.

21 David Edwin Harrell, *Oral Roberts: An American Life* (San Francisco: Harper & Row, 1985), 91, 102, 125, 212, 262, 299, 333; David Edwin Harrell, Jr., *All Things Are Possible: The Healing and Charismatic*

Revivals in Modern America (Bloomington, IN: Indiana University Press, 1975), 90; Spurgeon M. Dunnam, III, *God Is in the Now, He Will Meet Your Needs: An Interview with Oral Roberts* (Evanston, IL: Limited Edition Books, 1972), 1.

22   Candy Gunther Brown, "Healing Words: Narratives of Spiritual Healing and Kathryn Kuhlman's Uses of Print Culture, 1947–1976," in *Religion and the Culture of Print in Modern America*, edited by Charles L. Cohen and Paul S. Boyer (Madison, WI: University of Wisconsin Press, 2008), 271–297.

23   Brown, "Healing Words"; Kathryn Kuhlman, *I Believe in Miracles: Streams of Healing from the Heart of a Woman of Faith*, rev. ed. (Gainesville, FL: Bridge-Logos, 1962; 1992); Kathryn Kuhlman, *God Can Do It Again: Amazing Testimonies Wrought by God's Extraordinary Servant*, rev. ed. (Gainesville, FL: Bridge-Logos, 1969; 1993); Kathryn Kuhlman, *Nothing Is Impossible with God: Modern-Day Miracles in the Ministry of a Daughter of Destiny*, rev. ed. (Gainesville, FL: Bridge-Logos, 1974; 1999).

24   Kuhlman, *Nothing Is Impossible with God*, 73–100.

25   "Methodist Hospital Foundation," www.methodisthospitalfoundation. org/ (accessed April 15, 2013).

26   Cal Pierce, *Preparing the Way: The Reopening of the John G. Lake Healing Rooms in Spokane, Washington* (Hagerstown, MD: McDougal, 2001), 15, 105; "Meet the Directors," healingrooms.com/index. php?src=local&l=US1479&page=2 (accessed November 28, 2011); Candy Gunther Brown, *Testing Prayer: Science and Healing* (Cambridge, MA: Harvard University Press, 2012).

12 Spiritual Biography and Autobiography

TED A. CAMPBELL

INTRODUCTION

One of the most prominent means by which American Methodists disseminated their understandings of the Christian life was the genre of spiritual autobiography and related genres of death narratives, funeral orations, obituaries, and spiritual biographies. John Wesley had set a precedent for these works in his serially published *Journal of The Rev. John Wesley, A.M.* Wesley's theology of the "way of salvation" laid a foundation for understanding the spiritual life that was easily understood and could be applied in widely varying cultural contexts. Recent interpreters of American Methodism as a popular religious movement, such as John Wigger, David Hempton, and Lester Ruth, have utilized Methodist spiritual narratives as a means of understanding the impact that the Methodist movement had on nineteenth-century men and women of lower and middle social classes in the United States and elsewhere.[1]

THE WESLEYAN MODEL AND THEOLOGICAL
FRAMEWORK FOR SPIRITUAL BIOGRAPHY
AND AUTOBIOGRAPHY

John Wesley had been a reader of spiritual biographies from early on in his career. He indicated his sense of the importance of spiritual biographies in the following comment to a correspondent in 1771:

> Mr. Norris observes that no part of history is so profitable as that which relates to the great changes in states and kingdoms; and it is certain no part of Christian history is so profitable as that which relates to great changes wrought in our souls: these, therefore, should be carefully noticed and treasured up for the encouragement of our brethren.[2]

The principal purpose of disseminating spiritual autobiographies and biographies was for the encouragement of believers, but they also gave believers a kind of roadmap to the spiritual life and a vocabulary by which their own experiences could be understood.

The genre of spiritual autobiographies and biographies grew from sources in earlier Christian traditions. The fountainhead was Augustine's *Confessions*, in which Augustine of Hippo, writing in the 390s CE, had utilized the language of scripture, and especially of the Psalms, to craft a narrative of his own life in a first-person address to God. Medieval narratives of the lives of Christian saints also set a precedent for the genre of spiritual biography. Most immediately for the Methodist movement, Pietistic Puritans had developed the practice of keeping spiritual journals beginning with an account of their conversion, followed by narratives of the trials they faced as believers. They were encouraged to use these as a means of recounting their struggles to their pastors. An understanding of the *ordo salutis* as the out working of election ("effectual calling," justification, sanctification, and glorification) provided a sturdy framework for understanding a human life under the guidance of God.[3]

John Wesley himself set an example of spiritual autobiography that was well known to subsequent generations of Methodists. He published *The Journal of the Rev. John Wesley, A.M.* from 1740, though the first published fascicle contained material from as early as 1732, beginning with a really catchy line from a letter of that year:

> Sir,
> The occasion of my giving you this trouble is of a very extraordinary nature. On Sunday last I was informed (as no doubt you will be e'er long) that my brother and I had killed your son ...[4]

As Puritan biographies typically began with a conversion narrative, including an account of their preconversion life, the first fascicle of John Wesley's *Journal* began by laying out a narrative of Wesley's life prior to his conversion, ending with his observation "that I who went to America to convert others, was never myself converted to God."[5] The second fascicle began with an account of Wesley's Aldersgate Street experience of assurance.[6]

Wesley's *Journal* also set a precedent for honesty in reporting about his own spiritual struggles after the time of his Aldersgate Street experience. The following example was introduced as the thoughts of "One who had the form of godliness many years," but readers would scarcely have failed to recognize that Wesley was describing himself, and in fact a note in his private diary for this occasion stated, "Prayer, writ account of myself":

But that I am not a Christian at this day I as assuredly know as that Jesus is the Christ.

For a Christian is one who has the fruits of the Spirit of Christ, which (to mention no more) are love, peace, joy. But these I have not. I have not any love of God. I do not love either the Father or the Son.[7]

The writings of later Methodist people would account in great detail their own spiritual struggles, including their questioning whether they truly had Christian faith at all.

Wesley's *Journal* also exemplifies another characteristic taken up in later literature. Reflecting the popular genre of travel literature, the *Journal* was richly illustrated by accounts of travel, interesting places that Wesley had visited, and the people he met in those places. It was enlivened by accounts of attacks by angry mobs, rumors circulating about the evil intentions of Methodist people, and other intrigues. It included embedded stories of the conversions and spiritual triumphs of Methodist people. And it was full of Wesley's witty and sometimes rhetorically brilliant responses to the naysayers of the Methodist movement.

Just as the Puritan theology of the *ordo salutis* or "order of salvation" served as an intellectual framework for Puritan diaries, John Wesley's theology of "the way of salvation" served as a framework for works of spiritual biography and autobiography produced by Methodist people. Wesley could describe the "way of salvation" and various aspects of it in intricate detail, but he often summarized it in a three-fold pattern that recounted the state of a soul prior to justification, the moment of justification (usually accompanied by an assurance of pardon), and then the believer's struggles following justification. A well-known example comes from Wesley's *Principles of a Methodist Farther Explained* (1746), "Our main doctrines, which include all the rest, are three, – that of repentance, of faith, and of holiness."[8]

The three-fold pattern of the "way of salvation" proved to be a sturdy and easily comprehended framework. An early adherent of the African Methodist Episcopal Church, Jarena Lee, wrote that she heard the way of salvation explained by an African-American traveling preacher, William Scott, in the 1820s. Scott asked Lee:

if the Lord had justified my soul. I answered yes. He then asked me if he had sanctified me. I answered no and that I did not know what that was. He then undertook to instruct me further in the knowledge of the Lord respecting this blessing.... He told me the

progress of the soul from a state of darkness, or of nature, was three-
fold; or consisted in three degrees, as follows: – First, conviction for
sin. Second, justification from sin. Third, the entire sanctification
of the soul to God.[9]

In this one can see that the Wesleyan teaching of prevenient, justifying, and sanctifying grace – another way to state the three-fold pattern –
came to exercise a powerful force on popular imagination and gave
ordinary folk an extraordinarily helpful means of describing their own
spiritual experience.

PERSONAL TESTIMONY AS THE ROOT
OF SPIRITUAL AUTOBIOGRAPHY

John Wesley's *Journal* included within it a number of testimonies of
Methodist people. Although the Methodist class meetings were not supposed to focus on spiritual experiences, Methodist band meetings did
have this as a focus, and gatherings of Methodist societies in quarterly
love feasts and later quarterly conferences sometimes provided occasions
for testimonies.[10] There is evidence, moreover, that class meetings had
also come to serve as a venue for exchanging testimonies. Wesley had
heard testimonies at meetings like this and in private conversations, and
he included examples in his *Journal*. Consider the following references to
Joseph Norbury of London, from Wesley's *Journal* for November 1763:

> Tue. 15. I visited Joseph Norbury, a good old soldier of Jesus Christ.
> I found him just on the wing for paradise, having rattled in the
> throat for some time. But his speech was restored when I came in,
> and he mightily praised God for all his mercies. This was his last
> testimony for a good Master. Soon after, he fell asleep.
>
> ...
>
> Mon. 21. I buried the remains of Joseph Norbury, a faithful wit-
> ness of Jesus Christ. For about three years he has humbly and boldly
> testified, that God had saved him from *all* sin. And his whole
> spirit and behaviour, in life and death, made his testimony beyond
> exception.[11]

In this case, it was Norbury's testimony to entire sanctification that
Wesley found exemplary.

Later Methodist literature is replete with testimonies to the spiritual experiences of Methodist people. The following example is from
Homer Thrall's *History of Methodism in Texas*, published in 1872 but

recounting a story about the early Texas missionary to the Republic of Texas, Littleton Fowler, and his role in the conversion of William Kesee of Chappell Hill, Texas, who also became a Methodist leader. This event probably occurred around 1840:

> To have a private interview the two went out to a corn-crib. Here they prayed and held a class-meeting together, mutually exchanging experiences. When the two walked back again to the house, to one of them life presented a wonderfully changed aspect…. Fortunate is the theological seminary that can point to its students who fulfilled as faithfully and successfully the obligations of the Christian ministry as the one that Littleton Fowler graduated from Billy Kesee's corn-crib.[12]

This account suggests that by this time, "class meetings" had come to have a regular focus on testimonies: they "held a class-meeting together, mutually exchanging experiences."

The presence of these testimonies embedded in other works show that giving testimony to spiritual experience was a very common part of Methodist life. Methodist people would have been familiar with the formal theology of the "way of salvation" by way of sermons, which often included personal testimony on the part of the preacher.[13] Beyond sermons, Methodist people knew elements of the "way of salvation" by way of tracts, hymns (and the arrangement of hymnals), catechisms, and other works disseminated by Methodist denominations.[14] They also gained a vocabulary for describing spiritual experiences they learned from hearing the testimonies of other believers.

Sometimes the language used in personal testimonies differed from that of formal consensus. I have found, for example, that testimonies of Methodist constituents in the nineteenth century often preferred the term "conviction" over the more formal "awakening" or "the repentance of sinners." They often used "conversion" as a singular term to describe justification and the assurance of pardon. They came to use the word "sanctification" as a shorthand way of saying "entire sanctification," and that created a problem in finding vocabulary to describe the process of sanctification leading up to entire sanctification.[15]

SUSTAINED SPIRITUAL AUTOBIOGRAPHIES

Formal as well as popular sources for describing spiritual experiences gave Methodist people a rich framework and vocabulary for describing their own lives as Christians, and they produced voluminous writings doing so. These accounts took the form of sustained narratives of a person's spiritual journey and spiritual experiences, following the ways in which Methodists had typically described the "way of salvation." Some of these accounts were written for publication, but not all. Many were intended entirely for personal use, perhaps for sharing them orally in Methodist gatherings, although some of these eventually found their way into print. William Stevenson's *Autobiography* (see below) was written privately around 1844 and then published fourteen years later following Stevenson's death. The four other works listed below were all published by the authors, that is, they themselves put up the money for publication in the hopes of getting a return by selling copies of the books.

The following give a sample of five sustained accounts of personal religious history by American Methodists, here listed in chronological order:

William Apess, *A Son of the Forest: The Experience of William Apess, a Native of the Forest* (self-published originally in 1829).[16]

Jarena Lee, *The Life and Religious Experience of Jarena Lee, A Coloured Lady: Giving an Account of Her Call* (published for the author, 1836).[17]

Zilpha Elaw, *Memoirs of the Life, Religious Experience, Ministerial Travels and Labours of Mrs. Zilpha Elaw, An American Female of Colour, Together with Some Accounts of the Great Religious Revivals in America* (published by the author and sold by T. Dudley, 19 Charter-House Lane, and Mr. B. Taylor, 19, Montague St., Spitalfields, 1846).[18]

William Stevenson, *The Autobiography of the Rev. William Stevenson* (serialized in the *New Orleans Christian Advocate* between March 13 and April 24, 1858).[19]

Julia A. J. Foote, *A Brand Plucked from the Fire: An Autobiographical Sketch* (Cleveland, Ohio: published for the author by W. F. Schneider, 1879).[20]

This is a very diverse group of individuals. William Apess was a Pequot Indian from Massachusetts. He was part of the Methodist Episcopal Church until 1830, when he became one of the first clergy associated with the Methodist Protestant Church. Jarena Lee, Zilpha Elaw, and Julia A. J. Foote were all free black women from northern states, and all claimed a divine calling to preach. Lee was associated with the African Methodist Episcopal Church, having been converted under the influence of Bishop Richard Allen, the denomination's founder. Zilpha Elaw was associated with the Methodist Episcopal Church. Julia A. J. Foote was associated with African Methodist Episcopal Zion Church and also identified herself with the growing holiness movement within American Methodism. William Stevenson was an Anglo-American minister originally associated with the Methodist Episcopal Church, but he became part of the Methodist Episcopal Church, South, after its formation in 1845.

Despite the diversity of the authors of these narratives, the narratives share common features that mark them as examples of Methodist spiritual autobiographies. Each of them has a recognizable structure, covering the following five aspects of spiritual experience:

1. They all begin with an account of the pre-conversion life of the narrator, including an account of their conviction of sin and spiritual struggles prior to conversion. These could be dramatic struggles, although Zilpha Elaw indicated that her experience prior to conversion was not dramatic but involved a simpler sense of her having grieved God.[21]

2. They all have an account of the narrator's conversion, typically a dramatic experience accompanied by a sense of a direct, divinely-given assurance of the forgiveness of their sins. Zilpha Elaw's account is again an exception, for she notes that her own conversion was of a gentler nature, though it was followed by a vision of Christ in which she was assured of forgiveness.[22]

3. They all continue with stories of the struggles of the soul after conversion. These are often very severe struggles, matching those prior to conversion.[23]

4. All except William Apess include a testimony to the experience of entire sanctification.[24]

5. All five accounts include a narrative of the person's calling to be a preacher and (in the case of William Stevenson) an ordained minister.[25] In the cases of Lee, Elaw, and Foote, these discussions are tied up with their struggles with those who objected that women should not be preachers of the Gospel. In the case of Apess, the discussion was tied up with his struggle to be licensed to preach in the Methodist Episcopal Church and his perception that he had been denied a preaching license because he was an Indian.[26]

In addition to the similarities between the structures of these narratives, they often show resonances with elements of Wesley's *Journal* (perhaps transmitted via the *Life of Wesley* by Thomas Coke and Henry Moore), and many similarities to each other.

Julia A. J. Foote's title, *A Brand Plucked from the Fire*, recalls the biblical phrase (Zechariah 3:2) that John Wesley had used in his own branding (so to speak) and that he associated with his rescue from the Epworth rectory fire in February 1709.[27] Similarly, William Stevenson described an event in which he was working on a house and fell through the roof and through the floor below. He commented on this experience, "O my soul, love thou the Lord. Love thou the Lord, for thou hast been plucked as a brand from the burning."[28] On two occasions, William Apess had reference to a "warmed heart," evoking John Wesley's narrative of the Aldersgate Street experience in which he felt his "heart strangely warmed."[29]

There is a direct parallel between Jarena Lee's account of her experience of entire sanctification and an account of entire sanctification given by William Apess' wife Mary Apess. Jarena Lee wrote, "That very instant, as if lightening had darted through me, I sprang to my feet and cried, 'The Lord has sanctified my soul!'"[30] Mary Apess wrote, "I felt the mighty power of God again, like electric fire, go through every part of me, cleansing me throughout soul, flesh, and spirit."[31] Apparently the images of "lightening" and "electric fire" were common images used to describe the experience of entire sanctification. Zilpha Elaw and Julia A. J. Foote both wrote that they fell to the floor in their experiences of entire sanctification.[32] This gives the impression that personal testimonies and more sustained accounts of spiritual experiences not only gave a vocabulary by which one could describe their own spiritual experiences, but in some ways "scripted" the experiences, that is, the narratives suggested to participants how an experience like that of entire sanctification was supposed to occur.

Jarena Lee had been converted under the influence of Richard Allen, the founder of the African Methodist Episcopal Church. Allen's own autobiographical account, *The Life, Experience, and Gospel Labors of the Rt. Rev. Richard Allen*, played a particularly important role in the formation of African Methodism in the United States. Allen's work also reflects the typical points of Methodist spiritual narratives given above, recounting his struggles prior to conversion, and then his conversion:

> I was brought under doubts, and was tempted to believe I was deceived, and was constrained to seek the Lord afresh. I went with my head bowed down for many days. My sins were a heavy burden. I was tempted to believe there was no mercy for me. I cried to the Lord both night and day. One night I thought hell would be my portion. I cried unto Him who delighteth to hear the prayers of a poor sinner; and all of a sudden my dungeon shook, my chains flew off, and glory to God, I cried. My soul was filled. I cried, enough for me – the Saviour died.[33]

The volume went on to describe Allen's spiritual experience and his calling to ministry. Most critical, Allen's work contained a narrative of the exclusionary treatment meted out to black members of the St. George society in Philadelphia, the event that led to the separate existence of the AME Church. This narrative that has been re-told at the beginning of every volume of the *Doctrines and Discipline* of that denomination.[34]

Sustained narratives of personal spiritual experiences like these were published by the earliest Methodist publishing venture in North America, the Book Concern of the Methodist Episcopal Church, established in 1789, from very early in its history. From very early, the Publishing Concern carried the *Journal* of Francis Asbury, adding new volumes to its publication list as Asbury prepared them. By 1791 they listed *The Experience and Travels of Mr. Freeborn Garrettson* in their short list of publications. This followed the pattern of earlier Methodist spiritual autobiographies. The first chapter ("Part") of the work describes Garrettson's life, "From my Childhood till my Conversion." The second chapter describes his life, "From my Conversion till I entered the Connection as a Travelling Preacher." Subsequent chapters detailed Garrettson's preaching and travels through the eastern United States and Canada. The publishing house subsequently updated this work with new editions including descriptions of later periods in Garrettson's life.[35] In the middle of the nineteenth century, the publishing house of the Methodist Episcopal Church published Peter Cartwright's *Autobiography* (1856). Cartwright's *Autobiography* followed the general pattern of earlier Methodist autobiographies, though it also recounted in detail his virulent hatred of slavery and his abolitionist activities. The publishing house of the Methodist Episcopal Church, South, refused to sell the volume.[36]

In addition to autobiographical studies of American Methodist leaders, the Book Concern also offered personal narratives of British Methodists who had been associated with John Wesley. From at least 1793 its catalog listed a volume entitled *The Experience of Several Eminent Methodist Preachers, with an Account of their Call to, and Success in the Ministry*, a work giving the autobiographies of earlier British Methodist preachers associated with John Wesley. These are also autobiographical narratives following the general framework laid out above.[37] From 1804 the Publishing Concern offered *The Memoirs of the Rev. Peard Dickinson*, an autobiographical account of another preacher associated closely with John Wesley.[38]

The publishing houses of the Methodist denominations carried many autobiographical volumes through the nineteenth and early twentieth centuries, though these tended to be accounts of well-known leaders like Garrettson or Cartwright. Many more such accounts were published privately as we have seen in the cases of Apess, Lee, Elaw, and Foote, and some were published in denominational serial literature such as the *Autobiography of William Stevenson* serialized in the *New Orleans Christian Advocate*.

I conclude this section by noting one later autobiographical account published by the Methodist Episcopal Church, South, in 1898, José Policarpo Rodríguez's *"The Old Guide": Surveyor, Scout, Hunter, Indian Fighter, Ranchman, Preacher: His Life in His Own Words*. This is a work designed to appeal to men, a lively, macho tale recounting the remarkable life of Rodríguez, one of the earliest Hispanic preachers in the Methodist Episcopal Church, South. Like other Methodist autobiographies, it recounts Rodríguez's early life and eventually his conversion, though most of the book is taken up with the exciting details of his pre-conversion life, well summarized in the words of the subtitle, "Surveyor, Scout, Hunter, Indian Fighter, Ranchman." Toward the end, the work explains some of the workings of Methodist polity as Rodríguez described his process of obtaining a license to preach and becoming ordained.[39]

DEATH NARRATIVES, FUNERAL ORATIONS, AND OBITUARIES

"The question has been raised," wrote C. I. Scofield, "whether Moses wrote the account of his death" in Deuteronomy 34. Scofield rigorously followed Fundamentalist orthodoxy in concluding that Moses did indeed write the account of his own death in that chapter, by way of a special divine revelation, thus preserving the full doctrine of the Mosaic authorship of the Pentateuch.[40]

Other humans have not generally written accounts of their own deaths, but narratives of the faithful deaths of Methodist people were vastly important in early Methodist spirituality, so death narratives mark a transition from autobiography to biographical accounts in early Methodist literature. David Hempton has pointed out how consistently the (British Methodist) *Arminian Magazine* included stylized accounts of the faithful deaths of Methodist people. "To die a good and holy death, free from anguish and uncertainty, was the aspiration placed before the Methodist faithful in the pages of *The Arminian Magazine*."[41]

An account of John Wesley's death written by Elizabeth Ritchie, *Some Account of the Last Sickness and Death of the Rev. John Wesley*, published six days after John Wesley died, became the standard account of Wesley's death and provided an abiding example for subsequent narratives of the deaths of Methodist people.[42] Ritchie had served as Wesley's housekeeper in his last days, and it was her account of Wesley's last hours that included his attempts to say, "I'll praise ... I'll praise," suggesting that Wesley was trying to say "I'll praise my Maker while I've breath / and when my voice is lost in death, / praise shall employ my nobler powers." This was a testimony to a faithful death, commensurate with the witness Wesley had made through his life. A similar account of the death of John William Fletcher was written by Fletcher's wife, Mary Bosanquet Fletcher, in 1785.[43]

American Methodists continued this trajectory of writing accounts of the holy deaths of Methodist saints. An example appears in Ezekiel Cooper's 1799 *Funeral Discourse, on the Death of that Eminent Man the Late Reverend John Dickins*:

> When his speech was nearly gone, he was observed, by the friend that attended him, to be in fervent praise and prayer; and although but few of his words could be articulated, he was heard distinctly to say, "Glory! Glory! Come, Lord Jesus!" Those were his last words, that could be understood. Here was an evidence of his unshaken confidence, to the last.[44]

Unlike the death narratives given in *The Arminian Magazine*, this account appeared at the conclusion of a funeral oration. Lester Ruth has shown that Methodist people continued producing and disseminating accounts of happy and holy deaths through the nineteenth century.[45]

The funeral oration was itself an important genre for offering a narrative of the spiritual lives of Christians. John Wesley once again set a precedent in his sermon "On The Death of The Rev. Mr. George Whitefield" (November 1770), and Wesley's own death led to a plethora of funeral orations. In addition to the one preached by John Whitehead at Wesley's funeral on March 9, 1791, Methodist preachers Thomas Coke, James Kenton, Thomas Olivers, and Richard Rodda all published funeral orations celebrating Wesley's life and death. Anglican priests Elhanan Winchester, William Hobrow, and William Huntington also prepared funeral orations celebrating John Wesley that were subsequently published.[46]

The funeral oration offered a first occasion on which one could summarize the life of a Methodist. It might be grounded on personal knowledge or on written sources (e.g., diaries, journals, and death narratives) and tended to follow the pattern given above for sustained personal narratives, going light on the struggles of the soul prior to conversion and after conversion, placing more emphasis on the individual's conversion, their faithfulness and holiness, and very often their experience of entire sanctification and/or their experience of calling to ministry, with an added narrative of their faithful death.

Funeral orations prepared the way for more formal obituaries. John Lenton points out that obituaries of British Methodist preachers printed in the minutes of the Conference were at first very brief notices, but grew in length in the early nineteenth century.[47] By the middle of the nineteenth century, obituaries in American Methodist conference journals had grown into florid accounts of the spiritual experiences of ministers. An example appears in the journal of the New England Conference for 1878 celebrating the life of Hector Brownson (1791–1877). The obituary records some details of Brownson's early life, then his conversion: "He was powerfully awakened under a sermon by a pioneer Methodist preacher and converted soon after under a parlor exhortation given by a Mrs. Hanks, one of the noble Christian women of her day." It goes on to recount his marriage, his military service in the War of 1812, his calling to ordained ministry, and his various appointments. The obituary concluded with an account of his death:

> On the sabbath morning of April 30, 1877, he was seated in his rocking chair. His head reclined and his countenance lighted up with a pleasant smile. He seemed to have fallen into a restful sleep, but it was the sleep of death and the waking to eternal life.[48]

There are thousands of such obituaries of Methodist itinerant elders recorded in conference journals like this one.[49] They not only provide an example of Methodist spiritual narratives; they are a treasure trove of information for family historians and genealogists.

BIOGRAPHY AS A METHODIST GENRE

Early Methodist spiritual biographies tended to follow the same general framework as the spiritual autobiographies, funeral orations, and obituaries considered in the previous sections, and I will argue that biographies can be seen, among American Methodists, as a derivative of spiritual testimonies and more sustained autobiographical narratives. John Wesley himself had valued spiritual narratives, as indicated in the quotation given above. Of particular importance to him was the *Life* of Gaston Jean Baptiste de Renty (1611–1649), a well-educated Catholic layman who, inspired by Thomas à Kempis' *Imitation of Christ*, had given his life in service to the poor. Wesley included *The Life of de Renty* in his own

Christian Library, and the Publishing House of the Methodist Episcopal Church offered it for sale through the early nineteenth century.[50]

Just as John Wesley's *Journal* provided a pattern for the spiritual autobiography, so the *Life of the Rev. Mr. John Wesley, A.M.* by Thomas Coke and Henry Moore provided a frame of reference for Methodist biographical works. This biography was originally published in 1792, the year after John Wesley's death, and was published by the Book Concern of the Methodist Episcopal Church in the United States from at least 1793.[51] Coke and Moore prepared the book hastily. They did not have access to Wesley's personal diaries or to too many of his letters due to a conflict with John Whitehead, and their account thus relied heavily on John Wesley's own *Journal*. The work of Coke and Moore set the pattern for the subsequent retelling of Wesley's life in official Methodist circles. It emphasized the corruption of the Church of England in Wesley's time and dwelt on Wesley's Aldersgate Street experience unambiguously as Wesley's own conversion to Christian faith. It did not mention the ordinations of 1784 except in a subsequent section on the American Methodist mission. Although the two-volume *Life* that Whitehead published in 1793 and 1796 was far more nuanced and utilized a wider range of sources, Methodist leaders on both sides of the Atlantic objected to Whitehead's views of Wesley and strongly favored the *Life* by Coke and Moore. The biography by Coke and Moore thus became the standard interpretation of John Wesley's life and experience, and generations of Methodist people knew of Wesley principally by way of this work. It was apparently published before the Book Concern began to publish extracts of Wesley's *Journal*.[52]

The Publishing Concern also carried in its earliest lists of publications a biography of Thomas Walsh (1730–1858), an early Methodist preacher from Ireland whose death was blamed, at least partly, on attacks by ignorant mobs while Walsh was preaching. His biography by John Morgan, *The Life and Death of Thomas Walsh*, was a standard of early Methodist literature. It was apparently printed together with the *Journal* of another British Methodist, John Nelson, when published by the Book Concern of the Methodist Episcopal Church.[53]

Biography does not seem to be nearly as prominent a genre within Methodist circles as the other forms of spiritual autobiography considered above. It was only an exceptional group of influential Methodist leaders for whom the labor of producing a biography was expended. Lester Ruth's *Early Methodist Life and Spirituality: A Reader* (2005) gives an extensive list of publications of Methodist spiritual narratives, but only three of these were properly biographies, that is, accounts composed by someone other than the subject of the work.[54] I suggest, then, that biography should be seen as a derivative genre within the range of American Methodist narratives of spiritual experiences, an occasional outgrowth of the more common genres of spiritual autobiographies considered above.

THE PERSISTENCE OF METHODIST SPIRITUAL AUTOBIOGRAPHIES, BIOGRAPHIES, AND OBITUARIES

The confident, sometimes swaggering, spiritual biographies of American Methodists from the 1800s now seem like a thing of the past, though there are some areas of American Methodist life in which these genres have continued. Samuel Gardiner Ayres' *Methodist Heroes of Other Days* (1916) republished a great deal of heroic earlier Methodist biographies.[55] Similarly, Halford E. Luccock's *Endless Line of Splendor*, originally published in 1950, included brief biographies of Methodist and other Christian leaders and was published in a new edition (co-authored with Webb Garrison) as recently as 1992.[56]

The practice of giving personal testimonies remains alive in evangelically oriented Methodist congregations. In the 1960s and 1970s, United Methodist congregations in the United States hosted Lay Witness Missions, weekend-long evangelistic meetings that featured the testimonies of visiting laypersons.[57]

A contemporary instance of the genre of spiritual autobiography is that of United Methodist Bishop James K. Mathews (1913–2010), whose autobiography, *A Global Odyssey*, was published by the Abingdon Press, a division of the United Methodist Publishing House, in 2000. This book displays many of the characteristics of earlier American Methodist spiritual autobiographies. It does not detail Mathews' struggles of the soul prior to conversion except to note that, under the influence of a spiritual mentor, he once filled four pages of paper listing all of his known sins.[58] It does have an account of his conversion, following the conversion of his brother Joe, then a separate account of an experience of assurance that his sins had been forgiven.[59] It has a lengthy description of his sense of a calling to ministry and his subsequent struggles with related issues, for example, his decision to refuse election as a bishop in India.[60] Like earlier Methodist biographical and autobiographical literature, the work is replete with Mathews' accounts of travel, especially his many years in India. It does not recount an experience of entire sanctification, though it shows Mathews' consistent concern for the cultivation of Christian holiness.

This article has shown that more sustained accounts of spiritual experiences grew out of the practice of giving testimonies to one's experience in Methodist meetings. Accounts of the deaths of Methodists were added to these accounts, and then funeral orations and obituaries offered succinct biographical accounts of the lives of Methodist people. In a few exceptional cases, full-scale biographical works recounted the lives and experiences of Methodist leaders. In all of these ways, autobiographical and biographical accounts of the spiritual experiences of Methodist people like the ones considered here served as a powerful means to disseminate Wesleyan and Methodist understandings of the Christian faith to broad audiences

Notes

1   John Wigger utilizes a pastiche of testimonies and narratives of Methodist people to exemplify the affective religion of American Methodists in the nineteenth century in *Taking Heaven by Storm* (Urbana and Chicago, IL: University of Illinois Press, 1998), 104–124. David Hempton utilizes personal narratives of John Edwards Risley, Fanny Newell, and Hannah Bunting in *Methodism: Empire of the Spirit* (New Haven, CT: Yale University Press, 2005), 60–65. Hempton notes that these are only samples of a voluminous literature of personal narratives produced by Methodists. Lester Ruth illustrates Methodist life in the nineteenth century by way of a series of personal narratives in *Early Methodist Life and Spirituality: A Reader* (Nashville, TN: Kingswood Books, 2005), 309–322.

2   John Wesley, letter to "Miss March" dated 14 April 1771, in John Telford, ed., *Letters of the Rev. John Wesley, A.M.* 8 vols. (London: Epworth Press, 1931), 5:237.

3   William Haller, *The Rise of Puritanism, Or, The Way to the New Jerusalem as Set Forth in Pulpit and Press from Thomas Cartwright to John Lilburne and John Milton, 1570–1643* (New York: Columbia University Press, 1938), 86–92. See also my discussion of the Puritan understanding of the *ordo salutis* and the use of diaries in Ted A. Campbell, *Wesleyan Beliefs: Formal and Popular Expressions of the Core Beliefs of Wesleyan Communities* (Nashville, TN: Kingswood Books, 2011), 67–69.

4   In the first fascicle of the *Journal*, in W. Reginald Ward and Richard P. Heitzenrater, eds., *Journal and Diaries* (Bicentennial Edition of the Works of John Wesley; 1988–2003), 18:123.

5   *Journal* for 29 January 1738, in Ward and Heitzenrater, eds., *Journal and Diaries*, 18:214.

6   *Journal* for 24 May 1738, in Ward and Heitzenrater, eds., *Journal and Diaries*, 18:242–250.

7   *Journal* for 4 January 1739, in Ward and Heitzenrater, eds., *Journal and Diaries*, 19:29–30.

8   *The Principles of a Methodist Farther Explained*, ¶ VI:4–6, in Rupert E. Davies, ed., *The Methodist Societies: History, Nature and Design* (Bicentennial Edition of the Works of John Wesley, volume 9; 1989), 195.

9   Jarena Lee, recounting a conversation with William Scott, in William Andrews, ed., *Sisters of the Spirit: Three Black Women's Autobiographies*

of the Nineteenth Century (Bloomington, IN: Indiana University Press, 1986), 33.

10 On quarterly conferences as occasions for testimonies, see Lester Ruth, *A Little Heaven Below: Worship at Early Methodist Quarterly Meetings* (Nashville, TN: Kingswood Books, 2000), 107–112, 239–242.

11 *Journal* for 15 and 21 November 1763, in Ward and Heitzenrater, eds., *Journal and Diaries*, 21:438 and 439.

12 Homer Thrall, *History of Methodism in Texas* (Houston, TX: E. H. Cushing, 1872), 45. I would date the event roughly around 1840, because Fowler came to the Republic of Texas as a missionary of the Missionary Society of the Methodist Episcopal Church in 1837 and died in 1845. Thrall also refers to Kesee in *Chappell Hill in 1843*, 75.

13 Lester Ruth, "Liturgical Revolutions," in William J. Abraham and James E. Kirby, eds., *The Oxford Handbook of Methodist Studies* (New York: Oxford University Press, 2009), 322–323.

14 Campbell, *Wesleyan Beliefs*, 148–156.

15 Ibid., 163–165. Another example of autobiographical testimony is that of Catherine Livingstone Garrett, given in Russell E. Richey, Kenneth E. Rowe, and Jean Miller Schmidt, eds., *The Methodist Experience in America, vol. 2: A Sourcebook* (Nashville, TN: Abingdon Press, 2000), 94–95.

16 In Barry O'Connell, ed., *On Our Own Ground: The Complete Writings of William Apess, a Pequot* (Amherst, MA: University of Massachusetts Press, 1992), 1–97.

17 In Andrews, ed., *Sisters of the Spirit*, 25–48.

18 In Andrews, ed., *Sisters of the Spirit*, 49–52.

19 I have edited a text of Stevenson's *Autobiography* based on a typescript at Bridwell Library, Southern Methodist University, and checked it against the original publications in the *New Orleans Christian Advocate*.

20 In Andrews, ed., *Sisters of the Spirit*, 161–234.

21 William Apess, in O'Connell, ed., *On Our Own Ground*, 129; Jarena Lee, in Andrews, ed., *Sisters of the Spirit*, 29; Zilpha Elaw, in Andrews, ed., *Sisters of the Spirit*, 55; William Stevenson, *Autobiography* sections published on March 13 and 20, 1858; Julia A. J. Foote, in Andrews, ed., *Sisters of the Spirit*, 178 and thereabouts.

22 William Apess, in O'Connell, ed., *On Our Own Ground*, 121–127; Jarena Lee, in Andrews, ed., 27; Zilpha Elaw, in Andrews, ed., *Sisters of the Spirit*, 55–57; William Stevenson, *Autobiography* section published on March 20, 1858 (the conclusion of this section); Julia A. J. Foote, in Andrews, ed., *Sisters of the Spirit*, 180–181.

23 William Apess, in O'Connell, ed., *On Our Own Ground*, 130–132; Jarena Lee, in Andrews, ed., *Sisters of the Spirit*, 27–32; Zilpha Elaw, in Andrews, ed., *Sisters of the Spirit*, 58; William Stevenson, *Autobiography* sections published on March 27, and April 3, 1858; Julia A. J. Foote, in Andrews, ed.,; cf. the chapter titles on pp. 182 (chapter eight), 184 (chapter nine), and 186 (chapter ten), all of which reveal struggles of the soul following conversion.

24 Jarena Lee, in Andrews, ed., *Sisters of the Spirit*, 34; Zilpha Elaw, in Andrews, ed., *Sisters of the Spirit*, 66; William Stevenson, *Autobiography* section published on April 3, 1858; Julia A. J. Foote, in Andrews, ed., *Sisters of the Spirit*, 186–187.

25 William Apess, in O'Connell, ed., *On Our Own Ground*, 43–44 (beginning of chapter nine); Jarena Lee, in Andrews, ed., *Sisters of the Spirit*, 36 and following; Zilpha Elaw, in Andrews, ed., *Sisters of the Spirit*, 87 and following; William Stevenson, *Autobiography* section published on April 3, 1858; Julia A. J. Foote, in Andrews, ed., *Sisters of the Spirit*, 205 and following.

26 William Apess, in O'Connell, ed., *On Our Own Ground*, 51, and see O'Connell's note on this page about material that Apess removed from an earlier edition of the work relating to the issue of the licensing of an Indian to preach. Apess was granted a license to preach by the Methodist Protestant Church when he identified himself with that body in 1829/30.

27 On "a brand plucked out of the burning," see Richard P. Heitzenrater, *The Elusive Mr. Wesley*, 2nd ed. (Nashville, TN: Abingdon Press, 2003), 42–46.

28 William Stevenson, *Autobiography* section published on March 13, 1858.

29 William Apess, in O'Connell, ed., *On Our Own Ground*, 51 and 68.

30 Jarena Lee, in Andrews, ed., *Sisters of the Spirit*, 34.

31 Mary Apess, in O'Connell, ed., *On Our Own Ground*, 143.

32 Zilpha Elaw, in Andrews, ed., *Sisters of the Spirit*, 66; Julia A. J. Foote, in Andrews, ed., *Sisters of the Spirit*, 186–187.

33 Richard Allen, *The Life, Experience, and Gospel Labors of the Rt. Rev. Richard Allen* (Philadelphia: F. Ford and M. A. Ripley, 1880), 5.

34 Allen, Life, *Experience and Gospel Labors*, 14–15. Cf. *The Doctrines and Discipline of the African Methodist Episcopal Church, 2004–2008* (Nashville, TN: AMEC Sunday School Union, 2005), 5–6.

35 James Penn Pilkington, *The Methodist Publishing House: A History*, 2 vols. (Nashville, TN: Abingdon Press, 1968), 1:96, 101, and 102 (illustration). The version of Freeborn Garrettson's *Experience and Travels* I have consulted is the third edition, undated but believed to have been published in 1792 by John Dickens, the publisher of the M.E. Church, in Philadelphia.

36 Pilkington, *Methodist Publishing House*, 1: 391.

37 Pilkington, *Methodist Publishing House*, 1: 102 (illustration). The version I have consulted of *The Experience of Several Eminent Methodist Preachers* was published in New York in 1812. It is listed in the 1793 catalog of the Book Concern as "The Experience of about twenty British Methodist Preachers, well bound and lettered." This catalog also lists the *Journal* of John Nelson, another British Methodist preacher associated with John Wesley, apparently printed together with *The Life and Death of Thomas Walsh* (see below).

38 Pilkington, *Methodist Publishing House*, 1: 137.

39 José Policarpo Rodríguez, *"The Old Guide": Surveyor, Scout, Hunter, Indian Fighter, Ranchman, Preacher: His Life in His Own Words* (Nashville, TN, and Dallas, TX: Publishing House of the Methodist Episcopal Church, South, Smith and Lamar, Agents, 1898).

40 *The New Scofield Reference Bible* (1969), note on Deuteronomy 34:12.

41 Hempton, *Methodism*, 67.

42 Ritchie's work is presumed to have been published in London and is dated 8 March 1791. Wesley had died on 2 March. Cited in Richard P. Heitzenrater, ed., *"Faithful Unto Death": Last Years and Legacy of John Wesley* (Dallas, TX: Bridwell Library, 1991), items 1 and 2 (p. 15).

43   In Heitzenrater, ed., *"Faithful Unto Death,"* item 84 (p. 62).

44   Ezekiel Cooper, *A Funeral Discourse, on the Death of that Eminent Man, the Late Reverend John Dickins*, 2nd ed., (Philadelphia: R. Maxwell for Asbury Dickins, 1799), 27. Cf. Pilkington, 123.

45   See the accounts given in Ruth, ed., *Early Methodist Life and Spirituality*, 287–308.

46   In Heitzenrater, ed., *"Faithful Unto Death,"* items 6–13 (pp. 18–20).

47   John Lenton, *John Wesley's Preachers: A Social and Statistical Study of the British and Irish Preachers who Entered the Methodist Itinerancy before 1791* (Milton Keynes: Paternoster Press, 2009), 400–401.

48   *Minutes of the Seventy-Ninth Session of the New England Annual Conference of the Methodist Episcopal Church* (Boston, MA: James P. Magee, 1878), 42–43.

49   Through most of the nineteenth century in the Methodist Episcopal Church and the Methodist Episcopal Church, South, only itinerant elders were members of annual conferences, and consequently only their obituaries were consistently printed in conference journals. Local elders were minuted in quarterly conferences, but quarterly conference minutes were seldom printed and not nearly as many of these have survived.

50   Pilkington, *Methodist Publishing House*, 146, an illustration of the catalog of the Methodist Book concern from 1804 with the "Life of Monsieur de Renty" listed on the second page.

51   The book is listed among the publications of the Book Concern in 1793; cf. Pilkington, *Methodist Publishing House*, 102 (illustration). Cf. Frederick E. Maser, "The Early Biographers of John Wesley," *Methodist History* (January 1963), 34.

52   Pilkington, *Methodist Publishing House*, 143, mentions the publication of a second volume of John Wesley's *Journal* in 1804.

53   Pilkington, *Methodist Publishing House*, 1:102 (illustration). The listing in this 1793 catalog says simply, "Walsh and Nelson's Lives."

54   Ruth, ed., *Early Methodist Life and Spirituality*, 317–322. The only properly biographical studies in this extensive list of primary sources are the following: John Ffirth's biography of Benjamin Abbott, Richard A. Humphrey's *History and Hymns of John Adam Granade*, and John M'Lean's biography of Philip Gatch.

55   Samuel Gardiner Ayres, *Methodist Heroes of Other Days* (New York and Cincinnati, OH: Methodist Book Concern, 1916).

56   Halford E. Luccock and Webb Garrison, *Endless Line of Splendor*, 3rd ed., rev. (Nashville, TN: United Methodist Communications, 1992).

57   Lay Witness Missions originated with Presbyterian author and theologian Ben Campbell Johnson, but were licensed by the General Board of Discipleship of The United Methodist Church. The weekend events are described in Johnson's *A Road to Renewal: Preparation Manual for a Lay Witness Mission* (Atlanta, GA: Lay Renewal Publications, 1968).

58   James K. Mathews, *A Global Odyssey: The Autobiography of James K. Mathews* (Nashville, TN: Abingdon Press, 2000), 76.

59   Ibid., 76, 86–87.

60   Ibid., 233–234.

13 Education

STAN INGERSOL

"Methodism was cradled in a University ... [and] could not, therefore, be indifferent, much less hostile, to the education of the people," wrote Abel Stevens, Methodism's early historian.[1] John and Charles Wesley and Thomas Coke were in a select circle of early Methodists who enjoyed university educations in an age of widespread illiteracy. Still, John Wesley nourished the hope that Methodists would read, believing that "a reading people will always be a knowing people" and fearing that Christians would not "grow in grace unless they give themselves to reading."[2] So he fostered literacy, edited and published *The Arminian Magazine,* and reprinted scores of spiritual and theological works in the fifty-volume Christian Library series.

The Wesleyan vision led American Methodists to initiate an educational agenda that began with charity schools for poor children and a reading course for ministers, and then rose higher to embrace liberal arts education and graduate theological seminaries. These became features in all American Methodist branches – the central tradition comprising the Methodist Episcopal Church (MEC) and its successors, and dissenting traditions found in African Methodist, German Methodist, and Wesleyan-holiness sects. Over the course of their histories, Methodist churches utilized education to pursue various objectives: to uplift and enfranchise the illiterate; to advance human knowledge; to promote Christian discipleship, evangelism, social justice, and churchmanship; and to cultivate the theological and professional competence of their ministers.

CHARITY SCHOOLS AND SUNDAY SCHOOLS

In 1785, *The Arminian Magazine* circulated a letter by Robert Raikes promoting "Sunday charity schools" throughout England. It was no item of mere curiosity. Two years later, Methodism's founder noted that "eight hundred poor children [are] taught in our Sunday schools" in Bolton, England, "by about eighty masters, who receive no pay." Wesley's journals show that Sunday charity schools assumed an increasing role in Methodism's program to uplift and empower the poor, who were instructed in elementary education, moral values, and cultural improvements like singing.[3]

Americans encountered a different social and physical environment. There were urban poor, but most Americans inhabited an immense rural space that grew larger as the frontier shifted west, and, unlike Wesley's England, millions of Americans were slaves before 1865. Yet, early MEC *Disciplines* instructed ministers to "Preach expressly on Education." Should their lack of formal education make them feel inadequate to do so, still their *Discipline* instructed them: "you are to do it; else you are not called to be a Methodist-Preacher."[4]

Francis Asbury noted in 1790 that a Methodist conference in Charleston had "resolved on establishing Sunday schools for poor children, white and black."[5] Church officials and annual conferences urged preachers to encourage Sunday charity schools, yet much depended on laypersons like William Elliott, who organized Sunday schools on his Virginia plantation in 1785, teaching white and black children alike, though separately, to read the Bible. After sixteen years, Elliott moved his Sunday school site to a nearby Methodist church, where it continued.[6] Such local efforts were multiplied hundreds of times within Methodist spheres of influence, and Methodists in eastern cities joined other Protestants in municipal Sunday school unions that promoted general and religious education.

Nathan Bangs helped to organize the Methodist Sunday School Union in 1827 – a step toward systematizing MEC efforts and connecting them to the Book Concern, the church's publisher. A year later, there were over 1,000 affiliated Sunday schools and over 10,000 teachers serving 63,240 students. By 1830, an estimated 150,000 children attended Methodist Sunday schools, and by 1900 over 2.5 million. The Union urged that young people be instructed "particularly in the knowledge of the Holy Scriptures, and in the service and worship of God." Community schools were educating more American children, and charity schools were less vital, so the Union declared that "religious instruction is the grand and primary object of Sunday school instruction in our day and among our children."[7] The 1836 *Discipline* required Methodist Sunday schools to instruct children in vital Christian experience, too, including how they should fulfill their roles as baptized Christians. By 1840, Sunday schools were an integral part of congregational life and Quarterly Conferences were required to supervise the schools within their jurisdictions. Daniel Kidder, a college graduate, became the MEC's first Editor of Sunday School Books and Tracts in 1844. By 1876, the denomination had nearly as many Sunday schools as churches, and total Sunday school enrollment exceeded total church membership.[8] If the charity school sought to empower and civilize, the Sunday school aimed to Christianize.

The transformation of Sunday schools did not end the MEC's investment in basic education. The slavery issue divided mainline Methodism into regional churches until 1939 – the northern MEC and the Methodist Episcopal Church, South (MECS). After the Civil War, the northern church began educating southern blacks through its own Freedmen's Aid Society, organized in 1866. Within three years, it established and supported fifty-eight grammar schools and later expanded into colleges and universities.[9] MEC home missionaries were committed to reconstructing the South's social order but faced opposition from southern whites, who resented their presence and opposed black education. Some schools were forced to close. The Freedmen's Aid Society eventually concentrated on educating black preachers, believing that clergy were in the best position to lead their race.[10]

Reconstruction brought a significant shift in the fortunes of the African Methodist Episcopal (AME) and African Methodist Episcopal Zion (AMEZ) denominations, which originated in early-nineteenth-century Philadelphia and New York City, respectively. After the Civil War, both churches aggressively recruited members among the freedmen. Slaves had usually attended their masters' churches, so emancipation allowed significant realignment to occur throughout Southern religion, manifested particularly among Baptists and Methodists. African Methodists used Sunday schools to recruit members. Basic literacy was the primary mission of early postwar Sunday schools and remained an aspect of their work throughout the nineteenth century, especially where children of black rural sharecroppers worked in the fields and could be taught only on Sundays. African Methodist churches came to regard Sunday schools as effective means of evangelism because students comprised the bulk of those making professions of faith. Acting to solidify their roles in the New South, the AME placed its Sunday school agency in Nashville in the 1880s, while the AMEZ placed its board in Charlotte, North Carolina. The Colored (now Christian) Methodist Episcopal Church (CME) had originated within the MECS and relied on the latter's Sunday school materials until a CME publishing company was established in Jackson, Tennessee. By 1900, most AME and AMEZ members lived in the South, and by 1916 more than 40 percent of all Methodist Sunday schools in that region operated in AME, AMEZ, or CME churches.[11]

Sally McMillen's study of the southern Sunday school notes that black Methodist churches were more disposed than white ones to select women to supervise as Sunday school superintendents. The AME actually urged congregations to elect two Sunday school superintendents – a male and a female. The state and local Sunday school conventions conducted by African Methodists spoke out against social injustices, particularly against their race, and conventions became venues for publicly opposing disenfranchisement, segregation, and lynching.[12]

German constituents of the MEC also gravitated readily toward Sunday schools. Led by William Nast, they were especially numerous in the Midwest, stressed a devoted family life, and systematically established Sunday schools for their children. Some had religious weekday schools and constructed Sunday school libraries stocked with German and English books. German Methodist sects manifested the same interest. The 1835 general conference of the Evangelical Association (EA) (later Evangelical Church) urged all societies to conduct German Sabbath schools, and Rev. Henry Bucks insisted that teaching children was a better use of the pastor's time than preaching repeatedly "to old hardened sinners on whom all the efforts seem to be lost."[13]

The catechetical method of "question and answer" dominated early religious education but was gradually replaced through the influence of the International Uniform Lesson series. John H. Vincent, later bishop, promoted this development during his two decades heading the Methodist Sunday School Union. In 1872, he appealed to the International Sunday School Convention for coordinated lesson plans that crossed denominational lines. The convention appointed him to chair a committee to develop the idea. The uniform lesson plan meant that on any given Sunday, participating Sunday schools studied the same biblical text, regardless of age or denomination. In time, the curriculum included church history, the study of Bible lands, and theological topics. In Gerald McCulloh's apt phrasing, "the Sunday school, which had begun to outstrip the revival as an evangelizing agency of the church, came also to supply the means of Christian nurture for those who were being saved."[14] Vincent's southern counterpart, Atticus Haygood, resisted the move while editor of the *Sunday School Magazine*, wanting a strict Methodist-based curriculum. His successor shifted models, provoking the MECS bishops, with Haygood now among their number, to declare in 1890 that they preferred catechetical methods. They noted, though, that their own congregations did not seem to agree.[15]

By the twentieth century, general education theory influenced Sunday school education, and graded curriculum was developed for different age groups. Methodist publishers provided an array of Sunday school magazines and papers for teachers and students. As the Methodist class meeting declined, adult Sunday school classes became the locus of the small group experience. Church buildings were designed to provide educational space, one of the most influential schemes being the "Akron plan," pioneered by a Methodist church in Ohio that made Sunday schools a primary focus of its church program. The local church was understood as more than sacred space for worship. It was also a place to educate minds and hearts. The Sunday charity school, created to serve the poor, had evolved into the modern Sunday school, designed to promote the knowledge and experience of Christianity, embraced by Methodists of all ages and types, whether poor or affluent.[16]

Sunday school began declining in American Protestantism in the 1980s, partly due to secular pursuits, such as Sunday morning sports, especially those involving children. But adults also sought new approaches to Christian education, including small group studies unrestricted by a sixty-minute Sunday school hour or a particular day of the week. United Methodist bishop Richard Wilke's popular "Disciple Bible Study" series, developed in the 1980s, engaged participants in daily Bible readings and a weekly two-hour session, with the convener acting as a moderator rather than a lecturer.

THE COURSE OF STUDY

The evolution of congregational-based education had parallels in other areas. Methodist ministerial education originally consisted of a course of study pursued privately by candidates for ordination but directed by the annual conferences. In time, this gave way to a college experience, followed in many cases by further training in a graduate theological seminary, particularly after the mid-twentieth century.

The course of study was a required reading program for Methodist preachers. It was the dominant method of theological education throughout nineteenth-century Methodism and well into the twentieth century. It demanded self-motivated individuals, but the great physical demands placed on circuit riders generally limited the early Methodist ministry only to such persons. For Methodists, and perhaps for others, Francis Asbury epitomized the self-made preacher. Possessing only a basic grammar school education, he learned to read the Bible in Latin and in biblical Hebrew and Greek, and he developed a wide range of reading interests. He strove to read 100 pages a day when conditions permitted, though American roads made it very difficult to read on horseback, as

Wesley had done.[17] By his death in 1816, he was among America's most widely traveled men and a far better-read American than most.

The bishop and presiding elders determined the early course of study for the conferences, but by the mid-nineteenth century a universal reading list was formulated by the Board of Bishops and printed in the *Discipline*, and required texts were available through the Book Concern. The annual conferences examined the candidates and either passed or withheld them from advancement, thus holding them to the requirements. Candidates could hold preacher's licenses while undertaking the course of study, but they could not be ordained an elder or received as a minister in full connection until they passed. The reading list generally included books in English, rhetoric, American history, church history, Methodist history, systematic theology, homiletics, religious biography (including a life of Wesley), biblical studies, the denomination's particular *Discipline*, expositions of church polity, missions, ethics, and sermons (including Wesley's sermons). By 1912, the MEC's reading requirements underlined new sensitivities, with works on organizing and operating a Sunday school system, the psychology of religious experience, and the church's relation to social issues, including Walter Rauschenbusch's *Christianity and the Social Crisis*. The list retained many standard works, though, like John Wesley's *Plain Account of Christian Perfection*, an abridgement of Francis Asbury's journal, and books on evangelism, religious conversion, and the temperance crusade.[18]

African Methodist and Wesleyan-holiness churches had their own versions of the course of study that reflected their mainline Methodist roots. In the Church of the Nazarene (CN), ministerial candidates read Methodist writers on church history, pastoral care, preaching, and spiritual disciplines. They were introduced to John Wesley through his sermons, his writings on Christian holiness, and a biography. Until 1940, first year students were oriented to Wesleyan theology by Amos Binney's theological catechism, and in following years read the systematic theologies of MEC theologian John Miley or MECS theologian Thomas Ralston.[19]

The liberal arts degree increasingly became the twentieth-century norm for educating ministers, yet America's Methodist denominations still provide the course of study option for candidates whose circumstances warrant that approach.

COLLEGES AND UNIVERSITIES

America's competitiveness was evident in its religious life. Despite established churches in some colonies, religious dissent's creative edge could be observed everywhere. It was evident in New England's Free Will Baptists, who advanced during the Great Awakening; in the middle colonies among Quakers, Mennonites, Brethren, Presbyterians, and Roman Catholics; in the Carolinas, where German folk of Moravian, Lutheran, and Reformed bent mixed with Scotch-Irish Presbyterians; and in the Baptists, stretching from Rhode Island to Georgia, who would find their most congenial home in the South.

Denominational pluralism led Americans to quickly settle the issue of church and state; few harbored the desire to imitate the European model. Yet, pluralism also led to contests among denominations. The churches were united on some issues, like the necessity of winning the allegiance of Americans, who were overwhelmingly unchurched when the republic began. Likewise, the sects supported one another's revivals, and only after converts were harvested did sectarian differences come back into play. In public debates, Methodists opposed Presbyterians over predestination and election, Campbellites over baptismal regeneration, and Baptists on nearly every issue except the necessity of revivals. Methodists held their own, for they knew their Bibles, and the ministerial course of study was steeped in theology. Indeed, they believed that their doctrines had been worked out so thoroughly by Wesley and other scholars that even preachers without formal education could project them confidently.

The fact remained that Methodists and Baptists had lower educational standards for clergy than Episcopalians, Presbyterians, and others. This allowed them to field more preachers in shorter time and to hue more closely to the path of western settlement, leading them to grow more rapidly than other Protestant churches. In this context, the ministerial course of study seemed sufficient until the mid-nineteenth century, when the upward social and economic mobility of a rising middle class carried Methodist expectations with it, making colleges more desirable and relevant. Methodists "came late to the business, like Baptists, but, like them, once started, moved zealously forward," starting thirty-four schools between 1830 and 1861.[20]

The rise of Methodist schools advanced sectarian objectives. When Indiana Asbury University (now DePauw) was authorized in 1836, the Indiana Conference complained that most regional colleges were "in the hands of other denominations," so they sought "an institution under [their] control," from which they could "exclude all doctrines which we deem dangerous."[21] The classroom provided ministerial candidates a more social, intense, and mentored education, as it did for students pursuing other professions. The schools gathered young people of one or both sexes and educated them in an atmosphere of spiritual nurture bounded by Wesleyan beliefs. Chapel services generally were conducted once or twice daily throughout the nineteenth century and were customary weekly or more often at most Methodist-related colleges until the mid-twentieth century. Methodist colleges generated social and professional networks for their students, provided marriage opportunities, and made them alumni, often solidifying life-long relationships to Methodist churches and their institutions.

The colleges and the conferences stood in a unique relationship. The churches viewed their colleges as expressions of their religious culture and bearers of the denominational identity. They wanted the colleges to succeed because the church was successful when they did so. They saw the colleges as creations that benefited their children and grandchildren. The schools sought to attract students from other denominations but without losing their Methodist zeitgeist. They accepted the task of educating future clergy alongside future lay leaders in Methodist congregational life.

Colleges played another role in the overarching story that Methodism shared with other American churches. In the protracted effort to evangelize Americans and win their allegiance, Methodist colleges participated with other Christian schools in a sustained effort to civilize and Christianize the nation.

The first Methodist schools were academies, or secondary schools. The students had to possess the equivalent of a grammar school education before being admitted. There were also "seminaries," a term generally (but not always) referring to female academies. The MEC had twenty-eight academies, seminaries, and manual labor schools by 1840, each supported by annual conferences. Academies sometimes developed into colleges, while colleges, in other instances, added academies to their program.[22]

Several leaders in Methodist higher education began teaching careers at academies, like Wilbur Fisk, the first Methodist minister in New England with a college degree, earned at Brown University while he intended to be a lawyer. But Fisk entered the ministry instead, and he was a presiding elder in 1826, when he became principal of Wesleyan (later Wilbraham) Academy in Massachusetts. Five years later, he became founding president of Wesleyan University in Middletown, Connecticut, serving until his death. Twice elected bishop – by the Methodist Church of Canada in 1829 and by the MEC in 1836 – he declined both times. Fisk disputed theology with Calvinists and Unitarians, supported temperance reform, advocated a liberal arts education for preachers and missionaries, and viewed his work in higher education as a proper function of his ordained ministry. At Wesleyan, Fisk established the first Bachelor of Science degree, now offered universally.[23]

Though early, Wesleyan University was not America's first Methodist college. In 1822, Kentucky's legislature gave degree-granting authority to Augusta College, a joint venture of Methodist conferences in Ohio and Kentucky. Its alumni included Randolph Sinks Foster, Northwestern University president and bishop, and theologian John Miley. After graduating twenty-one classes, the MEC schism over slavery divided its sponsors, forcing its closure in 1849.[24]

Other Methodist colleges emerged on the heels of Wesleyan University. Randolph-Macon College opened in Virginia in 1832. Indiana Asbury University opened in 1837. A seminary in Lebanon, Illinois, was chartered as McKendree College in 1835 after a political battle in the state legislature, which did not want to authorize sectarian colleges. Methodists prevailed after forming a coalition with Baptists and Congregationalists, who wanted to open church colleges as well. Within a decade of Wesleyan's founding, Methodist colleges opened in Alabama, another in Virginia (Emory and Henry College), and female colleges opened in Delaware, Georgia, and Ohio, among others. By 1860, there were forty-nine Methodist colleges, more than any denomination

WESLEYAN UNIVERSITY, MIDDLETOWN, CONN.

Figure 10. **Advertisement for Wesleyan University (1883)**, Methodist Library Collection, Drew University, Madison, New Jersey.

except the Presbyterians.[25] The MEC created a Board of Education in 1868, and Methodist colleges and universities were federated under the board in 1892. That year, the MEC authorized a University Senate, composed of educators, to set educational standards and to exclude from official status schools that failed to meet them.[26]

In 1939, a three-way merger united the MEC, MECS, and Methodist Protestant Church (MPC). At that juncture, the MEC had six universities (American, Boston, Northwestern, Syracuse, University of Denver, and University of Southern California), forty-two colleges, and eleven junior colleges. The MECS brought three universities (Duke, Emory, and Southern Methodist University), twenty-three colleges, and sixteen junior colleges. The MPC brought three colleges and a junior college.[27]

Among German Methodist sects, the United Brethren in Christ (UBC) founded Otterbein College (now University) in 1847 and established others, including the University of Indianapolis. The EA founded several schools, including Albright College in Reading, Pennsylvania. Other colleges died or passed to other groups, but German Methodism's determination was evident in enterprises like Lane University, founded during the Civil War by UBC abolitionists at LeCompton, Kansas, stronghold of the state's pro-slavery faction, and named for James Lane, Kansas senator and ardent abolitionist. Dwight D. Eisenhower's parents met as students there and were married in the nearby home of her brother, a UBC minister, before Lane closed in 1902.[28] The surviving UBC and Evangelical schools became United Methodist institutions in 1968. They are among over 100 American colleges and universities that the Board of Higher Education lists as official schools of the United Methodist Church.

African Methodists pursued their own stake in higher education. The AME Church founded Union Seminary near Columbus, Ohio, in 1847 and merged it with Wilberforce University, an MEC institution near Xenia, Ohio, in 1858. AME leader Daniel Payne purchased the school outright in 1863. Payne was his denomination's outstanding advocate of higher education. Born a free black in South Carolina, he graduated from a Lutheran theological seminary in Pennsylvania and joined the AME Church in 1841, rising to become an outstanding bishop. Payne's purchase made Wilberforce the first black-controlled college in the nation. The AME Church planted seven more colleges, all in the South, before 1891. The AMEZ Church founded Livingstone College in 1879, now located in Salisbury, North Carolina. The CME Church founded Lane College in Jackson, Tennessee, in 1882, followed by other colleges in the South.[29] As repositories of historical memory, African

Methodist colleges help to sustain the identities of their denominations as progressive forces in African-American life and in the struggle for civil rights and social justice.

The nineteenth-century Wesleyan-holiness revival generated another network of Methodist schools. Dissenters from mainline Methodism, Wesleyan-holiness people sought their own press, publishers, and schools. Free Methodist Church (FMC) founder B. T. Roberts opened an academy at North Chili, New York, in 1866 that evolved into Roberts Wesleyan University, now in Rochester. The FMC has colleges in Michigan and Illinois, and Seattle Pacific University in Washington. Roberts had a particular interest in ministry to the poor, and scholars at FM schools still help to nourish and perpetuate his idealism today. The Wesleyan Church (WC) has a handful of universities, including Houghton College in New York, which began as an academy in 1883 and offered college courses fifteen years later. Indiana Wesleyan University is another of the WC's major schools. The CN supports eight American liberal arts institutions and a Bible college. Point Loma Nazarene University in San Diego originated in Los Angeles through the auspices of lay women associated with Phineas Bresee, the leading Nazarene founder. He became an early president of the school, which was known as Pasadena College until it relocated. Lay initiative and female enterprise are themes that run through the early histories of several Nazarene colleges.

Some Wesleyan-holiness colleges are not official church schools. John Wesley Hughes and H. C. Morrison were early leaders of Asbury College, an independent institution in Wilmore, Kentucky, that originated with deep ties to southern Methodism. Taylor College (now University) in Indiana originated as a Methodist female college, became co-ed in 1855, and remained affiliated with the MEC until 1922, yet it gravitated firmly to the Wesleyan-holiness camp in the late nineteenth century, to be renamed after Bishop William Taylor, a holiness movement stalwart. Azusa Pacific University, near Los Angeles, resulted from several college mergers, including FM and Church of God (Anderson, Indiana) schools. Wesleyan-holiness schools generally perpetuate a specific type of Wesleyan theology and a spiritual identity rooted in the holiness revival's concern for Christian perfection.

Methodist schools notably placed women in religion departments earlier than other denominations. Georgia Harkness studied philosophy and theology and taught applied theology at Garrett Biblical Institute for a decade beginning in 1939. She was the first woman to be a full professor at an American seminary. Before her death in 1947, Olive Winchester earned a divinity degree at Glasgow University (1912), a Th.D. at Drew (1925), taught biblical literature at three Nazarene colleges, was academic dean at one, and headed Pasadena College's religion department. Emily Ellyson and Mildred Bangs Wynkoop headed religion departments at other Nazarene schools before it became common.

National and regional culture has long affected the internal politics of Methodist schools, well illustrated in the public outcry in Georgia that led president James Dickey of Emory College to force the resignation of classics professor Andrew Sledd in 1902. Sledd's *Atlantic Monthly* article had condemned the lynching of African Americans, violating the white South's racial orthodoxy. Bishop Warren Candler, his father-in-law, could not save him. In North Carolina, John Kilgo, president of Trinity College, vowed not to be "rabbled" under similar circumstances and then was forced to prove this. Trinity's history professor, John Spencer Bassett, chastised segregation as a violation of southern manners and favorably compared Booker T. Washington to Robert E. Lee in Trinity College's own academic journal. North Carolina's leading newspaper launched a crusade to drive out Bassett, but Kilgo stood behind him, as did trustees and the Methodist family that later endowed the college handsomely, transforming it into Duke University. The Bassett Affair resulted in a milestone for academic freedom in the South.[30] Ironically, Dickey and Kilgo later served as MECS bishops.

The two cases underscore the ongoing conflicts between social conservatives and progressives that spill over into the church and even play out on Methodist campuses, which Sledd's subsequent career also attests. After earning a doctorate, he was president of the University of Florida and then of Methodist-affiliated Southern University (now Birmingham-Southern College) in Alabama. He returned to Georgia in 1914, joining the Candler School of Theology, where he taught New Testament until his death and influenced a generation of Methodist clergy that included theologian Albert Outler. Progressive Methodist clergy in Alabama and Florida formed the Andrew Sledd Study Club to promote interest in racial issues and civil rights.[31] Over and over, twentieth-century church colleges and seminaries became arenas where Methodists contended over race, voting rights, war, economic justice, the environment, and globalization.

Secularization also influences Methodist schools. With specific reference to higher education, historian George Marsden uses the term to characterize processes that lead church-affiliated schools to minimize, even terminate, relationships with their denominations. The contributing factors can include the need for financial support beyond the church and a desire by university leaders and alumni for higher status. The Vanderbilt University case was Methodism's most dramatic instance. The university was long fostered by MECS Bishop Holland McTyeire, but philanthropists provided the school with more reliable financial support than the church ever did. Under President James Kirkland, the school reduced the church's role in university governance and finally separated completely from the MECS after a nine-year legal battle that ended in 1914.[32] With less drama, Wesleyan University severed its Methodist ties in 1937, and the University of Southern California did so in 1952, as have others.

The evolution of some Methodist schools into major research universities necessarily entails the acceptance of religious pluralism on campus, but it does not always entail total separation from the church. Boston University, Duke, Emory, Southern Methodist University, and the University of Denver have large faculties and student bodies that represent many (or no) faith traditions, yet the universities remain church-related, though the public may not always see this. At the least, these institution's graduate schools of theology are unmistakably Methodist seminaries, but other evidences also may be apparent. Duke University, for instance, readily acknowledges Methodist roots and affiliation, and its Christian origins are clearly manifested in the primary campus's cruciform design, with its architectural focal point being Duke University Chapel, the home of a regular and devoted Sunday morning congregation that demands good preaching and good organ music.

The typical Methodist college, though, has a few thousand, or a few hundred, students and maintains good relations with the districts or conferences. For instance, Baker University offers its campus each summer for Institute, a multiple-week gathering of United Methodist youth across eastern Kansas, who gather for worship and education within the context of the Wesleyan "quadrilateral" (Scripture, reason, tradition, and experience). The conference operates the program, but the university hosts the event, which acquaints Methodist youth with their church's local university, cultivates ties to pastors and congregations, and strengthens alumni relations. The university chaplain is appointed by the Kansas Area bishop. In such ways, colleges in the Wesleyan tradition nurture and strengthen denominational ties.

THEOLOGICAL SEMINARIES

Methodist seminary dean and theologian Robert E. Cushman summarized a vision of graduate theological education. "What *is* a school?" he asked.

"Is it not a place, or better, a community where light is kindled and nurtured *in the meeting of minds*?" Yet, a theological seminary is much more, for it enshrines "a collective or corporate biography of faith in search of understanding."

> It is the hope and expectation for such a school that, in the meeting of minds, the light of faith burns brighter – perhaps bright enough, by God's grace, for men and women to find their way to fulfilling service in the Kingdom of God. No other kind of school either expressly aspires or presumes to attempt so much![33]

Despite such lofty visions, specialized theological education was initially resisted in virtually every branch of American Methodism.

Abel Stevens and Wesleyan University President Stephen Olin were among nineteenth-century Methodists who urged the creation of theological seminaries. Others strongly disagreed. In their era, a "theological seminary" was understood to be a Bible college with a curriculum restricted to theology and ministry, leading Wilbur Fisk to oppose the concept by arguing that ministers should receive a liberal arts education alongside laity. Nathan Bangs agreed. MEC bishops stated in 1840 that theological seminaries were unnecessary. Roman Catholics, Presbyterians, Moravians, Dutch Reformed, Lutherans, Congregationalists, Episcopalians, and Baptists – all organized seminaries between 1791 and 1817. William R. Cannon, Methodist historian and bishop, summarizing this situation, wrote that "in this regard, no other denomination in America was more backward" than the MEC.[34]

John Dempster, a former missionary, was determined to change this attitude. He opened Newbury Biblical Institute in Vermont in 1839. It relocated to Boston in 1868, becoming Boston Theological Seminary (now Boston University School of Theology). Drew Theological Seminary opened in New Jersey in 1867; a college developed later in conjunction with it. The MEC provided a seminary for Swedish-language pastors in Evanston, Indiana, in 1870, followed by a Norwegian-Danish seminary. By 1919, the MEC's nine seminaries included Garrett Biblical Institute in Chicago, Iliff School of Theology in Denver, and Maclay (now Claremont) School of Theology near Los Angeles. Gammon Theological Seminary originated at Clark College, an Atlanta school founded by the Freedmen's Aid Society. Despite the growing number of seminaries, the MEC did not allow a seminary diploma to waive the course of study requirement until 1928. The MECS had fewer theological schools. The first, Vanderbilt Divinity School, left the church in 1914, prompting the General Conference to authorize new seminaries in Georgia and Texas, affiliated with Emory University (Candler School of Theology) and Southern Methodist University (Perkins School of Theology).[35] Duke University Divinity School was added to the roster before the Methodist reunion in 1939. Methodist Protestants brought to that union Westminster Theological Seminary, founded in Maryland in 1882. It became Wesley Theological Seminary after relocating near American University in Washington, DC, in 1958. The 1956 General Conference authorized other seminaries for the Methodist Church: Saint Paul School of Theology in Kansas City, Missouri, and Methodist Theological School in Ohio in Delaware, Ohio.[36]

The UBC created Union Biblical Seminary (later Bonebrake Theological Seminary). The EA had Evangelical Theological Seminary in Illinois and Evangelical School of Theology in Pennsylvania. The two German Methodist denominations merged in 1946, creating the Evangelical United Brethren Church (EUB), and Bonebrake and Evangelical School of Theology merged eight years later, taking United Theological Seminary as the new name. The merger creating The United Methodist Church in 1968 led Evangelical Theological Seminary to merge with Garrett Biblical Institute, now Garrett-Evangelical Theological Seminary.[37]

Similar forces were at work in African Methodism. Wilberforce University had initiated Payne Theological Seminary by 1871. Livingstone College began offering the bachelor of divinity degree in 1903 and named its school of theology in 1906 for AMEZ Bishop James Hood, who had fostered higher education. The Interdenominational Theological Center in Atlanta, chartered in 1958, brought together six seminaries representing different denominations. Three of the six seminaries are Methodist: Gammon (UM), Turner (AME), and Phillips (CME).

Asbury Theological Seminary, founded in 1923, was the first seminary in the Wesleyan-holiness tradition. Today, evangelical United Methodists of various types comprise its primary constituency, though it has enjoyed FM and WC sponsorship, too. Its student body exceeded 1,200 students in 2000. Nazarene Theological Seminary opened in Kansas City, Missouri, in 1945, and its student body reached nearly 500 before peaking. The FMC has Seattle Pacific Seminary in Seattle, washington, and Northeastern Seminary at Roberts Wesleyan College in Rochester, New York. Wesley Seminary at Indiana Wesleyan University opened in 2009, the WC's first graduate seminary. Other Wesleyan-holiness seminaries include Anderson University School of Theology, connected to the Church of God (Anderson, Indiana), and George Fox Evangelical Seminary in Portland, Oregon. Azusa Pacific University School of

Theology is nondenominational, as is Wesley Biblical Seminary in Jackson, Mississippi, favored by Wesleyans who adhere to strict views of Scriptural inerrancy.

Methodist theological schools can cultivate distinct identities. Boston University's philosophy department and seminary were long associated with *personalism* through Borden Parker Bowne's influence. Claremont School of Theology became a primary place to study process theology through John Cobb, Jr.'s influence. Saint Paul School of Theology cultivated interests in various theologies of liberation during and after William McElvaney's presidency. Black theology is studied at African Methodist seminaries, while evangelical Wesleyan theology is the accent at Asbury Theological Seminary and at CN, FM, and WC seminaries. Duke Divinity School and Perkins School of Theology are fairly characterized as seminaries standing in a tradition of critical orthodoxy.

Methodist theological schools have spearheaded a Wesley studies renaissance that has influenced Wesleyan theological education for more than thirty years. Early groundwork was laid in studies published by Boston University's George Croft Cell, Drew University's Franz Hildebrandt, Candler School of Theology's William R. Cannon, and Perkins School of Theology's Albert Outler. A significant turning point occurred when Cushman, Outler, Hildebrandt, and Merrimon Cuninggim – representing four different institutions – agreed to sponsor a joint project to produce a modern critical edition of John Wesley's theological works and, in the process, to train Wesley specialists.[38] Frank Baker initially directed this project from Duke University, and he supervised the training of specialists who have now carried their interests to various Methodist schools. Perkins, in Outler's time and since, has emphasized historical studies on Wesley and Methodism, as does Drew University and Theological School, home to an extensive Methodist library and the official archives of the United Methodist Church. Church historian Paul Bassett's call in 1985 for "Re-Wesleyanizing Nazarene Higher Education" spurred faculty and administrators at Point Loma Nazarene University to found the Wesleyan Center for Twenty-First-Century Studies, while Northwest Nazarene University hosts the Wesley Center for Applied Theology and The Wesley Center Online. Duke University's Center for Studies in the Wesleyan Tradition is linked to the Wesley Works project. Ironically, through the cross-pollination that occurs now within Wesleyan theological education, John Wesley's relevance for contemporary Methodist churches is being appropriated more critically and earnestly in America today than in much of the nineteenth and most of the twentieth centuries.

Notes

1 Abel Stevens, *History of Methodism*, vol. 2 (New York and Cincinnati, OH: Methodist Book Concern, n.d.), 479.

2 John Telford, ed., *The Letters of John Wesley, A.M.*, vol. 8 (London: Epworth Press, 1931), 247.

3 *The Arminian Magazine* (January 1785), 41, and John Wesley, *Journal* (July 27, 1787); cited in Addie Grace Wardle, *History of the Sunday School Movement in the Methodist Episcopal Church* (New York and Cincinnati, OH: Methodist Book Concern, 1918), 18–22.

4 MEC, *Discipline*, 1787, 39; Wardle, *History of the Sunday School Movement*, 44–45.

5 Elmer T. Clark, ed., *Journals and Letters of Francis Asbury, Vol. 1: The Journal, 1771 to 1793* (London and Nashville, TN: Epworth Press and Abingdon Press, 1958), February 17, 1790, 625.

6 Wardle, *History of the Sunday School Movement*, 46–47; Wade Crawford Barclay, *History of Methodist Missions: Part One: Early American Methodism 1769–1844, Vol. 2: To Reform the Nation* (New York: Board of Missions and Church Extension of The Methodist Church, 1950), 15.

7 *Methodist Magazine* (1828), 352; *Methodist Magazine* (1827), 368; *Christian Advocate and Journal*, No. 33, 130–131, quoted in Wardle, *History of the Sunday School Movement*, 62–64; Barclay, 411, 414; Richard Cameron, *Methodism and Society in Historical Perspective* (Nashville, TN: Abingdon Press, 1961), 275.

8 Wardle, *History of the Sunday School Movement*, 76; Gerald O. McCulloh, "The Theology and Practices of Methodism, 1876–1919," *The History of American Methodism*, 3 vols., edited by Emory Bucke (New York and Nashville, TN: Abingdon Press, 1964), II: 643.

9 Cameron, *Methodism and Society*, 202, 203.

10 Paul Harvey, *Freedom's Coming: Religious Culture and the Shaping of the South from the Civil War through the Civil Rights Era* (Chapel Hill, NC: University of North Carolina Press, 2005), 29–33.

11 Sally G. McMillen, *To Raise Up the South: Sunday Schools in Black and White Churches, 1865–1915* (Baton Rouge, LA: Louisiana State University Press, 2001), 14, 22, 32, 73–74, 98.

12 McMillen, *To Raise Up the South*, 166, 175.

13 Barclay, *History of Methodist Missions*, 278; Raymond W. Albright, *A History of the Evangelical Church* (Harrisburg, PA: Evangelical Press, 1942), 191, (quote) 194.

14 McCulloh, "Theology and Practices," 643, (quote) 644; Cameron, *Methodism and Society*, 275.

15 McMillen, *To Raise Up the South*, 136.

16 McCulloh, "Theology and Practices," 644.

17 John Wigger, *American Saint: Francis Asbury & the Methodists* (New York: Oxford University Press, 2009), 19, 104–108, 353–354; Barclay, *History of Methodist Missions*, 433, 435.

18 MEC, *Discipline, 1876*, 351–353; MEC, *Discipline, 1912*, para. 570.

19 Stan Ingersol, "Methodism and the Theological Identity of the Church of the Nazarene," *Methodist History* (October 2004), 30–31.

20 Cameron, *Methodism and Society*, 232–233.

21 Quoted in Barclay, *History of Methodist Missions*, 380.

22 Cameron, *Methodism and Society*, 233–234.

23 Douglas J. Williamson, "Wilbur Fisk," in Charles E. Cole, ed., *Something More Than Human: Biographies of Leaders in American Methodist Higher Education* (Nashville, TN: United Methodist Board of Higher Education and Ministry, 1986), 91–106; William R. Cannon, "Education, Publication, Benevolent Work, and Missions," in Bucke, I: *History of Anglican Methodism*, 557.

24 Cannon, "Education, Publication," 554, 555.

25 Barclay, *History of Methodist Missions*, 404, 405.

26 Cameron, *Methodism and Society*, 242–244.

27 John O. Gross, "The Field of Education, 1865–1939," in Bucke, 3: 220–222, 238, 239, 242.

28 Don W. Holter, *The Lure of Kansas: The Story of Evangelicals and United Brethren* (n.p.: Kansas West Commission on Archives and History and Kansas East Commission on Archives and History, 1990), 49–52.

29 Milton C. Sernett, *Black Religion and American Evangelicalism: White Protestants, Plantation Missions, and the Flowering of Negro Christianity, 1787–1865* (Metuchen, NJ: Scarecrow Press and the American Theological Library Association, 1975), 140–145, 299; Carter G. Woodson, *The History of the Negro Church* (Washington, DC: Associated Publishers, 1921), 180–186.

30 Terry Lee Matthews, "The Emergence of a Prophet: Andrew Sledd and the 'Sledd Affair' of 1902," Ph.D. diss., Duke University, 1990.

31 Arthur W. Wainwright, "Andrew Sledd," in Cole, ed., *Something More Than Human*, 213–227.

32 George M. Marsden, *The Soul of the American University* (New York and Oxford: Oxford University Press, 1994), 276–287.

33 Robert E. Cushman, "Fifty Years of Theology and Theological Education at Duke," *Duke Divinity School Review* (Winter 1977), 4–5.

34 Cannon, "Education, Publication," 568–570, (quote) 571.

35 McCulloh, "Theology and Practices," 649–658.

36 Gerald O. McCulloh, *Ministerial Education in the American Methodist Movement* (Nashville, TN: United Methodist Board of Higher Education and Ministry, 1980), 14–147, 210–217.

37 J. Bruce Behney and Paul H. Eller, *The History of the Evangelical United Brethren Church* (Nashville, TN: Abingdon Press, 1979), 243–244, 362; Albright, 292, 406.

38 McCulloh, *Ministerial Education*, 297–308; see also Duke University's online Center for Studies in the Wesleyan Tradition.

Part III

Methodists and American Society

14   Methodists and Race

MORRIS L. DAVIS

From their earliest days in the colonies and the early U.S. republic, Methodists were both united as Christians together in multiracial gatherings and yet also divided along racial lines. These tensions have never disappeared. Rather, race and other similar culturally constructed markers of human difference such as ethnicity, nationality, and culture have remained central tensions in Methodist development, from individual relationships to congregational cultures to institutional differentiation. Throughout the two and a half centuries in which they have been present in American life, Methodists of all kinds have mirrored the dynamics of the larger American culture, particularly in the case of race. This does not mean that Methodists have been of one mind on conceptions of race and what those conceptions have meant; rather, Methodists, like the many groups in the larger and ever-evolving national American culture, have held and acted on vastly opposing views. From almost every angle of race thought, Methodists have participated in, instigated, or mimicked the dynamics in the rest of American culture. Among white Methodists, some joined or led the abolitionist movement, while others joined or led in defense of slavery. Numerous others fell somewhere in the middle, immobilized by an inability to simultaneously follow a principle of antislavery or proslavery and preserve family and social ties.[1] Among black Methodists, the choice to split institutionally in the face of racism, or remain in the denominational fold with sympathetic whites because of a theological discomfort with schism, has, over and over again, presented a painful dilemma. The power of race as an organizing principle and a tool of control shaped the way Methodists conceived and carried out evangelical outreach by forging the missions movement, and placing Native Americans, immigrants, and people around the world in mitigated relationships to denominational structures and full Methodist fellowship.

The central conceptual notion needed in order fully to understand the deep effects race has had on Methodist history is the power and ubiquity of whiteness. Whiteness and its explanatory power can best be understood by recognizing that there have always been Methodists who do not use any descriptive adjectives that qualify their claim to Methodism. White, English-speaking Methodists have never had to refer to themselves or their denominations with any qualifying language. White Methodists, in other words, have always controlled the privilege of understanding themselves and acting as "normal" Methodists. There have always been Methodists and black Methodists; holiness advocates and Black holiness advocates; the MEC and the AME; the MECS and the Colored Methodist Episcopal; the Oklahoma Conference and the Oklahoma Indian Conference. In this way, race is most powerful in its silent form – that is, the assumption that there are people without race, who are "normal," while those who must be identified or are forced to identify themselves as a qualifying adjective. Recognizing this can reveal how deeply race has effected Methodism, and why tracing racism or racist attitudes only marks certain of these effects, and masks the more difficult and intractable means by which race has managed to continue to haunt Methodists of all kinds.

Previous chapters in this volume have outlined much of the institutional history of denominational splits over race. A few of these, such as the stories of holiness abolitionists that formed the Wesleyan Methodist Connection, demonstrate how complicated the problem of race has been in this history. Why, for instance, did so few black Methodists join that denomination, when it took on the strongest antislavery stance? If understanding race and Methodism is as simple as tracing the history of those who had the most appealing view on slavery, and if those people represent a kind of "true" Methodist stance, why were they not more successful in healing the racial divide in the membership? Questions like this have yet to be adequately explored, but this chapter will focus on the era after the Civil War with a view toward understanding how race functioned with such persistence and malleability. This will show that it was not until after emancipation that Methodist denominations became more entrenched around racial divisions, shoring up boundaries that already existed, as well as creating new ones. This time period discloses the complex set of positions that Methodists generally took up in the face of more pronounced institutionalization in American Protestantism, and how this institutionalization provided both a means of another instantiation of race prejudice and a platform for antiracist activism. Methodism, by its vast national reach and high cultural profile, both reflected and greatly influenced the larger national dilemma of race.

FROM EMANCIPATION FROM SLAVERY
TO SEGREGATED FREEDOM

After the Civil War, Methodist denominations whose strength was
mostly or entirely in northern states, moved into the southern states
with great energy and resources to address the needs of the former slaves
and seek to establish churches among them. The MEC, AME, and AMEZ
all rushed southward to establish churches, address the physical needs of
former slaves, and build schools. In this era, Methodist denominations
played a major role in the rise across the United States of a system of
colleges and universities that became the largest in the world. Methodist
denominations were integral to the founding of scores of highly influential schools for African Americans, known to later generations as
"historic black colleges and universities." These schools, many born
out of this missionary effort, became central to the formation of black
American culture in the decades after emancipation.[2]

Much of this missionary fervor also created tension between
denominations, even to the point of legal battles over church property.
The AME and the AMEZ encountered some resistance from the newly
formed CME, which argued that its membership and territory were being
taken over by northern interlopers. Meanwhile, some in the much larger
and wealthier denominations often perceived the CME as too closely
tied to the parent white denomination of their former slaveholders, the
MECS. These tensions created divisions that persisted, and when, in
later decades, these three historically black denominations considered
a national merger, hard feelings and old scores remained part of the failure of these discussions.[3] Despite these tensions and debates, all four
of these Methodist churches gained members in the later nineteenth
century, and the imprint of this extension and outreach work would
be difficult to overstate. It is in this era that the MEC and the AME,
in particular, came to be powerfully centralized religious institutions
with global reach and a significant national prominence as representative Protestant churches in the United States. Both of these churches, in
different ways, evolved to be seen as custodial institutions of white and
black American Christian culture.[4]

If the divisions between the predominantly white Methodist denominations seemed intractable, the divisions between the different racialized denominations were even more so. While so many white-dominated
denominations remained separate – especially the two largest, the MEC
and MECS – merger discussions between white and black denominations were not possible. White denominations attempted merger talks

through the late nineteenth century, but they gained very little ground. The holiness movement was on the fringe of institutional influence in both the MEC and MECS, and so any discussions with schismatic holiness groups never gained much traction. Thinking that the end of slavery meant the end of the reasons for separation from the mother church, a few thousand members of the holiness and abolitionist Wesleyan Methodist Connection returned to the MEC after the Civil War, including some high-profile leaders such as Lucius Matlack. But for the most part those denominations continued on with their work without much further thought of where they came from. Race, in other words, held sway as one primary marker of identity for many Methodists, and so the institutional histories of these groups in regards to the issue are fairly static after the Civil War. There are two arenas that are especially helpful for learning more about race and Methodism: the struggles for racial equality in the MEC – the denomination which had the most multiracial membership of any Methodist denomination; and missions, that area of Methodist work that was common to all the Methodist denominations, and which was defined foundationally on race.

Toward the end of the Civil War, in 1864, the MEC created its first officially sanctioned conferences for black Methodists. The Baltimore and Washington conference was the first. And while these conferences – eventually nineteen in all by the creation of the Methodist Church in 1939 – are often referred to as the beginning of a larger and longer pattern of increased racial segregation in the MEC, the telling events in the story of race and American Methodism occurred much sooner than that. Slavery and the fracturing of Methodism along racialized denominational lines is, of course, the primary aspect of this story, but too often the history is told as prejudices defined by a matter of degrees. In this way, slavery has come to structure the historical narrative of race in a way that elides the much deeper and perhaps less insidious effects of racial thinking. It is more instructive to consider the ways in which the brutality of slavery and the conversion of slaves to Methodist Christianity are tied to other forms of prejudicial differentiation. The key to tying these together is the shifting identity among Methodists in regard to their changing sense of mission.

MISSIONS AND RACE

Methodist historian Wade Crawford Barclay argued persuasively many decades ago in his influential *History of Methodist Missions* that the early Methodist movement was inherently a mission movement, and thus did not need to differentiate within it a body of activity that was "missional."[5] He argues – and it has been widely accepted – that the reason the early movement was by definition a "mission movement" is because the primary focus of the movement was conversion. This conversionist orientation was general in that Methodists attempted to convert anyone they encountered. Well-known neighbors who were not understood as racially different were just as much the objects of Methodist mission at this stage as anyone else, and the work of conversion was not defined as a separate activity – a mission – that was different from the work of witnessing to a neighbor or family member for the purpose of conversion.

In the early nineteenth century, Methodists, along with other American Protestants, began to think differently and thus organize differently in regard to evangelical outreach. While evangelization remained a focus, certain forms of evangelical outreach came to be called "missions." The revivals of this period, and even the traveling preaching associated with it, were not labeled missionary work. But evangelical outreach that entailed Methodists leaving their communities and going to another people group was called missionary outreach. For Methodists, this shift is often narrated by the founding story of John Stewart, a former slave who went in 1815 to live among and evangelize the Wyandotte Indians in what was called the Ohio Territory. His mission was successful in the sense that he did find converts, and the news of that success spurred a new era in which certain forms of outreach from Methodists for conversion was characterized as "mission," while other forms were not. Put most starkly, organized evangelical outreach to white people was not generally considered missions, while organized evangelical outreach to nonwhites was. From their very inception, organized missions were defined not simply as work toward conversions in general, but work toward conversions of those people who were defined racially, and whose needs were beyond conversion. This does not mean that all mission work was necessarily racist; rather, it shows that race as an ideological power formed Methodist culture in a way that circumscribed nearly everything, including the central conceptualization of missions. For instance, the AME engaged in a massive missions effort to nonwhite populations in Africa, including Liberia, but sent no missionaries to convert whites anywhere.[6] This odd rendering of a New Testament command is only possible in a deeply racialized religious culture.

This set of needs, beyond a lack of the gospel, came to be described in terms of the language of civilization. Race was a central aspect of civilizational discourse, and usually considered by whites as an initial telling mark of one's civilizational state or progress.[7] In the nineteenth century, the heavily racialized discourse of "Christian civilization" became a primary and widely accepted mode of ascribing human difference. As the movement for missions organizing gained momentum, particularly toward the end of the nineteenth century, "spreading Christian civilization" became a nearly uncontested goal of U.S. Protestant missions, even while, by necessity, different Methodist denominations used the term in slightly different ways. Even in denominations such as the AME and AMEZ, in which missions were circumscribed racially, the language of "Christian civilization" was a common description of the larger goals of mission work, though with an obviously restated stance between missionaries and those to whom they were sent. Fundraising in the white-dominated Methodist denominations highlighted the civilizing effects of mission, and foregrounded stories and images of exotic races in need of Christian civilizational progress.[8]

To understand the fundamental linkage between the concept of missions and race, however, it will help to look carefully at the ways in which different forms of evangelization were categorized in the United States. As in many other Protestant denominations, Methodists eventually segregated their mission efforts into "home" and "foreign" missions. Foreign mission work received far more support among Methodists nationally, and many more missionaries were sent "overseas" than were assigned to mission activity within U.S. geographical borders. Outreach to Native Americans and immigrants in nearly all Methodist related denominations fell under the umbrella of "home" missions. In the MEC and the MECS, work with large populations of former slaves and their descendants in the American South continued under the rubric of "home missions" activity. Yet, while all the home mission efforts were racially defined, not all the missions' activity in the southern states was directed to African Americans. In the Appalachian Mountains, where people of European ancestry generally lived in isolated settlements or small farms, white-dominated Methodist mission boards sent missionaries to start schools and churches. These missions were defined, however, in explicitly racial terms in order to make sense within the widely accepted assumptions about missions. In a survey of Methodist mission work published in 1915 by eventual MECS Bishop John Moore, the various races to which the churches were sending missionaries were listed and described. Along with Mexicans, "Negroes," and Chinese, the people who lived in the southern Appalachian Mountains were defined as a distinct subset of white Europeans called "Southern Mountain People." Moore describes these people in standard race language by analyzing their genetic formation, arguing that their geographic isolation over time created a distinct race that had thus not progressed as far along the path to civilization as other Americans of European descent.[9] The missions at "home," in other words, even if they were to people who might look like the white Methodist missionaries, were directed at people who were not fully realized Americans.

A more direct example can be found in Methodist home mission activity to immigrants. Nearly all the Methodist-related denominations engaged in some kind of evangelical outreach to immigrants. In the western states, Nazarenes organized missions to immigrants from Asia and South and Latin America. In the major gateway for U.S. immigration, New York, MEC mission boards poured resources into the flow of new peoples from around the world. Some of the groups were big enough that they were given their own mission. This occurred with the large population of immigrants from Italy, whose converts were given membership in the Italian Mission conference. This effort, like so many others, was defined not simply in terms of national identity, but rather squarely within the prevailing narratives of human races. The problems particular to this mission, and the challenges faced by the missionaries, were framed by the MEC mission boards as issues stemming from the racial particularities of Italians – not national or cultural differences. Italians, like the Southern Mountain people, were described as genetically different and thus not as civilizationally evolved as U.S. white Methodists.[10]

MISSIONS NOT DEFINED AS "MISSIONS"

As an example of the kinds of racial differentiation that were assumed under the rubric of missions, one might look at a campaign common to nearly all the Methodist denominations: temperance. The war against alcohol was framed in Christian moral terms, and a significant portion of the resources and leadership for this international reform movement came from Wesleyan and Methodist Christians. The most famous of these reformers was the long-time president of the Woman's Christian Temperance Union (WCTU), Frances Willard.[11] Willard and the women she led are credited with a pivotal role in not only laying the groundwork for the amendment to the U.S. constitution that made alcohol illegal, but also the Nineteenth Amendment giving women the right to vote. The success of the temperance movement, to which Christian white women were particularly crucial, proved to men that women were a political force to be reckoned with, and made their pleas for full enfranchisement difficult to ignore. However, the ways in which the work of these women to fully Christianize the people of the United States could have been defined as missions, but were not. The efforts of the WCTU against alcohol consumption were not a simple moral crusade against inebriation. Their arguments were based on an analysis of the broad effects of alcohol consumption and the many ways in which they saw it undermining American Christian civilization. For the WCTU and their many supporters, the bedrock of Christian civilization was the nuclear family (the "Victorian" concept of family, as it has come to be called by many historians).[12] As these women analyzed poverty among American families, and the effect it had on families, they saw alcohol as a leading cause. And men consuming alcohol, almost exclusively, were the cause of the problems. To these reformers, alcohol was the first link in a chain of cause and effect that pulled loose the foundations of families: It took men away from their families as they spent time drinking or at bars; it took money away from families, often forcing women and children to work because the father was wasting money on alcohol; inebriation and drunkenness were themselves impediments to true moral and spiritual living; the poverty that ensued was itself an impediment to a full Christian life, as it prevented children and their parents from attending church; and it created a context in which people were tempted to break the law in order to survive.

All of these concerns were shared by mission organizers and were central to the work of mission boards, no matter which population was the object of that mission organizing. If this is so, then why was this powerful form of Christian outreach not described more readily as mission work? And why did the overlapping concerns of the WCTU and mission boards of various denominations not result in institutional cooperation? I would suggest that, because the primary focus of the WCTU was restoring white families and addressing the drinking problems of white (and supposedly Christian) men, it did not match the prevailing assumption that mission work was aimed at people outside of the intimate community and not known neighbors. The drinking of white men and the effect on families was a concern about white neighbors who were considered fallen from the established pinnacle of white Christian civilization. One should also remember that women in this time period were often the driving force in foreign mission organizing and fundraising, and also were often the majority of volunteers serving in missions fields – much of that work devoted to temperance. Thus, that their domestic reform work was not also called missions is even more striking.

Further evidence of this racial divide can be found in the refusal of the leadership of the WCTU to respond positively to overtures by African-American women – particularly Ida B. Wells – to make the political connections that would reflect the resonance between the women's rights arguments that were in the forefront for the WCTU, and larger human and civil rights arguments being made on behalf of African Americans.[13] By failing to join forces based on obvious common principles, the WCTU revealed itself as dependent upon the highly racialized constructs in place for what white Christians considered charity or evangelization, and what they thought required a different structural solution altogether. To conflate the objects of Christian relief work was, for these white Christians, to confuse white neighbor with nonwhite others.

A NARRATIVE EXAMPLE: THE CREATION OF THE METHODIST CHURCH

The most useful and high profile example of the ways in which race was thoroughly embedded into the fabric of Methodist life is the 1939 merger between the MEC, MECS, and MPC. And while this example is primarily about only three of the Methodist denominations, it is instructive because it is one of the few examples of Methodist denominational history in which there are significant representatives in the denominational conversation who are not white. The multiracial conversation – in this case white and black stakeholders and major players – that is the core of this narrative allows us to observe the way underlying assumptions about race emerge when the stakes for representation are high and the players represent different racial groups. One can observe, in other words, the ways that Methodists' opposing views about U.S. racial politics worked out when forced into the open. The example of an interracial denomination allows us to understand more clearly how Methodists conflated race with Christianity.

This denominational merger was the culmination of many decades of work because initial conversations between the MEC and the MECS about merger had begun as soon as the Civil War ended. And while there were specific technical institutional differences, as well as distinct differences in ethos and identity between the three denominations, the primary impediment to a reunion of these bodies was the issue of race. The central disagreements existed between the MEC and the MECS, and were concerned primarily with issues of structure and governance, such as the power and role of the episcopacy, and the related issues of conference design. But all of the progress on these matters, no matter how apparently bound by matters of polity, was tied to the question of "the status of the Negro" in the new church. Episcopacy, conference, jurisdictional conference, appointment power, and general conference delegate rights were all directly tied to the way in which the proposed new church would define the relationships between a human being's racial assignation and their status within a Christian denomination. The technical details of institutional merger were but distractions from the central problem of race, and instead provided cover for a systematic racialization of Methodist ecclesiology. In the end, what emerged in the form of the Methodist Church was an ecclesiastically Christianized racialism, or an ecclesiastically racialized Christianity, that embodied in its very structures a theology of the church based on the assumption of white supremacy.[14]

After many decades of gestures toward a merger, the MEC and MECS finally formed a large working group in 1915, with mandates from the respective General Conferences, which met regularly into the early 1920s. This Joint Commission on Unification, as it was called, was composed of fifty members, twenty-five from each church. All were white save two black delegates from the MEC: Robert Elijah Jones and I. Garland Penn. They represented the more than two hundred thousand black members of their denomination, many of whose families had been Methodists for generations. They were critical in the many weeks of debates over the years in which the Commission met, often the only delegates in the way of an agreement that would have seen all of the black members pushed out of their church to make way for a reunion of white Methodists in the three denominations.

From the beginning of the negotiations, it was clear that many of the delegates from the MECS thought that the only way a merger was possible was for the black membership to be cut out entirely. It was equally clear that many of the white delegates in the MEC would be willing to scale back the membership status of black Methodists in their denomination in order to meet MECS needs and facilitate a merger. From the very first meetings, several of the leading figures in the negotiations made it clear that they understood how the status of the black membership remained the central disagreement, and attempted to find ways to accommodate or facilitate a compromise by setting out principles and framing the debates in ways that would avoid deadlock. On the very first day, the first chair, Bp. Cranston of the MEC constructed a way forward for the Commission that would avoid debates about Scripture, doctrine, and history, since, he said, there would be no way that they all

Figure 11. **Bishop Robert E. Jones, the Methodist Episcopal Church,** Methodist Library Image Collection, Drew University, Madison, New Jersey.

could agree on these matters. No doubt he had in mind the intractable debates about the abolition of slavery in the 1840s that led to the split between the MEC and the MECS, in which each church read Scripture in opposing ways on the question of slavery. To avoid a similar fate, Cranston and like-minded delegates argued that the principle that they should follow was one of "expediency," because their ultimate goal was a reunited church. If the church were to remain divided, he argued, the future success of "American Christian civilization" would be put in jeopardy. All Americans were watching what they did, he said, and if the Commission could not find their way toward a merger, then the Methodists' place as the representatives of American Christian civilization would be permanently compromised. Many of the white delegates joined him in this concern: How could Methodists claim to represent the best of American civilization, and continue to lead in the spread of Christianity around the world, if they could not find a way to rejoin their own family, consolidate their resources, and function as "one in the spirit?"

And yet, as Jones and Penn and a few of the white delegates argued, how could they join the two institutions if not all Methodists were welcome? How could Methodists claim the mantle of the guardians of American Christian civilization if that reunion were only possible with the exclusion of black Methodist brothers and sisters? For nearly seven years the Commission debated this basic question. In the final few meetings, by which much of the initial careful and decorous debating had been abandoned, the delegates had given in to ad hominem attacks, with the white supporters of a merger without the black membership or a racially segregated membership accusing those blocking the possibility of such a compromise as lacking patriotism. Supporters of racial segregation argued finally that instead of racially segregated conferences and congregations, that the black Methodist conferences should be placed in a more natural relationship with mission conferences. Jones and Penn resisted this vociferously, finally giving in to a proposal in which all the regional annual conferences would be restricted for white congregations, while existing black congregations in the MEC would be organized inside separate sprawling annual conferences, with little regional consolidation. In this detail, it is not only that, again, mission conferences were conceived at a fundamental level in racial terms, but that even for the black delegates in this Commission, segregation in nonmission conferences was preferred as a matter of status and power, as well as the perception that mission conferences were reserved for Methodists who were not yet fully civilized as Christians.

While the MEC, MECS, and MP churches were unable to agree on the proposal in the immediate meetings following its release, the basic outlines of the plan became the basis of the eventual merger in 1939. The Methodist Church that was voted into existence by a majority of the delegates (save the black delegates who sat down and wept and refused to sing "We're Marching to Zion" as a celebration of the merger) was made palatable to the white supremacist factions and their more moderate enablers by the segregation of all Methodists into racialized annual conferences. The Central Jurisdiction, which was comprised of all the black annual conferences, remained in place until the merger of the Methodist Church with the EUB to create the United Methodist Church in 1968.

CONCLUSIONS

The emergence of the mission category in the unification debates helps us understand how race had become a part of the fabric of Methodist thinking in the United States. Because those who were the object of missions were not considered fully developed along a scale of civilizational progress, so then it felt natural for the opponents of a fully integrated church to suggest placing black Methodists into a category of mission – despite the fact that they were already converted Christians, and members of a church. In the same way, that AME mission work did not target white people as appropriate objects of mission also suggests that the categories for mission had less to do with the state of people's souls than their place in a hierarchy of human races.

It is impossible to escape the deep structural and systemic reach of race in U.S. history. Methodism is no different in that regard from other religious groups, except that its history is more nationally significant, because of the large number of members, multiple denominational bodies, its multiracial character, and its profound influence on American life. Because of this significance, it is difficult to understate the effect that Methodism's racial divisions as well as its principled advocacy for racial reconciliation have had on both American culture and the character of the Christianity that it helped spread around the world. Methodist history, doctrine, and polity cannot be understood without considering the ways race shaped each. This will require sorting out the complex array of opposing views on race and racial politics that were held by Methodists. More specifically, it will require an understanding of how the basic missional character of Methodism evolved from general evangelism to structured taxonomic mission design. In this newly evolved

mode of evangelization, the question "who is my neighbor?" became
more sharply posed as "who is my neighbor, and how is my neighbor different from me?" Much of Methodist energy after that was spent either
attempting to protect these divisions or break them apart – both in the
name of true Methodism.

Notes

1 See Donald G. Mathews, *Methodism and Slavery* (Princeton, NJ:
   Princeton University Press, 1965).
2 See Charles V. Willie, *The Black College Mystique* (New York: Rowan
   and Littlefield, 2005).
3 Roy W. Trueblood, "Union Negotiations between Black Methodists in
   America," *Methodist History* 8, no. 4 (July 1970): 18–20.
4 For a discussion of Methodists and the concept of "American Christian
   civilization" using the language of "custodianship" and an analysis of
   the ways that white Methodist identity was bound to ideas of Africa
   and Africans, see Jay Douglas Green's dissertation, "Africa Rediviva:
   Northern Methodism and the Task of African Redemption, 1895–1910
   (Kent, OH: Kent State University, 1998).
5 Wade Crawford Barclay and J. Tremayne Copplestone, *History of
   Methodist Missions*, vols. I–III (New York: Board of Missions and Church
   Extension of the Methodist Church, 1949).
6 For a full overview of AME missions in North America and Africa see
   James Campbell, *Songs of Zion: the African Methodist Church in the
   United States and South Africa* (New York: Oxford University Press,
   2005). The AME did send missionaries to Native Americans.
7 Ruth Bederman, *Manliness and Civilization: A Cultural History
   of Gender and Race in the United States, 1880–1917* (Chicago, IL:
   University of Chicago Press, 1995).
8 See Morris L. Davis, "American Methodist Missions: The Problems of
   'Home,'" *Methodist Review* 2 (2010): 33–67.
9 John. M. Moore, *The South Today* (New York: Missionary Education
   Movement of the United States and Canada, 1916).
10 See David F. Evans' dissertation, "The Methodist Melting Pot: Italian
   Immigrants in the White Protestant Imagination, 1909–1916" (Madison,
   NJ: Drew University, 2011).
11 A useful essay on this subject is Carolyn DeSwarte-Giffords' "For
   God and Home and Native Land: the WCTU's Image of Woman in
   the Late Nineteenth Century," reprinted in *Perspectives on American
   Methodism: Interpretive Essays*, edited by Russell E. Richey, Kenneth
   E. Rowe, and Jean Miller-Schmidt (Nashville, TN: Abingdon Press,
   1993), 309–321.
12 See for instance Gregory A. Schneider, *The Way of the Cross Leads
   Home: The Domestication of American Methodism* (Bloomington, IN:
   Indiana University Press, 1993).

13 For an account of the public accusations from Ida B. Wells and ensuing replies from Willard and others, see Ralph Luker *The Social Gospel in Black and White* (Chapel Hill, NC: University of North Carolina Press, 1991), 102–105.

14 For the complete history see Morris L. Davis, *The Methodist Unification: Christianity and the Politics of Race in the Jim Crow Era* (New York: New York University Press, 2008). For an in-depth overview of this time period in the MECS specifically, see Robert Watson Sledge, *Hands on the Ark: The Struggle for Change in the Methodist Episcopal Church, South, 1914–1939* (Madison, NJ: United Methodist Church, Commission on Archives and History, 1975).

15 African-American Methodists and the Making of the Civil Rights Movement

DENNIS C. DICKERSON

The civil rights movement of the 1950s and 1960s drew upon ideas and methodologies that reflected the influence of Wesleyan theology and Methodist social consciousness. Such activists as A. Philip Randolph, Archibald J. Carey, Jr., Sadie T. M. Alexander, Joseph A. DeLaine, James L. Farmer, James M. Lawson Jr., and others emerged out of African Methodist religious bodies which incubated theologies and tactics that emphasized "social holiness," rights rhetoric embedded in the Bible and the U.S. Constitution, and the techniques of nonviolent direct action. Historically, the African Methodist Episcopal Church (AME), the African Methodist Episcopal Zion Church (AMEZ), the Colored Methodist Episcopal Church (CME), and the separate African-American conferences and jurisdictions with the Methodist Episcopal Church (MEC) motivated their ministers and members to oppose unjust societal structures that attacked the humanity of African Americans. That tradition culminated in a significant presence of leaders and frontline participants in the black civil rights struggle whose background in African-American Methodism informed their activities against Jim Crow. Moreover, at pivotal points in the civil rights struggle black Methodists made indispensable contributions without which the crusade for African-American advancement would have been hindered. Missing from the scholarly literature on the "long" civil rights movement are accounts about how the Wesleyan black experience energized specific activists to fight against American apartheid. How African-American Methodism affected the modern civil rights movement and its ideology is the subject of this essay.

Embedded in the institutional culture of black Methodist bodies lay a theology and ethos focused on African-American liberation from slavery, segregation, and enforced inequality. One scholar has declared that when Richard Allen, the AME founder, led the walkout from St. George Church in Philadelphia in 1787, it became an emancipationist symbol

and a defining event for the black freedom struggle. The St. George incident, he said, was replicated and reenacted in both sacred and secular
settings and symbolized the determination of African Americans to
be free.[1] Additionally, one AMEZ historian has argued that ministers
in that denomination, beginning in the antebellum era, were expected
to be frontline freedom advocates. Also, the AME and AMEZ officials
made exclusive claims on Frederick Douglass, the iconic abolitionist
and peerless black spokesman, as belonging to their particular denomination. Although compelling evidence validates the assertions of each
Wesleyan group, the crucial issue was how the two African Methodist
bodies competed as militant defenders of African Americans through
their connection to Douglass. A liberty agenda, therefore, existed in
the institutional DNA of Wesleyan blacks from the eighteenth century
through the civil rights era of the twentieth century.

Scholars in civil rights studies usually cite the activities of Martin
Luther King, Jr., and the presence of movement centers in select southern
black Baptist churches as the main religious influences in the African-
American freedom struggle. Few are familiar with the emancipationist
ethos that Wesleyan blacks developed during the long span of their religious history in the United States. Recent discourse about Jacqueline
Dowd Hall's argument about "the long civil rights movement" provides
a framework that accounts for Wesleyan black liberationist impulses
that underlay the activism of a broad aggregation of insurgents. Hall
correctly contends that "the long civil movement" which drew from
"the liberal and radical milieu of the late 1930s, was intimately tied
to the 'rise and fall of the New Deal order,' accelerated during World
War II, stretched far beyond the South, was continuously and ferociously
contested, and in the 1960s and 1970s inspired a 'movement of movements' that de[fies] any narrative of collapse." This broader time span,
she contends, best includes a wide range of ideas and methodologies that
animated the movement.[2]

Hence, "the long civil rights movement," which transcends the
usual beginning point in 1954 with the Brown decision and deceleration
at the end of the 1960s, identifies when its ideology and tactics were ger-
minated, realized, and diffused into derivative efforts to broaden freedom for blacks and other subordinate populations. Hall's perspectives
build on the earlier scholarship of Harvard Sitkoff, Richard M. Dalfiume,
and other scholars who established the origins of the civil rights movement during the New Deal and World War II eras. Sitkoff argues that
New Deal reforms and the racial inclusivity of federal programs precipitated a transfer of black political loyalties from the Republicans to

the Democrats and buoyed their expectations for greater gains from the Roosevelt administration. Moreover, he said that blacks during the Second World War pressed militantly for civil rights through grassroots protests especially in the military and in the workplace. Dalfiume, in earlier publications, also documented the rise of black mass movements and militant agitation during the 1940s.[3]

Within this framework A. Philip Randolph, Archibald J. Carey, Jr., and Sadie T. M. Alexander spearheaded and reflected the racial militancy of the 1930s and 1940s and its aggressive push into a nascent civil rights movement that Sitkoff and Dalfiume chronicled. Though African-American activists drew from multiple intellectual and tactical sources and precedents, Randolph, Carey, and Alexander brought foundational ideas and methodologies to the black freedom struggle. Their ideological inheritance lay in two interactive areas. All three adopted the protest tradition, which Frederick Douglass and W. E. B. Du Bois respectively articulated in the nineteenth and early twentieth centuries. Douglass and Du Bois argued that blacks were American citizens and had an obligation and a God-given right to press their civic claims through a variety of protest activities and through efforts to enact and enforce laws that affirmed their legal equality. Douglass, unlike his contemporary Martin Delany, and Du Bois, in contrast to his antagonist Marcus Garvey, eschewed black nationalism and expatriation to Africa. Though Randolph embraced socialism, all three viewed racial integration as the ultimate objective of black rights initiatives.

Their activism also owed to a tradition of Wesleyan social holiness. Though none of the three ever named John Wesley as their theological forebear, they surely identified with Richard Allen as their model of Wesleyan-inspired insurgency. Allen, who attained iconic stature in the denomination to which Randolph, Carey, and Alexander belonged, grounded his understanding of personal renewal and the pursuit of societal transformation in the tenets of Wesleyan theology. Allen, born a slave in Philadelphia in 1760, but exposed to Methodism as an adolescent in Delaware, adopted the typical language of Wesleyan converts to describe his salvific experience. Moreover, he linked his deliverance from sin to an urgent necessity to be freed from slavery. So serious was Allen about this matter that he facilitated the conversion of his slaveowner to achieve the purchase of his freedom. Also, Allen believed, as Wesley himself taught and his many preachers declared, that slavery and other systems that subjugated fellow human beings were sinful. Additionally, the personal renewal that believers drew from Christian salvation generated efforts to achieve the same renewal in the broader society. Hence, Allen's ministry reflected social holiness in founding the AME Church, fighting against slavery, bringing relief to yellow fever victims, facilitating the escape of fugitive slaves, and providing refuge to fellow AME Morris Brown in the aftermath of Denmark Vesey's abortive slave revolt in Charleston.

Though theologian Andrew C. Thompson warns against linking social holiness and social justice, it remains true that African-American Methodists have conflated the two concepts. Whether their interpretations focused on AME founder Richard Allen and his wife, Sarah Allen, who worked with the Underground Railroad, or AMEZ abolitionists Jermain Loguen and Harriet Tubman, Wesleyan blacks believed that their salvific experiences merged social holiness and social justice. Inward holiness and personal renewal, gained through salvation and sanctification, motivated them to re-create in the larger society a reflection of what God intended for creation. Hence, social holiness, as understood within subordinate black Methodist communities, obligated adherents to transform oppressive social contexts into societies where justice and equity prevailed. These objectives, though at times articulated as social justice, involved believers in building the Kingdom of God because they were saved and sanctified people. Thompson declares that "those who are being transformed in love within the fellowship of Christian community will find themselves motivated to go out into the world and share that love more broadly with those who have not been recipients of grace in the same way." The Allens, Loguen, and Tubman validated this formulation of social holiness as meaning that they reflected God's divine love through the reformation of society so that all of creation would show that God was no respecter of persons. If that was social justice, then for these African-American Methodists it was social holiness by another name. This pursuit derived directly from their experience of salvation and sanctification and was informed by their interactions with other believers living out their faith within their marginalized Methodist bodies.[4]

Therefore, Richard Allen, after his death in 1831, was celebrated as a saint who showed the way to black liberation. As the founder of an enduring institution and as an exemplar of social and economic independence, Allen's hagiography was diffused through the denomination's annual celebrations of his birth, presentations of his likeness in AME material culture, and in the making of an oral and written tradition lauding his relevance to contemporary black freedom struggles. What AME ministers and members learned about Wesleyan social holiness was imparted through regular commemorations of Allen's life and ministry.

A twentieth-century AME bishop observed that Allen "was the first of great Christian preachers in America to stand up in principle and practice for full manhood rights for the black Christian." Similarly, those in the AMEZ tradition celebrated its insurgent origins and maintained its mandate to oppose oppressive structures that persisted into the twentieth century. Paul Robeson, the celebrated singer, actor, and persecuted activist, for example, acknowledged in the 1950s "the freedom-striving tradition" of the denomination in which his father and brother served as pastors. Speaking about Mother AMEZ Church in New York City, Robeson noted "a bond that joins me with the long, hard march that is my people's history in America." He added that "this very church could not abide the church of the Christian slavemasters," so "yes, I've got a home in that rock." When Rufus E. Clement, the president of Atlanta University, won election in 1953 as the first African American to the Atlanta Board of Education, fellow AMEZ clergy commended him for "living up to our Heritage." Another group of Zion churchmen, in tribute to his activist parents, Bishop George C. and Emma C. Clement and others, said that he had "fulfilled" the goals of these pioneers in "the fight for race freedom." Therefore, the institutional memory of AME, AMEZ, CME, and black MEC groups, maintained over two centuries, communicated a tradition of vigorous confrontations against forced racial segregation and discrimination. Whether the example was Allen or another black Methodist icon or institution, African-American Methodists inherited ecclesiastical bodies committed to an emancipationist ethos.[5]

Most historical accounts of African Methodism highlight bishops as the principal carriers of the AME tradition of social activism. Their record in maintaining Allen's social insurgency, with some exceptions, was either mixed or nonexistent. To examine how Randolph, Carey, Alexander, and others understood this Methodist ethos suggests that the crucial carriers of Wesleyan social holiness lay not in church hierarchies, but within the rank and file among lay and clerical activists. These three leaders, for example, encountered Allen through multiple streams of diffusion in denominational history and culture. Randolph admired Henry M. Turner, the Civil War chaplain, bishop, and militant critic of American racism, who emulated Allen's social consciousness. Carey was the son and namesake of an AME bishop who patterned his social and political involvements after both Allen and Turner. Sadie T. M. Alexander, a "true daughter" of African Methodism, was reared in the home of her grandfather, Bishop Benjamin T. Tanner, who molded the denomination's historical and theological identity through his prolific publications. She grew up immersed in the Allen legacy and grounded in AME social insurgency. Randolph, Carey, and Alexander expressed their salvific renewal through pursuits to perfect American society especially in matters of black civil rights and testified to Allen's influence within their vocations.

More than any other progenitor of the modern civil rights struggle, A. Philip Randolph developed tactical templates that characterized movement methodologies in the 1950s and 1960s. The emphasis on grassroots mass mobilization that later activists adopted in their various organizations owed to successful initiatives that Randolph inaugurated in the 1930s and 1940s. His ideas about organizing and mobilizing nonelite blacks drew from his socialist ideology and interactions, his commitment to the labor movement, and his awareness of Gandhian demonstrations aimed at ending British colonialism in India. Though wrongly accused of atheism and ecclesial irreverence, Randolph's advocacy of these movement tactics grew out of the social insurgency he learned from African Methodism. Born in Crescent City, Florida, Randolph called himself "one of the sons of African Methodism." The AME Church, described as "the single most effective organizational force for Florida's black residents," included Randolph's parents, James and Elizabeth, as two of its most militant adherents. The father, a veteran pastor to various rural churches, taught Randolph about Allen, and Turner modeled for his son the "soul of a fighting revolutionist." This heritage of AME social insurgency moved his mother to join his father to defend a black man whom the Ku Klux Klan had targeted for lynching.[6]

Examples of Wesleyan insurgency embodied in Allen and Turner, and perhaps in AME hero and slave insurrectionist Denmark Vesey, ripened Randolph into a trenchant critic of oppressive societal structures expressed in racial segregation and exploitative capitalism. When he embraced socialism, after settling in New York City, he grew impatient with religious acquiescence to the suppression of the working class. His persistent denunciation of clergy and churches and their indifference and opposition to black worker interests filled the pages of his coedited publication, *The Messenger*, founded in 1917. When he agreed to head the Brotherhood of Sleeping Car Porters (BSCP) in 1925 and lead its twelve-year battle for recognition, it intensified his annoyance with black religious support of employers. Despite charges of being anti-Christian, Randolph, according to his biographer, "consistently adhered to his own liberal religious beliefs, rooted in the socially conscious African Methodist traditions of his parents." Hence, Randolph viewed

"African Methodism as the 'religious reflection of the deep revolutionary currents set in motion by the French Revolution which had given rise to the doctrine of the Rights of Man.'" Moreover, the AME founder showed that "the dignity of the human personality was 'sacred'" and this view of Allen related to "Randolph's own Christian humanist and personalist perspective."[7]

Though Randolph's unionist activities were staunchly opposed by AME Bishop Archibald J. Carey, Sr., he was heartened when such fellow AME's as Joseph Gomez opened his Detroit church to BSCP meetings. Such pastors reminded Randolph that latent sources of support still lay among black clergy. He expressed his optimism in 1931 when he addressed a conference at Yale Divinity School on "Whither the Negro Church?" He told black seminarians that churches should facilitate the organization of unions and provide "moral support by going to and participating in the meetings. The minister should play a big part in the labor movement because 99 percent of his members are laborers." Randolph's acceptance of the Yale invitation showed his eagerness to draw black ministers into the labor cause. His expectations were surely buoyed after he established the March on Washington Movement (MOWM) to fight against employment discrimination. Though the AME Council of Bishops would "not endorse the movement of the 'March on Washington' because of the temper of the times," there were influential dissenters within their ranks. AME Bishop Richard R. Wright, Jr., Executive Secretary of the Fraternal Council of Negro Churches (FCNC), for example, favored Randolph's efforts and queried him on areas where MOWM and the FCNC could cooperate. Wright, a Ph.D. in sociology, had written several scholarly publications that chronicled and denounced discrimination against black workers. In place of a divided Bishops Council Randolph became an influential lay carrier and exponent of his denomination's emancipationist tradition.[8]

Randolph's MOWM proposed in 1941 to bring 100,000 demonstrators to Washington, DC, to pressure President Franklin D. Roosevelt to issue an executive order to protect black workers. After Roosevelt's Executive Order 8802 established a Fair Employment Practices Committee, MOWM monitored whether the agency enforced directives to withdraw federal contracts from employers guilty of racial discrimination. Randolph included clergy in the MOWM infrastructure and drew impressive support from such ministers as Archibald J. Carey, Jr., the socially conscious pastor at Chicago's Woodlawn AME Church. Carey, unlike his father, supported organized labor and attracted to Woodlawn Randolph's protégé, Willard S. Townsend, the president of the

United Transport Service Employees of America. "I became a member of this church," he said, "because I appreciate the leadership Archibald Carey has given the Negro people and the cause of labor." These activities showed that a developing network of black clergy and labor leaders, grounded in Wesleyan social holiness, were pressing for black civil rights and workplace equality.[9]

Crucial to the nascent civil rights movement was Randolph's experimentation with various forms of grassroots mobilization. Starting in 1925, Randolph developed the Brotherhood of Sleeping Car Porters into a cohesive organization and steered it to full recognition in 1937. He transferred this organizing momentum into the National Negro Congress (NNC) that drew together numerous African-American institutions into a federated front to advocate black inclusion in New Deal programs. The NNC, which elected Randolph as president, also supported the CIO organizing drives in 1936 and 1937 and urged black workers to join various industrial unions. Despite the pivotal presence of such leading black clergy as AMEZ Bishop William J. Walls, leftist forces plotted a takeover of the non-ideological NNC. "By 1940," Walls recalled, "communist influence had dwarfed the organization" and most of the members became "disillusioned." Like Walls, Randolph rejected the rise of the radical left and exited the group. Perhaps, the NNC's top-down methodology motivated Randolph's return to the grassroots organizing model he used in building the BSCP. Founding the MOWM was the fruit of his NNC experience.[10]

The prayer protests that Randolph employed in the MOWM, for example, showed that grassroots mobilization benefited from the institutional support and spirituality of black churches. In observing the success of Gandhian satyagraha in India Randolph understood that these same resources resided within black congregations and could invigorate a social protest movement. He was reminded that social change, grounded in spirituality, drew as much from Mahatma Gandhi as from the "the life of Jesus Christ." These beliefs derived, said his biographer, from "the moral and spiritual power of nonviolence" that Randolph inherited from his father's "high moral commitments" as an AME minister. MOWM, therefore, relied on networks of organizers in several cities who mobilized African Americans through black churches and other familiar institutions.[11]

Hence, Randolph's influence on civil rights activism in the 1950s and 1960s lay in normalizing grassroots mobilization as the standard tactic that the Congress of Racial Equality (CORE), Southern Christian Leadership Conference (SCLC), and the Student Nonviolent

Figure 12. **Truman Commission**: Channing Tobias (CME), Dorothy Tilly (ME), and Sadie Tanner Mossell Alexander (AME), Sadie T. M. Alexander Papers at the University of Pennsylvania.

Coordinating Committee (SNCC) adopted as their major methodology. Though the NAACP and the National Urban League maintained their emphases on working through government and corporate institutions, innumerable branches and affiliates in the two organizations focused on Randolph's tactics. Additionally, SCLC and other groups explicitly depended on religiously based activism as intrinsic to bus boycotts in the 1950s in Baton Rouge, Montgomery, and Tallahassee. SCLC, founded in 1957, emerged out of these local religious and community initiatives. Moreover, the massive march on Washington in 1963, Randolph's brainchild, generated pressure that helped to enact the landmark Civil Rights Act of 1964. Randolph himself attributed these movement contributions to his black Wesleyan inheritance. His biographer correctly observed that Randolph's "religiosity was a blend of an African Methodist social gospel and a Christian humanist perspective informed by a philosophical belief in the sacredness of human personality." Inadvertently, she identified the premise on which Wesleyan social holiness is based. Any societal structure that violated the integrity of divine creation required an activist onslaught against it. Randolph inherited this perspective from Richard Allen and consciously emulated the AME founder in pursuing Wesleyan social insurgency.[12]

Like Randolph, Archibald J. Carey, Jr., linked his social activism to Richard Allen. He was "a fighter against segregation," Carey said, and "a workman in the building of the Kingdom of God." Therefore, AME's should follow the founder and pledge "dedication not only to the calling of God but to the service of man ... [and] making a kingdom of men [into] a kingdom of heaven." Bishop Carey, despite his antiunionism, became a compelling example of Allenite activism. The bishop, beyond his extensive political involvements, embraced the same protest tradition that his contemporary W. E. B. Du Bois exemplified. The younger Carey, the successive pastor of two Chicago congregations, emulated his father and became the city's best-known clergy–activist. As a Chicago alderman and as an Eisenhower appointee, Carey used his political positions to fight racial discrimination in both housing and employment. In 1948 he sponsored the ill-fated "Carey Ordinance," which would outlaw bias in publicly financed housing. President Dwight D. Eisenhower appointed him vice chairman of the President's Committee on Government Employment Policy in 1955 and chairman in 1957. Before his term ended in 1961, Carey conducted hearings and recommended remedies for black federal employees who encountered discrimination in hiring and promotion.[13]

Though Carey focused on painstaking efforts to press black civil rights through local and federal bureaucracies, he never eschewed grassroots protests and demonstrations. His support of Randolph's NNC and MOWM presaged involvements in helping to birth and facilitate the activities of new civil rights organizations. Moreover, he parlayed his impressive oratorical abilities to aid in shaping compelling rhetoric for the civil rights cause. When a small interracial group of pacifists established the Congress of Racial Equality in 1942, they found an eager benefactor in Archibald Carey. James Robinson, a Catholic, was initially drawn to the AME pastor because of Carey's well-known activism. Bernice Fisher, a Baptist, was so impressed with Carey's militancy that she became Woodlawn's first Caucasian member. As Carey became better acquainted with other CORE founders, he allowed Woodlawn to become its first headquarters and the site of its first national convention. He supported CORE's protest against discriminatory treatment of black students at Northwestern University. Moreover, Carey, as he grew more familiar with Gandhian nonviolence, backed CORE's 1947 Journey of Reconciliation, which challenged segregated interstate travel. Carey, who sustained relationships with most of CORE's founders, cooperated primarily with Homer Jack, a Unitarian and head of the Chicago Council against Racial and Religious Discrimination. Jack, who drew Carey to the agency's advisory board, also supported Carey's antidiscrimination ordinance for public housing. Carey was especially proud as CORE emerged as a pivotal organization in the civil rights movement in the 1960s with James Farmer, another early protégé, as its national leader.[14]

Carey, a background benefactor for CORE, played a similar role for SCLC. Its leader, Martin Luther King, Jr., established it in 1957 to sustain momentum from successful bus boycotts in Baton Rouge, Montgomery, and Tallahassee. During the Montgomery bus boycott Carey chaired a Chicago committee that raised funds for the movement. Carey and King met in Montgomery when the Chicago pastor spoke in 1955 at a citizenship rally at Alabama State College. Later, King filled several preaching engagements at Carey's Quinn Chapel AME Church. During these interactions King probably learned about Carey's 1952 speech to the Republican National Convention. Carey's cadences concerning black freedom in moving metaphors of bells ringing from numerous mountaintops across the nation caught King's attention. These Carey couplets included: from every mountain side, let freedom ring; not only from the Green Mountains and the White Mountains of Vermont and New Hampshire; not only from the Catskills of New York; but from the Ozarks in Arkansas, from the Stone Mountain in Georgia, from the Great Smokies of Tennessee and from the Blue Ridge Mountains of Virginia. This rhythmic rhetoric reappeared in King's classic "I Have a Dream" speech at Randolph's 1963 March on Washington.[15] Though Carey functioned as a King confidante, they seemingly parted when charges of moral misconduct from FBI Director J. Edgar Hoover threatened the SCLC leader. Carey attempted to persuade Hoover to end his crusade to destroy King, but his failure did not prevent him from enlisting Hoover's help in pursuing a federal appointment for himself. This selfish behavior marred Carey's broader contributions to the civil rights movement, but never nullified his commitment to Wesleyan social holiness.[16]

Carey's involvement in the Eisenhower administration in the 1950s showed that presidential initiatives, as much as grassroots mobilization, advanced black civil rights. Eisenhower's predecessor, Harry Truman, building on gains during the Roosevelt administration and proposals of his own, promoted the 1948 election as "a coming of age of civil rights in American politics." His record of advocacy for a permanent

Fair Employment Practices Commission (FEPC), the desegregation of the military, and the hard-hitting report on black civil rights titled *To Secure These Rights* were some of the credits adduced to his presidency. Though Truman did not vigorously act on the findings of this report, *To Secure These Rights*, he helped to frame the program and rhetoric of his civil rights appeal. The two blacks on the Civil Rights Committee, Sadie T. M. Alexander and Channing H. Tobias, emphasized that black inequalities represented a case for national action. Moreover, they leveraged their appointment to the Truman commission to attack pervasive racial discrimination in American society and viewed their service as consistent with the liberationist thrust of their black Wesleyan heritage. They pressed Truman toward more vigorous action on black civil rights.[17]

The principles that Alexander and Tobias enunciated, despite Truman's periodic inconsistencies, clearly defined the objectives of the civil rights struggle. Alexander, for example, viewed Truman's Executive Order 9981 on military desegregation as derivative from the president's civil rights committee. The committee, Alexander said, "has pointedly stated that separate facilities are never equal and that without equality of opportunity democracy is an illusion." Her black Methodist identity compelled the articulation of this perspective. Born in Philadelphia in 1898 Alexander grew up in the home of her grandfather, the eighteenth AME Church bishop. Her four degrees, all from the University of Pennsylvania, included a Ph.D. and a LL.B. The AME Bishops Council appointed her as its general counsel, and the NAACP, the National Urban League, and the Philadelphia Human Relations Commission similarly drew upon her expertise. Tobias, like Alexander played a large role among Wesleyan blacks. Born in 1882 in Augusta, Georgia, Tobias became a minister in the CME Church, but developed vocations in the YMCA as head of the department on colored work and in the Phelps Stokes Fund as director. His prominence in these nonprofit organizations led to his election as chairman of the Board of Directors of the NAACP. In each venue, Tobias ferociously criticized Jim Crow as "an insult to the Creator." While serving on the Truman commission he affiliated with the National Emergency Against Mob Violence Committee.[18]

Though *To Secure These Rights* was lauded as an assault on pervasive racial discrimination, numerous internal battles to sharpen its language, content, and impact involved Alexander and Tobias. For example, they wanted to withhold "Federal appropriations to segregated schools" in any congressional bill for aid to education. Moreover, they and a few others insisted that "their votes (should be) recorded" on this issue. Alexander was especially forthright about a lynching in Greenville, South Carolina, and the FBI investigation of the crime. The incident showed why the Civil Rights Section in the Criminal Division of the Department of Justice required an upgrade to an assistant attorney general for civil rights who would administer regional offices "throughout the south." Tobias's sense of urgency about civil rights, according to Alexander, was revealed in his "conviction and frankness in committee deliberations where he "practice(d) no evasions, no indirection, (and) no splitting of hairs." Both stood together, for example, on employing "Negro personnel" for the committee. When neither was consulted on hiring someone they deemed unfit, they declared that "unnecessary criticism" of the committee might result. The two also pushed for committee hearings away from Washington (DC) because the group would be "carrying the influence" of the commission to other communities.[19]

Alexander and Tobias, though engaged in painstaking bureaucratic battles for civil rights, generated external pressure from the National Urban League (NUL), the NAACP, the National Council of Negro Women (NCNW), and other groups. Alexander was disappointed that "not a single organization working in the field of Negro concern" had submitted a memorandum. Therefore, she was "very anxious that the (National Urban) League have an opportunity to present the result of its work for 35 years." Because she dually served on the Truman committee and as secretary of the NUL national board, Alexander was convinced that League testimony "will be of great value to us." Executive Director Lester B. Granger was scheduled to appear before the committee as was Walter White, the head of the NAACP. Because Alexander was determined that the report should "pass into law and not relegated to governmental archives," she asked the venerable Mary McLeod Bethune, the NCNW founder, to urge President Truman "to present the recommendations to Congress and ... to appoint a permanent committee on Civil Rights." Alexander made the same request to William H. Gray, Jr., the president of Florida A & M College in Tallahassee. "I urge that you, every member of your faculty and every person whom you touch," she said, to endorse the recommendations. Additionally, Alexander enlisted allies in the American Friends Service Committee and the southeastern branch of the Methodist Women's Society of Christian Service to resurrect the expired FEPC.[20]

Though neither Tobias nor Alexander toiled in grassroots movement organizations, each recognized that Gandhian nonviolence was stirring the moral sensibilities and praxis of theorists and activists in the civil rights struggle. Tobias, for example, visited Gandhi in 1936 in India while attending the World Conference of the YMCA. Alexander traveled to India in 1952 in the American delegation to the International Conference of Social Work. Though Gandhi had been assassinated in 1948, Alexander encountered Indians who were applying his religious principles to the construction of a stable social order. Hence, Tobias and Alexander joined black contemporaries, namely, Benjamin E. Mays, Howard Thurman, Mordecai W. Johnson, and William Stuart Nelson, in anchoring their ideas about achieving black civil rights in Gandhian non-violence. Like these black religious intellectuals, Tobias and Alexander opposed sinful societal structures and viewed Gandhian satyagraha as an indispensable tool to dismantle these systems. Additionally, their embrace of Wesleyan social holiness led to their engagement with Gandhian thought. As heirs to black Methodist opposition to racial oppression, Tobias and Alexander readily accepted a developing consensus that Gandhi's fight against British colonialism could invigorate the black freedom movement.[21]

In grassroots settings in South Carolina and Alabama, respectively, J. A. DeLaine and Rosa Parks drew upon the iconic reputation of Richard Allen as a black Methodist freedom fighter to stir their insurgency against southern segregation. DeLaine, an AME pastor and a principal, requested school officials in Clarendon County, South Carolina, to provide buses to his students at the Scott's Branch School. After the rebuff, the NAACP aided him in spearheading a suit to rectify this inequity. DeLaine, who founded and revived the Manning-Clarendon County NAACP in 1943 and in 1947, responded to a state NAACP official who invited challenges to public school inequalities. Therefore, DeLaine persuaded James Pearson, the father of one of his students, to sue the Clarendon County school system for failing to provide bus transportation for his son and other black children. When a technicality nullified the Pearson suit, DeLaine initiated *Briggs v. Elliott*, which directly challenged the constitutionality of public school segregation. Though the Fourth Circuit Court of Appeals rejected *Briggs*, the NAACP merged it with similar suits from Virginia, Delaware, and one in Kansas, which included the aggrieved daughter of AME minister Oliver L. Brown. Ruling on these combined cases, *Brown v. The Board of Education of Topeka et al.*, in 1954 the Supreme Court said that public school segregation violated the Fourteenth Amendment and was therefore unconstitutional.[22] DeLaine attributed his activism to the example of Richard Allen and because "the AME Church has been in the forefront of the civil rights movement ever since its beginning." His visibility in the *Pearson* and *Briggs* cases drew Ku Klux Klan harassment, economic reprisals, and an incinerated home from which the DeLaines hurriedly escaped. Though his bishop transferred him to a different congregation to ensure his safety, a trumped-up criminal charge compelled him to flee South Carolina for New York. Though fellow clergy raised funds to help him establish a second AME congregation in Buffalo, he never attained any choice pastoral appointments or any broader denominational recognition for his landmark civil rights activities. A disappointed DeLaine scarcely realized that little-known clergy like himself had become the principal practitioners of AME social holiness and the church's major carriers of its emancipationist ethos.[23]

Rosa Parks, like DeLaine, held no high denominational position, but embraced the liberationist theology of the AME founder. Also, like DeLaine, Parks was prominent in her local NAACP and was active in investigating the rape of black women and promoting voter registration. As a stewardess at St. Paul AME Church in Montgomery, Alabama, Parks prepared the bread and the wine for the congregation's monthly Eucharist. This ritual of renewal affirmed her ongoing pursuit of inward holiness and the obligation this imposed to realize this same renewal in the broader society. Parks's devotional life as an AME in two Alabama congregations and a third in Detroit, Michigan, linked her personal salvific experience with her consistent efforts to challenge white societal structures that upheld American racism. In blending her church function as a stewardess to her civic role as a social activist led to Parks's refusal to relinquish her seat on a Montgomery bus to a white man in December 1955. This singular protest and her well-known moral reputation stirred the local black population to inaugurate a 381-day bus boycott. Parks's insurgency, which derived from her early exposure to the Richard Allen narrative, facilitated the rise of Martin Luther King, Jr., and energized a sustained nationwide movement for black civil rights.[24]

Because segregation was structured into the Methodist Church, African Americans, who remained in this majority white denomination, understood that racism conspicuously afflicted both church and society. African-American Methodists belonged to thirteen separate annual conferences organized between 1868 and 1927. Existing racial organizations enabled the 1939 merger of the MEC, the MECS, and a smaller Methodist sect to create a Central Jurisdiction that functioned as a segregated black body. The white Methodists who imposed this system upon blacks affirmed, according to one scholar, that "whiteness" represented "the pinnacle of human progress" and that "American Christian Civilization," both "nationalized and racialized" was what the merger asserted. Though black Methodists shared with other African Methodists an historic liberationist ethos, the creation of the Central Jurisdiction reenergized their insurgent protests against racism in both church and state.[25]

These developments spearheaded James Farmer's lifelong activism against racial segregation. The Methodist merger occurred during his matriculation at the School of Religion at Howard University. His father and namesake, himself a Methodist minister and biblical scholar, expected Farmer to emulate him. Because the unification boldly established a forced black separatism, Farmer wondered "how was I to preach Christ in a church whose structure" had surrendered to racism. Moreover, Howard Thurman, his principal professor, introduced him to Mahatma Gandhi and "loaned" him books about the Indian saint. Farmer became a pacifist and later a part-time Fellowship of Reconciliation (FOR) employee where he studied "nonviolence as a technique for social change." After he finished a thesis, under Thurman's direction, on "A Critical Analysis of the Historical Interrelationship between Religion and Racism," Farmer received his divinity degree and joined FOR's staff full-time. His father asked if he was ready for ordination, but Farmer refused to enter the ministry and vowed instead to work "to destroy segregation." He accepted a FOR assignment in Chicago where in 1942 he became cofounder of CORE. This interracial organization under Farmer's leadership in the 1960s accelerated civil rights activities through the freedom rides in 1961 and in intense voter registration campaigns among Mississippi blacks in 1964.[26]

James Farmer's insurgency drew from his simultaneous reaction to the jarring power play by white Methodists in creating the Central Jurisdiction and his introduction to the direct action philosophy and praxis of Gandhian satyagraha. This moral methodology, Farmer believed, could undermine white hegemony in the church and "destroy" it within the broader American society. James M. Lawson, Jr., who emerged from a more diverse Wesleyan background than did Farmer, shared with him a poignant encounter with pacifism and Gandhian nonviolence. Both found in Gandhian thought a proactive rather than a passive engagement against hegemonic forces embedded in violence and racial oppression. Lawson, who became a serious student of Gandhi, diffused his teachings through nonviolent training workshops in Nashville, Tennessee. These seminars both energized the Nashville civil rights movement and precipitated his expulsion from Vanderbilt Divinity School. Workshop graduates, however, seeded several other civil rights groups and activities throughout the American South.

As much as King himself, Lawson brought nonviolent direct action to the forefront of the civil rights movement. His Gandhian conversion derived from familial, religious, and pacifist sources. His father and namesake, an AMEZ pastor, served several congregations especially in Uniontown, Pennsylvania, where Lawson was born, and in Massillon, Ohio, where he grew up. The elder Lawson was steeped in the "freedom" precepts of the Zion Church that boasted the black rights heroism of abolitionist Sojourner Truth and protester Bishop Alexander Walters. Hence, wherever the senior Lawson served, he spearheaded the founding of a NAACP or an Urban League to advance the interests of his congregation and community. Though he later switched his affiliation to the Lexington Annual Conference in the Central Jurisdiction of the Methodist Church, the older Lawson established his own activist persona. His son followed him into the ministry of a segregated Methodist body and adopted his father's insurgent posture as a Wesleyan preacher. The methodology that the junior Lawson chose was influenced, however, by his mother. When he struck back at a white boy for calling him a racial epithet, Filane Lawson chastised her son for his pointless and equally hurtful response. The strength to love, forgive, and understand, she said, were better demonstrations of Christianity than physical revenge. This lesson ripened Lawson to embrace, years later at Baldwin-Wallace College, the teachings of visiting lecturer A. J. Muste, the founder of FOR. Because of Muste, Lawson was persuaded to become a pacifist and a voracious reader of books by and about Gandhi. Moreover, he was motivated to register at his draft board in 1950 as a conscientious objector to the Korean War. His refusal to join the U.S. Army landed him in federal custody, and he was incarcerated in minimum-security facilities. After his release, he went to India as a Methodist missionary to teach and coach athletics at Hislop College and to deepen his study of Gandhian philosophy and praxis.[27]

When he enrolled in the Graduate School of Theology at Oberlin College, Lawson met King who had come to speak. During their conversation King convinced him to move south to develop civil rights activities in Nashville. Therefore, Lawson transferred to Vanderbilt Divinity School and met with Kelly Miller Smith, a leading Baptist pastor. Smith and Andrew N. White, an AME denominational executive, in 1958 formed the Nashville Christian Leadership Conference as SCLC's first affiliate. They targeted segregation in downtown stores and recruited students from several local colleges as the principal demonstrators. To prepare the activists Lawson held nonviolent workshops at various black churches and taught them Gandhian principles and practical techniques to protect themselves from physical assaults. Lawson cited relevant biblical passages to undergird his instruction on nonvio-lence. He also drew from the example of John Wesley, who confronted mobs opposed to his teachings through nonviolent responses. Not only did students, during a few months of intense confrontations in 1960, successfully integrate local stores, but joined CORE-sponsored freedom rides violently halted in Anniston, Alabama. Lawson trainees boarded replacement buses and pressed on to Mississippi and incarceration in the notorious Parchman prison. Lawson's influence also extended to the founding conference of SNCC in 1960 where his position paper on non-violence helped to shape the tactical trajectory of this new civil rights organization. Additionally, Lawson workshop alumni and the teacher himself populated other movement activities including the fateful Memphis sanitation workers strike in 1968. Lawson, a major clerical leader in fighting for the union rights of mostly black garbage men, per-suaded King to lead demonstrations in the Bluff City. Though the SCLC leader was assassinated, the successful organization and hard-won rec-ognition of an African-American municipal union showed a largely suc-cessful application of nonviolent direct action in a city where militant, young demonstrators and white city officials paid scant attention to the Gandhian principles that Lawson and King articulated and practiced.[28]

Wesleyan social holiness, a foundational factor in the activism of African-American Methodists, blended with other methodologies to achieve black civil rights. The grassroots mobilization techniques and labor organizing of Randolph, the painstaking institutional and bureau-cratic efforts of Carey, Alexander, and Tobias, the singular, but militant initiatives of DeLaine and Parks, or the Gandhian praxis of Farmer and Lawson built on traditions of insurgency intrinsic to the Wesleyan black heritage. Whether the religious body was AME, AMEZ, CME, or black MEC, the civil rights struggle drew intellectual and activist energy from identifiable black Methodists who provided indispensable leader-ship and who understood themselves as heirs to an insurgent religious tradition that informed their involvement in the broader movement for African-American civil rights.

Notes

1   Eddie S. Glaude, Jr., *Exodus!: Religion, Race, and Nation in Early Nineteenth-Century Black America* (Chicago, IL: University of Chicago Press, 2000), 24–25; 58; David H. Bradley, Sr., *A History of the AME Zion Church* (n.p.: Parthenon Press, 1956), 107–108; Dennis C. Dickerson, *A Liberated Past: Explorations in AME Church History* (Nashville, TN: A.M.E. Sunday School Union, 2003), 33.

2   Jacqueline Dowd Hall, "The Long Civil Rights Movement and the Political Uses of the Past," *Journal of American History* 91 (2005): 1235.

3   Harvard Sitkoff, *A New Deal for Blacks: The Emergence of Civil Rights as a National Issue: The Depression Decade* (Oxford: Oxford University Press, 1981); Harvard Sitkoff, "Racial Militancy and Interracial Violence in the Second World War," *Journal of American History* (December 1971): 661–681; Richard Dalfiume, "The 'Forgotten Years' of the Negro Revolution," *Journal of American History* (1968): 90–106.

4   Andrew C. Thompson, "From Societies to Society: The Shift from Holiness to Justice in the Wesleyan Tradition," *Methodist Review* 3 (2011): 143,163, 168–170.

5   See Richard R. Wright, Jr., *Allen Day Address: Richard Allen, 1760–1831:Greatest Negro Born in America* (Philadelphia, PA: St. George Methodist Church, 1960), 9; *Paul Robeson Speaks*, edited by Philip S. Foner (New York: Brunner/Mazel, 1978), 387; Paul Robeson, *Here I Stand* (Boston, MA: Beacon Press, 1971), 1–2; quoted in Dennis C. Dickerson, *African Methodism and Its Wesleyan Heritage: Reflections on AME Church History*, (Nashville, TN: A.M.E. Sunday School Union, 2009), 148.

6   Larry Eugene Rivers and Canter Brown, Jr., *Laborers in the Vineyard of the Lord: The Beginnings of the AME Church in Florida, 1865–1895* (Gainesville, FL: University Press of Florida, 2001), xv; Cynthia Taylor, *A. Phillip Randolph: The Religious Journey of an African-American Labor Leader* (New York: New York University Press, 2006), 7, 11, 21.

7   Taylor, *A. Phillip Randolf*, 39, 50–52, 54, 84, 224.

8   "Whither the Negro Church?" Seminar held at Yale Divinity School, New Haven, Connecticut, April 13–15, 1931, 7; Taylor, *A. Phillip Randolf*, 167; Proceedings of the Mid-Summer Session of the Council of Bishops, African Methodist Episcopal Church in Avery Chapel AME Church, Oklahoma City, Oklahoma, June 26–27, 1941.

9   Taylor, *A. Phillip Randolf*, 138; 169–170; and Dennis C. Dickerson, *African American Preachers and Politics: The Careys of Chicago* (Jackson, MS: University Press of Mississippi, 2010), 97.

10 William J. Walls, *The African Methodist Episcopal Zion Church: Reality of the Black Church* (Charlotte, NC: A.M.E. Zion Publishing House, 1974), 522.

11 Taylor, *A. Phillip Randolf*, 157–159.

12 Taylor, *A. Phillip Randolf*, 225.

13 Dickerson, *African American Preachers and Politics*, 83, 99–103, 134–145.

14 Dickerson, 77–78.

15 Dickerson, 119; 169–171.

16 Dickerson, 171–177.

17 Harvard Sitkoff, "Harry Truman and the Election of 1948: The Coming of Age of Civil Rights in American Politics," *Journal of Southern History* 37 (1971): 597–616.

18 Sadie T. M. Alexander Statement, Sadie T. M. Alexander Papers, Box 40, Folder 6, University Archives & Records Center, University of

Pennsylvania, Philadelphia, PA; Dennis C. Dickerson, "Methodist Women and Civil Rights: Sadie T. M. Alexander and Dorothy R. Tilly," *AME Church Review* (April–June 2010), 32–38; Raymond R. Sommerville, Jr., *An Ex-Colored Church: Social Activism in the CME Church* (Macon, GA: Mercer University Press, 2004), 58–59.

19 Channing Tobias to Sadie T. M. Alexander, September 1, 1947; Box 39, Folder 40; Alexander to Robert Carr, April 21, 1947, Box 39, Folder 39; Alexander to William H. Gray, Jr., November 11, 1947, Box 39, Folder 40; Alexander to Tobias, February 18,1947; Tobias to Alexander, February 26, 1947; Alexander to Tobias, February 28,1947; Alexander to Tobias, May 23, 1947; Box 39, Folder 39; STMA Papers, Archives & Records, UP, Philadelphia, PA.

20 Alexander to Lester B. Granger, February 26, 1947; Alexander to Carr, March 15,1947; Carr to Members of the President's Committee on Civil Rights, April 10, 1947; Box 39, Folder 39; Alexander to Mary McLeod Bethune, November 5, 1947; Alexander to William H. Gray, Jr., November 10, 1947, Box 39, Folder 40; Alexander to Frank S. Loescher, January 19, 1949; Box 65, Folder 23, STMA Papers, Archives & Records, UP, Philadelphia, PA.

21 Dennis C. Dickerson, "African American Religious Intellectuals and the Theological Foundations of the Civil Rights Movement, 1930–1955," *Church History* 74 (2005): 217–235; Newspaper clipping (1952) Box 1, Folder 57, STMA Papers, Archives & Records, UP, Philadelphia, PA.

22 Dickerson, *A Liberated Past*, 185–191.

23 Dickerson, 192; 198.

24 Dickerson, *African Methodism and its Wesleyan Heritage*, 178–182.

25 James S. Thomas, *Methodism's Racial Dilemma: The Story of the Central Jurisdiction* (Nashville, TN: Abingdon Press, 1992), 46–47; Morris L. Davis, *The Methodist Unification: Christianity and the Politics of Race in the Jim Crow Era* (New York: New York University Press, 2008), 132.

26 James Farmer, *Lay Bare the Heart: An Autobiography of the Civil Rights Movement* (Ft. Worth, TX: Texas Christian University Press, 1985), 142–143, 146–147.

27 Interview with James M. Lawson, Jr., conducted by Dennis C. Dickerson and Larry Isaac, Clark Memorial United Methodist Church, Nashville, TN, 2007.

28 Lawson interview; Profile: James Lawson, civil rights advocate, United Methodist News Service, February 11, 2003.

16 American Methodist Women: Roles and Contributions

LACEYE C. WARNER

INTRODUCTION

John Wesley and Wesleyan/Methodist movements have generally supported women's ecclesial leadership and allowed for women's receipt of modest ecclesiastic rights. Alongside Quakers and other smaller Christian communities, early Methodism maintained a space for women to preach and lead within the movement. In early British Methodism, women assumed numerous roles from preacher, class and bandleader, sick visitor, nurse, prayer leader, Sunday school teacher, and school operator. This relative support for women's roles and contributions carried into American Methodism – including the Wesleyan/holiness movement that demonstrated significant support for women's recognized ministry roles. Indeed, Antoinette Brown Blackwell (1825–1921), the first woman to receive ordination in the United States, was ordained by a Wesleyan minister, Rev. Luther Lee, in 1853.[1]

According to scholars studying early American Methodism, particularly in Philadelphia, New York, and Baltimore, women made up the majority of members among Methodist small groups.[2] Barbara Ruckle Heck (1734–1804) is heralded as the mother of American Methodism having joined a Methodist society in Ireland in 1752 and later convincing her cousin Philip Embury to begin preaching in the fall of 1766 following their immigration to New York.[3] Women enjoyed the mutual community, fellowship, and spiritual formation of the societies or classes (essentially small groups) and from about 1770 to 1815 were appointed as class leaders in the Methodist Episcopal Church (MEC).[4] Similarly, in the African Methodist Episcopal Church (AME) before the Civil War, women assumed roles such as teacher, exhorter, evangelist, class leader, and on occasion, traveling preacher.[5]

In the following pages, we will survey women's contributions to American Methodism, including select missionary work both domestic and foreign, key figures within movements such as temperance, suffrage, and racial justice, as well as trace the narrative leading to ordination for women in American Methodist and related traditions.[6]

MISSIONARIES

A significant arena in which women responded to God's call to ministry was through mission work. Though mainly excluded from denominational efforts organized by men, women organized themselves into local auxiliaries and national networks to participate in outreach ministries and support other women and men in such work. Although women served in various unofficial capacities, not until the nineteenth century did they begin to organize on a relatively large scale with ecclesial endorsement.

The earliest mission work in American Methodism was organized in the African Methodist Episcopal Zion (AMEZ) and AME Churches called the Daughters of Conference dating from 1821 and 1828, respectively.[7] Prior to the formal organization of the AME group, Sarah Bass Allen (1764–1849), wife of Bishop Richard Allen, is credited with founding the AME Daughters of Conference. She is well known for gathering women to sew the preachers' clothes following the establishment of the AME Church in 1818. The efforts of these groups focused mainly on fundraising, though expanded their impact as they grew into subsequent organizations. In the AMEZ Church, Mary Roberts (d. 1861) founded the organization and served as president for forty years. She also helped to organize the Young Daughters of Conference in 1845, for which Ellen Stevens (n.d.) served as president.[8] In 1880, the AMEZ General Conference established the Ladies Home and Foreign Mission Society (LHFMS). General Conference eventually elected officers by 1884, but in the same year a ruling was adopted to prevent women from membership in the General Conference.[9] Mary J. Small (1850–1945), one of the first women to receive ordination in the AMEZ Church, served as president of the LHFMS for at least two terms.[10] In the AME Church, the Woman's parent Mite Missionary Society organized its first gathering in 1874 under Mary A. Campbell's (1817–1910) leadership as the first president. In 1893 the Women's Home and Foreign Missionary Society followed. In 1944, these two groups merged into the Women's Missionary Society and were led by the president, Lucy Hughes (d. 1945), after presenting a joint petition many years prior at the 1916 General Conference.[11]

The Woman's Foreign Missionary Society (WFMS) of the MEC was established in Boston in 1869 with only six Methodist women present.[12]

The WFMS published a periodical entitled *Heathen Woman's Friend* and used the slogan "Woman's Work for Woman."[13] The WFMS hoped to liberate native women in foreign lands from both spiritual and physical captivity. Like most missionary efforts of the time, while largely well intentioned, some ministries and interactions reinforced unhelpful colonial themes. By 1910, more than half of Protestant missionaries were women.

In 1869, Isabella Thoburn (1840–1901) and Dr. Clara Swain (1834–1910) represented the newly formed WFMS of the MEC as the first single female missionaries.[14] They made significant contributions to the education and medical care of indigenous women. Thoburn served in Lucknow[15] where her brother, Bishop James Thoburn, was newly appointed. In her first two terms, Isabella Thoburn established a boarding school for girls in Lucknow, served as principal of a girl's school in Cawnpore, as well as among Lucknow's poor teaching Sunday school and training "Bible reader" evangelists.[16] Thoburn continued to expand educational opportunities for women,[17] receiving a government charter in 1895 for a woman's college that would become Lucknow University.[18]

Upon graduation from the Woman's Medical College in Philadelphia in 1869 with the MD, Clara Swain agreed to serve an orphanage and attend to women in secluded zenanas in Barielly, India.[19] In 1871, a local prince more than fulfilled Swain's need for property to implement her vision.[20] By June 1873, she was offering medical training to young women, treating patients, and running a dispensary. Early the following year, she established a hospital. She also taught Sunday school, trained Bible women, and evangelized in zenanas.[21] After fifteen years, Swain became the personal physician to the rajah of Khetri, which led to further opportunities for medical care, training, and evangelism.[22]

In the Colored Methodist Episcopal Church (CME), later the Christian Methodist Episcopal Church, the General Conference eventually approved the organization of the Women's Missionary Society in 1886. This work grew from Mrs. Caroline Poe's (n.d.) leadership of similar work in the East Texas Conference and her persistent petitions to General Conference.[23]

In the Methodist Episcopal Church, South (MECS) a Woman's Missionary Society of the Board of Missions (later the WFMS) organized in 1878. Margaret Campbell Kelley (1805–1877) and Mrs. Willie Harding McGavock (1832–1895) led the effort proposing a WFMS to the General Conference. McGavrock served as secretary from 1878 until her death in 1895 and Juliana Gordon Hayes (1813–1895) served as president until her death, also in 1895.[24] In response to testimony from missionary

Lizzie M. Guthrie (d. 1880), supported through the Interdenominational Woman's Union Missionary Society, Methodist Protestant women voted to organize a WFMS in 1879.[25]

Women among the United Brethren in Christ (UBC) and Evangelical Association/Church (EA/C) organized missionary societies after 1870.[26] The UBC General Conference voted to approve such work through a vote of commendation for The Woman's Missionary Association in 1872.[27] However, the EA/C was more equivocal, refusing a petition to organize such work in 1878, though authorizing a Woman's Missionary Society (WMS) following a subsequent request from Minerva Strawman (1869–1924) in 1883.[28] The WMS was organized, but with the stipulation that women's groups could only organize locally and must be supervised by the presiding preacher. In 1899 the WMS finally received approval for a periodical.[29]

In 1880, following General Conference of the MEC, approximately fifty women gathered to form the Woman's Home Missionary Society (WHMS). Lucy Webb Hayes (1831–1889), Mrs. Rutherford B. Hayes, served as president. In 1884 the WFMS and WHMS were both recognized and made agencies of the church, giving the denomination some control. In 1886 the Woman's Department of the Board of Church Extension, later the Woman's Parsonage and Home Mission Society (and still later the Woman's Home Missionary Society) was established in the MECS.[30] Across Methodist/Wesleyan traditions women implemented other home missionary efforts through numerous local auxiliaries and national networks – for example, the Ladies and Pastors Christian Union and the national and international organization of the Woman's Christian Temperance Union.

In 1940 following the union of the MEC, MECS, and Methodist Protestant Church (MPC), women's missionary work amalgamated largely following the model of the MECS's Woman's Missionary Council combining foreign and home missionary work into one organization.[31] When the UBC and EA/C joined to become the Evangelical United Brethren Church (EUBC), the women's missionary work resembled the EA/C with the formation of the Women's Society of World Service, which also combined foreign and home missionary work at the national level.[32] In 1968, the Methodist Church (MC) and EUBC joined to form the United Methodist Church (UMC) at which time women's missionary work was organized in the Women's Division protecting their efforts and eventually allowing for the establishment of United Methodist Women local organizations that followed the Wesley Service Guild and Women's Society of Christian Service models.[33]

WOMEN IN CHURCH AND SOCIETY

Women contributed significantly to various movements within American society such as Temperance, Suffrage, Abolition, and feminist movement. These contributions most often grew from the woman's vocations for ministry, including advocacy for the disenfranchised, teaching, preaching, and ordination.[34] The following section features three key female figures within American Methodism and their contributions to important movements of the time: Frances Willard, Jesse Daniel Ames, and Mary McLeod Bethune.

Frances E. Willard

Frances E. Willard's (1839–1898) ministry vocation led her to facilitate women's evangelistic ministry within the National Woman's Christian Temperance Union (NWCTU) encouraging aspects of a woman's church.[35] One of the most influential women of her time, and one of the few women honored in the U.S. Capitol's Statuary Hall,[36] Willard was a committed member of the MEC. Willard's Christian faith, informed by the Wesleyan theme of holiness, grounded her roles as educator and reformer. Invited to serve as the president of the newly founded Evanston College for Ladies in 1871, Willard was the first woman in America to confer a college degree.[37] But it was her work with the NWCTU that reflected her greatest influence. Elected president of the NWCTU in 1879, Willard served in that role, challenging and leading the organization, until her death almost two decades later.

The NWCTU organized following the Woman's Crusade against liquor dealers. Started in Ohio during the winter of 1873–1874, the Crusade quickly spread to neighboring states, then across the country, and finally linked with other movements across the world.[38] Recognizing the systemic implications of intemperance, Willard strategically expanded the NWCTU's horizons to address a wide range of issues affecting women – suffrage, poverty, ecclesiastic rights, marriage, and labor. Willard guided the growth of the NWCTU from a small, precarious organization with a simple focus of temperance to the largest women's organization in the nation with a complex agenda of social reform.[39]

Blocked from leadership in higher education and frustrated by a seemingly unanswerable call to ordained ministry, Willard channeled her Christian vocation into the trajectory of the NWCTU. Prior to her election as president in 1879, Willard experienced what she would refer to as a "conversion" to woman's suffrage, linking her faith to participation in causes beyond temperance reform.[40] Within the NWCTU Willard engaged in and facilitated women's evangelistic ministries. While advocating for woman's suffrage and ecclesiastic rights within the MEC, Willard implemented ecclesiological elements in the programs of the NWCTU. In her text *Woman and the Pulpit*, Willard argued for the ordination of women and suggested that if the current disenfranchisement persisted, women should consider ordaining themselves, effectively proposing a woman's church.[41] Willard's proposal did not materialize, as some had feared and others hoped, through a massive exodus of female church members from mainline Protestant and evangelical denominations. However, the NWCTU did provide women with Christian vocations to preach and to attain other ministry roles with training and practice.

Jesse Daniel Ames

Jessie Daniel Ames (1883–1972) was an activist for women's suffrage and antilynching. Ames was largely ambivalent toward the MECS, in which her mother was a devoted participant.[42] Graduating from Southwestern University in 1902, Daniel married a friend of her father's who was a military physician thirteen years her senior, Roger Post Ames, in 1905.[43] Because of his service in Central America, the couple lived separately for most of their nineteen-year marriage.[44] After her husband's death in 1914, Jessie Daniel Ames organized a county suffrage association in 1916.[45] Her effort led to Texas becoming the first southern state to ratify the Nineteenth Amendment.[46] Ames was involved in numerous political organizations (devoted to women's legislative platforms): Texas Equal Suffrage Association (as protégé of president Minnie Fisher Cunningham) later renamed the Texas League of Women Voters (president), National Democratic Party Convention (delegate at large), American Association of University Women (founder, president), Joint Legislative Council (executive committee member), the Texas Committee on Prisons and Prison Labor (executive committee member), and the Texas State Federation of Women's Clubs (political science chairman).[47]

Realizing the limitations and contradictions created by racial injustice, Ames focused her attention there,[48] first with the Commission on Interracial Co-operation as regional president, director of Women's Work.[49] Her major contribution to racial justice was through an organization she founded in 1930, the Association of Southern Women for the Prevention of Lynching (ASWPL).[50] The ASWPL challenged the reasoning for mob violence against African-American males by working to abolish the stereotype of white woman's vulnerability and need for protection.[51] With a decrease in the number of lynchings, the ASWPL dissolved in 1942, eventually contributing to Ames' reluctant retirement from women's rights and interracial work.[52]

Mary McLeod Bethune

Mary McLeod Bethune (1875–1955) was the first African-American woman to establish a four-year institution of higher learning and[53] to found a national organization to lobby the federal government,[54] and the first African American to hold a high-level government appointment as director of the Negro Division of the National Youth Administration.[55] She advised three presidents and received numerous awards.[56] Between 1933 and 1945, Bethune was arguably the most powerful African-American *person* in the United States.[57] According to Bethune, this was largely due to the exercise of her Christian faith.[58] Bethune's Christian faith and the ministry it inspired is most clearly demonstrated in her educational contributions, which are intimately related to her commitment to political action, specifically civil rights and racial justice.

Bethune committed her life to education after struggling with its inaccessibility as a result of race and class discrimination. Raised in a loving Christian family, Bethune gladly accepted educational opportunities in Christian mission contexts, initially through a small local school staffed by a Presbyterian missionary. Bethune later attended Scotia Female Seminary and eventually received admission to what would become Moody Bible Institute. She interpreted such opportunities as a setting apart. Although she felt a call to missionary work in Africa, the Presbyterian Foreign Mission Board denied her participation. As a result, she redirected her vocational trajectory to serve among African Americans in the South.

McLeod Bethune served in a number of missional and Christian education roles living in Georgia, South Carolina, and Florida while caring for her aging parents, meeting and marrying Albertus Bethune in 1898, and giving birth to her only son, Albert, in 1899.[59] After working with a Presbyterian minister who invited her to organize a school in connection with his local church in Palatka, Florida, she moved to Daytona Beach late in the summer of 1904.[60] In October of that same year she opened Daytona Educational and Industrial School for Negro Girls.[61] Although opened with no sponsorship (religious or otherwise), Bethune nurtured the school into a junior college by 1924. At this point she decided to seek denominational support and inquired into sponsorship from Presbyterian, Episcopal, and Methodist Churches. The MEC responded first to Bethune's request. With sponsorship, the MEC proposed a merger with Cookman Institute, a Methodist coeducational school. Although initially reluctant to consider such a merger, Bethune accepted the proposal and the invitation to serve as president of the new institution.[62]

Following the MEC's sponsorship of Bethune-Cookman College, Bethune became very involved, participating at all levels of church life. Within five years of her joining the MEC, she was elected as a delegate to General Conference, the denomination's national policy-making body.[63] Between 1928 and 1952, she served as a delegate to each General Conference and as a delegate to each Annual and Jurisdictional Conference from 1924 until her death in 1955.[64] In 1938, preparations were in process for the reunification of the MEC, MECS, and MPC. Although the divisions were caused largely as a result of polity issues, these issues were not void of theological and ethical implications. While the MPC divided from the MEC in 1820 as a result of stronger democratic tendencies, the role of race in the separation of the MEC and MECS from each other in 1844 was more apparent.[65] At the 1938 Methodist Episcopal General Conference, 250 African-American leaders, including Bethune, met to protest the provisions for segregation and creation of a Central Jurisdiction based solely on race, one of six jurisdictions, the remaining five determined by geography.[66] Bishop Robert E. Jones, Bishop Matthew W. Clair, and Mary McLeod Bethune voiced opposition to this plan to institutionalize segregation within the MEC.[67] In 1939, the merger occurred and the Central Jurisdiction was established, institutionalizing segregation. While many rejoiced at this ecumenical accomplishment, standing and singing "We're Marching to Zion," others, mainly African Americans and their friends, grieved in their seats, and some wept.[68]

ORDINATION OF WOMEN IN METHODIST AND WESLEYAN TRADITIONS

The first woman ordained within Methodism was most likely Helenor Davison (b. 1823). In 1866 Davison received ordination as Deacon in the Northern Indiana Conference of the MPC.[69] Anna Howard Shaw (1847–1919), an advocate for women's ordination and suffrage, received ordination in the New York Annual Conference of the MPC in 1880 though she was affiliated more closely with the Methodist Episcopal Church. Although the Methodist Protestant General Conference voted in 1884 that Shaw's ordination was unauthorized by church law, the New York Annual Conference continued to recognize her ordination.[70] By 1890 the

MPC began to be known as a Methodist denomination in which women could be ordained.[71]

In the UBC tradition women received ordination from 1889.[72] Prior to this, women received other forms of endorsement such as Charity Opheral's vote of commendation and Lydia Sexton's license to preach.[73] The first woman ordained in the UBC tradition in 1889 was Ella Niswonger who became a member of the Central Illinois Conference. Niswonger had been the first female graduate of the regular theological course at Bonebrake, later United Seminary, in Dayton, Ohio. In 1901 she also became the first woman to serve as a ministerial delegate to the UBC GC. By 1901, ninety-seven women were listed in the UBC ministerial directory.[74] However in the process of union with the EA/C in 1946 the issue of women's ecclesiastic rights was tabled.[75] According to at least one source, UBC women lost their clergy privileges in 1946 with the union that formed the EUB – until the UMC was formed in 1968 as a result of the amalgamation of the Methodist Church and the EUB.[76] According to Schmidt, offering a more subtle narration of circumstances, no additional women were ordained in either until 1968.[77]

As early as 1876 the word "male" was omitted from the AMEZ Book of Discipline when relating to ministry orders, theoretically allowing the possibility of women to assume such roles.[78] Bishop James Walker Hood of the AMEZ ordained Julia A. Foote (1823–1901) a deacon of the New York Annual Conference in 1884.[79] Mary J. Small (1850–1945) was ordained as a deacon ten years later in 1894, followed by ordination as elder in 1895 to the Philadelphia and Baltimore Annual Conference.[80] Foote was ordained an elder in 1899.[81]

In the AME Bishop Henry McNeal Turner ordained Sarah A.H., placing her name on the role of deacons. However, following this action at the 1887 session of the North Carolina Annual Conference, the presiding bishop overruled the action declaring it was contrary to church law.[82] In the meantime, alternative ministry roles for women in the AME were opened. For example, in 1868, the General Conference created the role of stewardess among the lay leadership of congregations.[83] In 1888, the role of female evangelist was established, drawing women into preaching; it was followed by the role of deaconess in 1900.[84] In 1948 the AME's Book of Discipline provided for the inclusion of women in ordination to the local diaconate.[85] In 1956, the General Conference voted to approve adding the words "and local elder."[86]

Jarena Lee (b. 1783, fl. 1818–1849) was the first known woman to preach in the AME.[87] Converted during Richard Allen's preaching, she shared her call to preach with him. He explained that provisions did not allow for women to preach. One day during a sermon in which it appeared that the preacher had lost the spirit, Lee stood up and began exhorting. Following Lee's contribution, Richard Allen endorsed her call to preach.[88] Influence of the holiness movement may be recognized in the preaching of Lee. The rise of the Wesleyan/holiness movement in America signaled a shift for women's preaching with the possibility of prophetic, if not priestly, preaching roles. While they did not receive license to preach or ordination, Phoebe Palmer (1807–1874) of the MEC and Amanda Berry Smith (1837–1915) of the AME were widely recognized Wesleyan/holiness preachers within American Methodism, as well as on the international landscape.[89]

Women in the CME were permitted license to preach and to do evangelistic work from 1894, though they were not yet ordained.[90] This decision followed the General Conference's creation of the role of stewardess in 1890, offering an alternative space for women to practice their vocations to ministry.[91] In 1918, the CME General Conference authorized the licensing of women as local preachers.[92] In 1966, the first woman ordained to the traveling ministry was Virgie Jackson Gant as an elder in the North Arkansas Annual Conference.[93]

Maggie Newton Van Cott (1813–1914), recognized within the Wesleyan/holiness movement, was the first woman to receive a license to preach in the MEC.[94] Anna Oliver (1849–1892), most likely the first female graduate of a theological institution, received a license to preach in 1876 and was recommended for ordination in 1880.[95] The MEC General Conference not only decided against women's ordination, but also rescinded the approximately seventy preaching licenses held by women (including Anna Howard Shaw) across the connection. Licenses to preach would not be extended to women in the MEC again until 1920.[96] In the meantime, women cultivated alternative spaces to fulfill their vocations to ministry through such avenues as the Deaconess movement, founded by Lucy Rider Meyer (1849–1922) in 1885 and recognized by the Methodist Episcopal Church in 1888.

The MECS made its decisions regarding women lay preachers and lay delegates to General Conference and Annual Conference as well as full ecclesiastic rights for women generally later than the other traditions that now form the UMC. However, Belle Harris Bennett deserves mention for her contributions to the mission of the MECS in the early twentieth century. Isabel "Belle" Harris Bennett (1852–1922) continued the work of Lucinda Helms, who formulated the plan for the Woman's Department within the MECS, as well as advocated for women's ecclesiastic rights and social reform.

Figure 13. **Phoebe Palmer, the Methodist Episcopal Church,** Methodist Library Image Collection, Drew University, Madison, New Jersey.

Bennett presented the idea of establishing a missionary training school for women to the Woman's Board for Foreign Missions (MECS) in 1889 and was promptly appointed as their agent for the project.[97] From these efforts Scarritt Bible and Training School was established in Kansas City in 1892.[98] For more than twenty-five years, Bennett served as president of the MECS's Woman's Home Missionary Society, and its new governing body, Women's Board of Home Missions, after 1898 (1896–1910), and its successor the Woman's Missionary Council (1910–1922).[99] With Bennett's leadership the first church settlement house opened in Nashville in 1901.[100] She helped to establish as many as forty Wesley Community and Bethlehem Houses, the latter for work among African Americans.[101]

These efforts coincided with Bennett's petition to the MECS General Conference for the office of Deaconess, which was recognized in 1902.[102] Bennett, among others, launched the campaign for women's laity rights that initially came to a vote at the MECS General Conference in 1910,[103] following the denomination's amalgamation of missionary work that resulted in the loss of autonomy among women's missionary organizations.[104] Although women were granted laity rights in 1918[105] and Bennett was elected as the Kentucky Annual Conference's first female delegate to General Conference in 1922, she was too ill to attend; dying that summer.[106] Following the campaign for laity rights, petitions for full clergy rights for women were before the MECS General Conference from 1926.[107] These finally came to fruition several decades later in the Methodist Church.

The year 1920 marked significant progress for the MEC and its recognition of women's ecclesiastic rights. In that year, not only did the U.S. ratify the Nineteenth Amendment granting woman suffrage, but the Methodist Episcopal Book of Discipline officially extended to women local preacher's licenses, the first step to ordained ministry. Winifred Willard and Witlia Caffray were among those initial women to receive such rights.[108]

In 1924, Methodist Episcopal women received limited clergy rights or "local" ordination.[109] Georgia Harkness (1891–1974), the first woman to serve on the faculty of a Methodist theological institution (Boston University School of Theology and later Garrett Evangelical Theological Seminary), was a local elder.[110] Harkness never sought ordination as an elder, although she was a leading proponent of women's clergy rights.[111] According to Harkness,

[The crux of the matter] is that women cannot enter a field where they are not welcome. Ordination is desirable, I believe, to put the stamp of the Church's approval upon the admission of women to its ministry. But what is needed even more is a general recognition by pulpit and pew of the legitimate place of trained women in this field. Women will never find welcome in the ministry until the press and our present religious leadership have remoulded [sic] public sentiment. Ordination is a step in this direction, but it is a step – not the final goal.[112]

If need arose women were sent as local pastors. Many women pursued theological education despite the lack of opportunities for women to serve as ordained ministers under appointment. In the MEC petitions for full clergy rights of women were sent to General Conference from 1928, interestingly, lagging behind the MECS by two years.[113]

By the time the Methodist General Conference met in Minneapolis in 1956 it had received over 2,000 petitions asking for full clergy rights of women.[114] A compromise recommendation was narrowly reached in committee and presented to General Conference. However, it contained a stipulation: "only unmarried women and widows may apply." By a vote of 389 to 297 the provision that married women could not apply was removed. "Then by an overwhelming show of hands" the delegates passed the historic motion putting into the Discipline the following simple but momentous words: "Women are included in all provisions of the Discipline referring to the ministry."[115] Although full clergy rights were granted in 1956, male pronouns for clergy remained in the Discipline until 1968.[116]

Maud Keister Jenson (1904–1998) was the first woman ordained in the Methodist Church on May 18, 1956. She was the first among many with the staggering of Annual Conference dates. She was ordained in the Central Pennsylvania Annual Conference, although from New Jersey. A graduate of Drew, she and her husband served the majority of their professional ministry in missionary service in Korea.[117] The second woman, Grace Huck (b. 1916), was admitted by the North Dakota Annual Conference and ordained on May 22.[118] Emma Hill Burrell (b. 1912) was admitted by the Washington Conference of the Central Jurisdiction on May 26, 1956, making her the first African-American woman to receive full clergy rights in the Methodist Church. A total of twenty-four women were received into full membership and received clergy rights that spring.[119]

Margaret Henrichsen (1901?–1976) was the first woman appointed as a district superintendent (DS) in the MC.[120] She served as the DS of the Bangor District in the Maine Annual Conference from 1967.[121]

In 1980, Marjorie Swank Matthews (1916–1986) served as the second female DS and the first female bishop of the UMC. She entered the ministry as a second career and was appointed bishop at age sixty.[122] In 1984, Leontine Kelly (b. 1920) was the first African-American woman bishop in the Methodist tradition.[123] Kelly was elected to the Episcopacy by the Western Jurisdiction, though nominated and endorsed in the Southeastern Jurisdiction as a member of the Virginia Annual Conference. In 1996, Charlene Kammerer (b. 1948) was the first woman elected to the episcopacy by the Southeastern Jurisdiction of the UMC.[124] In 2000 the AME elected Vashti McKenzie (b. 1947) as bishop.[125] The AMEZ elected Dr. Mildred "Bonnie" Hines (b. 1955) as their first female bishop.[126] Similar to Kelly, Hines served congregations mostly in North Carolina until her penultimate pulpit in Los Angeles from where she was elected bishop.[127] The CME followed in 2010 electing the Dr. Teresa Snorton (b. 1954?) to the episcopacy.[128]

While much progress has been made in church and society to allow for the contributions of women in ecclesial leadership, there is still much more work to be done. In the last ten to fifteen years the attrition rate for women leaving local church ministry in the UMC remains high, higher than men.[129] With women consisting of 40–60 percent of seminary students, only 10–15 percent of clergy in UM annual conferences are women. Several systemic issues are described as contributing to the attrition rate: some are personal choice relating to circumstance/familial, others related to supervision and congregational dynamics.[130] On a more positive note, the number of women elected to the episcopacy, appointed to the district superintendency, as well as those serving larger membership congregations in the UMC continue to steadily increase. As Harkness wisely stated in a statement quoted earlier, "ordination is a step ... but not the final goal."

Notes

Many thanks to Rev. Laura Rodgers Levens and Donyelle McCray, both excellent scholars and current students in the Doctor of Theology program at Duke University Divinity School, for their skillful research assistance with this project.

1   Beverly Zink-Sawyer, *From Preachers to Suffragists: Woman's Rights and Religious Conviction in the Lives of Three Nineteenth-Century American Clergywomen* (Louisville, KY: Westminster John Knox Press, 2003), 36.

2   Jean Miller Schmidt, *Grace Sufficient: A History of Women in American Methodism 1760–1939* (Nashville, TN: Abingdon Press, 1999), 52–53.

3   Schmidt, *Grace Sufficient*, 55.

4   Schmidt, *Grace Sufficient*, 53, 63.

5   Jualynne E. Dodson, *Engendering Church: Women Power and the AME Church* (New York: Rowman & Littlefield Publishers, 2002), 45.

6   For more on the women discussed here, see Laceye C. Warner, Saving Women: Retrieving Evangelistic Theology and Practice (Waco, TX: Baylor University Press, 2007), chapters 4 and 6. Also see my articles on "Jessie Daniel Ames," "Belle Harris Bennett," "Winifred Chappell," "Lucy Rider Meyer," "Phoebe Palmer," "Anna Howard Shaw," "Carla Swain," "Isabella Thoburn," and "Margaret Ann Newton Van Cott," in *The Westminster Dictionary of Women in American Religious History*, ed. Susan H. Lindley (Louisville: Westminster John Knox Press, 2008), 5, 17, 38, 148, 166, 196, 216, 219, 226, 236.

7   Dodson, *Endangering Church*, 45; David Henry Bradley, *A History of the A.M.E. Zion Church Part II, 1796–1872* (1956), 224. Dodson links the official group with the unofficial women's group started by Sarah Allen, Bishop Allen's wife, during the formation meeting of the AME Church in 1816.

8   Bradley, *History of A.M.E. Zion Church*, 2: 224, 225.

9   Bradley, *History of A.M.E. Zion Church*, 2: 232.

10 Bradley, *History of A.M.E. Zion Church*, 2: 233.

11 Octavia W. Dandridge, *Eleven Decades of Historical Events: Featuring The Women's Missionary Society, African Methodist Episcopal Church, 1874–1984* (Washington, DC: Women's Missionary Society A.M.E. Church, 1985), 1, 4. See also Charles Spencer Smith, *A History of the African Methodist Episcopal Church 1856–1922* (Philadelphia, PA: Book Concern of the A. M. E. Church, 1922), 303.

12 Schmidt, *Grace Sufficient*, 158–159.

13 Schmidt, *Grace Sufficient*, 159. In January 1896 the periodical title was changed to *The Woman's Missionary Friend*.

14 Dana Robert, *American Women in Mission: A Social History of Their Thought and Practice* (Macon, GA: Mercer University Press, 1997), 162; James Mills Thoburn, *Life of Isabella Thoburn* (New York: Jennings and Pye, 1903), 51–54.

15 Thoburn, *Life of Isabella Thoburn*, 75ff.

16 Thoburn, *Life of Isabella Thoburn*, 89–91, 116–122, 131, 92–93, 122–123, 160–180.

17 Robert, *American Women in Mission*, 161; Thoburn *Life of Isabella Thoburn*, 273ff.

18 Thoburn, *Life of Isabella Thoburn*, 74, 193.

19 Dorothy Clark Wilson, *Palace of Healing: The Story of Dr. Clara Swain* (New York: McGraw Hill, 1968), 16–18.

20 Robert, *American Women in Mission*, 164; Wilson, *Palace of Healing*, 42–43.

21 Robert, *American Women in Mission*, 164.

22 Robert, *American Women in Mission*, 165; Wilson, *Palace of Healing*, 60–75.

23 Othal Hawthorne Lakey, *The History of the CME Church* (Memphis, TN: The CME Publishing House, 1996), 270.

24 Schmidt, *Grace Sufficient*, 168–169.

25 Schmidt, *Grace Sufficient*, 172.

26   Schmidt, *Grace Sufficient*, 173.

27   Schmidt, *Grace Sufficient*, 173.

28   Schmidt, *Grace Sufficient*, 173–174. Later Minerva Strawman Speng.

29   Schmidt, *Grace Sufficient*, 174.

30   Schmidt, *Grace Sufficient*, 168–169.

31   Schmidt, *Grace Sufficient*, 270–271.

32   Schmidt, *Grace Sufficient*, 290–291.

33   Schmidt, *Grace Sufficient*, 291.

34   Zink-Sawyer, *Preachers to Suffragists*, 68.

35   The NWCTU, based mostly in small town congregations, claimed the largest number of participants in nineteenth-century women's organizations. See Lori D. Ginzberg, *Women and the Work of Benevolence: Morality, Politics, and Class in the 19th-Century United States* (New Haven, CT: Yale University Press, 1990), 204.

36   Nancy A. Hardesty, *Women Called to Witness: Evangelical Feminism in the Nineteenth Century*, 2nd ed. (Knoxville, TN: University of Tennessee Press, 1999), 2.

37   Hardesty, *Women Called to Witness*, 4–5; *Writing Out My Heart: Selections from the Journal of Frances E. Willard, 1855–96*, edited by Carolyn Gifford (Urbana, IL: University of Illinois Press, 1995), 6; and Frances Willard, *Glimpses of Fifty Years: The Autobiography of an American Woman* (Chicago, IL: Woman's Temperance Publication Association, 1889), 198–225.

38   By April 1874, more than one thousand saloons had been closed, and beer production in at least one state was estimated at one-third less. Barbara Leslie Epstein, *The Politics of Domesticity: Women, Evangelism, and Temperance in Nineteenth Century America* (Middletown, CT: Wesleyan University, 1981), 100. The World's Woman's Christian Temperance Union was organized in 1884.

39   Gifford, *Writing Out My Heart*, 7.

40   Willard, *Glimpses of Fifty Years*, 351. Hardesty, *Women Called to Witness*, 6. See also Zink-Sawyer, *Preachers to Suffragists*, 4–6, 171–216.

41   Willard, *Woman in the Pulpit* (Washington, DC: Zenger Publishing Co., 1978), 56.

42   Jacquelyn Dowd Hall, *Revolt against Chivalry: Jessie Daniel Ames and the Women's Campaign against Lynching* (New York: Columbia University Press, 1993), 29, 59–60.

43   Hall, *Revolt against Chivalry*, 9.

44   Hall, *Revolt against Chivalry*, 11–14.

45   Hall, *Revolt against Chivalry*, 31.

46   Hall, *Revolt against Chivalry*, 44.

47   Hall, *Revolt against Chivalry*, 32–34, 44, 48–50, 52.

48   Hall, *Revolt against Chivalry*, 53–54.

49   Hall, *Revolt against Chivalry*, 109–112, 123–128.

50   Hall, *Revolt against Chivalry*, 159–64.

51   Hall, *Revolt against Chivalry*, 194–197, 201–206.

52   Hall, *Revolt against Chivalry*, 255–256, 260.

53   Bethune-Cookman College, located in Daytona Beach, FL.

54   The National Council of Negro Women lobbied primarily on behalf of African-American women and children.

55 Bethune held this post during the presidency of Franklin Delano Roosevelt.

56 Herbert Hoover, Franklin Delano Roosevelt, and Harry S. Truman. See Clarence G. Newsome, "Mary McLeod Bethune and the Methodist Episcopal Church North: In but Out," in *This Far by Faith: Stories in African American Women's Religious Biography*, edited by Judith Weisenfeld and Richard Newman (New York: Routledge, 1996), 125.

57 Newsome, "Mary McLeod Bethune."

58 Newsome, "Mary McLeod Bethune."

59 Audrey T. McCluskey, "Introduction," in *Mary McLeod Bethune: Building a Better World, Essays and Selected Documents*, edited by Audrey T. McCluskey and Elaine M. Smith (Bloomington, IN: Indiana University Press, 1999), 5; see also Newsome, 127–129.

60 McCluskey, "Introduction."

61 McCluskey, "Introduction," 5.

62 Newsome, "Mary McLeod Bethune," 133.

63 Newsome, "Mary McLeod Bethune," 130.

64 Ibid.

65 See Frederick A. Norwood, *The Story of American Methodism: A History of the United Methodists and Their Relations*, (Nashville, TN: Abingdon Press, 1974), 164–209; for primary source material see Russell E. Richey, Kenneth E. Rowe, and Jean Miller Schmidt, eds., *The Methodist Experience in America: A Sourcebook*, vol. II (Nashville, TN: Abingdon Press, 2000).

66 African Americans had applied and received autonomy in separate annual conferences in the Methodist Episcopal Church from 1864 and in the (currently named) Christian Methodist Episcopal Church from 1870. However, despite the application of these African Americans, their creation along with the creation of the Central Jurisdiction imposed by the white majority all evidence the systemic sin of racism. For further explanation, see James S. Thomas, *Methodism's Racial Dilemma: The Story of the Central Jurisdiction* (Nashville, TN: Abingdon Press, 1992), 9–47.

67 Alice Knotts, *Fellowship of Love: Methodist Women Changing American Racial Attitudes, 1920–1968* (Nashville, TN: Kingswood Books, 1996), 135.

68 Thomas, *Methodism's Racial Dilemma*, 43.

69 Schmidt, *Grace Sufficient*, 181.

70 Schmidt, *Grace Sufficient*, 194.

71 Schmidt, *Grace Sufficient*, 194.

72 Schmidt, *Grace Sufficient*, 194.

73 Schmidt, *Grace Sufficient*, 109.

74 Schmidt, *Grace Sufficient*, 194.

75 Schmidt, *Grace Sufficient*, 284.

76 Russell E. Richey, Kenneth E. Rowe, and Jean Miller Schmidt, *The Methodist Experience in America* (Nashville, TN: Abingdon Press, 2001), 1:407.

77 Schmidt, *Grace Sufficient*, 284.

78 Bradley, *History of A.M.E. Zion Church*, 2: 240.

79 William Andrews, *Sisters of the Spirit: Three Black Women's Autobiographies of the Nineteenth Century* (Bloomington, IN: Indiana University, 1986), 10; Bradley, *History of A.M.E. Zion Church*, 2:384, 393–394.

80 Bettye Collier-Thomas, *Daughters of Thunder: Black Women Preachers and Their Sermons, 1850 – 1979* (San Francisco, CA: Jossey Bass, 1998), 59, 91.

81 Collier-Thomas, *Daughters of Thunder*, 59.

82 Jeane B. Williams, "The Clergywoman," in *Women on the Way: African Methodist Episcopal Women Maximizing Their Human and Spiritual Potential* (n.p.: *Committee on Research and Status of Black Women, Women's Missionary Society, A.M.E. Church, 1983), 50–53.

83 Dodson, *Endangering Church*, 58.

84 Dodson, *Endangering Church*, 96.

85 Williams, "The Clergywoman," 52.

86 Williams, "The Clergywoman," 52.

87 Collier-Thomas, *Daughters of Thunder*, 45.

88 Williams, "The Clergywoman," 50.

89 For more information about Phoebe Palmer, see Susan Hill Lindley, *"You Have Stept Out of Your Place": A History of Women and Religion in America* (Louisville, KY: Westminster John Knox Press, 1996), 118–120. For more information about Amanda Berry Smith, see Collier-Thomas, *Daughters of Thunder*, 48–53. For more information about women within the Wesleyan/Holiness movement, see Susie C. Stanley, *Holy Boldness: Women Preachers; Autobiographies and the Sanctified Self* (Knoxville, TN: University of Tennessee Press, 2002).

90 Lakey, *History of the CME Church*, 414.

91 Lakey, *History of the CME Church*, 271, 414.

92 Lakey, *History of the CME Church*, 414.

93 Lakey, *History of the CME Church*, 661.

94 Richey, Rowe, and Schmidt, *Methodist Experience in America*, 1: 242; Schmidt, *Methodist Experience in America*, 181–182.

95 Schmidt, *Grace Sufficient*, 188.

96 Schmidt, *Grace Sufficient*, 191–192.

97 Schmidt, *Grace Sufficient*, 209; Mrs. Robert W. MacDonell, *Belle Harris Bennett, Her Life Work* (Nashville, TN: Board of Missions, Methodist Episcopal Church, South, 1928), 55–57.

98 Schmidt, *Grace Sufficient*, 209; MacDonell, *Belle Harris Bennett*, 69.

99 Schmidt, *Grace Sufficient*, 171; MacDonell, *Belle Harris Bennett*, 85ff, 141ff.

100 Schmidt, *Grace Sufficient*, 172; MacDonell, 92–93.

101 MacDonell, *Belle Harris Bennett*, 95. For more on Bennett's work with African Americans see MacDonell, *Belle Harris Bennett*, 121–140.

102 Schmidt, *Grace Sufficient*, 210; MacDonell, *Belle Harris Bennett*, 96.

103 Schmidt, *Grace Sufficient*, 229; MacDonell *Belle Harris Bennett*, 232ff (239).

104 Schmidt, *Grace Sufficient*, 228–229; MacDonell records Bennett's opinions on the merger (234–236).

105 Schmidt, *Grace Sufficient*, 230; MacDonell, *Belle Harris Bennett*, 248–252.

106 Schmidt, *Grace Sufficient*, 231; MacDonell, *Belle Harris Bennett*, 253–255.

107 Schmidt, *Grace Sufficient*, 281.

108 Schmidt, *Grace Sufficient*, 273.

109 Schmidt, *Grace Sufficient*, 274.
110 Schmidt, *Grace Sufficient*, 283.
111 Schmidt, *Grace Sufficient*, 283.
112 Schmidt, *Grace Sufficient*, 274.
113 Schmidt, *Grace Sufficient*, 281.
114 Schmidt, *Grace Sufficient*, 281.
115 Schmidt, *Grace Sufficient*, 282.
116 "Both men and women are included in all provisions of the Discipline which refer to the ministry." *The Book of Discipline of the United Methodist Church* (Nashville, TN: The United Methodist Publishing House, 1968), section IV, Provision 308.2.
117 Schmidt, *Grace Sufficient*, 282–283.
118 Schmidt, *Grace Sufficient*, 283.
119 Schmidt, *Grace Sufficient*, 283.
120 "Timeline of Women in American Methodism." http://archives.umc.org/interior.asp?ptid=1&mid=2619 (accessed June 6, 2011).
121 Barbara Troxell, "Honoring One Another with Our Stories: Authority and Mutual Ministry Among United Methodist Clergywomen in the Last Decade of the Twentieth Century," in *Spirituality and Social Responsibility*, edited by Rosemary Skinner Keller (Nashville, TN: Abingdon Press, 1993), 289.
122 Richey, Rowe, and Schmidt, *Methodist Experience in America*, 1: 466; Barbara Troxell, "Ordination of Women in the United Methodist Tradition," *Methodist History* 37.2 (1999), 128.
123 Richey, Rowe, and Schmidt, *Methodist Experience in America*, 466. Kelly's daughter authored a moving biography of her mother: Angela Current, *Breaking Barriers: An African American Family & the Methodist Story* (Nashville, TN: Abingdon Press, 2001).
124 Barbara Troxell, "Ordination of Women," 128.
125 Dodson, *Endangering Church*, 1: 3.
126 "AME Zion Welcomes First Female Bishop," *Los Angeles Sentinel*, July 24, 2008, http://www.lasentinel.net/A.M.E.-Zion-Welcomes-First-Female-Bishop.html (accessed July 31, 2011).
127 "AME Zion Welcomes First Female Bishop."
128 "CME Church Elects First Female Bishop," *Chicago Defender*, July 19, 2010, http://www.chicagodefender.com/article-8304-cme-church-elects-first-female-bishop.html (accessed July 31, 2011).
129 See also Rolf Menning, "United Methodist Ordained Ministry in Transition (Trends in Ordination and Careers)," in *The People(s) Called Methodist: Forms and Reforms of Their Life*, edited by William B. Lawrence, Dennis M. Campbell, and Russell E. Richey (Nashville, TN: Abingdon Press, 1998), 132–138.
130 "Chapter Three: Cooperating with Grace," under the United Methodist Clergywomen Retention Study, compiled by the Anna Howard Shaw Center of Boston University http://www.bu.edu/shaw/publications/the-clergy-womens-retention-study/united-methodist-clergywomen-retention-study-3/ (accessed June 2, 2011).

17 Methodists and War

ANDREW J. WOOD

As other chapters in this volume indicate, the study of American Methodism is now a multidisciplinary undertaking in which a wide range of Wesleyan and Methodist traditions must be taken into account, including Methodist Episcopal, African-American, and Wesleyan-holiness traditions.[1] Similarly, the study of war is a growing field in historical studies that now features a wide range of approaches and concerns, including war and society, the social history of warfare, the impact of war on societies, and the role that a society's composition, history, beliefs, and values play in shaping wars. Given the scope and complexity of each of these areas of scholarly inquiry, a comprehensive account of American Methodists and war is simply not possible here. Thus, the goal of this chapter is to provide a framework for thinking about American Methodists and war. Invariably, broad strokes will be necessary. Furthermore, the focus will be on what did happen, not what should have happened. In other words, the aim is not to chart the history of Methodist virtue and vice on this issue.

A general overview of the terrain reveals that Wesleyans have a mixed record regarding war, whether support for it (prior to or during war) or the actual fighting of it. Amid the diverse ways in which American Methodists have responded to war, however, a basic pattern or principle can be observed. American Methodists have been most likely to support (a) war when they thought it advanced, extended or protected civilization.[2] With this in mind, the remainder of this essay will explore Methodists and war in the nineteenth century and then in the twentieth century, paying close attention to salient differences.

METHODISTS AND WAR IN THE NINETEENTH CENTURY

Civilization has often been compared to and contrasted with barbarism; in this, Wesleyans have been no exception. If Methodists viewed an idea, action, or policy to be "barbaric," then they generally considered

Figure 14. **Bishop Matthew Simpson, the Methodist Episcopal Church,**
Methodist Library Image Collection, Drew University, Madison, New Jersey.

it to be a threat to civilization. From John Wesley's commentaries on
the American Revolution to the wartime activities of Bishop Matthew
Simpson, Methodists wrestled with questions of the national well-being
as well as that of the church.[3]

American Methodists functioned with a fusion of "little r" republican and Protestant notions of civilization. These notions were largely
inherited from and informed by British developments, especially the
history of Protestantism in Britain, traditional English understandings
of "liberty," and the political theology of the British state. Such views
were characterized by a concern for literacy, free speech, freedom of religion, the rule of law, moral and spiritual seriousness and discipline, the

need for vigilance in the face of immorality and tyranny, the fragility of free, just, and honest government, and a persistent tendency to fear religious and political decline matched with a robust hope for progress. In other words, American Wesleyans behaved as though human persons and human societies were both readily corruptible and readily perfectable. It could go either way and *would* go one way or the other. Thus, Methodists were responsible, not just for having the right opinion or theory about this or that religious, social, moral, or political issue but also for doing something about it. For American Methodists, doctrine and ethics must be translated into polity and praxis.[4]

Such assumptions, when added to the vigorous growth of the various Methodisms by 1850, encouraged Methodists to assume the attitude of a "State church." That is, they were primary care takers of civilization and the moral, social, and political order. Whether or not Christians should engage in *war* is a theological question. Whether or not American Christians should support *a war* has often been viewed as a political question.

One major question for Wesleyans, one that has implications far beyond the subject of war and is perhaps especially important for United Methodists, is why has Methodism so often behaved like a state church? Few churches, if any, so consistently claims the mantle of moral authority over the national life as does the United Methodist Church. This tendency certainly characterized the Methodist Episcopal Church (MEC) and Methodist Episcopal Church, South (MECS). Perhaps it is simply a question of size and access to power creating a corresponding sense of responsibility and prerogative. The MEC was the "most extensive national institution in Antebellum America other than the federal government."[5] By 1868, Ulysses S. Grant could remark that there were three great parties in the United States: the Republican, the Democratic, and the Methodist Church. Smaller Wesleyan denominations have seemed far less confident about their ability to shape the course of history and national affairs.

On that note, then, the question is not just "what war?" or "what Wesleyans?" but also "what Wesleyans in what war?" As a general proposition, it seems that very few Methodists have liked the idea of war. If many could imagine a *necessary* war, fewer could imagine a *desirable* one. But for most Wesleyans – state church assumptions aside – the question of whether or not "we should be in this war?" was a pointless question simply beyond their ability to control or influence. After all, the government has not been in the habit of calling special elections with one question on the ballot – "should we go to war?" The presidential elections of 1860 ("yes we should") and 1916 ("no we shouldn't") seem to be the closest parallels. While public opinion is relevant, the recent U.S. census did not ask for a response to the question "what should our foreign policy be toward North Korea, Syria, and Iran?" It is worth noting that, if a state church has such influence with the government, most of its *members* do not. Interestingly, for much of the nineteenth century, many Methodist ministers did not vote as a matter of principle.

Of course, Methodist opposition to war was related to the death and harm wars brought to participants and spectators alike. But people get hurt and die in peacetime, too. No peace treaty can put a stop to traffic accidents and cancer. So there were other reasons to oppose war. Methodist polity required the same tools that businesses did; safe and reliable travel and the predictable functioning of the mails. Communication was necessary, congregations and conferences had to be able to meet, bishops (i.e., itinerant general superintendents in the Methodist system) had to be able to itinerate. Nineteenth-century wars were often very disruptive to the functioning of Methodist piety.[6]

War could be opposed for other reasons including assumptions about what army life would do to a pious young man. In other words, many worried about what army life would contribute to the moral and spiritual habits of young men. The moral habits of nineteenth-century armies were likely no better than those today (and perhaps much worse).

The role of women has been an important one. If Methodist interest in war revolved around civilization, women's civilizing roles – as the sustainers and teachers of civilization, the storytellers, and first ethicists – should be noted. It seems likely that further research into the relations between soldiers and their wives, mothers, sisters, and so on (mostly through their wartime letters) would reveal that Methodist women had as large a role to play in sustaining armies in the field as that played by any other Methodists. What is known of such letters during the Civil War suggests that Methodist women carefully weighed the political, theological, and pastoral meanings of war.

Methodists debated the competing responsibility of clergymen on the eve of war. Wars often created professional and personal crises for Methodist preachers. Should they resign (or "abandon") their homefront charges to follow the armies off to war? If so, should they go as noncombatants, or should they take up a weapon and stand a post? What should they say about God's will to those who came to them for counsel?

Wesleyans were likely to react to war as they would any other unwelcome current event, life trouble, or disaster. For example, as the bloodshed and suffering of the Civil War increased, Methodists amped up their introspection. Most thought the war was divine judgment for sin, but in addition to being a judgment of either the institution of slavery itself, or the un-Christian practices of individual slaveholders, some thought that it might also be a judgment of white treatment of American Indians or any number of social vices such as corruption, gambling, materialism, and so on. In other words, wars functioned in this case the same way any really bad news in a person's life might; they provoked the question "Why?"[7]

The nineteenth-century American experience of war was generally unlike the twentieth-century experience of war. Most nineteenth-century American wars were homefront or continental wars. Even the Indian Wars and the Mexican War were attempts to extend or secure the contiguous territory under the control of the U.S. government. American civilians often saw war up close in the nineteenth century. Beginning with the Spanish-American War and Philippine-American War, most American wars were interventionist wars fought overseas; they were a global extension of American power, not wars fought to secure the borders or the survival of the government itself as with the Civil War (this essay, frankly, overlooks early, primarily naval, conflicts and extensions of U.S. naval power that occurred before the Spanish-American War).

The American Civil War brought home the complicated tensions of war to every wing of Methodism. Northern Methodists demonstrated their unwavering support for the Union war effort by placing the American flag in church sanctuaries, and through Bishop Matthew Simpson's passionate eulogy of Lincoln as "Martyr."[8] The 1860 election had provided opportunity for many northern Methodists to identify "the arrival of the kingdom of God with the success of a particular political party."[9] Perhaps not surprisingly, in much of northern Methodism, being antiwar was often understood as equal to being proslavery. White southern Methodists had a more complicated task, as many were initially "reluctant Confederates." As the war progressed, they would have fewer tendencies to triumphalism than their northern counterparts.[10] Methodists were 38 percent of Union Army chaplains, and 47 percent of Confederate chaplains.[11]

In 1864, the Wesleyan Church, rooted in abolition, declared,

> Resolved, that in the spirit of patriots and of Christians, we affirm for ourselves and our churches our unqualified loyalty to the government, and our readiness to incline and make all the sacrifices necessary to the overthrow of the rebellion, and the destruction of slavery, its guilty cause.[12]

Yet emancipation itself – clearly a result of the war – was more important for the history of Methodism than prewar Methodist abolitionism. Emancipation made possible the dramatic expansion of black Methodism in the decades after 1865. This most dramatic religious transfer and expansion was perhaps the most important in the history of American Protestantism: the mass exodus of African Americans out of the MECS and other southern bodies controlled by whites. Thousands of African-American members of the MECS left for African-American communions or for the freedmen's ministries of the MEC. The near wholesale secession of blacks from the MECS would be among the most dramatic religious migrations in American history. It was well underway before the war ended and would culminate in the formation of the Colored Methodist Episcopal Church (CME) in 1870 (later renamed the Christian Methodist Episcopal Church) in agreement with the MECS. By the time the CME was organized, most black former-MECS members had long since left for other bodies in a flurry of movement marked by self-determination and racial and sectional religious competition.[13]

After the war and emancipation, most African-American Methodists left the MECS for the African Methodist Episcopal Church (AME), African Methodist Episcopal Church, Zion (AMEZ), both of northern origins, or the (CME). The African-American membership in the MECS declined dramatically during this period, and interracial worship became far less common than it had been before the war. Many African-American Methodists enjoyed the privileges, responsibilities, and freedoms of church leadership for the first time during the Reconstruction era, while white Methodists increasingly grew to maturity without any religious experience with their fellow African-American Methodists. Jim Crow legislation may have been encouraged by the socioreligious divide within Methodism during this period. Before the Civil War, the institutions of the South were largely biracial. Between the end of the war in 1865, the exodus of black Methodists out of the southern Methodist church was nearly complete.[14]

At the end of the Civil War, the MECS found itself in a sorry state. Church buildings had been badly damaged, left to decay, or destroyed altogether. More serious, Methodism embraced a hierarchical government in the context of popular idiom and a high stress upon "conference," the social function that built identity and knit the system into a whole. The functions of church life, especially those that bound the communion together, had largely ceased or had been severely curtailed. Church conferences at the local, district, annual conference, and general levels had not met for years. Few church papers had been published during the war, and many clergy and laity alike had been scattered by forced migration or wartime service, or had simply stopped meeting with one another. Bishops had been unable to confer with one another or to make clergy appointments, and Methodist itinerants had had to decide on their own whether to remain in their assignments or to seek opportunities elsewhere. Thousands of Methodists had died in the war, and many more had lost substantially in financial means. For a voluntary organization that believed the eternal destiny of millions depended on its functioning, such dislocations and disruptions meant that no less than the cause of Christ was threatened. Because of the peculiarities of its system, Methodism may have suffered a greater blow from the war than any other religious body. The prospect for recovery, especially regaining the operations of ministry, was as daunting as it was urgent.

Adding to this sense of crisis, thousands of members had disappeared, lost in the upheavals of war. Others had found their way into other denominations, especially the rival "Campbellites" and Baptist churches whose localism and congregational form was less dependent on ease of travel and communication. Religious bodies that could function during the war had not been idle; rebuilding the MECS would entail renewed competition for the religious opinions and alliances of a battered and anxious population.

Tensions between the MEC and MECS grew as the war came to the South. Sectional issues between the MEC and MECS then were not merely the results of extraecclesial social and political issues. Real matters of fraternal relations and philosophical differences (influenced heavily by antebellum debates over slavery) had grown worse since the cessation of formal hostilities. In the twenty years after 1865, the secular and religious newspapers enabled a war of words with accusations of moral degeneracy, violations of trust, heresy, and slander between the two largest branches of Methodism whose 1840s split had been more amicable that its postwar spats would suggest. From the vantage point of the MECS, these were not old wounds but new ones caused by new outrages. Most galling of all, many properties and even whole congregations had been confiscated and appropriated by the MEC under the force of Union arms. During the war, MEC Bishops Edward Ames and Matthew Simpson convinced Secretary of War Edwin Stanton to use the power of the federal armies to confiscate the church properties in the hands of the disloyal MECS and turn them over to bishops of the MEC.[15] The southern response to the MEC's methods of movement into the South was not surprising. In this context, while sharing a general distrust for northerners, many white southern Methodists would come to distrust northern Methodists in particular.

The MEC's view of itself as a national or state church of sorts was especially strong during the war with Bishop Matthew Simpson claiming simply that "Methodism is loyalty." American flags made their first appearance in sanctuaries among northern Methodists during the Civil War. Many in the MEC considered the MECS heretical and seditious, engaged in criminal acts for an immoral cause supported by religious untruth. Therefore, they overturned the agreement of 1844 whereby the MECS was considered a legitimate branch of Methodism. Undermining MECS legitimacy became then a marker of political and religious devotion for many northern Methodists. Securing "loyal" preachers to reform the religious, political, and moral lives of wayward white southerners became a focal point of MEC efforts in the South. MEC leaders were quite willing to utilize the military of the United States as an instrument of MEC intra-Methodist "ecumenical" policy toward the MECS.[16]

METHODISTS AND WAR IN THE TWENTIETH CENTURY

The memory of particular wars was a powerful force in affecting Methodist views toward future wars. Most Wesleyans joined in the heady talk about World War I (WWI), though there were a few exceptions. One was Nazarene editor B. F. Haynes – previously an MECS pastor and editor for thirty-eight years – who called repeatedly for universal disarmament before, during, and after WWI. Haynes claimed to have become convinced of pacifism at age thirteen after walking the bloody Civil War battlefield of Franklin, Tenn., the day after the battle.[17]

Methodist pacifism after WWI was linked to the judgment that it had been largely a waste of lives; in addition to casualties, it had interrupted missionary activity. Though the loss of American lives and destruction of American property was much greater during the Civil War, its accomplishments were unavoidable. The Union was held together, slavery was ended, and even white southern ex-Confederates believed that their cause had been well defended, their protest well heard even if it had ultimately failed. The Great War had few such merits – many would later consider it a total failure of the civilized nations of the West. Heading into World War II (WWII), Methodist clergy were determined to take a more cautious approach to patriotism feeling that WWI's defense of civilization against barbarism had been all too often barbaric itself and with none of the benefits to civilization that "good wars" had provided. Unlike WWI, the rights of conscientious objectors would be closely guarded.[18]

In the first half of the twentieth century, holiness denominations such as the Church of the Nazarene spoke more frequently on issues of war and peace. D. Shelby Corlett, editor of the Nazarenes' *Herald of Holiness* during the difficult latter years of the Great Depression and WWII, was drafted and then wounded during WWI. Corlett called upon Nazarenes in the early days of WWII to remain true to their purpose and aims: "In a time of war the church will be tempted to divert its efforts. ... To this temptation the church must not yield. The church must be the church in time of war, just as in time of peace."[19]

The importance of civilization contra barbarism showed in Methodist discussion during WWII. Reflecting the widespread pacifism of the 1920s and 1930s, the Methodist General Conference of 1940 had taken a strong peace stand. The 1944 General Conference of The Methodist Church moderated that stand. During the 1944 debates about The Methodist Church's position on war, those who rejected pacifism asserted that "we are well within the Christian position when we assert the necessity of the use of military forces to resist aggression which would overthrow every right which is held sacred by civilized men." Those urging a stronger antiwar stand countered "War is a crude and primitive force ... when the teachings of Jesus are fully accepted, war as a means of settling international disputes will die, and dying will set the world free from a cruel tyrant."[20] Bishop Bromley Oxnam, himself a supporter of the war and defender of the bombing of civilians as a military necessity, would publish a guide for conscientious objectors.[21]

Until 1945, most Americans who went to war did so as part of a temporarily expanded military. The post-WWII era brought a truly new development, namely, a large "peace time" standing military. Many Americans had an unfavorable or at least mixed view of the small peacetime armies of the nineteenth century. This is perhaps a useful point in noting the distinction between "Wesleyans and the military" and "Wesleyans and war." Since 1945, many service members have experienced one without the other. Before 1945, for most, they were one and the same. This "federalization" of American society, politics, and "militarization" of many American families was new indeed.

The Cold War intensified the links between American wars and American civilization. Western success in the Cold War depended as much on competitive foreign policy as on clashing armies. A Free, Religious West versus a Soviet, Atheistic East meant that Methodists would have a compelling interest in the newspaper battles of the Cold War. Methodist involvement in Civil Rights efforts played out in this Cold War context. Communist rhetoric critical of American treatment of African

Americans had proved effective in appealing to third world nations. Denying Communists an accurate and painful critique of American civilization made the civil rights of African Americans a "war" issue.

After Vietnam, many white Methodists started to deemphasize and even delegitimize military careers. Simultaneously, African Americans began to find increasing career advancement opportunities in the military, a trend more recently extended to a growing number of Latinos and women. Some might say that post-WWII, the military was viewed as a legitimate career, until rich whites stopped viewing it that way. If that view is accurate, it may be an ironic return to a nineteenth-century model – smaller, "overworked," volunteer, mostly poor, immigrant armies with an image problem. Military members may not need to be told of the high price of war. But given the growing military suicide rates among combat veterans of Iraq and Afghanistan, Wesleyans may have a number of pastoral issues to consider.

Since Vietnam, pacifism has received widespread attention among Methodist theologians and ethicists, including those in the holiness churches.[22] In 1986, the Bishops of the United Methodist Church issued a statement entitled *In Defense of Creation: The Nuclear Crisis and a Just Peace*, which argued from the threat of nuclear winter to the need for a more robust embrace of Methodism's peacemaking heritage.[23] The reaction from Paul Ramsey, in conversation with Stanley Hauerwas, criticized the bishops' statement as "disappointing" and "inadequate." Hauerwas labeled it, in a brief moment of understatement, "quite unremarkable."[24]

Herman Will's *A Will for Peace* dealt with the urge for peace in Methodist history. Will charted Methodists' history of war up to 1900 in a single chapter titled "The 'War Spirit' in the New Nation" arguing that peacemaking was a distinct minority position among Wesleyans despite the views of Wesley and Asbury. Writing in 1984, Will asserted "Until the last 50 years ... those prepared to reject all war have been a very small minority, often unnoticed historically."[25] Will's account thus put heavy emphasis on twentieth-century developments, especially those related to official Methodist organizations. Since the 1980s, theological and ethical commentary on war has received considerable attention from Methodists, perhaps most notably in the writings of Stanley Hauerwas.[26]

Yet for all this attention from Wesleyan academics, Methodists remain divided. In a September 2010 article in *Christianity Today*, United Methodist Bishop and Hauerwas colleague William Willimon expressed his frustration with the Bush and Obama administrations' war policies. But he also chided the Methodists under his care who were unwilling to accept his teachings on war. The fact is, as Willimon's article indicates,

war remains a contested issue, and the Wesleyan academic and episcopal elite may not have the same views as the membership.

AN EXAMPLE FROM 1880–1890S
MECS/NASHVILLE *CHRISTIAN ADVOCATE*

As noted earlier, Methodists commonly supported an ongoing war
with all of its passions and, often, personal and familial complications.
However, the late nineteenth century provides an interesting transitional
moment in American Methodist thought. Most southern Methodists
writing in the 1880s and 1890s had seen the Civil War up close. They
knew of its viciousness to soldier and civilian alike. Most had been in
uniform in what was the highest mobilization by percentage and age
range in American history. A war of that scale fought on familiar ground
was not readily forgotten. But it seems many southern Methodists had
not yet embraced a triumphalist version of the progress of American civilization, or at least, not progress by means of American military power.
Editors Oscar Penn (O. P.) Fitzgerald (1829–1911, editor 1878–1890) and
Elijah Embree (E. E.) Hoss (1849–1919, editor 1890–1902) spoke through
the pages of the *Christian Advocate*; both would be elected to the episcopacy of the MECS from the editor's desk.[27]

In 1888, the editors of the Nashville *Christian Advocate*, the central
and most important newspaper of the MECS, declared that "international arbitration is the next great step in the forward march of humanity" adding that "the vocation of the soldier among the civilized States
is passing away."[27] In 1889 they declared, "The law of retaliation long
ago ceased to control real Christians. The time hastens when it will
cease to control parties, nations, and races. True Christianity will bring
this to pass."[28] They continued,

> The masses of mankind will not submit to the silliness and barba-
> rism of war much longer. The burden of the expense of it and the
> hazard of life fall upon the rank and file, and they will not stand it
> much longer. The Geneva arbitration marked the first step toward
> the new era. What will be the next?[29]

In October 1889, they commented that "despotism and war ought to
be buried in the same grave, and the world will be ready for the funeral
sooner than some think."[30] They then added,

> The men who flippantly talk of religious wars and race wars in this
> republic are enemies to all religions and all races. Reason, persua-
> sion and patience will solve every problem before us. The only real

problem is whether we, as a people, are rational enough to patiently rely on moral agencies to accomplish moral results.[31]

Long before carpet-bombing or nuclear weapons, the editors of the *Advocate* cried, "The gospel of Christ will compel disarmament sooner or later. That is the only hope of the world."[32] Concluding a discussion of European militarism, the editors urged substituting "Arbitration, God's method for settling difficulties, for War, which is Satan's own."[33] The editors affirmed statements from the British government that "The Security of Modern Civilization" cannot rest on "brute force," and noted that "the final civilization of the world which will abide, must be that which John saw, 'the holy city, the new Jerusalem coming down from God out of heaven.'"[34] Reviewing the rise of arbitration, they declared,

> We hail such movements as the first rays which proclaim the dawn of the day when the nations of the earth shall learn war no more. May they shine unto that perfect day. War is the sum of all villanies, and ought never to arise between civilized states. It is a custom entailed from a semi-barbarous age, when rulers were wicked and the people ignorant.... The time of that ignorance has passed. The people are no longer servants. Princes must settle their feuds ... as other men do.[35]

Further showing the links between war and civilization they concluded in 1890 that the national increases in lynching and mob violence were lingering "satanic" effects of war.[36]

SPANISH-AMERICAN WAR

If the South is often thought to be a militaristic region, these Methodists wondered aloud about the wisdom of the Spanish-American War, and while many southern Methodists would later support American involvement in WWI, they added support for the League of Nations.[37] President McKinley, a Methodist from Ohio, had reservations about leading his country to war against Spain. MECS Editor and later Bishop E. E. Hoss warned of war against Spain including the tax burdens he felt would invariably accompany an expansion of the U.S. military.

Editor Hoss wrote passionately of his opposition to "'yellow' journals" and their "satanic" methods, saying,

> We have not yet recovered from the vast demoralization of our last war. Another one at the present time would stimulate everything in our civilization that needs repression. In spite of the fanatical jingoism that cries aloud for an instant declaration of hostilities,

we plead for an honorable peace. As a citizen and as a minister of the gospel, we enter our solemn protest against the taking of any step that is likely to bring on the horrors of military strife. Two weeks later, Hoss would write we exhort the people to be quiet. Let Christians everywhere pray the Lord to avert the horrors of war.[38]

Having praised the patience of President McKinley on March 17th and April 14th against his "cowardly" and "fire eating" critics, Hoss declared his commitments to peace in full after the war had finally come. "The readers of this ADVOCATE do not need to be told that we are a man of peace," Hoss began.

Having seen the horrors of war as they were exhibited in a border state during the unhappy period of 1861–1865, we are profoundly adverse to the shedding of human blood if it can possibly be avoided. When General Sherman said 'war is hell,' he spoke only the naked truth. It turns loose all the worse passions of men, and is accompanied by ten thousand evils of the most appalling character. The vast expenditure of money which it involves is the least thing that can be said against it. There is not a sin or vice which it fails to breed. That it furnishes the opportunity for the display of certain magnanimous virtues, is unquestionably true; but it is equally true that there is occasion for the development of these same virtues in the pursuits of peace. Heroism may find as appropriate a theatre for action in civil life as on the field of battle.[39]

Having praised McKinley's magnanimity and warned of possible lengthy entanglements and lingering troubles after victory over Spain, Hoss directed his closing comments to the clergy:

The pulpits of our country can do their best service in the present emergency, not by screaming out sentiments of hate and contempt for our enemies, but by teaching, with unwonted vigor, the lessons of Christian morality. Malevolent passions are never justifiable. Not to stimulate them, but to restrain them, is the business of Christian ministers. Though we have drawn the sword against Spain, we must still deport ourselves, not as savages, but as believers in the gospel of the Prince of Peace.[40]

CONCLUSION/SUMMARY

Methodists discussions of war were often heavily inflected with concern about civilization – its advance, extension, or protection. Much more research is needed concerning American Methodists and war, an area of need much related to the general lack of Wesleyan self-awareness concerning their own political history. If social and political historians are left to this task alone, they will continue to produce good work. But these historians cannot do Methodists' self-reflective work for them. They will not answer how Wesleyans have done with each other on the subject of war – undoubtedly a painful and controversial topic. They cannot do the intra-Methodist ecumenical and connectional work – the conferencing – around the history and meaning of war and politics and civilization in the Methodist tradition. Methodists must do that with their own resources and for themselves.

Notes

1   In this chapter, the terms "Methodist" and "Wesleyan" will be used interchangeably to refer to this wider tradition in America.

2   This is also true of Methodist involvement in politics generally. Intra-Methodist notions and discourse about civilization and barbarism shape Methodist thought and practice on many other social and political issues, including slavery, lynching, temperance and prohibition, gambling, immigration, dancing, polygamy, crime and punishment, abortion, public education, civil rights, higher education, and global health.

3   For further explorations of the American Revolution, see Jessie Shuman Larkins, "John Wesley among the Colonies: Wesleyan Theology in the Face of the American Revolution," *Methodist History* 45:4 (July 2007), 232–243; Dee Andrews, *The Methodists and Revolutionary America, 1760–1800* (Princeton, NJ: Princeton University Press, 2000) and *History of American Methodism*, edited by Emory C. Bucke (Nashville, TN: Abingdon Press, 1964), I: 145–184.

4   Fuller treatments of Methodist republicanism include A. Gregory Schneider, *The Way of the Cross Leads Home: The Domestication of American Methodism* (Bloomington, IN: Indiana University Press, 1993), especially Chapter 2, "Republicanism and Reform," and Russell E. Richey, *Early American Methodism* (Bloomington, IN: Indiana University Press 1991), especially Chapter 6, "The Four Languages of Early American Methodism."

5   C. C. Goen, *Broken Churches, Broken Nation: Denominational Schisms and the Coming of the Civil War* (Macon, GA: Mercer University Press, 1985), 57.

6   George C. Rable, *God's Almost Chosen Peoples: A Religious History of the American Civil War* (Chapel Hill, NC: University of North Carolina Press, 2010). Daniel Stowell, *Rebuilding Zion* (New York and Oxford: Oxford University Press,); Christopher Owen, *The Sacred Flame of Love* (Athens, GA: University of Georgia Press, 1998); and Hunter Dickinson Farish, *The Circuit Rider Dismounts: A Social History of Southern Methodism, 1865–1900* (Richmond, VA: The Dietz Press,

1938), especially Chapter 2, "The Status of Southern Methodism as the Close of the Civil War," 22–61.

7   Rable, *God's Almost Chosen Peoples.*

8   Karen B. Westerfield Tucker, "The American Flag in Methodist Worship: A Historical Look at Practice," General Board of Discipleship, 2002 http://www.gbod.org/site/apps/nlnet/content3.aspx?c=nhLRJ2PMKsG &b=5690503&ct=3842125.

9   Richard J. Carwardine "Methodists, Politics and the Coming of the Civil War," in, *Methodism and the Shaping of American Culture,* edited by Nathan O. Hatch and John H. Wigger (Nashville, TN: Abingdon Press, 2001), Chapter 10, 341.

10 Daniel Crofts, *Reluctant Confederates: Upper South Unionists in the Secession Crisis* (Chapel Hill, NC: University of North Carolina Press, 1989). Owen, *Sacred Flame of Love.* Hunter Dickinson Farish, *The Circuit Rider Dismounts: A Social History of Southern Methodism, 1865–1900* (1938).

11 Herman Norton, *Struggling for Recognition: The United States Army Chaplaincy, 1791–1865* (Washington, DC: Office of the Chief of Chaplains, 1977). *The Spirit Divided: Memoirs of Civil War Chaplains,* 2 vols. edited by John Brinsfield, and Ben Maryniak (Macon, GA: Mercer University Press, 2006); John Brinsfield, William C. Davis, *Faith in the Fight: Civil War Chaplains* (Mechanicsburg, PA: Stackpole Books, 2003). Frank Hieronymus, "For Now and Forever: The Chaplains of the Confederate States Army" (Ph.D. diss., University of California, Los Angeles, 1964); William W. Sweet, *The Methodist Episcopal Church and the Civil War* (Cincinnati, OH: Methodist Book Concern, 1912).

12 Donald and Lucille Dayton, "An Historical Survey of Attitudes toward War and Peace within the American Holiness Movement," in *Perfect Love and War: A Dialogue on Christian Holiness and the Issues of War and Peace,* edited by Paul Hostetler (Nappanee, IN: Evangel Press, 1974), 141.

13 Clarence E. Walker, *A Rock in a Weary Land: The African Methodist Episcopal Church during the Civil War and Reconstruction* (Baton Rouge, LA: Louisiana State University Press, 1982). Stowell, *Rebuilding Zion;* Reginald Francis Hildebrand. *The Times Were Strange and Stirring* (Durham, NC: Duke University Press, 1995). *Sacred Flame of Love.*

14 For the expansion of existing and creation of new African American denominations after the war, see William E. Montgomery, *Under Their Own Vine and Fig Tree: The African-American Church in the South, 1865–1900* (Baton Rouge, LA: Louisiana State University Press, 1993).

15 William Warren Sweet. *The Methodist Episcopal Church and the Civil War* (Cincinnati, OH: Methodist Book Concern, 1912.) Charles C. Goen, *Broken Churches, Broken Nation: Denominational Schism and the Coming of the Civil War* (1985). Donald G. Jones, *The Sectional Crisis and Northern Methodism: A Study in Piety, Political Ethics, and Civil Religion* (1979). Bucke, *History of American Methodism* (Metuchen, NJ: Scarecrow Press, 1964), vol. I: 187–193, 206–256. Stephen Ward Angell, *Bishop Henry McNeal Turner and African American Religion*

in the South (Knoxville, TN: University of Tennessee Press, 1992), Chapter 2 "A.M.E. Pastor and Army Chaplain," 33–59.

16 For other responses, see Frederickson, *The Inner Civil War* (Urbana, IL: University of Illinois Press, (1993). For northern views of the South during the war, see Reid Mitchell, *The Vacant Chair* (New York: Oxford University Press, 1995) and Earl Hess, *The Union Soldier in Combat* (Lawrence, KS: University Press of Kansas, 2005). For the northern evangelical sense of moral superiority to southern evangelicals and its relation to the ideology of the Republican Party, see Eric Foner, *Free Soil, Free Labor, Free Men* (New York: Oxford University Press, 1995).

17 B. F. Haynes, *Tempest-Tossed on Methodist Seas* (1921). "The Horrors of War," *Herald of Holiness* (August 12, 1914), 1–2.

18 Gerald L. Sittser, *A Cautious Patriotism: The American Churches and the Second World War* (Chapel Hill, NC: University of North Carolina Press, 1997). *Chaplains of World War II: A Pictorial Record of Their Work* (Washington, DC: Methodist Commission on Chaplains, 1948). W. Ward Smith, *A Study Revealing the Attitudes toward War During the Periods of 1914–1918 and 1934–1938 as presented in the Official Organs of the Church of the United Brethren in Christ.* (Thesis, B.D., Bonebrake Theological Seminary, 1939). Nazarene General Superintendent William M. Greathouse was a conscientious objector during WWII though he changed his position later, coming to conclude that Nazi gangsters were too dangerous to be left in power. The foundational document of the EUB merger in 1946 – later to become a United Methodist "standard of doctrine" – included a sharp antiwar statement. For religion and foreign policy in the WWI era, see Malcolm D. Magee, *What the World Should Be: Woodrow Wilson and the Crafting of a Faith-Based Foreign Policy* (Waco, TX: Baylor University Press, 2008), and Robert David Johnson, *The Peace Progressives and American Foreign Relations* (Cambridge, MA: Harvard University Press, 1995).

19 "We Are at War," *Herald of Holiness*, December 20, 1941, 3. For more on Nazarenes in the World Wars, see *Our Watchword and Song: The Centennial History of the Church of the Nazarene*, edited by Floyd Cunningham (Kansas City, MO: Nazarene Publishing House, 2009), especially 329–339, which pays close attention to the relationship between the wars and Nazarene missions in Asia.

20 Herman Will, *A Will For Peace: Peace Action in the United Methodist Church, A History* (Nashville, TN: General Board of Discipleship, 1984), 72–73.

21 G. Bromley Oxnam, *Conscience, the Church and Conscription: Guidance for Conscience Objectors* (Chicago, IL: Methodist Commission on World Peace, 1943); Will, *A Will for Peace*, 65–66.

22 *Perfect Love and War: A Dialogue on Christian Holiness and the Issues of War and Peace*, edited by Paul Hostetler (1974). The book was the result of a June 1973 meeting at Winona Lake, Indiana, sponsored by the Christian Holiness Association and the Brethren in Christ Church.

23 *In Defense of Creation: The Nuclear Crisis and a Just Peace* (Nashville, TN: Graded Press, 1986).

24 Paul Ramsey with epilogue by Stanley Hauerwas, *Speak Up for Just War or Pacifism: A Critique of the United Methodist Bishops' Pastoral Letter 'In Defense of Creation'* (University Park, PA: Pennsylvania State University Press, 1988).

25 Will, *A Will For Peace*, 7.

26 Examples include D. Stephen Long, *Living the Discipline: United Methodist Theological Reflections on War, Civilization, and Holiness* (Grand Rapids, MI: Eerdmans Publishing Co., 1992), Stephen Wendell Rankin, "John Wesley and War: Guidance for Modern Day Heirs?" *Methodist Review* 3 (2011): 101–139, Robert L. Wilson, *Biases and Blind Spots: Methodism and Foreign Policy since World War II* (Wilmore, KY: Bristol Books, 1988), Joseph L. Allen, *War: A Primer for Christians* (Nashville, TN: Abingdon Press, 1991), Stanley Hauerwas, *The Peaceable Kingdom: A Primer in Christian Ethics* (Notre Dame, IN: University of Notre Dame Press, 1983), and John M. Swomley, *War, Peace and Justice: The Prophetic Record* (Kansas City, MO: Saint Paul School of Theology, 1985).

27 NCA December 8,1888, p.8; NCA December 15, 1888, p.1.

28 NCA March 21, 1889, p.1.

29 NCA June 13, 1889, p.8.

30 NCA October 3, 1889, p.1 and p.9.

31 NCA October 10, 1889, p. 8.

32 NCA December 11, 1886, p.1.

33 NCA February 8, 1890, p.1.

34 "The Security of Modern Civilization," NCA January 29, 1887, p.8.

35 NCA September 17, 1887, p.1.

36 NCA February 22, 1890, p.1.

37 Robert Watson Sledge, *Hands on the Ark* 1975, pp. 172–175. Kenneth MacKenzie's study of Methodism during the Spanish American War focused on the MEC. Kenneth M. MacKenzie, *The Robe and the Sword: The Methodist Church and the Rise of American Imperialism* (Washington, DC: Public Affairs Press, 1961).

38 "The Prospect of War," NCA March 17, 1898, p.1. "The Suffering Cubans," NCA March 31, 1898, p.8.

39 "The Prospect of War," NCA March 17, 1898 p.1; "The President's Message," NCA April 14, 1898, p.8.; "The War with Spain," NCA April 28, 1898, p.1.

40 "The War with Spain," NCA April 28, 1898, p.1. See also p. 2 of April 28, 1898, for war reporting and other commentary at the beginning of military mobilization through the American South.

18 American Methodists and Popular Culture

CHRISTOPHER J. ANDERSON

> In the motion picture the world has a new instrument that can tell the truth, and if you of the church were to control it, you would have an instrument of extraordinary power.
>
> David Wark Griffith, Hollywood filmmaker,[1]
> *The (New York) Christian Advocate*, June 26, 1919

Popular culture, in its multiple forms, has been interwoven into the fabric of American Methodism. For nearly three centuries, Wesleyans have reached out to the masses by addressing the social and cultural situations of the hearer. This approach has been evidenced in multiple ways from John Wesley preaching to English miners to circuit riders evangelizing North America to late-nineteenth-century New York City Methodists showing motion pictures during the Sunday evening service. American Methodism and its denominational varieties regularly intersect with popular culture, resulting in perpetual tensions with the popular and cultural practices of those they attempt to reach. In turn, those reached by Methodist teachings and practices have helped shape and reshape the movement since its inception. American Methodists in particular have produced, promoted, and reacted against popular culture in multiple mediums including film, radio, television, the Internet, and social media. These forms of mass media, invented and professionalized outside of Methodism, have been adopted and used by the local church. Scholarship on Methodism often investigates theologies and theologians, institutions and denominations, as well as doctrinal standards and church polity. Yet the origins and substantial growth of the Methodist movement formed in the midst of the culture of the people and was largely the result of John and Charles Wesley and the many ministers and laity from all over the world who have taken "the church" to the people.

In 2008, the author presented a paper titled *Miss America and Methodism: Twentieth-Century Beauty Pageants as Christian Mission* at the Annual Meeting of the American Academy of Religion. The presentation explored a largely untouched area within the academic discipline of Wesleyan and Methodist Studies – namely, American Methodism and popular culture. The paper analyzed the ways in which American Methodists have constructed, situated, and modified beauty pageants in order to select certain women as world missionaries. The topic was quite different than what some expected and attendees, most of whom were scholars of Wesleyan and Methodist Studies, seemed intrigued. This chapter follows a similar path and identifies the ongoing relationship and inherent tensions between American Methodists and popular culture. More specifically the chapter identifies how Methodists have interacted with popular culture in the form of mass media, particularly the early years of the American silent film industry.

POPULAR CULTURE, MEDIA,
AND AMERICAN METHODISM

Several authors present snapshots of the interplay between religion and popular culture. Bruce David Forbes in his edited book *Religion and Popular Culture* suggests that an examination of religious movements through the lens of popular culture helps us learn more about how religion is perceived and how participation in religion plays certain roles in the lives of people. Forbes suggests that religious practices influence the culture surrounding a movement while at the same time adherents chip away and alter the ways in which that movement is practiced."[2] Forbes' insight is helpful toward a better appreciation of the complex historical relationship between American Methodism and popular culture. The everyday lives of Methodists were shaped by the theological, philosophical, historical, and social influences surrounding them. At the same time the ways in which Methodists reacted against and fully embraced forms of popular culture provides insight into how certain forms of popular culture were used to both promote Christianity and specifically reshape American Methodist culture.

In *Between Sacred and Profane: Researching Religion and Popular Culture* Gordon Lynch maintains, "Popular culture provides a framework through which understandings of religion can be shaped or maintained: it gives us a way to evaluate in the presence of others who we are, what we believe and do, and why."[3] Lynch's framework can be used to interpret American Methodism as a lens through which Methodist-related denominations examine and embrace various forms of popular culture. The way in which nineteenth-century Methodists reacted to certain entertainments such as card playing, dancing, and the theater helped shape the perceptions that other Christians and those nonreligious had of American Methodists. In the same way the approval of some Methodist ministers of projecting hymns in church or the incorporation of motion pictures into Sunday evening services publicly demonstrated that some Methodists were willing to embrace certain forms of popular culture. Not all Methodists reacted negatively to theatrical performances or embraced motion pictures. These divergent positions presented a continual conundrum for those looking on – and complicated how one understood the Methodist tradition.

The study of mass media is one of several approaches to the academic study of popular culture. Visual historian David Morgan posits that media functions as a space for meaning making – a location where worlds are created and shaped.[4] Media functions as a stage used by its creators to instruct, interpret, and shape the ways listeners, viewers, and readers learn about the world. American Methodists have been significant players in the history and uses of media, particularly mass media. From lantern slide projection to radio and to film, Methodists have incorporated these forms of media into the work and life of the church. For Methodists the message that emerged from these mediums brought additional members into the denominational fold. Learning how to effectively generate and use radio, film, and television meant that Methodists could create their own programming and content in order to protect adherents from participating in what was considered more "negative" forms of popular culture.

As creators of content American Methodists held a position of power to help shape and mold its followers historically and theologically. Media historian Stewart Hoover argues that by developing and using media churches have the power to control and define its own symbols.[5] These symbols, when placed within the semantics of Methodist theology and denominational social standards provide churchgoers with safe places to practice their faith. Lantern slide shows featuring the work of Methodist missionaries, radio sermons using familiar Wesleyan theological language, and film showings evidencing the history of American Methodism were broadcasted in Epworth League youth meetings and Methodist churches throughout the United States. These media helped shape the ways Methodist viewers and listeners were informed about the history of the church and presented historical and theological grand narratives passed down to several generations of Methodists.

Wesleyan and Methodist scholarship is replete with texts on the theology of John Wesley and other Methodist divines as well as on the study of institutional development and structure. Less work though has been done on American Methodists and popular culture, though several works include essays that examine the interplay between the history of the Methodist movement and popular culture. In 1993, Russell E. Richey, Kenneth E. Rowe, and Jean Miller Schmidt published an edited volume titled *Perspectives on American Methodism: Interpretive Essays.* The text offers several chapters that investigate "how and in what ways Methodism appealed to the common folk and how it figured itself as a folk movement."[6] Several essays analyze print media and social religious practices among other topics. In 1997, several additional volumes appeared in the series *United Methodism and American Culture.* The editors of the series, Russell E. Richey, Dennis M. Campbell, and William B. Lawrence, sought "to provide a careful, fresh estimate of the history of Methodism in America" with a "view to the church's effective participation in American society and the world in the future."[7] Chapters examine a range of topics from church architecture to campus ministry to public education. In volume 4, M. Garlinda Burton asks, "Why Can't United Methodists Use Media?" furthering the necessity of future academic work on Methodism, popular culture, and media studies.

Additional texts touch on American Methodism and popular culture including *The Democratization of American Christianity*[8] by Nathan Hatch as well as his coedited work with John Wigger titled *Methodism and the Shaping of American Culture.*[9] Wigger's *Taking Heaven by Storm: Methodism and the Rise of Popular Christianity*[10] and *American Saint: Francis Asbury and the Methodists*[11] explore the development of Methodism in the United States by looking for ways in which Methodists shaped popular culture and how forms of popular culture shaped and reshaped the church. Dee Andrews' *The Methodists and Revolutionary America, 1760–1800: A Shaping of an Evangelical Culture*[12] and J. Gordon Melton's *A Will to Choose: The Origins of African American Methodism* examine how early American Methodists helped shaped the colonial and national periods of the United States.[13] Most recently, the 2011 volume *Methodist Experience in America*[14] provides the most comprehensive sketch to date on American Methodist history. For students of popular culture the volume provides snapshots of the exchanges between Methodism as a movement and the adherents who shaped and were shaped by the varieties of Wesleyan traditions.

John Wesley, with encouragement from the Reverend George Whitefield, sought ways to preach and interact with people outside the walls of the local Anglican church. Taking Christianity from the church building to the homes and work places of the people opened opportunities to connect the fledging Methodist movement with the popular cultural practices of the day. In turn, those practices would shape and reshape the activities and messages of Methodist ministers and laity.

Early American Methodist ministers and laity regularly interacted with popular culture. Tradition holds that Barbara Heck, an early New York City Methodist, reacted strongly to games that used cards. Harry Hosier traveled thousands of miles on horseback with Francis Asbury in order to reach out to free and enslaved black Americans with the message of Christianity. There were reasons an appalled Heck tossed playing cards into a blazing New York City fireplace just as there were motivations for Hosier and Asbury to travel throughout the United States in order to preach to the masses. Methodism was a movement toward the people, interested in the lives of people, and as a result evidenced the inherent tensions that result when religious practice and expectations are blended with the surrounding cultures in American society.

As American Methodists wrestled with how to present Christianity to the people it was important for clergy to make decisions regarding which social and cultural activities were considered appropriate and which were not. Which amusements pleased God and which amusements were considered inappropriate for Methodists in good standing? The amusement question is examined further in this volume but because of its close ties with popular culture a few connections can be made between American Methodists, amusements, and popular culture. A snapshot of these tensions surfaced in the various Methodist doctrinal rulebooks called *Doctrines and Discipline*. Additional reactions were highlighted in the church press including denominational newspapers. Methodist books of church discipline both spelled out and remained vague regarding which forms of popular amusement were not permissible for members. Popular amusements of the nineteenth century and early twentieth century such as card playing, attending the theater, and dancing were nonnegotiable for American Methodists. Products of mass media on the other hand, when wrapped in purposes that sanctioned the church and evangelization, were generally embraced as a means to promote the work of Methodist-affiliated denominations and as tools of mission to reach people with the word of God.

The books of church law of the African Methodist Episcopal Church (AME), African Methodist Episcopal Zion Church (AMEZ), Free Methodist Church (FMC), Methodist Episcopal Church (MEC), and Wesleyan Methodist Church all contained the "Society Rules" established by John Wesley in 1744. These rules warned early Methodists of avoiding drunkenness, brawling, and unprofitable conversations that might present a negative perception of Methodists and their societies. These rules were transcribed into the various books of discipline for Methodist-related denominations in the United States beginning with the MEC in 1784. Similar language in all denominational disciplines included the phrase "taking such diversions as cannot be used in the name of the Lord Jesus."[15] Diversions in this sense were many and most likely meant by John Wesley to include the societal concerns faced by British Methodists in eighteenth-century England. In nineteenth-century America the diversions of card playing, the theater, and dancing were supplemented by concerns over church suppers, lantern slide projections, and alcohol. Popular cultural venues including the saloon with drinking and poker, the ballroom with dance, and the theater were social and cultural locations prevalent in American society. These forms of popular culture presented American Methodists with theological and ecclesiastical challenges. Ministers sought out the unconverted, those who could be found in the saloon and theater, and yet they did not have similar forms of amusement to help bring the same people into the church. And, for many Methodist clergy and laity, the church as structure represented a holy space – a house set apart for the worship of God – a place to get away from the diversions of society at large. As a result, Methodist clergy and laity faced a difficult compromise. They needed to either accept some forms of popular culture in their sanctuaries and fellowship halls or they needed to protest the use and practice of such forms of amusement. They did both.

MOTION PICTURES

American Methodists experienced a complicated relationship with entertainments including the film industry since the emergence of motion pictures into American society in the mid-1890s. Methodist disciplines were not specific in the critique of motion pictures, per se, focusing rather on other amusements. Yet while Methodist traditions historically linked with the holiness movement were critical or highly suspicious of the mass medium, other Methodist affiliations embraced film as a way to educate and inform church audiences on biblical characters, health-related issues such as tuberculosis, and photoplays of revered Methodist leaders including John Wesley and Francis Asbury.

The following section examines how six Methodist traditions with historic and theological roots to John Wesley interacted with and responded to the American silent film industry. Denominations including the FMC, Wesleyan Methodists, and MECS cautioned against or were suspicious of the use of motion pictures in the local church. Other Methodist denominations including the AME, AMEZ, and MEC seemed to embrace the use of film as a medium for education and church entertainment.[16]

A brief glance at the reactions of Methodist denominations and Methodist ministers between 1895 and 1920 reveal the contentious relationship between clergy and celluloid. American Methodists found film to be of use in church services as forms of entertainment and also as illustrations for sermons. Films were used as educational tools to both instruct Sunday school pupils and entertain Sunday night churchgoers. This broadcast medium had its antecedents in glass lantern slide technology and the work of traveling exhibitors for Epworth League youth programs as well as Methodist resort centers including Ocean Grove, New Jersey.

Several Methodist ministers published books lamenting the acceptance and implementation of forms of entertainment into the local church. Reverend Henry Brown, a presiding elder with the Columbia Conference of the MEC, argued that sinful amusements caused some members to become "broadminded" and that if Methodists gave in to certain forms of popular culture they should quietly leave the church. For Reverend Brown, those who were unable to abide by the restrictions against forms of popular culture set in place by church law should "get out."[17] He did not clarify if that meant joining another denomination or leaving Christianity altogether.

Reverend Beverly Carradine, minister with the St. Louis Annual Conference of the MECS, presented a strong stance against the educational value of amusements in the local church. In his book *Church Entertainments: Twenty Objections*, Carradine wrote as his sixteenth objection, "Oh, church of the living, holy God, how glorious has your work become! The drift, or educational tendency, of the entertainment, I emphatically repeat, is toward evil, and to grave evils all the while." Carradine amplified this objection with a forewarning for other Methodist readers, "But what follies and evils may we not expect to flow from the entertainment, which is itself the child of such parentage as Covetousness and Worldliness! What may we expect of such a child! And what will the grandchildren be!"[18] Carradine's textual metaphor was ironically prophetic in his own life as his grandson, actor John Carradine, would go on to a career in motion pictures including the role of biblical character Aaron in Cecil B. DeMille's epic film *The Ten Commandments* (1956). His great-grandson, actor David Carradine, had

Figure 15. **Chicago Methodists viewing a film at Community Methodist Episcopal Church,** General Commission on Archives and History, Madison, New Jersey.

a long career in film and television including playing popular culture icon Kwai Chang Caine on the 1970s martial arts hit *Kung Fu.*

Two Methodist bodies were also critical of the use of motion pictures. Clergy of the FMC spoke little of motion pictures in the weekly newspaper *The Free Methodist.* But, when they did, there was little doubt of denominational opinion. In 1914, the editor of *The Free Methodist* wrote, "Satan is always on the lookout to ensnare the young and lead them into sin and crime. Prominent among the devices he uses in these days is the moving picture show."[19] The editor cited a study from the periodical *Christian Herald* identifying how crime and debauchery by children and young adults had been the result of viewing films about murder, arson, and theft. According to the study, the viewer watches the film and is inclined to echo what has been seen on the screen.

The Wesleyan Methodist Church also expressed reservation about motion pictures but was willing to give the film industry the benefit of the doubt. An article in the denominational newspaper *Wesleyan Methodist* explained, "we have watched the development of this institution with interest" and asked "could it be that the development of modern science should make possible the introduction of something combining pleasure, fascination, amusement, recreation, and instruction in such a manner as to elevate the morals and go a long way toward revolutionizing society?"[20] Wesleyan Methodists were willing to consider the possibility of motion pictures as agents of education and instruction. Yet, there was a murky side to the industry that concerned clergy and laity. The article cited the *Detroit Daily News* and the author's concern about nudity and low morals in films projected as forms of art. Denominational leaders were not so ambivalent in a 1916 article published in the *Wesleyan Methodist*. The author of the essay "The Gates of Hell Shall Not Prevail" wrote,

> The rites of heathen religions, false religious systems of the past and present, Christian Science falsely so-called, Russellism, organized secrecy, superficial Christianity, the open saloon, the tobacco vice, worldly pleasures, the dance hall, the theatre and motion picture craze, the gambling table, social impurity – these and innumerable others dressed in the most attractive and fashionable modern garb, fawn and entice and deceive and ruin their millions.[21]

Criticism and cautious acceptance were the public opinions of Free Methodists and Wesleyan Methodists. Being in the world but not of it made evangelization a creative balancing act for these Methodists. The denominational newspapers of historically black Methodist traditions including the AME Church and AMEZ Church suggest general acceptance of films in the church. In his chapter "Race, Region, and Rusticity: Relocating U.S. Film History" Robert C. Allen notes that little is known concerning how films and moviegoing affected the everyday lives of African Americans during the early twentieth century, though evidence suggests that movie theaters were segregated resulting in little, if any, shared space between white and black audiences.[22] This segregation resulted in the creation of black theaters and additional space for black filmgoers to attend movies. African-American Methodist churches functioned as alternate locations for black moviegoers and by doing so packed church sanctuaries for special showings of illustrated lectures and motion pictures.

The AME Church newspaper *Christian Recorder* was largely silent with regard to motion pictures between 1895 and 1904. In September 1904 several articles appeared identifying a film producer and exhibitor named Dr. R.C. Richardson. On September 29, 1904, the *Christian Recorder* printed a picture of Richardson along with a promotional piece identifying that he and his wife had been to the St. Louis World's Fair and planned to give a series of talks with accompanying films in Washington, DC, New York, and Philadelphia. The following month an article titled "The Great Richardson Religious Show" highlighted Richardson's event at the Bethel AME Church in Philadelphia. Hundreds of moviegoers waited in line for the opening of the church doors to get in to the show. The event "brought forth loud applause, screams of delight, and shouts of joy."[23] The minister of the church, Reverend Dr. Fickland, realized the show's potential to draw in large crowds and promised Richardson he would host another showing on November 16th.

The same series of articles in the *Christian Recorder* emphasized the connection between motion picture shows and the AMEZ Church. Reverend Richardson's lecture and film were also presented at the Wesley African Methodist Episcopal Zion Church in Philadelphia. The author of the article noted its success stating, "notwithstanding the enormous seating capacity of the edifice and the intelligent and cultured audience assembled, there is really no building large enough to accommodate the patrons of this meritorious show."[24] Some churchgoers were refused entrance into Wesley AMEZ due to capacity restrictions. As with Richardson's show at Bethel AME a second performance was scheduled for Wesley AMEZ. Motion pictures, for these two Methodist churches, drew large crowds and evidenced that black Methodist ministers promoted films and congregations enjoyed watching films in church.

During the late nineteenth and early twentieth centuries clergy and laity of the MEC purchased and operated slide and film projection systems in the local church to illustrate the exploits of missionaries, to project short films as sermon illustrations, and to show sacred hymns during congregational worship. Yet, these activities were often viewed with caution by the leadership of the denomination. The 1896 General Conference of the MEC reaffirmed the denominational ban on many popular amusements including circuses, horse races, and theaters. *The Doctrines and Discipline of the Methodist Episcopal Church*, the official document of Methodist rules and regulations, recorded that if members were found guilty of indulging in such questionable activities of leisure and did not show "real humiliation" after a series of confrontations they "shall be expelled" from the church.[25]

This harsh position and ban on the use of amusements only went so far as some Methodist ministers and congregants decided to project and view films in their churches regardless of the potential for controversy. On October 27, 1896, only six months after the first public exhibition of film in the United States at Koster and Bial's Music Hall in Herald Square, New York City, congregants at Harlem's Trinity Methodist Episcopal Church watched motion pictures projected onscreen by an Edison Vitascope.[26] This early example of the use of film in a M. E. Church suggests some ministers within the denomination found value in silent films even though tensions were evident throughout American Methodism.

In 1898, these tensions surfaced once again while itinerant evangelist and motion picture exhibitor Henry H. Hadley toured the eastern United States with his motion picture and slide projection equipment. When Hadley attempted to utilize his "modern" motion picture machine in the Methodist-owned Tabernacle at Ocean Grove, New Jersey, he was turned down and asked to leave the facility. This banishment required Hadley to rethink his plans for his revival and film showing. To accommodate the concerns of New Jersey Methodists Hadley constructed a large circus tent in nearby Asbury Park to hold outdoor revivals and to project his version of the recently released New York-produced Jesus film *Passion Play of Oberammergau.* Hadley's mission to present the message of Christian salvation through the use of technology did not stop following his tent revivals. By the end of fall 1898 he continued to exhibit his Jesus film inside the sanctuaries of churches throughout the Northeast.

While some Methodists justified banning amusements and other Methodists encouraged the use of film, Charles Musser and Carol Nelson note in *High Class Moving Pictures* that a variety of Methodist ministers used motion pictures extensively in their parishes. Musser and Nelson confirm that in the late nineteenth century the Methodist Epworth League youth organization and other Methodist ministers frequently sponsored traveling film exhibitors. These viewings included exhibitors such as Lyman H. Howe, who traveled throughout the United States projecting slides, films, and songs for church audiences. At Howe's performances one might view the controversial film *The May Irwin Kiss* exchanged between Broadway actors Irwin and John Rice, view clips of sporting events, or observe "Spanish bullfights." Musser and Nelson note the irony of Methodist film shows and point out, "church-sponsored events were among the few ways Methodists could find legitimate entertainment."[27]

In 1897, for example, Howe presented a motion picture exhibition for viewers using his projector, the Animotiscope, at National Bank Hall in Cohoes, N.Y. This showing was sponsored by the Epworth League of the Cohoes MEC. Methodists and others who attended the viewing were so enthusiastic about the performance Howe was asked to extend his film show for another evening.[28] In April 1897, Howe regularly projected films at the Simpson MEC in Scranton, Penn. as Methodists continued to find the films of traveling exhibitors interesting to view and helpful toward raising funds for churches or church-sanctioned groups such as the Epworth League.

To successfully project motion pictures before Methodist audiences, ministers, and sponsoring agencies, such as the Epworth League, needed to provide films that would entertain and educate rather than solely amuse and provoke controversy. Ted Ownby in *Subduing Satan* identifies the anxieties of some Methodist parents in the early twentieth century who regularly checked the evening newspapers for soon-to-be released films. In one case the child of a Methodist minister was forbidden to attend any films with popular actors Mary Pickford and Charlie Chaplin.[29] For these Methodists certain films and film stars promoted the spiraling decadence evident in American culture by showing onscreen violence and debauchery that they believed intended to "inflame the passions and leave an indelible blot on the minds of the young."[30] By 1919, the movies of Mary Pickford, controversial only a few years prior, were a popular addition to the selection of films presented before thousands of eager Methodists desiring to see the star on the Centenary Celebration exposition screen in Columbus, Ohio.[31]

Musser and Nelson highlight these concerns and suggest Christian denominations such as the MEC developed "positive programming" that embraced the exchange of acceptable films by national film studios for use in the church.[32] By adopting films for regular use in the church Methodists, as well as other Protestant groups including Congregationalists and Baptists, converted their auditoriums and sanctuaries into what Vincent Rosini calls the "Sanctuary Cinema."[33] These sanctuary cinemas functioned as converted theaters at which motion picture projectors, fire proof projection booths, and muslin screens became standard fare.

Books such as Christian F. Reisner's *Church Publicity* (1913) and Arthur E. Holt's *Social Work in the Churches* (1922) suggested locations for ministers and church leaders to purchase the most up-to-date technology such as the Simplex motion picture projector from the New York-based Precision Machine Company and movie screens from United Theater Equipment.[34] Reisner, a Methodist minister from New York City, emphatically believed in the "tremendous possibilities" of motion pictures for his congregants and directed other ministers to consider purchasing the hand-crank Motiograph, manufactured at Enterprise Optical Manufacturing Company in Chicago. This machine, Reisner noted, "has fulfilled all its promises" after an investigation into its durability revealed the device was "less likely to be easily damaged and yet at the same time renders excellent service."[35]

For Reisner and his parish, Grace MEC, durable machinery and an adequately functioning church cinema were essential as his film programs regularly drew hundreds of moviegoers every week.[36] The venue advertisement for Saturday night events read,

> Every Saturday night five reels are shown. No admission is charged, but an offering is taken at the door. It is notably true that the regular church members do not attend the Saturday night entertainment. It is largely strangers.[37]

At Grace MEC, Reisner hoped "strangers" would attend his film services, and this was made possible through a connection with the New York-based General Film Company to provide films "devoid of objectionable features" for several hundred children who "shout with glee and applaud with wildest enthusiasm" at an assortment of silent films projected in the auditorium of the church for the Sunday school hour.[38] Throughout the 1910s Methodist ministers continued to promote the use of films in the church for educational and entertainment value. By providing films as supplements for Sunday school curriculum or as complimentary illustrations for Sunday evening sermons many Methodist clergy and laity became accustomed to viewing films in church auditoriums and sanctuaries.

In May of 1920 the General Conference of the MEC met in Des Moines, Iowa to conduct not only quadrennial denominational business but to support the use of motion pictures; already a multimillion dollar industry in American popular culture. *The Christian Advocate* provided readers with a vivid narrative of the film *The Expanding Years* projected onto a large screen in front of the delegates. The report explained,

> When the velvet draperies drew back to show the first title it became evident that something decidedly unique was to be seen. After rapidly sketching the history of Methodist Episcopal home missions from 1819, an animated chart of the reorganized board appeared, indicating the tasks of the several departments and bureaus. This was followed by pictures of the Mexican invasion into the border states, the Negro migration from the Southland and scenes from army cantonments and naval stations.[39]

Segments from the film also identified the role of Methodism in the Americanization of indigenous peoples and included the successes of

Methodist missionaries within non-Protestant American religions. *The Christian Advocate* explained,

> A transformation was seen (on screen) of a young Indian brave into an American citizen, and then into a member of the American Expeditionary Forces. The Mormon menace was stamped in no uncertain way ... (as well as) the arrival of the immigrant family partaking of the sacrament of the Lord's Supper in an American church.[40]

The audiences in attendance at the General Conference enthusiastically received the silent film. *The Christian Advocate* recorded, "It was a wonderful forty-five minutes! Those who saw it were unusually favored."[41] The film was so well received that it was repeated several times before General Conference adjourned and was later provided for Methodist churches throughout the country to view during missions conferences and educational settings.

Following the successful use of motion pictures at the 1920 General Conference the MEC decided to enter the film industry to produce and provide films for Methodist churches across the country. *The Christian Advocate* identified the general feeling across Methodism concerning motion pictures when the periodical proclaimed,

> Their (films) educational value is almost limitless. They combine amusement, entertainment, education, and spiritual appeal. They stimulate interest, quicken imagination and can be made a financial asset to the churches ... the pictures quicken our imagination and our sympathies. Through them we can gain a new inspiration and join in a common desire ... to help solve the problem of evangelizing the world.[42]

Methodists called for the involvement of the church in the film industry. Concerned with Hollywood and New York-based motion picture companies and suspicious of their motives, J. E. Crowther, author and producer of the Broadway pageant *The Wayfarer*, beckoned in his 1919 article "Methodism and the Theater,"

> The Church should rescue from the hands of vicious men the dramatic medium of education and restore it to its rightful place of honor. There is too much gun-toting; too much mere sensationalism; too much sloppy sentimentalism. And all this is the more regrettable when we remember the youthfulness and therefore impressionableness of the audience.[43]

The MEC moved toward the production of films more suited for church audiences in the spring of 1921. The Department of Stereopticons, Motion Pictures, and Lectures relocated from New York to Chicago, and the agency "rented lofts in Chicago for the production of still and motion pictures to be employed in the educational propaganda of the Church."[44] The agency emphasized that contrary to rumors printed in popular magazines such as *Variety* and *Education Film Magazine* they did not plan to produce films for entertainment, but rather to "inform the Methodist public concerning the organized work of the denomination in all lands."[45] In fact, the *Christian Advocate* reported, the MEC did not have enough money to produce entertaining motion pictures on a level with the silent film industry in Hollywood. Yet Methodists were able to provide alternative films for audiences concerned that popularly produced celluloid offerings corrupted audiences "by such defiling and dissipating exhibitions as are nightly spread before millions of people in the name of entertainment."[46] While not attempting to replace the sermon by use of the screen Methodists were interested in providing films that offered information and appealed to the emotions.

To achieve this end the MEC worked with the International Film Corporation to produce a motion picture that would inform audiences of the history of Methodism in the United States and provide moving entertainment that would encourage viewers to support the Methodist Book Concern. The 1921 Methodist-produced film *Along the Years from Yesterday* was the result. The film was distributed to Methodist Churches throughout the United States and described in an article by John Wesley Jackson in *The Christian Advocate*:

> To see John Wesley actually rise from behind his library table and greet Robert Williams is a treat that has been reserved for our day and generation. *Along the Years from Yesterday* makes this possible, for not only does this motion picture of the history of the Methodist Book Concern bring life to the parting scene between Wesley and Robert Williams, as the latter is about to start to America as a missionary; it also brings before the eye other notable events which heretofore never have been presented in livelier form than the printed page or fervid oratory.[47]

The film was well received by the author of the article. Jackson was impressed that Methodist forerunners often discovered textually in books, such as John Wesley and Francis Asbury, were now suddenly transformed from printed pages into larger-than-life human projections. He noted that he was so moved by the reality of the film that he was tempted "to reach out for one of the books" which the circuit rider took from his saddlebags.[48] This film is only one example of the direction taken by some Methodist churches to provide educational and moral films for its denominational audiences. This example also evidences Methodist forays into the popular cultural practices of American society.

SUGGESTIONS FOR FURTHER STUDY

The interplay between Methodism and popular culture is found in the earliest work and public disapproval of Methodists in England. David N. Hempton notes British Methodism's relationship with popular culture was complicated and complex. Importantly, Hempton confirms, "Wesley and his followers cut across many aspects of popular culture, which of course made Methodism more appealing to some, but also much less appealing for many others."[49] This was also the case in American Methodism as clergy and laity navigated difficult cultural waters while finding ways to bring Wesleyan teachings to the people of American society. Through the use of lantern slides, radio, television, and film, American Methodists both informed and were informed by the people they attempted to reach.

The many American Methodist denominations that trace their theological and institutional lineage to John and Charles Wesley have been informed and reshaped by the very people brought into the Methodist tradition. Analyzing how American Methodists both reacted against and embraced forms of popular culture, such as motion pictures, provide glimpses into the tensions that have been at work for the past three hundred years. Additional scholarship is needed that examines not only early silent film but other forms of popular culture including radio, television, and social media. This chapter brings attention to these forms and suggests further work is needed to discover the way in which popular culture informs how Methodists are perceived and how they continue to reach out to the masses and to the cultural influences both inside and outside the local church.

Notes

1 "World to See Centenary Celebration," *The (New York) Christian Advocate* (June 26, 1919), 4. In 1919, D. W. Griffith was a well-known American director and silent filmmaker. His film *Birth of a Nation* was arguably the most controversial motion picture of the early twentieth century. Griffith was raised in Kentucky and his family belonged to the Methodist Episcopal Church, South.

2   *Religion and Popular Culture in America*, edited by Bruce David Forbes and Jeffrey H. Mahan (Berkley, CA: University of California Press, 2005), 2.

3   *Between Sacred and Profane: Researching Religion and Popular Culture*, edited by Gordon Lynch (London: I. B. Tauris, 2007), 11.

4   David Morgan, "Religion, Media, Culture: The Shape of the Field," in *Key Words in Religion, Media and Culture*, edited by David Morgan (London: Routledge, 2008), 3.

5   Stewart Hoover, "The Cross at Willow Creek," in *Religion and Popular Culture in America*, 149.

6   Russell E. Richey, Kenneth E. Rowe, and Jean Miller Schmidt, *Perspectives on American Methodism: Interpretive Essays* (Nashville, TN: Kingswood Books, 1993), 14.

7   *Connectionalism: Ecclesiology, Mission, and Identity*, edited by Russell E. Richey, Dennis M. Campbell, and William B. Lawrence (Nashville, TN: Abingdon Press, 1997). The series includes five volumes published between 1997 and 2005.

8   Nathan Hatch, *The Democratization of American Christianity* (New Haven, CT: Yale University Press, 1989).

9   *Methodism and the Shaping of American Culture*, edited by Nathan O. Hatch and John H. Wigger (Nashville, TN: Kingswood Books, 2001).

10 John H. Wigger, *Taking Heaven by Storm: Methodism and the Rise of Popular Christianity in America* (Urbana, IL: Univeristy of Illinois Press, 1998).

11 John H. Wigger, *American Saint: Francis Asbury and the Methodists* (New York: Oxford University Press, 2009).

12 Dee Andrews, *The Methodists and Revolutionary America, 1760–1800: The Shaping of an Evangelical Culture* (Princeton, NJ: Princeton University Press, 2000).

13 J. Gordon Melton, *A Will to Choose: The Origins of African American Methodism* (Lanham, MD: Rowman & Littlefield, 2007).

14 Russell E. Richey, Kenneth E. Rowe, and Jean Miller Schmidt, *The Methodist Experience in America, Volume I* (Nashville, TN: Abingdon Press, 2010).

15 The language "The taking such diversions as cannot be used in the name of the Lord Jesus" is the same for the AME Church (1896 and 1924 editions), The FMC (1895), and The Wesleyan Methodist Church. The AMEZ Church Discipline uses slightly altered language "... and taking such diversions as cannot be done in the name of the Lord Jesus – such as dancing, card-playing, lottery, policy, and other games of change..." (1896 and 1925 editions).

16 The author realizes this brief sketch of six American Methodist traditions does not cover the wide extent of denominational and ministerial positions on motion pictures. It is likely that further study will reveal that film was both accepted and resisted by each ecclesiastical body.

17 Henry Brown, *The Impending Peril* (original edition, n. p.: Jennings & Pye, 1904; reprint edition, Charleston, SC: BiblioBazaar, 2011), 248–252.

18 Beverly Carradine, *Church Entertainments: Twenty Objections* (original edition, n.p.: A. W. Hall, 1898; reprint edition, Salem, OH: Allegheny Publications, 1989), 71–74.

19 "The Moving Picture Show," *The Free Methodist* (February 10, 1914), 9.

20 "Rottenness in the Movies," *Wesleyan Methodist* (September 27, 1916), 1.

21 "The Gates of Hell Shall Not Prevail," *Wesleyan Methodist* (March 1, 1916), 1.

22 Robert C. Allen, "Race, Region, and Rusticity: Relocating U.S. Film History," in *Going to the Movies: Hollywood and the Social Experience of Cinema*, edited by Richard Maltby, Melvyn Stokes, and Robert C. Allen (Exeter, NH: University of Exeter Press, 2007), 36–37.

23 "Moving Picture Exhibition," *The Christian Recorder* (September 29, 1904), 3; "A Religious Show," *The Christian Recorder* (October 27, 1904), 4.

24 "The Great Richardson Religious Show," *The Christian Recorder* (October 13, 1904), 4.

25 *The Doctrines and Discipline of the Methodist Episcopal Church* (New York: Eaton and Mains, 1896), 136–137.

26 *Harlem Local Reporter* (October 24, 1896), 2. Cited in an essay by Alison Griffiths and James Latham, "Film and Ethnic Identity in Harlem, 1896–1915," in *American Movie Audiences: From the Turn of the Century to the Early Sound Era*, edited by Melvyn Stokes and Richard Maltby (London: BLF Publications, 1999), 47.

27 Charles Musser and Carol Nelson, *High-Class Moving Pictures: Lyman H. Howe and the Forgotten Era of Traveling Exhibition, 1880–1920* (Princeton, NJ: Princeton University Press, 1991), 72; See also *Scranton Tribune* (April 14, 1897).

28 Musser and Nelson, 67–68.

29 Ted Ownby, *Subduing Satan: Recreation, Religion and Manhood in the Rural South, 1865–1920* (Chapel Hill, NC: University of North Carolina Press, 1990), 199.

30 Ownby, *Subduing Satan*, 199.

31 The Centenary Celebration of American Methodist Missions was a missionary exposition similar in nature to the popular World's Fairs of the nineteenth and twentieth centuries. The 1919 fair included a ten-story motion picture screen and dozens of films related to missionary work. Popular films were also included in the showings although they had been heavily edited by a censoring committee of Methodists. See Christopher J. Anderson, "The World Is Our Parish: Displaying Home and Foreign Missions at the 1919 Methodist World's Fair" (Ph.D. diss., Drew University, 2006).

32 Musser and Nelson, *High Class-Moving Pictures*, 10.

33 Vincent Rosini, "Sanctuary Cinema: The Rise and Fall of Protestant Churches as Film Exhibition Sites, 1910–1930" (Ph.D. diss., Regent University, 1998).

34 Arthur E. Holt, *Social Work in the Churches* (Charleston, South Carolina, BiblioLife, 1922), 122–128.

35   Christian F. Reisner, *Church Publicity: The Modern Way to Compel Them to Come In* (New York & Cincinnati: Methodist Book Concern, 1913), 159.

36   Reisner, *Church Publicity*, 157.

37   Reisner, *Church Publicity*, 159.

38   Reisner, *Church Publicity*, 297.

39   "The Expanding Years: Home Missions in Motion Pictures at the General Conference," *The (New York) Christian Advocate* (10 June 1920), 778.

40   *The Expanding Years*, 778.

41   *The Expanding Years*, 778.

42   J. T. Brabner Smith, "Visualizing the Truth: Motion and Stereopticon Pictures in Churches," *The (New York) Christian Advocate* (April 1, 1920), 457.

43   J. E. Crowther, "Methodism and the Theater," *The (New York) Christian Advocate* (September 18, 1919), 1191.

44   "The Church and Films," *The (New York) Christian Advocate* (March 17, 1921), 340–341.

45   "The Church and Films," 341.

46   "The Church and Films," 341.

47   John Wesley Jackson, "Along the Years from Yesterday: Early Methodism Made Real in Motion Pictures," *The (New York) Christian Advocate* (October 7, 1920), 1343.

48   "Along the Years from Yesterday," 1344.

49   David N. Hempton, "Wesley in Context," in *The Cambridge Companion to John Wesley*, edited by Randy L. Maddox and Jason E. Vickers (Cambridge: Cambridge Univeristy Press, 2010), 65–68.

Index

Abingdon Press, 256
abolitionism, 73, 320, 340
Abraham, William, 34, 198
Advent Christian Church, 233
African-American and German
    Evangelical-Pietist churches, 2
African-American tradition, 335
African-American Central
    Jurisdiction, 107–108
African-American Church of God in
    Christ, 105
African-American denominations, 66
African-American Methodists, 55–56,
    60–61, 66–67, 75–76, 81, 107,
    108–109, 113, 176, 180, 263–264,
    266, 270, 281–282, 284, 290,
    293, 296–297, 299, 300, 301,
    310–311, 313, 340
African-American women,
    82, 233, 289
African Americans, 44–45, 48, 60,
    66–67, 71–72, 75, 76, 81, 102, 107,
    109, 111–112, 123, 175, 180–181,
    184, 189–190, 193, 231, 233, 272,
    283, 286, 289, 296–297, 303, 310,
    322–323, 327, 340, 344, 356, 360
African Methodist colleges, 271
African Methodist Episcopal Church
    education in, 177–179
African Methodist Episcopal
    Church (AME)
    Allen Temple, 66
    American culture, 87, 88
    authors in, 4
    baptismal regeneration, 142
    birth of, 251

bishops in, 66, 81, 102, 109, 112,
    197, 299–301, 302, 307
black liberation theology, 30
black Methodists, 45, 181, 282, 296,
    299–300, 340
churches in, 270, 302, 306, 310
civil rights movement,
    309–310, 313
class meetings, 167
deaconess, 200
division in, 75
ecumenicism, 111
education in, 181, 270, 275
executives in, 312
expansion in, 66–67
figures in, 248, 297, 302, 305
founder of, 11, 250, 296, 299,
    302, 310, 317
healing, 231
holiness, 299
laity concerns, 197
lay clergy, 172
leaders in, 13, 66, 109, 270
ministries in the South, 76
mission of the church, 100
missionaries in, 86
missions in, 69, 83, 285–286, 293
motion pictures, 358, 360–361
music in, 81
office of deaconess, 103
on lynchings, 81
on slavery, 56, 60, 72, 73–74,
    76, 283, 299
ordination, 189
ordination and the Lord's
    Supper, 175

African Methodist Episcopal
    Church (AME) (*cont.*)
ordination of women, 103,
    176, 199, 324
pastors in, 88, 102, 303, 309
racial issues, 107
reconstruction, 263
second subgroup, 97
social activism, 305
Social Gospel movement, 102
social holiness, 310
social insurgency, 301, 305
Society Rules, 356
Sunday school, 263–264
temperance, 182, 183
textual authorities, 18
thanksgiving rites, 140
theology in, 9
war, 88
way of salvation, 245
weddings, 149
Womanist theology, 30
women and healing, 231, 233
women and local licenses, 200
women and missions, 201, 317
women bishops in, 329
women in, 301, 310, 316–317, 325
women in ministry, 324
women preachers, 82, 325
worship, 197
African Methodist Episcopal Church,
    Zion (AMEZ)
abolionists in, 299
American culture, 87–88
bishops in, 109, 303
black Methodists, 45, 181, 296,
    299–300, 340
Book of Discipline, 324
churches in, 300
civil rights movement, 312, 313
class meetings, 167
clergy in, 300
conferencing, 61, 160, 162
deaconess, 103
ecumenicism, 111
education in, 81, 179, 181, 270, 275
expansion in, 66
figures in, 248, 297

General Conference, 317
historians in, 297
lay clergy, 172
lay women, 103
leaders in, 102
ministries in the South, 76
missions in, 286
motion pictures, 358, 360–361
on slavery, 72, 73–74, 76, 283
ordination, 189
ordination and the Lord's
    Supper, 175
ordination of women, 103, 176,
    199, 317, 324
pastors in, 312
race issues, 107
reconstruction, 263
second subgroup, 97
Society Rules, 356
Sunday school, 263
superintendent, 61
textual authorities, 18
unity in, 107
weddings, 149
women and misssions, 317
women bishops in, 329
women in, 317
women preachers, 82
African Methodist preachers, 60
African Methodist seminaries, 276
African Methodist social gospel, 304
African Union churches, 189
African Unionists, 190
African Zoar, 55
Alabama State College, 306
Albright College, 270
Albright, Jacob, 57, 66
alcohol, 1, 15, 22, 79, 182–183, 209,
    287–288, 357
Aldersgate Renewal Ministries,
    32, 113, 198
Aldersgate Street experience,
    244, 250, 255
Alexander, Sadie T. M., 109, 296, 298,
    300–301, 307–310, 313
Allegheny College, 80
Allen Temple AME Church, 66
Allen, Ethan O., 232–233

Allen, Richard, 3, 11, 17, 51, 55–56, 66, 111, 180, 231, 248, 250–251, 296, 298–302, 305, 309–310, 317, 325
Allen, Sarah Bass, 299, 317
Along the Years from Yesterday, 366
AME Church Review, 179
American Academy of Religion, 353
American Anti-Slavery Society, 72
American culture, 1–2, 4, 15, 64, 87, 100, 140, 281, 283, 293, 363
American Methodist sermons, 124
American Methodist theology, 10
American Methodist women, 4
American Methodist preachers, 121
American Protestantism, 265, 282, 340
American Revolution, 125, 336
American seminary, 23
American society, 4, 60, 64, 72, 79, 80, 90, 131, 159, 166, 184, 301, 307, 311, 320, 329, 343, 355, 356, 357, 366–367
American Sunday School Union, 59
American University, 88, 270, 275
Ames, Jesse Daniel, 320, 321–322
ancient ecumenical Christianity, 24, 31
ancient ecumenical faith, 18, 36
ancient ecumenical sources, 29
Anderson University School of Theology, 275
Andrew, James O., 73, 163, 164
Anglican theological tradition, 17
Annual Conference (1860s), 74
Annual Conference (AC), 48, 53, 54, 55, 58, 60, 63, 64, 68, 71, 72, 75, 101, 113, 126, 160–162, 163–165, 173, 174, 179, 180–182, 189–191, 198–199, 202–203, 265, 268, 292–293, 310, 325, 328–329, 340
Annual Conference EA (1807), 57
annual conferences, 161
Anti-Saloon League, 104
antislavery, 55
Apess, William, 248–250, 252
Apostolic Constitutions, 200
Arminian Magazine, 54, 228, 253, 261–262

army life, 338
Articles of Religion, 12, 17
Asburian conference (1780), 49
Asbury College, 86, 271
Asbury Seminary, 86
Asbury Theological Seminary, 105, 208, 275–276
Asbury, Francis, 10, 13, 26, 45, 47–51, 53–56, 57, 58–59, 63–66, 70, 71, 74, 122, 127, 159, 164–166, 171, 172–173, 180, 189, 190, 198, 210–212, 231, 251, 262, 265, 266, 344, 356, 357, 366
asceticism, 4, 209–210, 213–214
Asian-American liberation, 30
Assemblies of God, 105
Association for Holding Union Holiness Conventions, 235
Association for the Advancement of Colored People, 102
Association of Southern Women for the Prevention of Lynching (ASWPL), 322
Atlanta University, 300
Augusta College, 20, 269
Augustine of Hippo, 244
Azusa Pacific University, 271
Azusa Pacific University School of Theology, 276
Azusa Street Revival, 89, 105–106

Baily, Joanna, 230, 231
Baker University, 273
Baker, Frank, 276
Baldwin-Wallace College, 312
Baltimore and Washington Conference, 284
band meetings, 246
Bangs, Nathan, 14, 20, 59–60, 68, 77, 131, 179, 218, 262, 274
baptism, 138–148, 149, 151, 192
    adult, 138, 142
    infant, 56, 138, 140–144, 145, 148
baptism of the Holy Spirit, 85, 89
Baptismal Covenant, 142
baptismal regeneration, 142–143, 267
Baptists, 67–68, 74, 127, 143, 181, 214, 263, 266–267, 269, 274, 297, 341, 363

Barclay, Wade Crawford, 284
Bassett, Paul, 276
Bennett, Belle Harris, 191, 325–327
Bethune, Mary McLeod, 320, 322–323
Bethune-Cookman College, 323
Between Sacred and Profane:
 Researching Religion and Popular
 Culture, 353
bible and preaching, 10
bible schools, 18
Birmingham-Southern College, 272
black and Womanist theology, 179
black filmgoers, 360
black liberation theology, 30, 299
black Methodism, 340
black Methodists for Church
 Renewal, 111
Black Pentecostal Holiness
 Church, 106
black separatism, 311
Blackwell, Antoinette Brown, 316
Board of Bishops, 266
Board of Global Ministries the
 Women's Division, 202
Board of Higher Education, 270
Board of Lay Activities, 195
Board of Missions, 201–202, 318
Boardman, Richard, 47
Boardman, William E., 234–235
Boards of Ordained Ministry, 203
Boehm, Jacob, 56–57, 66
Boehm, Martin, 46
Bonebrake Theological
 Seminary, 110, 275
Book Concern, 59, 68, 251,
 255, 262, 366
Book of Common Prayer (BCP),
 50, 138, 140
Book of Discipline, 18, 29, 44–46,
 50–53, 55, 57–59, 98, 110, 112,
 143, 156–158, 165, 166–167, 176,
 198, 213, 214, 217, 222, 262, 266,
 324–325, 327, 328, 357
Book of Worship, 140
Bostock, Bridget, 229
Boston Personalism, 21–23, 31, 32, 83
Boston Theological Seminary, 179
Boston University, 22, 23,
 270, 273, 276

Boston University School of Theology,
 83, 274, 327
Bourne, Hugh, 231
Bowne, Borden Parker, 25, 83,
 84, 87, 276
Bresee, Phineas, 87, 271
Brethren, 115, 350
Brethren in Christ, 85
Brett, Pliny, 56
Briggs v. Elliott, 309
British Methodism, 44, 85, 166, 251,
 254, 316, 367
British Methodist Conference, 123
British Methodist Episcopal Church, 74
Brotherhood of Sleeping Car Porters
 (BSCP), 301, 302, 303
Brown University, 268
Brown v. The Board of Education
 of Topeka, 309
Brown, Henry, 358
Browne, Borden Parker, 21–23
Brunson, Alfred, 69
Buckley, James Monroe, 191, 235–236
Burning Bush, 85
Burrell, Emma Hill, 328
Bushnell, Horace, 84

California German Annual
 Conference, 101
Calvinism, 18
Calvinists, 17, 67, 70, 268
camp meetings, 3, 52, 65, 68, 69, 77,
 84–85, 100, 124, 126–132, 133,
 162, 177, 233, 235
Campbellites, 67, 143, 267, 341
Canadian Congregational
 Churches, 108
Candler School of Theology, 272, 276
Cane Ridge Revival, 127
Carey Ordinance, 305
Carey, Archibald J., Jr., 109, 296,
 298, 300–301, 302–303,
 305–307, 313
Carey, Archibald J., Sr., 88, 302
Carradine, Beverly, 358–359
Carradine, John, 358
Cartwright, Peter, 63, 64, 65, 67–68,
 70–72, 73, 74, 79, 80, 85, 127, 177,
 198, 251–252

Case, Riley, 188, 196–198
Catholic University of America, 88
Centenary Celebration of Methodist
  Missions, 195
Central Christian Advocate, The, 108
Central Illinois Conference, 324
Central Jurisdiction, 181, 202, 293,
  310–312, 323, 328
Central Pennsylvania Annual
  Conference, 328
Chalcedonian Definition, 18, 31
Charismatic movement, 239
charity schools, 262
Chautauqua Assembly, 83–85, 100
Chicago Council against Racial and
  Religious Discrimination, 306
Chicago Deaconess Home, 200
Chicago Training School, 82
Chicago Institutional Church and
  Social Settlement, 102
Choctaw Mission Conference, 101
Christ's divinity, 12
Christian Advocate, 59–60, 68, 179,
  191, 235, 345–346, 364–366
Christian and Missionary Alliance, 85
Christian Herald, 359
Christian perfection, 77
Christian Recorder, 179, 360, 361
Christianity Today, 344
Christmas Conference (1784), 3,
  17, 44, 50–53, 106, 125, 159,
  171, 172, 173
Church Extension Society, 83
church membership, 12
Church of England, 17–18, 47,
  49, 50
Church of God, 161, 233
Church of God (Anderson, Ind.), 16,
  85, 89, 197, 271, 275
Church of God (Cleveland, Tenn.), 89
Church of God in Christ, 105, 106
Church of the Nazarene (CN), 4,
  16, 87, 98, 105, 143, 144, 146,
  161, 163, 172, 197, 232, 266,
  271, 276, 343
circuit riders, 68
circuits, 52, 53, 54, 56, 64, 65,
  125–127, 131, 162, 165, 173,
  174, 188, 192

City of Faith Medical and Research
  Center, 237
civil rights, 102, 108–109, 111, 271,
  272, 289, 296–298, 301, 303,
  305, 307, 308
Civil Rights Act of 1964, 304
civil rights movement, 4, 15, 183, 296,
  297–298, 303, 309, 311, 312
Civil War, 56, 66, 71, 74, 76, 77, 80,
  101, 104, 180, 182, 220, 263,
  270, 282, 283, 284, 289, 300, 316,
  338–339, 340, 342, 345
Claflin College, 75
Claremont School of Theology, 276
Clark College, 75, 274
Clark, John, 69
class meetings, 52, 65, 79, 157,
  166–167, 174, 188, 190,
  192–193, 246–247
clergy education, 176–179
clerical authority, 171
Coke, Thomas, 10, 13, 50–51, 53–56,
  58, 159, 163, 165, 166, 172, 249,
  253, 255, 261
Coker, Daniel, 55, 69, 180
Cokesbury College, 54
Cold War, 343
colleges, 18, 68, 81, 83, 108, 133,
  177–179, 181, 218,
  267–271, 273, 312
colleges and universities,
  263, 270, 272, 283
Collins, Kenneth, 34
Colored Deaconess Home, 100
Colored Methodist Episcopal Church
  or Christian Methodist Episcopal
  Church after 1954 (CME)
  birth of, 76
  black Methodists, 181, 282,
    296, 300, 340
  civil rights movement, 313
  class meetings, 167
  ecumenicism, 111
  education in, 110, 177–179,
    181, 270, 275
  lay clergy, 172
  leaders in, 109
  mission of the church, 100
  on slavery, 283

Colored Methodist Episcopal Church
or Christian Methodist Episcopal
Church after 1954 (CME) (*cont.*)
ordination and the Lord's
Supper, 175
ordination of women, 103, 199
pastors in, 307
racial issues, 107
second subgroup, 97
Sunday school, 263
temperance, 183
textual authorities, 18
unity in, 107
women bishops in, 329
women missionary societies, 318
women preachers, 325
Columbia Conference, 358
Commission on Pan-Methodist
Cooperation, 111
Commission on Religion and Race, 111
Commission on the Status and Role
of Women, 202
Committee to Study
Homosexuality, 112
Common Lectionary, The, 134
Communists, 343, 344
conference superintendent, 162
Confessing Movement, 32, 113
confirmation, 145, 147–148
Congregational Churches, 108
Congregationalists, 56, 67–68,
269, 274, 363
Congress of Racial Equality (CORE),
303, 305–306, 311, 313
connectionalism, 157, 158
Consultation on Church Union
(COCU), 111, 112
conversion, 12
Cookman Institute, 323
Cooper, Ezekiel, 58
Course of Study, 59, 60, 265–266
Covenant Discipleship, 167
Cox, Melville B., 69
Cranston, Bp., 290–292
Crawford, A. J., 69
Crooks, Adam, 73
Crowther, J. E., 365
Cullis, Charles, 235

cultic life, 4
Cyclopaedia of Methodism, 80

Daughters of Conference, 317
Davison, Helenor, 323
Daytona Educational and Industrial
School for Negro Girls, 323
deaconess, 200–201, 236, 327
Deaconess movement, 236, 325
deacons, 53, 55, 60, 103, 171, 173–174,
175, 180, 324
death and dying, 150–151
death narratives, 253
DeLaine, J. A., 296, 309–310, 313
Democrats, 298, 337
demonic healing, 230
Dempster, James, 47
Dempster, John, 179
denominational pluralism, 267
Detroit Daily News, 360
Disciple Bible Study, 113
District Superintendent (DS), 189,
329
divine healing, 85, 89, 227–229,
230–235, 236, 238
doctrinal commitments, 3, 12
doctrinal diversity, 3, 213
doctrine, 9, 12
Doctrine and Doctrinal Standards, 29
Doctrine and Doctrinal
Statements, 29
*Doctrines and Discipline of
the Methodist Episcopal
Church, The*, 361
Douglass, Frederick, 297–298
Dow, Lorenzo, 56, 70–71, 85, 89
Dreisbach, John, 57–58, 66
Drew Theological Seminary, 133, 274
Drew University, 81, 272, 276
Du Bois, W. E. B., 298, 305
Duke Divinity School, 275, 276
Duke University, 81, 270,
272–273, 276
Duke University Chapel, 273
Dutch Reformed, 274

East Ontario Conference, 217
East Texas Conference, 318

Ecumenical Affairs, 111
ecumenical Charismatic
   renewals, 236
ecumenical dialogue, 18
Ecumenical Movement, 146
ecumenical sensibilities, 36
ecumenicism, 109, 111
Edwards, Jonathan, 120, 131
Eisenhower administration, 306
Eisenhower, Dwight D., 305, 306
Elaw, Zilpha, 248–250, 252
elders, 50, 52, 53, 54–55, 57–59, 60,
   61, 64–65, 68, 71, 73, 87, 103,
   127, 146, 148, 161–162, 163, 171,
   173, 174–176, 180, 189–190, 198,
   203, 254, 266
Elliot, Maggie, 103
emancipation, 51, 102, 263, 282–283,
   296–297, 300, 302, 310, 340
Emory College, 272
Emory University, 269, 270, 273
Emory University Candler School of
   Theology, 275
emotionalism, 129
employment discrimination, 302
English Methodists, 121–122, 123,
   127–128, 236
Enterprise Optical Manufacturing
   Company, 363
entire sanctification, 14, 36, 56, 76–78,
   79, 85, 86, 104, 227, 230, 232–233,
   245–247, 249–250, 254, 256
episcopacy, 163, 167, 190
Episcopalians, 112, 267, 274
Epworth League, 83, 194–195, 354,
   358, 362–363
Evangelical Association (EA), 66
   brotherhoods, 194
   conferencing, 57
   deaconess, 200
   division in, 75
   education in, 270, 275
   episcopacy in, 86
   expansion in, 65
   German American movement, 56
   German language, 58
   German Methodists, 181
   holiness, 86

   laity representation, 190
   leaders in, 58
   mainline, 97
   mission of the church, 101
   missions in, 70, 83
   music in, 84
   office of deaconess, 103
   ordination of women, 199
   organizations for service and
   fellowship, 194
   polity, 190
   relationship to UBC, 57
   Sunday school, 264
   textual sources, 68
   theological libralism, 21, 25
   unity and division, 27
   unity in, 56, 108
   war, 88
   women in missions, 201
Evangelical Association/
   Church (EA/C)
   ordination of women, 324
   women's missionary societies, 319
Evangelical Church (EC)
   laywomen representation, 190
   ordination of women, 103
   racial issues, 108
   unity in, 108
   women representation, 191
Evangelical Friends, 85
Evangelical Lutheran Church of
   America, 112
evangelical renaissance, 32
Evangelical School of
   Theology, 110, 275
evangelical sensibilities, 10–14,
   15, 20
Evangelical Theological
   Seminary, 101, 275
Evangelical United Brethren
   Church (EUB)
   diaconate, 174
   education in, 110, 275
   German Methodists, 181
   infant dedication, 144
   laity in ministry, 188
   lay clergy, 172
   ordination of women, 103, 199, 324

Evangelical United Brethren
    Church (EUB) (cont.)
    racial issues, 108, 109
    unitity and division, 27, 28
    unity in, 99, 108, 111, 293
    women in ministry, 188
    women in missions, 202
    women missionary societies, 319
Evangelicals, 190
evangelism, 10
Evanston College, 320
Evening Light Saints, 89
evolution of Methodism, 3
Ewha Women's University, 83
ex opere operato, 141–142
Expanding Years, The, 364
experiential knowledge, 13–14
explanatory Notes to the
    Discipline, 10

Fair Employment Practices
    Commission (FEPC), 307, 308
Fair Employment Practices
    Committee, 302
Farmer, James L., 296, 311, 313
Federal Council of Churches, 111
Federal Council of Churches and
    Social Creed, 102
Federation for Social Service
    (MFSS), 200
Fellowship of Reconciliation
    (FOR), 311, 312
female clergy, 190
feminist movement, 320
feminist theologians, 30
feminist theology, 34, 179, 202
Finley, James, 128
Finney, Charles G., 77, 126
Fire-Baptized Holiness
    Church, 89, 106
Fisk, Wilbur, 268–269, 274
Five Points Mission, 69
Florida A & M College, 308
Florida Conference, 101
Fluvanna conference (1779), 49
Foote, Julia A. J., 82, 103,
    248–250, 252, 324
Forbes, Bruce David, 353

foreign missionary society, 201
foreign missions, 69, 83, 87, 88, 89,
    101, 107, 108, 172, 181, 184
Foundation for Evangelism, 110
Foundation for Theological
    Education, 32, 113
Francis Asbury, 3
Frank, Thomas Edward, 202–203
Fraternal Council of Negro Churches
    (FCNC), 302
Free Methodist Church (FMC)
    asceticism, 217
    authors in, 4
    birth of, 79
    conferencing, 160, 162
    dedication of infants, 143, 144
    diaconate, 174
    divine healing, 232
    education in, 87, 179,
        270–271, 275–276
    entire sanctification and divine
        healing, 232
    episcopacy in, 163
    expansion in, 98
    founder of, 15
    holiness, 80, 86
    holiness denominations, 104
    itinerancy, 174
    lay clergy, 172
    motion pictures, 358, 359, 360
    on slavery, 182
    on temperance, 85
    ordination of women, 82, 103
    pearchers in, 217
    Society Rules, 356
    tobacco, 220
    third subgroup, 98
    weddings, 149
    women in ministry, 176
Free Methodist Church (FMC)
    ordination of women, 103
Free Methodist, The, 359
Free Will Baptists, 267
Freedmen's Aid Society, 75, 263, 274
Freedom's Hill, 73
French Revolution, 302
Fundamental Methodist Church, 107
Fundamentalism, 27–28

funeral orations, 253–254, 257

gag rule, 73
Gammon Theological Seminary, 274
Gandhi, Mahatma, 303, 309, 311–313
Gandhian nonviolence, 305,
    308, 309, 311
Gandhian satyagraha, 303, 309, 311
Garrett Biblical Institute, 80,
    271, 274, 275
Garrett Evangelical Theological
    Seminary, 275, 327
Garrett Theological Seminary, 82, 133
Garrettson, Freeborn, 251–252
Garrison, William Lloyd, 72, 220
Geeting, George, 56
gender equality, 4
General Biblical Institute, 133
General Board of Global
    Ministries, 111
General Camp Meetings, 130
General Commission on Christian
    Unity and Interreligious
    Concerns (GCCUIC), 112
General Commission on the
    Status and Role of Women
    (GCSRW), 112
General Conference (1744), 121
General Conference (1779), 138
General Conference (1787), 53
General Conference (1792), 53, 54, 163
General Conference (1796), 53, 55
General Conference (1800), 55
General Conference (1804), 55
General Conference (1808), 55, 58
General Conference (1816), 57,
    58, 63, 177
General Conference (1820), 68
General Conference (1826), 61
General Conference (1828), 189
General Conference (1836), 72
General Conference (1844),
    73, 163, 164
General Conference (1845), 73
General Conference (1857), 199
General Conference (1860), 79
General Conference (1868), 191, 324
General Conference (1872), 191, 194

General Conference (1880), 82,
    191, 317, 319
General Conference (1884), 317
General Conference (1886), 318
General Conference (1888), 82
General Conference (1890), 325
General Conference (1892), 88, 190
General Conference (1896), 361
General Conference (1907), 190
General Conference (1916), 318
General Conference (1920), 364, 365
General Conference (1932), 110
General Conference (1936), 110
General Conference (1938), 323
General Conference (1940), 343
General Conference (1944), 343
General Conference (1952), 110
General Conference (1956),
    275, 325, 328
General Conference (1972), 29
General Conference (1976), 112
General Conference (1988), 30, 112
General Conference (2012), 203
General Conference (GC), 53, 54,
    58–59, 60, 63, 64, 73, 86, 103,
    106, 107, 113, 139, 159, 160–162,
    163–164, 172, 188–191, 194, 195,
    197, 199–200, 274, 290, 319, 323,
    324, 325–327, 365
General Conference AME (1948), 103
General Conference CME (1918), 325
General Conference Commission on
    Finance, 195
General Conference EA (1835), 264
General Conference EA (1839), 70
General Conference MEC (1928), 328
General Conference MECS, 327
General Conference MECS (1894), 105
General Conference MECS (1910), 327
General Conference MECS (1922), 327
General Conference MECS (1926), 327
General Conference MPC (1884), 324
General Conference UBC, 319
General Conference UBC (1815)
    unity in, 57
General Conference UMC, 176
General Conferences (1820s), 71
General Conferences (1840), 72

General Rules, 47
general superintendency, 164
Genesee Annual Conference,77, 79
George Fox Evangelical Seminary, 275
German Methodism, 81, 261,
    264, 270, 275
German Mission Annual
    Conference, 69
German Reformed, 56
German Reformed Theological
    Seminary, 130
Glasgow University, 272
glossolalia, 98
God's Bible School, 89
Good News, 32
Good News Memphis
    Declaration, 113
Good News's Renew, 113
Graduate School of Theology, 312
Grayson, William J., 210, 212
Great Awakening, 267
Great Depression, 106, 343

Hadley, Henry H., 362
Hall, Jacqueline Dowd, 297
Hammet, William, 56
Harkness, Georgia E., 23, 327–328
Harriett Holsey Normal, 100
Hartshorne, Charles, 31
Hauerwas, Stanley, 344–345
Haynes, Benjamin Franklin,
    26–27, 342
healing, 4
Heck, Barbara Ruckle, 316, 356
Henrichsen, Margaret, 329
Henry College, 269
Herald of Holiness, 26
Herborn Pietism, 46
higher education, 4
Hines, Mildred "Bonnie," 329
Hislop College, 312
Hogue, Wilson Thomas, 217
holiness, 2, 44, 52, 56, 65, 67, 76–78,
    85–88, 98, 100, 104, 105–106,
    157, 171, 173, 179, 182, 196–
    197, 199, 245, 254, 256, 266,
    281–282, 284, 320
holiness adherents, 89, 98,
    105, 114, 282

Holiness Association Meetings, 100
holiness camp meetings, 86
holiness churches, 16, 79, 87, 143,
    172, 176, 344
holiness colleges, 105
holiness denominations, 27, 80, 86,
    87, 89, 97, 98, 104, 105, 109, 111,
    112, 113, 160, 232, 343
holiness doctrine, 86
holiness figures, 85
holiness leaders, 86, 105
holiness movement, 3, 15, 26, 29, 30,
    77, 79, 86–87, 90, 188, 196, 197,
    212, 217, 218, 219, 221, 232, 248,
    261, 271, 284, 316, 325, 357
holiness preachers, 85, 88, 325
holiness radicals, 89
holiness revivals, 87, 133, 271
holiness traditions, 144
holiness Union, 89
holiness women, 89
Holy Club, 44
home and foreign missions, 286
Home Missioner, 200
homosexuality, 112, 113, 183, 184
Hood, James Walker, 87, 324
Hoover, J. Edgar, 306
Hoover, Stewart, 354
Hosier, Harry, 51, 356
hospital movement, 236
Hoss, E. E., 346, 347
Houghton College, 271
Houston Declaration, 112
Howard University, 311
Howe, Lyman H., 362–363
Huck, Grace, 328
Hudson Conference, 219
Hughes, Lucy, 318

Iliff School of Theology in
    Denver, 274
Illinois Conference, 82, 103
Indian Mission Annual Conference, 69
Indian Wars, 339
Indiana Asbury College, 80
Indiana Asbury University, 267, 269
Indiana Conference, 267
Indiana Wesleyan University, 271, 275
Industrial College, 100

Industrial Institute, 100
infant dedication, 140, 143–145
Inskip, John, 85
Institute on Religion and
    Democracy, 32
Interdenominational Theological
    Center, 110, 275
Interdenominational Woman's Union
    Missionary Society, 319
International Association of Healing
    Rooms (IAHR), 239
International Film Corporation, 366
International Holiness Union and
    Prayer League, 89
International Lesson Plans, 84
International Sunday School
    Convention, 264
inward holiness, 299, 310
Irwin, B. H., 88–89
Italian Mission Conference, 101, 287
itinerancy, 47, 57, 125, 164–167,
    171, 174–175
itinerating preachers, 46

Jackson, Rebecca Cox, 231
Japan Mission Conference, 101
Jarratt, Devereux, 48
Jennings, Theodore, 34
Jenson, Maud Keister, 328
Jim Crow, 4, 15, 75, 296, 307, 340
John Wesley Fellows, 32
Joint Commission on
    Federation, 106–107
Joint Commission on Unification,
    290
Journey of Reconciliation, 305

Keller, Catherine, 34
Kelly, Leontine, 329
Kentucky Annual Conference, 327
Kimball School of Theology, 101
King, Martin Luther, Jr., 23, 297, 306,
    310, 312, 313
Knapp, Martin Wells, 88–89
Ku Klux Klan, 106, 301, 310
Kuhlman, Kathryn, 236–238

Ladies and Pastors Christian
    Union, 319

Ladies Home and Foreign Mission
    Society (LHFMS), 317
Ladies' and Pastors' Christian
    Union, 194
Lane College, 270
Lane University, 270
Lane, James, 270
Large Minutes, 44, 45, 48, 53
Lawson, James M., Jr., 296, 311–313
lay representation, 188, 189–191, 201
Lay Witness Mission, 198
Laymen's Missionary Movement
    (LMM), 195
Lee, Jarena, 180, 245,
    248–250, 252, 325
Lee, Jason, 69
Lee, Jesse, 53, 54
Lee, Luther, 103
letter writing, 10
liberal arts colleges, 185
liberation theology, 30–31, 33, 179
Liberian Mission, 69
Liberty Party, 73
life-cycle rituals, 4
Lincoln, Abraham, 67, 74, 75,
    80, 339
literal Biblicist, 104–106, 113
liturgical life, 4
Liturgical Movement, 144, 146
Livingstone College, 270, 275
Lord's Supper, 48, 112, 138, 140,
    144–148, 149, 150, 151, 174, 175,
    192, 310, 365
Louis Annual Conference, 358
Lucknow University, 318
Lukyns, George, 230
Lutherans, 36, 57, 267, 274
Lynch, Gordon, 353

M'Gready, James, 126
M'Gready, John, 126
M'Gready, William, 126
Maclay (now Claremont) School of
    Theology, 274
Maddox, Randy, 34
Manship, Andrew, 121
March on Washington Movement
    (MOWM), 302–303, 305
marriage rites, 148–150

Mary J. Platt School, 101
Mason, Mary Morgan, 59
Masons, 86
mass media, 352–353, 354, 356
Matthews, Marjorie Swank, 329
McConnell, Francis, 132
McGavock, Willie Harding, 319
McKendree College, 269
McKendree, William, 56, 58–59,
    63, 64, 69
McKenzie, Vashti, 329
McKinley, William, 88, 89,
    106, 346–347
Mead, Stith, 210, 212
medical healing, 227, 229, 234, 236
Meeting for the Promotion of
    Holiness, 77
Meharry Medical College, 75
Mennonite Brethren, 85
Mennonite Pietism, 46
Mennonites, 46, 267
metaphors, 13
Methodism studies, 1–3
Methodist Church (MC)
    bishops in, 268
    black Methodists, 181, 293, 340
    Central Jurisdiction, 312
    church and state, 337
    churches in, 239
    clergy rights for women, 108
    confirmation, 148
    diaconate, 174
    education in, 110, 179, 275
    episcopacy in, 162, 164
    evangelism, 109, 110
    infant baptism, 144
    Korean Methodists, 182
    laity in, 199
    lay clergy, 172
    missions in, 202
    on sickness, 150
    ordination and the Lord's
        Supper, 175
    ordination of women, 103,
        176, 324, 328
    pacifism, 343
    polity, 199
    racial reconciliation, 201

racial segregation, 284, 310
racialism, 290
Social Gospel movement, 110
Sunday school, 238, 262, 265
supply pastors, 175
tobacco, 213
thanksgiving rites, 140
unity in, 111, 293
women clergy rights, 327, 328
women District
    Superintendent, 329
women missionary societies, 319
Methodist dogmatics, 35–36
Methodist Episcopal Church (MEC)
    African Americans, 75
    African Unionists, 190
    American culture, 87
    American society, 78, 81
    asceticism, 217, 222
    authority in, 71, 255
    baptismal regeneration, 142
    biographies in, 255
    bishops in, 66, 268, 341
    black Methodists, 55, 60,
        66–67, 181, 282, 290, 292,
        296, 300, 340
    Book Concern, 251
    Book of Discipline, 44, 46, 57
    brotherhoods, 194
    church and state, 337, 342
    churches in, 87, 88, 364
    civil rights movement, 313
    class meetings, 79
    clergy, 171
    conferencing, 52, 57, 58, 61,
        63, 159
    deaconess, 103, 200
    Deaconess movement, 325
    dedication of infants, 143
    diaconate, 180
    diversity in, 2
    division in, 71, 74, 75, 79, 98, 292,
        293, 323, 341, 342
    education in, 68, 81, 88, 177,
        178, 261, 262, 268, 269, 270,
        271, 274, 323
    elders in, 83, 84, 87, 358
    entire sanctification, 232

entire sanctification and
  healing, 232
episcopacy in, 51, 163, 164
expansion in, 63, 64, 65, 75, 125
figures in, 18, 248
Freedmen's Aid Society, 75
General Conference, 189, 364
Genesee Annual Conference, 77
German Methodists, 181
German ministry, 65, 66
healing, 231
holiness, 85, 86, 98, 196
holiness denominations, 104, 105
holiness movement, 197, 284
institutional segregation, 323
institutionalization in, 83
itinerancy, 175, 233
laity in, 188, 248
lay clergy, 172
lay ministry, 122, 190
lay women, 103
laymen representation, 191
leaders in, 102, 127, 131, 183
Lord's Supper, 146
luxuries, 218
Metropolitan Holiness
  Association, 197
mission of the church, 100
missionaries in, 86
missions in, 69–70, 83, 86, 184, 263,
  286–287, 364
motion pictures, 358, 361–362,
  363, 365, 366
music in, 84
officials, 77
on slavery, 55, 56, 72, 74,
  76, 182, 283
ordination of women, 82, 103,
  189, 199, 324
organizations for service and
  fellowship, 194–195
pastors in, 77, 89
Philadelphia Conference, 56
polity, 289
preaching licenses, 249
presiding elders, 189
Primitive Methodists (PM), 56
racial equality, 284–285

racial issues, 107–108, 180–181
racial segregation, 283, 284, 310
revival or missionary movement, 63
revivalism, 121
Simpson Chapel, 89
Social Gospel movement, 110
Society Rules, 356, 357
Sunday school, 262–263, 264, 266
Sunday School Union (SSU), 262
Sunday Service, 138, 139, 142
supply pastors, 175
temperance, 183
textual authorities, 18
textual sources, 59–60, 68, 179,
  251, 255, 266
theological libralism, 21
theology in, 9
tobacco, 212, 217, 218
Union support in, 75
unity in, 56, 57, 97, 106–107, 108,
  289–292, 323
weddings, 148, 149
Wesleyan Methodist Connection
  (WMC), 73, 284
Wesleyanism, 217
women and local licenses, 199
women and missions, 318
women clergy rights, 327–328
women in, 316, 320, 323, 325
women in ministry, 175–176, 200
women in missions, 201
women missionary societies, 319
women preachers, 325
women representation, 191
women's suffrage, 321
worldliness, 232
Methodist Episcopal Church,
  South (MECS)
African Americans, 76
American culture, 87, 88
birth of, 73
bishops in, 264, 272, 345, 346
black Methodists, 181,
  282, 290, 340
church and state, 337, 342
class meetings, 79
Confederate support in, 75
conferencing, 159

Methodist Episcopal Church,
South (MECS) (*Cont.*)
deaconess, 103, 200
decline, 75, 340–341
dedication of infants, 143
division in, 75, 107, 292, 293,
    323, 341–342
education in, 81, 177,
    269–270, 273, 274
episcopacy in, 164
evangelists in, 237
figures in, 18, 249
General Conference, 327
Hispanic Methodists, 181
holiness, 85, 86–87, 105, 196
holiness denominations, 105
holiness movement, 197, 284
influence of, 75, 76
institutionalization in, 83
lay ministry, 190
lay women, 103
laymen representation, 191
leaders in, 102
Lord's Supper, 266
mainline, 97
ministries in the South, 76
mission of the church, 101
missionaries in, 86
missions in, 83, 86, 184, 286
motion pictures, 358
on slavery, 74, 182, 283
ordination of women, 103
organizations for service and
    fellowship, 194–195
pastors in, 342, 358
polity, 289
prayer of committal, 151
racial issues, 107, 108
racial segregation, 283, 310
Sunday school, 263
supply pastors, 175
temperance, 76
textual authorities, 18
textual sources, 251, 252, 266, 345
theological libralism, 26
tobacco, 213, 218
unity in, 106, 108, 289, 290, 323
Woman's Board for Foreign
    Missions, 327

Woman's Home Missionary Society
    (WHMS), 327
women and missions, 201, 327
women clergy rights, 328
women in, 321, 327
women missionary
    societies, 318, 319
women preachers, 325
women representation, 191
Methodist Episcopal General
    Hospital, 236
Methodist Episcopal tradition, 335
Methodist Federation for Social
    Action (MFSA), 110
Methodist Federation for Social
    Service (MFSS), 102, 110, 195
Methodist Magazine, 59, 128, 179
Methodist Minute Men, 195
Methodist Protestant Church
    (MP/MPC)
    birth of, 71
    clergy in, 248
    clergy rights for women, 108
    conferencing, 101
    congregationalism, 190
    deaconess, 103, 200
    dedication of infants, 143
    diaconate, 174
    division in, 71, 74, 75, 107, 293, 323
    education in, 110, 270, 275
    episcopacy in, 86
    female clergy, 190
    itinerancy, 175
    laity in ministry, 188
    lay and clergy
        representation, 60, 191
    laywomen representation, 190
    Lord's Supper, 266
    mainline, 97
    missions in, 83
    on sickness, 150
    ordination of women, 82, 103,
        199, 323, 324
    racial issues, 107
    Reformed movement, 56
    Stilwellites, 60
    supply pastors, 175
    textual authorities, 18
    textual sources, 68

union societies, 189
unity in, 74, 107, 108, 289, 323
women and missions, 201
women in ministry, 176
women missionary societies, 319
Methodist Quarterly Review, 179
Methodist Reform, 70
Methodist Review, 179
Methodist Social Creed, 110
Methodist Sunday School Union, 264
Methodist Theological School, 275
Methodist Women's Society of
    Christian Service, 308
Metropolitan Holiness
    Association, 197
Mexican War, 339
Meyer, Lucy Rider, 81, 325
Miles College, 100
Miley, John, 18–20, 35
military careers, 344
Miller, George, 57
Ministerial Education Fund
    (MEF), 110
*Miss America and Methodism:
    Twentieth Century Beauty
    Pageants as Christian
    Mission*, 352
Mission Conference, 101
Mission Society of the Methodist
    Episcopal Church, 69–70, 113
Missionary Church Association, 85
Missionary Society, 59, 194
Missionary Society of the EA, 70
missions and evangelism, 109
Mississippi Theological and Industrial
    College, 100
Mite Missionary Society, 317
Mix, Sarah Ann Freman, 233–234
Mobile Conference, 101
Model Deed, 47
Modernist and Fundamentalist
    debates, 100
Moody Bible Institute, 322
Moore, Henry, 255
Moravians, 145, 267, 274
Morgan, David, 354
Mormons, 67, 68
Morrison, Henry Clay, 86
motion pictures, 352–354, 357–367

Musser, Charles, and Nelson,
    Carol, 362, 363
Muste, A. J., 312
*Mutual Rights of Ministers and
    Members of The Methodist
    Episcopal Church, The*, 60, 71

Nashville Christian Leadership
    Conference, 312
Nation, Carry A., 85
National Association for the
    Advancement of Colored People
    (NAACP), 102, 109, 183, 304,
    307–308, 309, 310, 312
National Camp Meeting Association
    for the Promotion of Holiness,
    85, 196, 235
National Council of Churches, 28
National Council of Negro Women
    (NCNW), 308
National Emergency against Mob
    Violence Committee, 307
National Negro Congress
    (NNC), 303, 305
National Urban League (NUL),
    304, 307, 308
National Woman's Christian
    Temperance Union
    (NWCTU), 320–321
natural theology, 20–21, 33, 36
Nazarene Theological
    Seminary, 275
Neo-Orthodoxy, 179
Nevin, John, 130
new birth, 14, 67, 77, 139–143,
    144–145, 227
New Deal, 297–298, 303
New England Conference, 72, 254
New York Annual Conference,
    217–218, 324
Newbury Biblical Institute, 274
Newcomer, Christian, 56, 66
Nicene Creed, 18, 31
Niebel, Henry, 58
Niswonger, Ella, 82, 103, 199, 324
North Arkansas Annual
    Conference, 325
North Carolina Annual
    Conference, 324

North Dakota Annual
   Conference, 328
Northeastern Seminary, 275
Northern Indiana Conference, 323
Northwest Nazarene University, 276
Northwestern University,
   269, 270, 305
Norwegian-Danish seminary, 274
Notes on the New Testament, 17

O'Kelly, James, 53, 54–55, 70, 89,
   163, 172, 189
Oberlin College, 312
obituaries, 10, 254, 257
odination of women, 323–329
Oklahoma Conference, 282
Oklahoma Indian Conference, 282
Oklahoma Native American
   Conference, 181
Oklahoma-Nebraska Conference, 101
Oliver, Anna, 176, 325
Oneida Conference, 179
Ordaining Women, 82
ordination, 12, 173, 189, 201
ordination of women, 70–7, 323–329
ordo salutis, 244, 245
Otterbein College, 270
Otterbein, Philip, 56–57, 66, 190, 198
Otterbein, William, 46
Outler, Albert C., 28–30, 31,
   198, 272, 276
Oxnam, Bromley, 343

pacifism, 311, 342–343
Palmer, Phoebe, 3, 77, 82, 105, 196,
   232, 234, 236, 325
Pan-Methodist Commission on
   Union, 111
Parham, Charles Fox, 88, 89,
   105, 232
Parks, Rosa, 309, 310, 313
parlor holiness, 77
Pasadena College, 271, 272
Passmore, Alderman John, 216
Payne Theological Seminary, 275
Payne, Daniel Alexander, 13,
   81, 87, 270
Pentecostal adherents, 114

Pentecostal Assemblies of the
   World, 106
Pentecostal Church of the
   Nazarene, 26
Pentecostal denominations, 97, 104,
   109, 111, 113
Pentecostal Holiness Church,
   85, 106, 237
Pentecostal Ministerial Alliance, 106
Pentecostal movement, 98,
   197, 233, 276
Pentecostalism, 90, 98, 105
Perkins School of Theology, 227, 275
personal conversation, 10
personal sanctification, 22
Personalism, 179, 276
*Perspectives on American
   Methodism: Interpretive
   Essays*, 355
Philadelphia and Baltimore Annual
   Conference, 324
Philadelphia Conference, 57, 130
Philadelphia Human Relations
   Commission, 307
Philippine-American War, 339
Phillips School of Theology, 110
philosophical theology, 10
Phoebus, William, 61
physical healing, 47–48, 230, 232, 238
Pietism, 46, 100, 101
Pilgrim Holiness Church, 16, 85, 98,
   105, 197, 232
Pillar of Fire, 85
Pilmore, Joseph., 156–159
Plan of Union, 111
playing cards, 356
Point Loma Nazarene
   University, 271, 276
polity, 4, 55, 71, 86, 98, 156–159,
   161, 162, 166, 167, 168, 190, 195,
   198–199, 252, 266, 290, 293, 323,
   337, 338, 352
poor and oppressed, 15
postmillennialism, 76, 106
poverty, 15
pragmatic concerns, 162
Prayer Book, 142
preaching, 4, 10, 12–13, 193

Precision Machine Company, 363
premillennialism, 104–105, 106
Presbyterians, 67–68, 74, 127, 130,
    214, 216, 266–267, 270, 274
preservationist theology, 19
presiding elder, 52
Primitive Methodist Magazine, 231
Primitive Methodists (PM), 56, 231
Primitive Physick, 228, 230–231
Process theology, 31–32, 34, 179, 276
proclamation of the Gospel, 10
progressive theology, 20
Promotion of Holiness, 196
Protestant Episcopal Church, 151
Protestant nuns, 200
Protestant scholasticism, 13
Publishing Concern, 255
Puerto Rico Mission, 101
Puritan biographies, 244
Puritanism, 1
Puritans, 1, 101, 224, 244, 245

quadrilateral, 29–30, 33
Quakers, 267, 316
quarterly meetings, 47, 52, 64–65, 127,
    132, 146, 160, 162, 192, 262
*Quarterly Review of the Methodist
    Episcopal Church, South*, 179

race and class discrimination, 322.
racial discrimination, 102, 109, 180,
    300, 302–303, 305–306, 307
racial divisions, 282, 293
racial reconciliation, 201, 293
racial segregation, 81, 106, 183, 284,
    292, 296, 300, 301, 311
racism, 66, 70, 75, 80, 88, 99, 106, 108,
    183, 201, 281, 282, 285, 298, 300
radical holiness associations, 85
radical holiness traditions, 111
radical sensibilities, 14–17, 30, 36
Randolph, A. Philip, 109, 296,
    298, 300–306
Randolph-Macon College, 269
Rankin, Thomas, 47–49
Reconciling Congregations, 112
Reconciling Ministries Network, 112
Reconstruction era, 340

Reformed, 36
Reformed Church, 108
Reformed Methodists, 56, 189
Reimagining Conference, 113
Reisner, Christian F., 363–364
religious emotionalism, 128
Religious Intelligencer, 60
Religious Right, 185
religious societies, 46
RENEW, 202
Republican Methodist Church, 172
Republican Methodists, 86
Republican National Convention, 306
Republican Party, 181
Republicans, 297, 337
Restrictive Rules, 17, 58, 161, 164
revivalism, 3, 56, 84, 100, 119, 121,
    122, 131–132, 133, 196
revivals, 17, 25, 27, 47, 76, 85, 100,
    119–120, 121, 125–129, 131, 132,
    133, 134, 198, 267, 285, 362
revivals and awakenings, 9–10, 12,
    14, 17, 33
Richard M. Dalfiume, 297–298
Richardson, R. C., 360–361
Rider, Lucy Meyer, 87
Ridge Revival, 128
Rio Grande Conference, 181
Rituals or Books of Worship, 139
Roberts Wesleyan College, 275
Roberts Wesleyan University, 271
Roberts, B. T., 77–80, 82, 89,
    103, 271
Roberts, Oral, 236–237
Rock River Conference, 219
Rodda, Martin, 47, 49
Rodda, Webb, 49
Roll of Preparatory Members, 140
Roman Catholicism, 71, 113
Roman Catholics, 88, 267, 274
Roosevelt administration, 298, 306
Roosevelt, Franklin D., 302
Rush, Benjamin, 215–216
Rush, Christopher, 61
Rust College, 75

sacraments, 4
Saint Paul School of Theology, 276

Salvation Army, 16, 85, 172, 176
sanctification, 12, 27, 76–77, 79,
    87, 89, 98, 105, 123, 124, 214,
    232–235, 238, 244, 247, 299
sanctificationist mysticism, 21
Sawyer, Mike, 208–209,
    213–214, 222–223
Scarritt Bible and Training School, 327
Scotia Female Seminary, 322
Scott, Orange, 72–73, 89
Scriptual images, 14
Scriptural concepts, 14
Scriptural metaphors, 13, 14
Scriptural reasoning, 10
Seattle Pacific Seminary, 275
Seattle Pacific University, 271, 275
secessionist groups, 231–232
Second Great Awakening, 126
seminaries, 32, 80, 83, 110, 133, 171,
    177–180, 247, 261, 265, 268, 273,
    274, 275, 276
Seventh-Day Adventists, 85
Seybert, John, 58, 66
Seymour, William Joseph, 88,
    89–90, 105
Seys, John, 69
Shadford, George, 47–48
Shaw, Anna Howard, 82, 103, 176,
    199, 323–324, 325
sickness, 150
simplicity and intelligibility, 10–12
Simpson, Matthew, 80–82, 85, 87,
    336, 339, 342
Sims, Albert, 217, 219, 220–222
Sitkoff, Harvard, 297–298
slavery, 4, 15, 16, 56, 66, 70, 71–74,
    79, 98, 101–102, 104–105, 109,
    182, 213, 220, 221, 251, 263, 269,
    270, 281, 282, 284, 292, 296, 298,
    339, 341, 342
Small, Mary J., 317
Smith, Joseph, 68
Snethen, Nicholas, 55, 89
Snorton, Teresa, 329
Social Creed, 110
Social Gospel movement, 101–103,
    104, 110, 147, 183, 200
social holiness, 98, 101, 104, 108, 228,
    296, 299, 310

social justice, 98, 113, 184,
    261, 271, 299
social media, 352
societies, 52, 65
Soule, Joshua, 58–59, 61, 73
South Carolina Annual Conference
    (1865), 76
Southeastern Jurisdiction, 329
Southern Christian Leadership
    Conference (SCLC), 183, 303–305,
    306, 312–313
Southern Methodist Church, 107
Southern Methodist University,
    3, 270, 273
Southern University, 272
Southwestern University, 321
Spanish-American War, 88,
    339, 346–347
spiritual sanctification, 227, 230
Spring Arbor University, 29
State church, 337
Stevens, Abel, 124
Stevenson, William, 248–250
stewardess, 324, 325
Stewart, John, 69
Stilwell, William, 60–61
Stilwellites, 60
Stockton, William, 60
Strackbein, Gilbert, 238
Strawbridge, Robert, 47–48, 70, 138
Student Nonviolent Coordinating
    Committee (SNCC), 304, 313
Summers, Thomas O., 17–20, 35
Sunday charity schools, 261–263,
    265
Sunday school, 59–60, 68, 76, 83–85,
    100, 132, 193–194, 238, 261–265,
    266, 318, 358, 364
Sunday School Advocate, 68
Sunday School Books and Tracts, 263
Sunday school conventions, 264
Sunday school libraries, 264
Sunday School Magazine, 264
Sunday school superintendents,
    193, 194, 264
Sunday School Union (SSU),
    59, 194, 262
Sunday Service, 139, 141, 142,
    145–146, 148, 150, 151

Sunday Service of the Methodists in North America, The, 138
superintendent, 50–52, 53, 61, 65, 159, 162–163, 164, 166, 171, 173, 174, 209
Swain, Clara, 318
Syracuse University, 270
systematic theology, 10

Taylor College, 86, 271
Taylor, Felson, 82
Taylor, William, 86
television, 352
temperance, 76, 82, 85, 104, 182, 266, 268, 287, 288, 317, 320–321
temperance movement, 82, 287
temperance society, 183
Tennessee College, 75
testimonies, 13, 246–247
Thanksgiving of Women after Child-Birth, 140
theological knowledge, 13
theological languages of American Methodism, 9, 33–34
theological libralism, 20–28
theological sensibilities, 2–3, 9–10, 24–25, 26–27, 30–31, 35, 36
theology, 9, 12
theology and other disciplines, 20
Thirty-Nine Articles of Religion, 17, 50
Thoburn, Isabella, 318
Thoburn, James, 318
Thompson, Andrew C., 299
Thurman, Howard, 311
Tigert, John J., 158, 159, 162
tobacco, 15, 79, 183, 208–214, 215–223
Tobias, Channing H., 307–309, 313
Tomlinson, Betsy, 231–232
Tract Society, 194
Transylvania University, 20
travel literature, 245
Trinity College, 272
Truman, Harry, 306–307
Trust Clause, 47
Tuesday Meetings, 196
Tuesday Meetings for the Promotion of Holiness, 232
Turner, Henry M., 81, 300–301

twenty-four Articles of Religion, 50

UBC Home and Foreign Mission Society, 70
Underground Railroad, 299
Union Biblical Seminary (now United), 199, 275
Union Seminary, 270
Unitarians, 67, 268, 306
United (Bonebrake) Seminary, 82, 275
United Brethren in Christ (UBC)
  birth of, 46
  black Methodists, 45
  Book of Discipline, 57
  brotherhoods, 194
  church and state, 337
  clergy in, 172
  conferencing, 57
  confessional statement, 57
  deaconess, 103, 200
  decline, 112
  division in, 75, 197
  education in, 270, 275
  episcopacy in, 57
  expansion in, 57, 65–66
  expulsion of, 56
  German-American movement, 56
  German language, 58
  German Methodists, 181
  German ministry, 65
  holiness, 86, 196–197
  itinerancy, 233
  lay leadership, 190
  lay ministry, 188
  lay representation, 190
  lay women, 103
  laywomen representation, 190
  leaders in, 102
  mainline, 97
  Masonic membership, 86
  mission of the church, 101
  missions in, 83
  ordination of women, 82, 103, 199, 324
  organizations for service and fellowship, 194
  polity, 190, 198–199
  racial issues, 108
  relationship to EA, 57

United Brethren in Christ
(UBC) (cont.)
speaking in tongues, 89
textual sources, 68
unity and division, 27
unity in, 56–57, 107, 108
women and local licenses, 199
women in ministry, 176
women in missions, 201
women missionary societies, 318–320
United Evangelical Church (UEC)
congregationalism in, 86
episcopacy in, 86
holiness, 86
mainline, 97
unity in, 108
*United Methodist Book of
Worship*, 140
United Methodist Church (UMC)
adolescent rite, 148
authors in, 4
baptismal regeneration, 142
bishops in, 112, 185
black Methodists, 181
churches in, 208
class meetings, 167
Common Lectionary, The, 134
conferencing, 160–162
confirmation, 148
contentment, 223
deaconess, 200, 201
decline, 184
diaconate, 174
diversification of leadership, 112
division in, 97, 113
ecumenicism, 112
education in, 110, 179, 270, 275, 276
elders in, 2, 237
episcopacy in, 163, 164
ethinic diversity, 182
feminism, 202
homosexuality, 112, 184
infant baptism, 144
itinerancy, 174
lay and clergy representation, 191
lay clergy, 172
lay preachers, 192
Lord's Supper, 267, 146

mainline, 97
missions in, 184
ordination, 176
ordination and the Lord's
Supper, 175
ordination of women, 176, 324
organizational structures, 111
organizations for service and
fellowship, 194
pacifism, 344
polity in, 158
quadrilateral, 30
renewal, 112, 113, 114
renewal movements, 68, 198
social debates, 184
temperance, 183
tensions in, 203
testimonies, 256
textual sources, 179
theological diversity, 179
theology in, 9
unity and division, 28
unity in, 99, 111, 293
weddings, 149–150
Womanist theology, 30
women bishops in, 329
women District
Superintendent, 329
women education, 329
women in, 325
women in leadership, 329
women in ministry, 112
women representation, 191
women's missionary
societies, 319, 320
United Methodist Men, 195
United Methodist Publishing
House, 256
United Methodist Women
(UMW), 112, 202
United Theater Equipment, 363
United Theological
Seminary, 110, 275
Uniting Conference (1939), 109–110
Uniting Conference (1968), 111
United Brethren in Christ (UBC), 108
Universalists, 67
universality of sin, 12

universality of the Gospel, 14–15, 31
universities and seminaries, 25, 84
    108, 261, 273
University of Denver, 270, 273
University of Florida, 272
University of Indianapolis, 270
University of Pennsylvania, 307
University of Southern California, 22,
    87, 270, 273
University Senate, 270
unlimited atonement, 17

Vacation Bible Schools, 100
Van Cott, Maggie Newton, 325
Vanderbilt Divinity School,
    274, 311, 312
Vanderbilt University, 76, 81,
    133, 273
Varick, James, 60–61
Vasey, Thomas, 50
Vincent, John Heyl, 83–84, 87–88
Virginia Annual Conference, 329

Walk to Emmaus, 113, 198
Walker, David, 72
Walls, William J., 303
Walsh, Thomas, 255
Walters, Alexander, 109, 312
Washington Conference, 101, 328
Watkins, W. P., 220, 221
Watson, David Lowes, 193
way of salvation, 165, 166, 168, 243,
    245, 247, 248
Wayfarer, The, 365
Weekly Recorder, The, 130
Welch, Dr. Thomas, 84
Wells, Ida B., 81–82, 102, 289
Wells-Barnett, Ida B., 109
Wesley Biblical Seminary, 276
Wesley Center for Applied
    Theology, 276
Wesley Center Online, The, 276
Wesley Seminary, 275
Wesley Service Guild, 320
Wesley Theological
    Seminary, 110, 275
Wesley Works project, 276
Wesley, Charles, 229

Wesley, John, 17, 28–29, 30, 31, 34,
    36, 44–46, 47–53, 56, 59, 105,
    111, 119–122, 123, 131, 145–151,
    156, 157–159, 163, 164–166, 171,
    172, 173, 175–176, 189, 191, 212,
    214–215, 216, 217, 223, 232,
    236, 237, 238–239, 243–246, 249,
    250, 251–255, 261–262, 266–267,
    271, 276, 298–299, 313, 316,
    336, 344, 352, 354, 355, 356,
    357, 366–367
Wesley, John and Charles, 44, 47,
    209–210, 261, 352, 367
Wesleyan (later Wilbraham)
    Academy, 268
Wesleyan Church (WC), 4, 103, 139,
    163, 174, 271, 275–276, 339
Wesleyan holiness, 271
Wesleyan holiness churches, 158,
    161, 164, 167, 266
Wesleyan holiness colleges, 271
Wesleyan holiness people, 271
Wesleyan holiness revival, 271
Wesleyan holiness scholars, 32
Wesleyan holiness seminaries, 275
Wesleyan holiness traditions, 9
Wesleyan Methodist, 359, 360
Wesleyan Methodist Church, 172,
    176, 179, 232, 356, 359–360
Wesleyan Methodist
    Connection (WMC)
    abolitionists, 282, 284
    birth of, 73, 77
    division in, 73
    elders in, 89
    episcopacy in, 86
    expansion in, 98
    holiness, 86
    holiness denominations, 104
    on slavery, 74
    ordination of women, 82, 103
    pastors in, 73
    textual sources, 68
    third subgroup, 98
    Women's Rights Convention, 73
Wesleyan Pietism, 46
Wesleyan Repository, 60
Wesleyan Service Guild, 201–202

Wesleyan social holiness, 298, 299, 300, 303, 304, 306, 309, 313
Wesleyan Theological Journal, 32
Wesleyan Theological Society (WTS), 32
Wesleyan University, 268, 269–270, 273, 274
Wesleyanism, 47
Western imperialism, 109
Western Jurisdiction, 329
Westminster Theological Seminary, 275
Whatcoat, Richard, 50, 53
white supremacy, 293
Whitefield, George, 47, 120, 215, 355
Whitehead, Alfred North, 31, 255
Wilberforce College, 81
Wilberforce University, 270–271, 275
Wiley, Orton H., 27–28
Will, Herman, 344
Willard, Frances E., 82, 102, 103, 176, 191, 194, 287, 320–321
Williams, Robert, 47–48, 366
Willimon, William, 344
Wills, Mary, 82, 103
Wilson, George W., 25–27
Wofford College, 177
Woman in the Pulpit, 82
Woman's Board for Foreign Missions, 327
Woman's Christian Temperance Union (WCTU), 82, 102, 103, 104, 191, 194, 287–289, 319
Woman's Crusade, 320
Woman's Department of the Board of Church Extension, 319
Woman's Division of Christian Service, 201
Woman's Foreign Missionary Society (WFMS), 83, 201–202, 318
Woman's Home and Foreign Missionary Societies, 194, 317
Woman's Home Missionary Society (WHMS), 191, 201–202, 319, 327
Woman's Medical College, 318
Woman's Missionary Association, 319
Woman's Missionary Council, 319, 327
Woman's Missionary Society (WMS), 201, 317, 318–319
Woman's Parsonage and Home Mission Society, 319
woman's suffrage, 321, 323
Womanist theology, 30
women clergy, 175–176
women in Methodism, 102–104, 123
women in ministry, 16
Women's Auxiliary, 59
Women's Board of Home Missions, 327
Women's Division of Christian Service, 108
Women's Division of the General Board of Global Ministries, 112
women's ordination, 15
women's rights, 15
Women's Rights Convention, 73
Women's Society of Christian Service, 320
Women's Society of World Service, 319
women's suffrage, 320, 321, 323
Wood, Charles, 2
Woodworth-Etter, Maria Beulah, 88–89, 233
work of the Holy Spirit, 12, 13–15
World Council of Churches, 28, 109, 111, 144
World War I (WWI), 342–343, 346
World War II (WWII), 297–298, 342–344
Wright, Milton, 86
Wright, Richard R., Jr., 47, 302

Young Daughters of Conference, 317
Young Men's Christian Association (YMCA), 307, 309
Youth's Instructor and Guardian, 59